BIOGRAPHICAL MEMOIRS OF FELLOWS, II

BIOGRAPHICAL
MEMOIRS
OF FELLOWS
II

Published for THE BRITISH ACADEMY
by OXFORD UNIVERSITY PRESS

Oxford University Press, Great Clarendon Street, Oxford OX2 6DP

Oxford New York
Auckland Bangkok Bogotá Buenos Aires Cape Town Chennai
Dar es Salaam Delhi Hong Kong Istanbul Karachi Kolkata
Kuala Lumpur Madrid Melbourne Mexico City Mumbai Nairobi
São Paulo Shanghai Singapore Taipei Tokyo Toronto

British Library Cataloguing in Publication Data
Data available

ISBN 0–19–726302–X
ISSN 0068–1202

Typeset in Times
by J&L Compostion, Filey, North Yorkshire
Printed in Great Britain
on acid-free paper by
Antony Rowe Limited
Chippenham, Wiltshire

The Academy is grateful to Professor P. J. Marshall, CBE, FBA
for his editorial work on this volume

Contents

HILARY ARMSTRONG

Arthur Hilary Armstrong
1909–1997

I

HILARY ARMSTRONG changed the subject of ancient philosophy by devoting much of his long life to promoting study of the Neoplatonist philosopher Plotinus. When Armstrong graduated from Cambridge University in 1932, Plotinus was widely regarded in the English speaking world as an obscurely mystical thinker, a minority interest at best, and certainly not a philosopher remotely comparable in intellect and rigour to Plato and Aristotle. Today, thanks to Armstrong's prolific output, especially his seven-volume text and translation of the *Enneads*, no serious scholar of ancient philosophy can afford to neglect Plotinus. Armstrong by intellectual and emotional temperament had a remarkable affinity for Plotinus' extraordinary mind and imaginative complexity. His books and articles are more than a fine scholarly achievement. They also express Armstrong's enthusiasm for the spirituality and theism that drew him to Plotinus, and they publicise that philosopher with a subtle combination of sympathy and criticism. One of his greatest achievements was his ability to exhibit Plotinus' creative use of the preceding philosophical tradition. Hence Plotinus has become essential reading not only for those particularly interested in Neoplatonism but also for anyone engaged with the afterlife and interpretation of the Presocratics, Plato, Aristotle, and Stoicism.

As well as being a leading scholar of ancient philosophy, Armstrong was a devout, active, and increasingly idiosyncratic Christian; or perhaps better, a free-thinking Christian Platonist. His religious outlook, catholic

Proceedings of the British Academy, **120**, 3–17. © The British Academy 2003.

with a small c (though he espoused Roman Catholicism for much of his life), consistently informed his view of Plotinus. As he grew older, he became increasingly ecumenical, critical of eccesiastical hierarchy, and sympathetic to the religious experience of other faiths. He published extensively both on contemporary theological issues and also on early Christian thought and its relation to Greek philosophy, especially Platonism.

II

Armstrong was born at Hove in Sussex on 13 August 1909, the youngest of four children. His father, an Anglican priest in the Chichester diocese, had read theology at Cambridge, and collected antique Bibles. There was another clergyman in the family, Armstrong's maternal uncle Arthur Shirley Cripps. This man became an Anglican priest in Rhodesia where he built a mud-brick church, practised poverty, and became revered as the local saint. Cripps also wrote religious verse. Religion, then, was a central part of Armstrong's early experience and probably reinforced by his reputedly strict and dominating father whose political sympathies were high Tory. His mother is remembered as a submissive figure. His father would not have sympathised with the feminist leanings evident in some of Armstrong's later publications.

As a young child, he was precocious and made to read *The Times* at the age of six. With his sister Dorothy he developed a love of gardening that remained a strong interest throughout his life, and he became a keen photographer, which reflected the feeling for natural beauty that is constantly evident in his writings and a basic feature of his personal religion. Of his two brothers, John became a distinguished artist (ARA), painting in a Daliesque style, while the other, Ronald, disappeared. Whether through nature, nurture or both, Armstrong and his brothers shared a character that would be marked by streaks of rebelliousness and unorthodoxy.

At the age of thirteen he went to Lancing where Evelyn Waugh was an older contemporary. Like Waugh, Armstrong was strongly attracted to Roman Catholicism. Before converting to that faith in 1932, he collaborated with David Jones, an engraver, on his first publication—*A Dominican Calendar* (Ditchling Press, 1928), consisting of hand-written Greek and Latin texts to accompany engravings for each month of the liturgical year. He studied the Classics tripos at Jesus College, Cambridge, where he was a mainstay of the chapel; and after graduating with first-class honours he spent a year at the University of Vienna. In 1933 he was appointed librarian in charge of the new library of the Cambridge Classical Faculty in Mill Lane, a position that gave him a virtual research fellowship. There he began the work on Plotinus that became his first monograph, *The Architecture of the Intelligible Universe in the Philosophy of Plotinus* (Cambridge, 1940; reprinted Amsterdam, 1967; French translation with critical preface, Ottawa, 1984). At Cambridge he was a very close friend of Arthur Peck, who became a Fellow of Christ's College in Classics, and with whom he shared an unlikely interest in Morris dancing as well as ancient philosophy. Another dancing friend was Joseph Needham. In 1933 he married Deborah Wilson, whom he had met in Vienna. Deborah was one of the first women graduates of the University of Birmingham. She was of Quaker background, but converted on her marriage to Roman Catholicism.

In 1936 Armstrong was appointed Assistant Lecturer in Classics at University College Swansea. His first writings on Plotinus appeared at this time: 'Plotinus and India', *Classical Quarterly*, 30 (1936), 22–8, and 'Emanation in Plotinus', published surprisingly for the period in the leading philosophical journal *Mind*, 46 (1937), 61–6. Shortly before the outbreak of war, he accepted the position of Professor of Latin Literature and Classical Greek at the Royal University of Malta in Valletta. By this time he had three young children. The family travelled to Malta by way of Italy and Sicily. This was a traumatic experience, but much worse was to occur when the island came under siege in 1942 and was bombed by the Italians. The Armstrongs, seriously depleted in weight and forced to sell all their possessions, were evacuated to Britain by military plane. Before they left Hilary ruefully observed someone wearing his pyjamas. He enjoyed his years in Malta. Before the privations of war became severe, he had a lively social life there, and he later wrote an article for *The Downside Review* on the fauna and flora of the island.

On returning to England in 1943, Armstrong first taught sixth-form Classics at Beaumont College, Old Windsor. That same year he delivered a series of lectures on ancient philosophy at the London headquarters of the Newman Association, a society of Roman Catholic university graduates. These lectures were the foundation for his most widely read book, *An Introduction to Ancient Philosophy* (London, 1947, frequently reprinted, translated into Italian, Spanish, and Japanese, and running to a fourth edition in 1965). In about 250 pages, the book surveys the entire period of ancient philosophy, starting with the Presocratics and concluding with the later Neoplatonists and Augustine. This was a very bold project for a scholar in his thirties to undertake, and one that showed a remarkable command of the subject in one so young. It would be forty years before a book of comparable scope and accessibility appeared—Terence Irwin's *Classical Thought* (Oxford, 1988).

Comprehensive though Armstrong's *Introduction* is, it is no even-handed synopsis. Half the book is devoted to post-Aristotelian philosophers. This treatment of material that was quite unfashionable at the time adds much to the work's appeal; the later chapters devote far more space to Neoplatonism and early Christian thinkers than a more conventional study would have allotted. The book was and remains a masterly treatment, elegantly written, forthright in judgement, and attractively personal. Such criticisms as can be brought against it are few as compared with the strictures Armstrong himself pronounced against his work in the introduction he attached as preface to the fourth edition. Some of his comments are worth quoting at length because they give a revealing glimpse of the author's mentality.

He describes the book as bearing 'the stamp of what is now a rather old-fashioned sort of Roman Catholic onesidedness and complacency . . . the musty smell of a period when educated Catholics could still talk about the Perennial Philosophy (meaning Thomism) . . . More serious is the failure to show any sign of realizing that contemporary philosophy has important criticism to offer of some of the traditional positions described with approval.' Armstrong berates himself for 'narrowness in the whole planning of the book'. What he refers to is 'the assumption that the only really important and interesting movements of thought derived from ancient Greek philosophy in the mediaeval period were those of the Latin West', as distinct from Byzantium and the world of Islam. As editor of *The Cambridge History of later Greek and Early Medieval Philosophy* (Cambridge, 1967), Armstrong took steps to rectify these self-confessed omissions by commissioning chapters on Early Islamic Philosophy (R. Walzer) and a chapter including Byzantium (I. P. Sheldon-Williams).

He finds another limitation of the book in its 'Cambridge' approach, especially in the chapters on Plato. He alludes here critically, though also deferentially, to the influence of F. M. Cornford, saying that his own 'account of Plato's metaphysics is perhaps too clear-cut and simplified even for an elementary introduction'. As an alternative, he recommends his readers to explore 'Oxford' ways of looking at Plato, especially the books of I. M. Crombie, referring to Crombie's *An Examination of*

Plato's Doctrines (London, 1962) and *Plato, the Midwife's Apprentice* (London, 1964).

Current readers of Armstrong's *Introduction* will probably think he was too hard on himself. The book is rewarding in part because of its one-sidedness. His critical comments are chiefly interesting for the light they shed on his own capacity for rethinking his positions and priorities. Right up to the end of his long life he remained a remarkably open-minded thinker, albeit staying constant to his unshakable theistic intuitions.

III

The appearance of this book, seven years after the publication of Armstrong's still indispensable monograph on Plotinus, must have done a lot to launch his reputation as a scholar of ancient philosophy. Together with E. R. Dodds (FBA), Regius Professor of Greek at Oxford, who strongly supported him, he was now the leading British expert on Plotinus. In 1946 he returned to full-time university teaching first as Lecturer and then as Senior Lecturer in Latin at University College, Cardiff. Then, in 1950, he succeeded A. C. Campbell as Gladstone Professor of Greek at the University of Liverpool, remaining there as head of the Department of Greek until taking early retirement in 1972. F. W. Walbank (FBA) was already there in the chair of Latin. When Walbank soon moved sideways to the Rathbone Chair of Ancient History, R. G. Austin, who had been Armstrong's former boss at Cardiff, replaced him as Professor of Latin. No provincial university in England had a more illustrious trio of Classics professors.

The Armstrongs, now parents of five children, began living in the Wirral. Hilary denounced their West Kirby home as bourgeois (his wife had wanted something grander), and they moved to an attractive house in one of Liverpool's older residential districts, quite close to the university. Classics at Liverpool was organised in three departments, Latin, Ancient History, and Greek. Small though each of these was, they cherished their autonomy, and cooperation between them was less evident than the uneasy coexistence that this curious, though then common, administrative practice encouraged. (The situation was scarcely different during my own tenure of the Gladstone Chair from 1973 to 1983.) From the outset, it seems, Hilary took no interest in university committees, leaving the running of the department to his junior colleagues as far as he could. At routine meetings he would sometimes groan and wave his hands in desperation; and at home he was much the same, so helpless when the lights fused during a party he was hosting that all he could manage was to jump up and down, calling 'do something'. As a teacher, however, he was kindly and much appreciated, but in an era without computers, e-mail, and university assessment demands, he stood out for his lack of practicality. He did not type or drive, and it is hard to imagine how he would have coped without the unremitting support of his staunch Greek department colleagues, Henry Blumenthal and John Pinsent. Their devotion to him (including regular visits to his Shropshire home after he retired) shows the warmth and even charisma of a personality that those who did not know him well or shared his interests tended to find aloof. By the time he retired from the Gladstone Chair, aged sixty-three, he had become so remote from the university community in general that I rarely heard his name mentioned by colleagues outside Classics.

During his earlier Liverpool years Armstrong forged close ties with two colleagues in other departments, A. C. Lloyd (later FBA) and R. A. Markus (later FBA). Lloyd, who held the Liverpool chair of Philosophy from 1957 to 1984, shared Armstrong's passion for Plotinus and Neoplatonism, but in temperament the two men were strikingly different except for their disinclination for university administration. In contrast with Armstrong's religiosity, Lloyd was fiercely agnostic, and his personal tastes as well as his bachelor life-style and vigorous wit made him a striking contrast to his reclusive colleague. Yet, they cooperated successfully and greatly respected one another. With Markus, a leading medieval historian, Armstrong shared a strong interest in Augustine and Christianity. They jointly published a short book *Christian Faith and Greek Philosophy* (London, 1960, translated into Portuguese and Polish), based on lectures they gave under the auspices of the university's Extra-Mural Department; and Marcus wrote the chapters on Marius Victorinus and Augustine for Armstrong's *Cambridge History of Later Greek and Early Medieval Philosophy*. Lloyd was responsible for the chapters on the Later Neoplatonists. Another Liverpool contributor to this large volume was the medieval historian H. Liebeschütz, author of the entire part on Western Christian Thought from Boethius to Anselm. With Armstrong himself writing the part on Plotinus, this *Cambridge History* was very much a Liverpool volume, registering the fact that at the time of its composition that university was the British centre for the study of the book's subject matter. Its status in this regard was further enhanced with the appointment of Henry

Blumenthal, the leading British Neoplatonist scholar of his generation, to the Greek department.

The *Cambridge History of Later Greek and Early Medieval Philosophy*, though excellent in its treatment of Neoplatonism and that movement's influence, is too narrowly focused to do justice to the 'Later Greek' of its title. The volume includes only a perfunctory treatment of Stoicism, bypasses Scepticism, and says little about the commentators on Aristotle. In partial defence of Armstrong's editorial decisions, it is fair to say that all three of these subjects, now very much to the fore, were being little studied in Britain in 1967. Another relevant consideration must have been length, since the volume runs to over 700 pages. Yet, Armstrong made a poor decision in assigning the long first part of the book, surveying Greek philosophy from Plato to Plotinus, to the turgid pen of Philip Merlan; and throughout Armstrong's work one finds a tendency to depreciate Stoicism. With the recent publication of numerous works on that philosophy, including *The Cambridge History of Hellenistic Philosophy* (ed. K. Algra *et al.*), the shortcomings of Armstrong's *Cambridge History* appear much less significant than the book's undoubted strengths.

Fruitful though Armstrong's collaborative work was, his most important contribution to ancient philosophy in his Liverpool years was the preparation and partial publication of his seven-volume translation and edition of Plotinus for the distinguished Loeb Classical Library series of Harvard University Press. He kept in close touch with Continental experts on Neoplatonism, especially P. Henry and H.-R. Schwyzer, and it is their great editorial work on Plotinus (3 vols., Oxford, 1964–82), that he used as the basis for his own text. Armstrong's first two volumes appeared in 1966, followed the next year by volume 3. By 1976, shortly after his retirement from Liverpool, he was ready with volumes 4 and 5, but for reasons outside his control these were not published until 1984. Volumes 6 and 7 appeared in 1988, supported by grants from the British Academy and the Leverhulme Trust. His original intention was to publish six volumes, each containing nine treatises (enneads) in accordance with Porphyry's edition of Plotinus' work. In fact, he found that he needed two volumes (6 and 7) for the sixth and most demanding ennead.

The Loeb series publishes texts of Greek and Latin authors accompanied by translations. Volumes are typographically complex. The left-hand page contains the original text and brief textual apparatus. The right-hand page gives the corresponding translation. Footnotes may also be included. Volumes of the series vary considerably in their scale of annotation and explanatory material. Armstrong strikes a fine balance. His pages are less cluttered than those of some recent volumes in the series, but he introduces each of the fifty-four treatises with a helpful synopsis, and his volume 1 includes text and translation of Porphyry's *Life of Plotinus*.

Prior to Armstrong, English readers of Plotinus were dependent on the translation by the maverick and brilliant Irishman Stephen MacKenna (1872–1934). MacKenna had literary genius. His version of the *Enneads* will never be surpassed in its intuitive feeling for the original; but as a translation for scholars it is too free, insufficiently sharp in rendering technicalities, and based on an inadequate Greek text. Armstrong's great achievement is his accuracy and complete immersion in Plotinus' philosophy.

Plotinus concludes *Ennead* 1.6, adapting Plato, by describing the soul's ascent to ultimate goodness. Here is MacKenna's version:

> So, mounting, the Soul will come first to the Intellectual-Principle and survey all the beautiful Ideas in the Supreme and will avow that this is Beauty, that the Ideas are Beauty. For by their efficacy comes all Beauty else, by the offspring of Being and of the Intellectual-Principle. What is beyond the Intellectual Principle we affirm to be the nature of Good radiating Beauty before it. So that, treating the Intellectual-Cosmos as one, the first is the Beautiful: if we make distinction there, the Realm of Ideas constitutes the Beauty of the Intellectual Sphere; and the Good, which lies beyond, is the Fountain at once and Principle of Beauty: the Primal Good and the Primal Beauty have the one dwelling-place and, thus always, Beauty's seat is there.

And now Armstrong's rendering:

> First the soul will come in its ascent to intellect and there will know the Forms, all beautiful, and will affirm that these, the Ideas, are beauty; for all things are beautiful by these, by the products and essence of intellect. That which is beyond this we call the nature of the Good, which holds Beauty as a screen before it. So in a loose and general way of speaking the Good is the primary beauty; but if one distinguished the intelligible [from the Good] one will say that the place of the Forms is the intelligible Beauty, but the Good is That which is beyond, the 'spring and origin' of beauty; or one will place the Good and the primal beauty on the same level: in any case, however, beauty is in the intelligible world.

MacKenna's translation has poetry and rhythm (as Plotinus' original does not); but it fails to convey the difficulty Plotinus wants to state concerning the limitations of language for expressing the relationship of beauty to the intelligible world on the one hand and to the highest reality, the Good, on the other hand. For anyone grappling with the obscurities of Plotinus' thought, Armstrong's version is distinctly preferable. He also indicates, as MacKenna does not, that the words 'spring and origin' (rendered by MacKenna 'Fountain and Principle') are a quotation from Plato's *Phaedrus*.

The difficulties of Plotinus' Greek are extreme. One may wish that Armstrong had said more about them in the introduction to his first volume and that he had given a fuller account of his policy as translator. He also missed an opportunity to discuss the rhetoric of the *Enneads*. There is no question, however, but that his Loeb Plotinus is a towering achievement. In 1970, three years after the publication of his third volume, he was elected Fellow of the British Academy. This belated honour in Britain gave him great pleasure, though he had long been recognised in Continental Europe as a major scholar.

A detailed assessment of Armstrong's interpretative work on Plotinus would be out of place in this memoir and far beyond my competence.[1] Many of his articles as well as his early monograph have become classics, including the large number of them cited in the bibliography of *The Cambridge Companion to Plotinus* (Cambridge, 1996), edited by L. P. Gerson. From the beginning of his work, as is evident in *The Architecture of the Intelligible Universe*, Armstrong resisted the reduction of Plotinus' philosophy to a completely consistent system. While he did a great deal to lay out the structure of Plotinus' metaphysics and its rationalistic underpinnings, he was also receptive to the 'wild' and visionary passages, finding Plotinus in some ways more like the romantic poets and painters he so deeply influenced than he was like an academic philosopher. Armstrong's sensitivity to ambiguity and flexibility in the *Enneads* stands as a salutary warning, reminding those who work on these fascinating texts that, for all that they share with earlier Greek thought, they are a strikingly original guide to, and even a record of, an all-embracing inner experience, combining rationality, intuition, and erotic yearning for ultimate union with the ineffable and transcendent One or Good or God, which is the source of everything. Armstrong lived long enough to see the *Cambridge Companion to Plotinus* in print, and it must have given him great satisfaction. Globally speaking, he was one among several eminent Neoplatonic scholars of the twentieth century, but without his impetus the subject would hardly have developed in the English-speaking world to the high point it has reached today.

---

[1] I refer, instead, to the following publications: H. J. Blumenthal and R. A. Markus, eds., *Neoplatonism and Early Christian Thought* (London, 1981); H. J. Blumenthal, 'Plotinus in the light of twenty years' scholarship, 1951–1971', in *Aufstieg und Niedergang der römischen Welt*, II. 36. 1 (Berlin/New York, 1987), 528–70; and K. Corrigan and P. O'Cleirigh, 'The course of Plotinian scholarship from 1971 to 1986', ibid. 571–623.

While Plotinus remained the main focus of Armstrong's scholarship throughout his life, he was very active during his Liverpool years as a contributor to Catholic journals, including *The Downside Review*, *The Heythrop Journal*, and *The Tablet*. In these publications he was principally interested in comparing Platonic and Plotinian conceptions of divinity, salvation, love, and human status with Christianity. He collected some of these articles, together with his earliest papers on Plotinus, in a volume entitled *Plotinian and Christian Studies* (London 1979). Although some of the material on Plotinus is strictly exegetical, the general impression that the book conveys is the author's dialectical manoeuvering between what he calls 'the critical Hellenic spirit' and traditional Christianity, often to the advantage of the former. Armstrong makes such remarks as 'I always thought that I was a Christian of a sort'; but he wonders 'what the history of Christianity would have been like if Our Lord's first contact with Graeco-Roman civilisation had been of a rather different kind—if, instead of being summarily crucified by a second-rate Roman official he had been cross-examined by a genuinely Socratic Greek philosopher' (XIV, p. 45). He writes approvingly of 'reflective Hellenic piety', finding in it a basis for rejecting 'the anthropocentrism which has been characteristic of at least the later Christian and post-Christian centuries of our era, the setting of men (in or out of the Church) apart from the non-human material world which is regarded as wholly profane, mere raw material for human exploitation' (XIV, p. 46). (One recalls Armstrong's love of gardens.) It would require a lengthy study to explore the complexity of his religious outlook, celebrating what he calls 'the divine self-manifestation in the glorious diversity of the universe', while equally committed to the idea of divine transcendence. Neither Neoplatonists nor Christian philosophers seem to have completely satisfied his essentially undogmatic temperament. Instead, he consistently engaged with both movements, not only studying them historically and analytically but also in terms of their applicability to a modern theistic sensibility. In due course, unhappy with ecclesiastical hierarchy and dogmatism, Armstrong renounced Roman Catholicism, and returned to the Church of England.

IV

By this time he had already embarked on a fresh teaching and research career as Professor of Classics and Philosophy at Dalhousie University in Halifax, Nova Scotia, a position he held from 1972 to 1983. This institution is older than most British and American universities, with a Faculty of Arts dating back to 1818. At Dalhousie Armstrong was instrumental in founding a new journal *Dionysius*, managed by the Department of Classics, and specialising in work on later ancient philosophy and patristic studies. His renown as an expert in these fields brought him many graduate students with whom he established strong relationships for the rest of his life. I have the impression that he was much happier with the atmosphere of Dalhousie than with Liverpool, where he had few students with whom he could work intensely on his favourite topics.

Before retirement from Liverpool, the Armstrongs moved to a wonderful Elizabethan house near Ludlow, to which he returned during each of his Canadian years. The house had a large garden, which Hilary used not only for cultivating flowers and fruit but also for philosophical thought. Throughout the 1980s he continued to publish numerous articles and to give lectures on Plotinus, other Neoplatonists, and early Christianity. He assembled these later publications in a second volume of papers, *Hellenic and Christian Studies* (London, 1990). By 'Hellenic' Armstrong says in his introduction that he means 'someone who holds to the old ways of worshipping and thinking about the Divine, in more or less conscious opposition to Christianity'. While much of his work in this volume is a historical engagement between Platonism and early Christian thought (as in his previous collection), Armstrong here, more clearly than anywhere else, affirms his conviction that debate between the Hellenic and Christian traditions has consequences and relevance for contemporary ways of thinking about divinity.

The collection starts with a remarkable paper entitled 'Some advantages of polytheism'. Placed at the beginning of the book, this paper is essentially programmatic, since it registers Armstrong's constant insistence on the need for pluralism and openness in approaches to religious experience. He characterises himself as one who 'can only say that awareness of God in the natural world is the heart and foundation of any religion I have'. In this article and elsewhere in the book, his writing shows a wit and lightness scarcely evident in his earlier work, and one glimpses his love of English poetry, especially Blake, and art. The tone of the polytheism article can be partly gauged by the following quotation from its first page: 'I have sometimes been sufficiently irritated by the way Christians talk about Greek heathenism to think about setting up in my garden a statue of Priapus or of Diana of the Ephesians.'

Of especial interest in the book are four long papers which Armstrong gave as contributions to the annual Eranos conference at Ascona from

1986 to 1989. By the time he delivered the last one of these he was eighty years old, but they read as the work of someone at the height of his powers. The organisers of Eranos made an inspired choice in inviting him, and he found the Eranos setting and tradition, inspired by Jung, much to his liking: 'There seems to be a presence there of gods too real for theology which generates a sort of freedom and seriousness (not necessarily solemnity) not far from the spirit of Plotinus as I understand him' (p. x). One has the sense that Eranos treated him as a guru, and that he played the role both superbly and ironically. (Though not exactly handsome, Armstrong was a big man with a strong face and winning smile.)

Eranos sets its contributors a general theme for them to develop according to their speciality. The expansiveness of the occasion gave Armstrong opportunities to show his deep interest in Greek literary texts as well as his familiar Platonists. His first Eranos lecture was entitled 'The divine enhancement of earthly beauties: the Hellenic and Platonic tradition'. He begins with a brilliant survey of Greek literary representations of beauty, ranging over Homer, the Homeric Hymn to Demeter, Sappho, Sophocles, and Theocritus (clearly a favourite author). By the end he is comparing the principles of light and dark in late Neoplatonism with Yin and Yang. In the heart of the paper, he argues persuasively that the Platonic Forms, because they are neither in space nor in time, should not be regarded (in spite of some of Plato's language) as 'beyond' or 'outside' the material world but rather as the ground of its existence. In similar vein, he interprets the 'ladder' of love in the *Symposium* as including descent to see lower beauties enhanced by the divine presence of Beauty Itself.

This study deserves to be much more widely read than its somewhat obscure publication has probably made possible. The same applies to Armstrong's other Eranos papers: 'The hidden and the open in Hellenic thought', 'Platonic Mirrors', and 'Itineraries in late antiquity'. Of all Armstrong's later writings, the last of these papers gives the clearest and strongest impression of his final religious outlook.

The theme of that Eranos session was crossroads; he chose to speak about 'the spiritual crossroads of late antiquity', meaning the period 200–700 CE, but he begins his article with the present situation, as he sees it, in which Christianity's 'dominance' is over, and a new way needs to be found 'if we are to survive at all as properly human beings'. He constructs his argument around the crossing of 'three itineraries'. The first of these he calls 'the ancient piety of folk religion', referring to a sense of 'harmony and integration with the gods of nature'. And he warns of 'the grave psychological consequences if it disappears from experience and consciousness', because of our need, as he sees it, to establish unity with the divine in nature. His second itinerary (Jerusalem) is Christianity (in which he includes Judaism), characterising it as 'intransigent and exclusive monotheism', an outlook that led to the exclusion of the feminine from the sphere of divinity. The third itinerary is, of course, Athens, or Greek philosophy, culminating in Neoplatonic, 'non-exclusive' monotheism.

Armstrong was never a merely bland defender of Christianity, but, given his earlier Catholic phase and involvement with numerous Catholic circles at home and abroad, his comments on the victory of that religion over the Way of Athens would make the Vatican shudder. He writes tartly about the Church's grabbing of wealth and power, and he assigns the triumph of Christianity to 'internal power-politics' as distinct from 'the inevitable result of a great spiritual movement marching irresistibly to its goal'. Calling that victory 'fatal', he looks to a 'future in which all that is reasonably certain seems to be that no religious group will be of much service to the world unless it is prepared to accept equality with others, to practice mutual hospitality' (XIV, p. 131). For his own part, having returned to the Church of England, he occupied a prominent forward pew at the Sunday morning service of St Lawrence's, Ludlow.

His broad interest in all forms of religion made him a highly appropriate editor of the volume on *Classical Mediterranean Spirituality* (New York, 1986) in the series *World Spirituality. An Encyclopedic History of the Religious Quest*.[2] For this large book, he enrolled a team of scholars from Germany and France as well as Britain and North America, including several of his former students. The chapters include not only treatments of Greek and Roman religion and the contributions of leading ancient philosophers, but also studies of Egyptian cults, the civic contexts of religion, and the piety of ordinary men and women in late antiquity. As the author of the chapter on Epicureans and Stoics, I corresponded with Armstrong and found him enthusiastic about my proposed interpretation of the Epicurean gods (chiefly developed by my collaborator David Sedley in fact) as a theory of human idealisation and projection, anticipating Feuerbach, rather than as metaphysically independent entities. Knowing only Armstrong's work on Plotinus at this time, I was surprised by his enthusiasm, but I now see that it was symptomatic of his sympathy for the most diverse religious experience.

[2] Armstrong was also the obvious choice to write the survey article on 'Greek philosophy and Christianity', for M. I. Finley's new edition of *The Legacy of Greece* (Oxford, 1981), pp. 347–75.

V

Armstrong was a very unusual man. Though seeming to be unworldly and incapable of being practical, he was intensely aware of what he found important in everyday experience, and always receptive to new ideas in the spheres that interested him. He felt things deeply, and he could be as troubled by a bad frost ruining his plants as he would be annoyed by a papal encyclical. His writings are most generous in their acknowledgements of what he learnt from others, whether these people were illustrious scholars or MA students that he taught. He never resorts to polemic, and his expository manner is more tentative than assertive.

Next to Plotinus, his sympathy was strongest for Plato's dubitative Socrates. Armstrong's religiosity, for those who do not share that outlook, is an impediment to reading some parts of his large output, and his writing style, though sometimes arresting, can be verbose but also unduly elliptical. Sometimes too his enthusiasms ran away with him, as when he claims that there was continuity between Hellenic philosophical monotheism and 'archaic peasant religion' (*Hellenic and Christian Studies*, XIV, p. 111).

The scholarly world has taken the measure of his great work on Plotinus and the Platonic tradition, but he was also a creative religious thinker (with some affinity to Teilhard de Chardin) and a more interesting one than has probably been widely recognised. Filtered through his religious orientation, the negative theology of Plotinus (one of his favourite topics), i.e. the impossibility of attaching any positive attributes to the ultimate divine principle, becomes an affirmation of 'faith in and dim awareness of the Unknowable Good, which I cannot and do not want to get rid of, but which remains tentative, personal, not absolute or excessive, and making no demands on others' (*Hellenic and Christian Studies*, VII, p. 50).

In addition to his service at Dalhousie University, Armstrong's North American experience included a visiting professorship at Manhattanville College, Purchase, NY; and in 1979 he was Professor of Christian Philosophy at Villanova University, Pennsylvania. The American Catholic Philosophical Association awarded him its Aquinas Medal in 1973. He was a pioneer founder of the quadrennial Oxford Patristic Conference. His former Liverpool colleagues, Blumenthal and Marcus, edited a Festschrift in his honour, appropriately titled *Neoplatonism and Early Christian Thought* (London, 1981).

Though obviously an assiduous scholar, Armstrong had many other interests. Besides the gardening and photography already mentioned, he

was passionately devoted to classical music and ballet, regularly attending concerts at the Liverpool Philharmonic during his years in that city.
He enjoyed walking and travel, and he remained a pipe-smoker to the end
of his life, undeterred by the fact that he once set his house on fire with a
discarded pipe. He suffered a stroke in 1989, which made further work
difficult, but he remained a voracious reader with a remarkable gift of
recall, and he continued to cherish close contact with scholarly friends
and former students. One of these, Kevin Corrigan (an expert on Plotinus),
has written about Armstrong's liking to be taken out for a pub lunch,
which could involve a drive of a hundred miles to and from his favourite
place.

Armstrong died on 16 October 1997. His ashes are interred with those
of his wife in the Ludlow churchyard which is also the last resting place
of A. E. Housman. He is survived by two sons and a daughter.

A. A. LONG
Fellow of the Academy

Note.   My face to face experience of Armstrong was limited to a single day we spent
together in the Cambridge area in the early 1980s. What I chiefly remember about the
occasion was the effortless flow of conversation and our mutual delight in the beauty
of Ely Cathedral. I am indebted to the Reverend Christopher Armstrong for telling
me much about his father's background and early life. Others whose reminiscences
have been helpful to me are Jay Bregman, Kevin Corrigan, Barry Fleet, and the late
Henry Blumenthal.

MAX BELOFF

Max Beloff
1913–1999

I

MAX BELOFF was born in London on 2 July 1913. His parents, Simon and Mary Beloff, were Russian Jewish immigrants who had come to England in 1910. Simon Beloff prospered as an agent in the export trade and so it was a comfortably affluent and cultivated household in which his son Max grew up. The family became quite large with Max the eldest of five, alongside three sisters (deceased) and a brother (John) who has survived him. All were to achieve distinction in later life in the varied fields in which they worked. It was also a liberal household in its approach to the Jewish faith, maintaining many of the Jewish family customs, but not at all committed to regular religious observance. This may go some way towards explaining why in later years Beloff had a secularist view of religion and did not regard himself as part of Anglo-Jewry as that term was understood in the earlier part of the twentieth century, though this never affected the sympathetic ties with the Jewish community in Britain that he always retained. His parents continued to speak Russian in the home, but they must have anglicised themselves fairly quickly since Beloff's first language was English, and only later did he learn Russian and some Hebrew. Beloff was sent to St Paul's School in London where he thrived on the rigorous and challenging academic education for which the school was well known. Whilst there he was sent to Switzerland on health grounds for a term and this enabled him to become fluent in French. At St Paul's he also acquired an interest in cricket that was to endure throughout his life. He

Proceedings of the British Academy, **120**, 21–40. © The British Academy 2003.

concluded his school career by winning a scholarship at Corpus Christi College, Oxford to which he went in 1932 to read Modern History. Before embarking on his university studies Beloff spent some time in 1931 in Berlin in order to learn German.

At Oxford Beloff quickly achieved academic distinction. He gained a first in Modern History finals in 1935, this being preceded by winning the Gibbs Scholarship in Modern History in 1934, and followed by a Senior Demyship at Magdalen College in 1935. Whilst an undergraduate Beloff, who had in those days like so many middle-class young men at Oxford strong Socialist sympathies, joined the Oxford Union, spoke wittily there, and became its Librarian. When the famous 'That this House would not fight for King and Country' debate took place in 1933 Beloff acted as teller for the ayes. In a re-enactment of the debate fifty years on he was game enough to speak on the opposite side of that motion. In 1937, after completing a B.Litt. thesis at Magdalen, he went back to Corpus Christi as a research fellow, and after two years in that capacity left Oxford in 1939 for an Assistant Lecturership in the Department of History at Manchester University. At this time Lewis Namier was head of department and Alan (A. J. P.) Taylor one of Beloff's colleagues. Judging from a story told many years later by Professor John Clarke of the University of Buckingham in a commemorative address, the young Beloff did not get on well with Namier. In response to an encomium on him delivered by the American Cultural Attaché in 1976 on the occasion of the two hundredth anniversary of the Declaration of Independence, Beloff could not contain his profound disagreement and with characteristic honesty told him that Namier was 'a bad historian and a horrible man'.

Beloff's time at Manchester was soon interrupted by the outbreak of war. He was called up and served for a short time in the Royal Corps of Signals before being invalided out in 1941. His military service took him to the North Wales coast where, as he was to recall nearly sixty years later when addressing the House of Lords during the debate on the Second Reading of the Government of Wales Bill 1998, he was part of the 'ultimate deterrent' against a German invasion that fortunately never took place. Beloff then returned to Manchester and began to concentrate on American history, a subject that was to become one of his abiding interests. But there cannot have been many students about, and from 1944 onwards he must have spent considerable time in London after he had agreed to work for the Royal Institute of International Affairs on a detailed historical account of Soviet foreign policy. Within a year of the war ending he was offered the newly founded position of Nuffield Reader in the Comparative Study of Institutions at Oxford and so returned to his *alma mater* where he was to spend the next twenty-eight years.

In the opening pages of his collection of essays *An Historian in the Twentieth Century: Chapters in Intellectual Autobiography* (1992) Beloff remarks that he had always seen his career prospects in terms of becoming an historian. From an early age he pursued this ambition with remarkable single-mindedness. Reportedly taking his cue from a schoolmaster at St Paul's who advised his pupils to read a book a day Beloff became an omnivorous reader of historical material of all kinds. He was also assiduous in making notes on most of what he read, a habit maintained until old age. After graduating he embarked on research for a B.Litt. and chose on the advice of the historian G. N. Clark, a topic in late seventeenth-century English history with both social and political facets. It was the results of this work that were published in 1938 as *Public Order and Popular Disturbances, 1660–1714*, the first of well over twenty books which Beloff was to write in the course of his academic career. This first book was a scholarly monograph offering a fluently written and perceptive account of the fragility of public order in the period after the Restoration. It may well be that this first substantial piece of academic writing in which Beloff explores some of the practical and material limitations affecting all efforts to maintain 'peace, order and good government' foreshadows his later concern with the early stages in the development of the modern state in Europe. Another characteristic of all Beloff's later writing is clearly present in this first book. He had been educated and subsequently trained as an historian in an intellectual environment in which the scholar was expected to range widely within his subject and to be capable of presenting his findings elegantly and in a manner comprehensible to an educated, non-specialised reader. This imperative to write lucidly and to bring together both the historical evidence and the relevant explanatory arguments in a coherent narrative was to remain a powerful influence throughout Beloff's career.

Yet in terms of disciplinary location within the university it was not strictly speaking as an historian that Beloff returned to Oxford in 1946. The post he took up was new and intended to encourage the study of contemporary political institutions. Its first holder was by statute required to be a specialist in American institutions, and within a year of taking up the appointment Beloff was elected to a Faculty Fellowship at Nuffield College, then a fledgling graduate college intended to promote the study of the social sciences. But the Oxford of those days was a tolerant and eclectic place and few doubted that politics (one of the three elements in the School of Philosophy, Politics and Economics) had to be studied on an historical foundation. Indeed, for many years after 1945 politics as taught and studied at Oxford consisted mainly of papers in modern or contemporary history. Organisationally too the dividing lines between faculties were not as sharp as they later became and Beloff was a member of both the Social Studies and Modern History faculties, supervising graduates from both and offering lectures addressed to students from both faculties. The effect of the commitment to contribute to the teaching of politics on Beloff's intellectual development and his professional career was almost certainly to push his historical interests firmly into the twentieth century and to reinforce a conviction that contemporary political issues and problems could only be analysed and understood from an historical perspective. But whilst he continued to work on historical topics and to publish books that have to be described as works of historical scholarship, he was also developing a strong interest in public affairs and in particular in the ways in which foreign policy was formulated in Britain as well as in the United States and in other countries in Europe and beyond. Inevitably this meant over the years following that disinterested historical concerns were sometimes overshadowed in his work by particular current practical and political preoccupations. History was to run the risk of becoming the launching pad for a political argument.

From 1946 until 1974 Beloff led the life of a successful Oxford don. After his return to Oxford Beloff acquired a large house towards the end of the Woodstock Road in north Oxford where he and his family lived. He had married Helen Dobrin, the daughter of Russian émigrés in 1938, and they later had two sons. He was active both in college affairs (until 1957 at Nuffield, and thereafter at All Souls) and in the conduct of business in the two faculties to which he belonged, and especially in the Modern History faculty. He was too a diligent lecturer and gave much care to the supervision of graduates, a category steadily growing in size and importance during his years at Oxford. But he was not one of those Oxbridge academics who are content to be absorbed by teaching duties and the sometimes beguiling engagements of college or faculty administration. His passion was scholarship and research and it was to these activities that he resolutely devoted most of his time. This, therefore, seems an appropriate point at which to survey Beloff's academic output both during his Oxford years and after.

II

The results of his work on Soviet foreign policy for the Royal Institute of International Affairs appeared in two volumes entitled *The Foreign Policy of Soviet Russia* and published in 1947 and 1949 respectively. The first covered the years 1929 to 1936, the second 1936 to 1941. The focus was narrow and Beloff concentrated on a detailed description derived from a wide range of sources, including such Soviet documents as were then available, of the conduct of Soviet foreign policy in the era of Litvinov and down to the German invasion of Russia. The outcome was an extensive pioneering exercise in what was basically diplomatic history. The presentation was clear and concise, very much in what became the typical Chatham House style. Inevitably such work lacked the prophetic insights of someone like George Kennan who was also thinking and writing roughly at this time about Soviet foreign policy, and it is arguable too that it gave insufficient attention to the impact of Stalin's dictatorship on the making of Soviet foreign policy. Nonetheless, it was a remarkable contribution to laying the foundations for a better-informed approach to understanding Russian foreign policy in the post-war world. Very soon after these two books had appeared, a third volume entitled *Soviet Policy in the Far East 1944–51* followed (1953). Here again Beloff demonstrated his capacity to organise a large and disparate amount of very recent historical material into a coherent and lucid account of Soviet ambitions and interventions in a little known part of the world and thus to provide what he described as a structural framework for considering the deeper movements of change in the region and in Soviet policy. It is also noteworthy that all this work demonstrates political detachment in the handling of the material as well as a shrewd awareness of practical issues and problems.

The very recent history of Soviet foreign policy was, however, not Beloff's only historical preoccupation at this time. He was also reaching back into the past and meeting some of the specific obligations of his new post at Oxford. In 1948 he published *Thomas Jefferson and American Democracy*, and also an edition with critical introduction of *The Federalist or, The New Constitution.* Then in 1954 he brought out a short historical account of the early stages in the evolution of the modern state in Europe entitled *The Age of Absolutism 1660–1815.*

The book on Jefferson, relatively short and based mainly on the voluminous secondary literature on him, came out in a 'teach yourself history' series edited by A. L. Rowse. Whilst it opens with a broad survey of

Jefferson's long life and varied achievements, the main focus is on the contribution made by Jefferson to the establishment of the United States and to the shaping of its democratic traditions and ideals. Beloff's analysis of all this is succinct and shot through with many penetrating insights into the tensions in Jefferson's own political career and in his efforts to combine a strong commitment to natural law doctrines with the need in politics to provide practical answers to the challenges presented. This awareness of the difficulties inherent in reconciling practice with doctrine is expressed again in Beloff's commentary on *The Federalist* when he underlines a basic duality in that remarkable document between the empirical and sceptical account of social relations on which many of its institutional recommendations rest and the system of natural rights to the protection of which, so it proclaims, government should be dedicated. *The Federalist* was soon followed by *The Debate on the American Revolution* (1949), a striking collection of extracts from varied sources of American political arguments in the period 1760 to 1783.

The *Age of Absolutism* is a cross between a modest introductory textbook and a critical essay. A passage in the preface is worth quoting for the sake of the light it throws on Beloff's views on history (or more precisely historiography) as well as on the study of politics. Noting in the preface that he had not written a compendium he remarked: 'I have tried instead to emphasise some elements in the society and politics of the period which appear to be of most consequence from the point of view of those whose interest in history is the *pragmatic one of trying to understand their own times*' (author's italics). This observation indicates clearly that Beloff already at this stage in his career regarded history as in some sense a source of practical lessons and, as a consequence, was satisfied that the study of politics as a practical activity had always to proceed on the basis of relevant historical understanding.

Between 1954 and 1970, a space of sixteen years, Beloff's published output in book form appeared to reflect a shift in the centre of gravity of his research and writing away from straightforward historical work to various aspects of politics and public affairs. This does not mean that he pushed his historical interests out of view—far from it—and towards the end of this period he was working intensively on what was to become the first part of his attempt to delineate the decline and fall of the British Empire. But for a while it was foreign policy-making, both in the United States and in Britain, and the beginnings of economic and political integration in Western Europe that figured prominently in his work. In 1955 *Foreign Policy and the Democratic Process* came out. This reproduced a series of lectures given at Johns Hopkins University in which Beloff examined the various ways in which the fact of being a democracy had a profound impact on the making of American foreign policy. There followed a work of a quite different kind, *Europe and the Europeans: an International Discussion* (1957). This was the outcome of Beloff's collaboration with a number of study groups set up by the Council of Europe to consider what evidence there might be for the existence of something like a common and shared European consciousness—what some Germans, especially back in the 1950s, were fond of designating *'abendländische Kultur'*. Out of what must have been somewhat rambling investigations and discussions Beloff hammered out an incisive and wide-ranging account of the different strands in what might be called the European political, economic, and cultural space. Much of the analysis he offered was historical and he gave short shrift to many myths about the ways in which Europeans somehow or other composed a unity. On the contrary diversity and difference were vital elements in the European evolution, especially in the cultural sphere to which he devoted a chapter in which he brilliantly synthesised a wide range of evidence drawn from literature and art. The practical conclusions drawn in this book were, not surprisingly, somewhat thin, a fact emphasised in retrospect when one notes that it was written just before the Treaty of Rome was signed. At this time there was little experience of the potential for the drawing together of the separate national economies in Europe. Beloff's presentation of the consciousness of what it means to be European does, however, already reflect in a restrained and entirely non-ideological way the scepticism about the larger enterprise of European unification that he was to express so strongly in later years. It was essentially his keen historical awareness of how Europe had for both good and ill evolved in the past that led him even in the 1950s to pour a certain amount of water into the wine of the enthusiasts for the creation of some sort of common European identity. A collection of previously published essays appeared in 1959 under the title *The Great Powers*. Many of these again reflect his interest in how American foreign policy has to reflect many of the internal structural conditions of American government and politics, but there are also articles on European integration and on problems in comparative political analysis and the relevance of historical study to it.

In *New Dimensions in Foreign Policy: A Study in British Administrative Experience 1947–59* (1961) Beloff sought to show how British administrative methods and arrangements had been adapted in the post-war world to cope with the growth in commitments to a wide range of new international bodies, especially in Europe. He emphasised the importance for foreign policy makers of finding points of balance amongst competing and often conflicting interests stemming from the more complex international environment in which they had to operate. This excursion into the field of British administration may have reflected Beloff's feeling that after his election in 1957 to the Gladstone Chair of Government and Public Administration at Oxford he ought to make more explicit his concern with contemporary British public administration as a specific field of study. In 1963, however, he was back with American foreign policy and its approach to European unity in *The United States and the Unity of Europe*, a book based on lectures given at the Brookings Institution. In it he traced the significance of the theme of unity in Europe in American foreign policy and the material contributions made by the United States to the economic and political reconstruction of Western Europe after 1945. It was clear in his view that United States governments, whilst ostensibly keen to promote 'unity' in Europe were never quite sure why and how the pursuit of this cause related to American national interests. He also discussed the position of Britain in relation to these developments, laying particular emphasis on the constraints stemming from Commonwealth ties and interests that motivated the British refusal to embrace economic integration in Europe.

In this middle phase of Beloff's academic career there is yet another book on what can be described as the general context of foreign policy, *The Balance of Power* (1967). This was based on the Beatty Memorial lectures given at McGill University in Canada. Here he ranges widely over both theoretical and practical issues bearing on the conditions under which states have to co-exist. He believed that the balance of power in Europe in some nineteenth-century sense had plainly been destroyed both as a result of war and of ideology. The tensions between *Realpolitik* and moral commitments could be seen, so he argued, in the inability of the Americans to decide whether they wanted to see a united Europe as an adjunct to their own power or as an independent power in the world. Whilst it is doubtful how far Beloff succeeded in this volume in clarifying some of the conceptual muddles affecting the very notion of balance as applied to politics in general and international politics in particular, he did as usual illustrate his arguments from a wide range of experience. There is, for example, a perceptive chapter on the impact at that time of the absence of a counterweight in the Far East to China, a situation prompting both the Soviet Union and the United States (though for different reasons) to favour support for India. These lectures are peppered too with acerbic comments on such matters as contemporary moral reluctance to make use of the notion of a balance of power in world politics, and the self-righteousness and lack of realism then discernible, for example, in the Indian approach to foreign policy. Yet another book appearing in 1969, *The Future of British Foreign Policy,* testified to his preoccupation at this time with the difficulties facing Britain as it struggled to find a new direction in foreign policy in the face of the loss of empire and the gradual but steady progress of economic integration in Europe. He saw the difficulties of any project of European federation, but eschewed all polemics on the relations between Britain and the European Economic Community.

One other work in this middle period underlined Beloff's abiding concern with American political institutions. This was *The American Federal Government* (1959), a short textbook in which he set out lucidly and perceptively the main features of the political institutions and practices of the United States. Overall the output of these years between 1954 and 1969 illustrates the very wide span of Beloff's interests in and knowledge of contemporary politics—international, British, and American. Yet whilst he continued to display impressive erudition and an acute sense of what was significant in all the topics he handled, there are signs of some sacrifice of focus and of scholarly quality in his output. The publication in 1969 of *Imperial Sunset Vol. I: Britain's Liberal Empire 1897–1921* reaffirmed, however, his reputation as an historian. It underlined not only Beloff's voracious appetite for work, but also his underlying belief that only through an understanding of historical experience can we make sense of where we are now and devise intelligent responses to present day practical political problems. He acknowledges in the introduction that he received the impetus to embark on this work from Harold Macmillan's decision in 1961 to apply for membership of what was then known generally as the Common Market. Perhaps unconsciously echoing Edward Gibbon's famous remarks about what prompted him to set to work on his own great history, Beloff states that he intends to trace the profound changes in British attitudes and power since that apogee of empire in 1897, when it would have been inconceivable that Britain would contemplate joining 'a set of economic arrangements . . . inspired by the ideal of a United Europe'. With his keen eye for historical drama—or perhaps for irony?—he notes in the Introduction that Churchill, a subaltern in the Indian army in 1897, the year of the Diamond Jubilee, had survived to vote on the motion approving the application to join the European Economic Community in 1961: 'The decline and fall of the British Empire had been consummated within a single active lifetime.'

Yet despite these echoes of Gibbon's *Decline and Fall* Beloff's *Britain's Liberal Empire 1897–1921* and its eventual successor volume, published in 1989 under the title *Dream of Commonwealth 1921–42*, are very different works. Gibbon set out on his vast canvas events in the distant past with which at any rate the educated classes in Europe were vaguely familiar and the remains of which could still be contemplated in many countries. The decline of Rome could draw on plenty of nostalgia for greatness lost. In contrast (and no doubt Beloff was keenly aware of this) the decline of the British Empire, though well advanced, was still going on and remained a matter of contemporary political controversy. In addition there can be no doubt that there were influential voices in British public life that welcomed the dissolution of empire: it was still far too early for anything like the revisionism in favour of a more charitable assessment of the benefits of the imperial mission for the nations previously subject to British rule and of which Beloff's work contained more than a hint. It is striking, however, that apart from some references early in volume 1 of *Imperial Sunset* to his desire to focus on those aspects of the decline of the Empire which would throw light on what was then perceived as the choice between Europe and the Commonwealth, Beloff then provides a judicious and wide-ranging historical account of the various streams of development within the Empire and in the world to which it was exposed which within a quite short period eroded belief amongst the British ruling elites in the feasibility of maintaining the whole vast structure. After all, British governments had themselves established self-governing 'Dominions' and it was not surprising that most of these assumed ever greater autonomy in the management of their foreign, defence, and trade policies. Perhaps what was really surprising was the fact that even on the eve of the Second World War something like an 'imperial system' still survived, taking its lead from London and bringing all the major self-governing dominions into the war (apart from Eire which had placed itself in a different category altogether). It was characteristic of Beloff's sharp eye for historical turning points that he then brought volume 2 to a close in 1942, the year in which Singapore fell to the Japanese invaders. For him that event was final proof that the Empire had effectively come to an end. No matter what restoration appeared to take place after 1945 Britain would no longer have the resources or the will to keep the Empire going, whether as political reality or as a mere ideal.

Beloff's work on the passing of the British Empire was never completed as he originally envisaged it. There was to be a third volume taking the story down to 1961, but as he reports in the concluding pages of volume 2 he realised that he was by 1989 too old ever to carry out the task, but he hoped that some day a younger scholar might continue where he left off. Whether in the near future anybody will be ready to embark on such a wide-ranging historical synthesis does, however, seem to be doubtful. Historical scholarship in relation to the imperial experience has, like so much else in the academic world, become both specialised and segmented. Meanwhile Beloff's work stands as an impressive testimony to his powers of historical synthesis, his capacity for shrewd judgements on political events, his awareness of the realities of power in material terms, and the fluency of his pen. But whilst the titles of the two volumes suggest the contemplation of a sad decline from greatness, the content of them reveals virtually nothing of such emotional self-indulgence. Instead what Beloff provides is a clear, no-nonsense historical narration of what he saw as crucial stages in the rapid political decline of what for a few decades had been the most extensive empire the world had ever seen.

After 1970 the flow of publications slowed down a little, no doubt to a large extent because other non-academic preoccupations were beginning to emerge and to make increasing demands on Beloff's time and attention. Most important of these were his involvement in the founding of what was to become the independent University of Buckingham, and later his membership of the House of Lords and the immersion in public affairs that this brought. However, before dealing with these matters it is convenient to conclude this survey of Beloff's principal academic writings. In 1970 he published a collection of articles and essays already in print under the title *The Intellectual in Politics and other essays*. The articles are arranged under six headings, though this device does little to confer thematic unity on the book. Perhaps the most interesting section consists of three essays on what he called the Jewish predicament. These are examples of the comparatively rare occasions (another occurs in his later collection of essays *An Historian in the Twentieth Century*) on which he dealt with aspects of modern Israeli politics and the difficulties faced by the Jewish state in a hostile environment. He appeared to write on these matters with some diffidence and a certain degree of detachment. This may have been a consequence of his lack of sympathy for Zionism as a political ideology, but it may also have owed something to the difficulties he had in coming to terms with a society as brash, energetic, and disputatious as modern Israel. Nevertheless he did visit Israel on several occasions, lectured at the Hebrew University, and was proud of being a governor of Haifa University. In 1980 what turned out to be a highly successful textbook on British government appeared, *The Government of the*

United Kingdom: Political Authority in a Changing Society. This was written jointly with Gillian Peele of Lady Margaret Hall at Oxford who contributed very substantially both to the assembling of research material and to the final shape of the text. The book went into a second edition in 1980 and into a third in 1995, though on the latter occasion without Beloff's participation. Something like an historical supplement to the book on British government is provided by Beloff's 1984 publication, *Wars and Welfare: Britain 1914–1945*. This provides a brisk and judicious summary of the impact of war and welfare policies on British politics and methods of government.

As already mentioned the second part of *Imperial Sunset* came out in 1989. After that there were only two more books to appear. One was *An Historian in the Twentieth Century: Chapters in Intellectual Autobiography* (1992) and the other was *Britain and the European Union: Dialogue of the Deaf* (1996). The former is interesting chiefly for the light it throws on Beloff's family background and his experience in the House of Lords as well as for incisive comments on the writing of history and a variety of other topics. It contains too an essay, entitled 'The Jewish Experience', in which Beloff provides a remarkably sympathetic and perceptive exploration of the social and moral foundations of the Israeli state. In the book on Britain's difficult relationship with the European Union he set out in detail the grounds for what was by 1996 his confirmed and profound hostility to the manner in which the European Union was developing and the implications of this for the political and constitutional integrity of the United Kingdom. Of all the intellectuals in politics Beloff had become perhaps the most convinced Euro-sceptic to be found amongst them. Once again, however, his arguments are not to be dismissed as merely cranky. They rested on persuasive historical grounds as well as expressing his own deep commitment to what he saw as the inherent virtues of the British system of government and British notions of the rule of law. The survival of all this was in his view under threat as the political pretensions of the European Union became ever more ambitious.

III

Despite the fact that Beloff was intensely devoted to research and academic writing, he began in the later 1960s to develop interests which eventually led him into something like a new career in public affairs. This was to last for best part of a quarter of a century down to his death in 1999.

In 1957 he had left Nuffield College for All Souls on his appointment as Gladstone Professor of Government and Public Administration. This was a prestigious position which gave to its holder opportunities to engage in public life if he cared to take them. It may well be that the greater emphasis in Beloff's publications during the 1960s on the practical aspects of government, especially in the field of foreign relations reflected a desire on his part to demonstrate that he was not just an academic historian, but also a keen student of government. Then in the later 1960s came student dissent and a growing taste for iconoclasm amongst the young. Though the manifestations of student radicalism at Oxford were relatively tame compared with those experienced elsewhere even in Britain, they upset many of the more traditionally minded senior members of the University, including Beloff and the then Warden of All Souls, John Sparrow. All Souls, perhaps just because it had no students, was an easy target for the Young Turks who denounced it as a reactionary bastion of privilege. Beloff and Sparrow reacted adamantly and did not conceal their feelings of outrage, though curiously the former was committed to internal reforms in All Souls such as the admission of graduates which the latter came to oppose. After only a few years the storm blew over, not least because many dons at Oxford reacted more calmly and sought some kind of dialogue with the student radicals. But these years disillusioned Beloff considerably (he was from time to time the object of personal vilification) and All Souls was not reformed in the ways he had hoped for. All this may well have stimulated his concern about the position of universities in Britain generally and the question-marks hanging over their future. At any rate he felt strongly enough about these matters to write an article for the journal *Minerva* in 1967 entitled *British Universities and the Public Purse*. This offered restrained and sensible comments on the impending threat that the Comptroller and Auditor General would be given access to university accounts. Beloff did not see this as worth a lot of fuss, but focused instead on the much more diffuse challenges to the autonomy of universities stemming from their increasing dependence on public funds and the tendency of the bodies providing them to foist their priorities on the universities. In so far as the article contained a plea, it was for British universities to be more active in seeking private funds in emulation of their American counterparts.

The effect of this contribution to public debate was to make Beloff well known as someone worried about the drift towards a completely state funded university system and sympathetic to efforts to marshal private resources in support of academic institutions. The initiative then passed for a while to others, notably Professor Harry Ferns of Birmingham University and Mr Ralph Harris (later Lord Harris of High Cross), the Director of the Institute of Economic Affairs (IEA) and a strong advocate of free markets. It was a paper by Ferns, published by the IEA in 1968, that launched the proposal for a private and wholly independent university. But Beloff was quickly back in the centre of the discussions which then took place and led soon after to the setting-up of a Planning Board for an Independent University. In that context he was active and successful in engaging the support of several eminent people, including his brother-in-law, Sir Ernest Chain, holder of a Nobel Prize for biochemistry. Furthermore, his preference for a relatively tradition-alist university with an Oxbridge flavour as opposed to a large city-centre foundation, originally preferred by the radical free marketeers amongst the founding fathers, had a major influence on what finally emerged, though from the very beginning finance was also a major con-straint. However, largely as the result of a generous (and at that time anonymous) gift from the businessman, Lord Tanlaw, the scheme for the building of a university in the small town of Buckingham became feas-ible, and despite the many obstacles in the way of achieving the desired objective the University College at Buckingham was able to open its doors to students at the end of 1975. But well before that event Beloff had been persuaded by the Provisional Council of the fledgling institu-tion to accept appointment as its founding Principal. So in 1974 he resigned from his chair at Oxford and left All Souls for the distinctly Spartan surroundings of what was mainly a building site in a modest market town.

Without doubt Beloff showed outstanding courage and dedication in taking up this challenge at the age of 61. He knew that he faced much opposition from the Labour Government that took office in 1974, from many parts of the bureaucratic education establishment, and even from people who on political grounds should have been supportive. Neverthe-less, he set about bringing together a nucleus of talented academic and administrative staff, solicited and gained at least enough financial support to allow the dismal site in Buckingham to be transformed, and played a major part in the design of the initial courses to be offered. In this con-nection he was very much in favour of courses combining at least two subjects or disciplines and opposed narrow specialisation. He became too a vigorous and effective publicist for the new venture. Once students had arrived he took his duties towards them very seriously, giving lectures, talking with them and providing academic advice when needed. When he retired in 1979 he could be confident that his successor, Professor Sir Alan Peacock, was taking over a going concern. Though Beloff's time at Buckingham was short, his contribution was crucial to the success of the whole undertaking. He conferred academic distinction on the new institution and above all applied his formidable capacity for hard work and tenacity of purpose to pushing it forward. It was a source of gratification to him that in a changed political climate the new University College received a royal charter in 1983 and was thus enabled to confer degrees in the normal way.

The last phase of Beloff's career took him into public life and service. For most of his life he had been a supporter and sometimes active member of the Liberal party. But he parted company from the party in 1972 and moved steadily towards the Conservative party which he joined in 1979. In particular he was attracted by the libertarian and free market thinking that was being propagated by several 'think-tanks' close to the Conservative party and its new leader, Margaret Thatcher. On her advice he received a knighthood in 1980, and then in 1981 accepted a life peerage, taking the title of Baron Beloff, of Wolvercote, the village near to the end of the Woodstock Road in Oxford where he had lived for many years. In offering him the peerage Mrs Thatcher made no bones about her expectation that he would support the Conservative Party in the House of Lords. For the most part Beloff remained faithful to his side of the bargain, though he was far too independent in his judgement ever to be a mere party man and there were to be many occasions on which he did not hesitate to criticise and oppose measures put forward by the government he supported. One reason for his readiness to take up a critical stance is to be found in the distance that always existed between him and the inner circle of Conservative politicians. This in turn stemmed from the fact that he lacked conventional political instincts and skills, was too honest and outspoken in the expression of his opinions and convictions to be a comfortable partner in deliberations about policy and tactics, and was probably too sharply focused in respect of the causes that mattered to him in public affairs—foreign policy, education and especially the higher end of it, and the British constitution—to relate comfortably to the free-wheeling generalists who dominate British political life. Nevertheless, perhaps for a very short time in the early 1980s Beloff hoped that he might exert real influence on the party's policies for education as a result of an advisory position in the Conservative Research Department to which he had been appointed. But he had an uneasy relationship with Sir Keith Joseph and was effectively sidelined by 1983.

The House of Lords did, however, provide a stage on which Beloff could play the kind of part in public life for which he was eminently suited—that of a thought-provoking and often provocative critic. What is more, the procedural framework suited him. Unique amongst legislative chambers the House of Lords conducts most of its business in plenary session by debate on the floor of the House. It is able to do this chiefly because, knowing that its decisions can always be overridden by a government with a majority in the House of Commons, most members of the Lords exercise self-restraint and tone down party commitment. This is one of the reasons why it has a reputation for rational and well-informed debate: it is indeed rather like a high-grade debating society of the kind that Beloff had known in his youth at Oxford. So most of Beloff's work in the Lords was done through speaking in debate, asking questions, and proposing motions on the floor of House. He was never much of a committee man, though he did serve a short stint (1981–2) on the Select Committee on Science and Technology and in 1995–6 was a member of an ad hoc Select Committee on Relations between Central and Local Government. His record of attendance in the House was impressive, amounting occasionally to over 200 daily attendances in a session. This meant that he got into the habit of coming up to London for at least three days a week. He travelled from Brighton (to which he and his wife retired), stayed overnight at the Reform Club, and then went over to his office in the Lords in the morning and into the chamber later on. Colleagues have recalled that he was a rather solitary figure in the House, sometimes to be found working in the library, sometimes just sitting in a corner thinking. This no doubt helped him to develop an outstanding ability to deliver without notes short and pithy speeches, peppered often enough with sardonic and sometimes humorous remarks. Within the somewhat esoteric environment of the Lords he could perhaps be described as a 'crowd-puller'. Like many other peers he concentrated on topics in which he was keenly interested. He spoke often on education and especially on the universities, and vigorously opposed some features of the Education Reform Act 1988 which he saw as undermining academic freedom. Similarly he opposed in the same year the introduction of student loans, joining forces with critics from the opposition parties and the cross-benches. Foreign affairs often brought him into action, and during the 1990s that often meant opposition to the European Union and to legislation (for example on the Maastricht treaty) stemming from British membership. He maintained too a vigilant eye on all measures and proposals with a bearing on British constitutional arrangements. Not surprisingly he was a persistent and trenchant critic of most of the constitutional changes introduced after 1997 by the Blair Government. He opposed human rights legislation with perfectly defensible arguments, but his attempt to defend the right of hereditary peers to sit in the House of Lords on the grounds that the hereditary principle was a factor in many social practices, including the inheritance of property between the generations, struck many as quixotic. For Beloff the eighteen years he spent in the Lords may have sometimes seemed like a personal 'imperial sunset'. Yet they were also years of unremitting toil, imposing a burden that he nonetheless accepted without complaint even though in the end Parkinson's disease was steadily taking its toll and reducing his mobility. But in accepting such burdens, which also included regular attendance at meetings of the Association of Conservative Peers, he was remaining faithful to his own austere sense of duty and commitment to public service.

Alongside his activity in the House of Lords Beloff remained very active as a writer, though the flow of books diminished in his later years. But if he wrote fewer books, he was even more heavily engaged than earlier in his life in writing for newspapers, particularly *The Times*. He was also ready to give the occasional lecture, sometimes to bodies like the Conservative Political Centre or the Centre for Policy Studies, sometimes within an academic framework as at All Souls where he gave three lectures in 1997 in commemoration of the fiftieth anniversary of Amery's *Thoughts on the Constitution*. Beloff had remarkable fluency as a contributor to the press and, though much of his journalism was polemical, it was never superficial or trivial. He felt strongly on many issues and in the expression of his views he could sometime appear to be insensitive and tactless. But whatever the issue with which he was dealing he always believed that it had to be treated seriously, and often enough that meant putting it into an historical context. He did this even in what must have been the last thing he wrote for *The Times* shortly before his death on 22 March 1999. This was an article in which, prompted by reading volume 1 of Ian Kershaw's *Hitler*, historical comparisons were drawn between the ways in which Hitler and Tony Blair had each built up support for their 'projects'. Not surprisingly this piece elicited cries of outrage from many, though, as I wrote to Beloff at the time, if he had put the emphasis squarely on techniques of propaganda alone, he might have been less exposed to indignant criticism. But he was never one for toning down a vigorous polemic.

Beloff received many honours and tokens of recognition. He was elected to a Fellowship of the British Academy in 1973. He held six honorary

doctorates and was a D.Litt. of the University of Oxford. He was an
Honorary Fellow of Corpus Christi College and of Mansfield College,
Emeritus Fellow of All Souls, and between 1975 and 1984 a Supernu-
merary Fellow of St Antony's College. He was an honorary professor at
St Andrews University, and naturally retained strong links with the University of Buckingham, in the development of which he continued to
maintain a keen interest. He was for some time a governor of his old
school, St Paul's, and also of the University of Haifa in Israel.

IV

A fair assessment of Beloff's work as an historian and political scientist
(though he disliked that term) is not easy to make. This is in part because
whilst much of what he wrote was history, much of it was also what might
be called 'public affairs from an historical standpoint'. Inevitably this
meant that what was intended to be straightforward historical analysis
sometimes ran the risk of being too heavily influenced by current preoccupations arising in the sphere of public affairs. Yet this idea that the historian should be concerned with public affairs was very much to the fore
in the 1930s when Beloff was at Oxford, and to some extent his ideal
became and remained that of the scholar-historian who brings his knowledge to bear on the problems and controversies of his own times. As to
his views on what being an historian really involves, they were plain and
down-to-earth. Beloff had no taste for theoretical or philosophical speculation on questions such as: what is the status and validity of historical
knowledge? He took the practical line that historical facts were generally
ascertainable and that once they had been gleaned from the records of the
past and put together intelligently, the historian could claim something
like objectivity for the account he presented. There is interesting confirmation of this view in a passage in *An Historian in the Twentieth Century*
where he contrasts it with the conclusions of Professor Sir Michael
Howard (whom Beloff admired) in favour of a more sceptical view of
what degree of historical objectivity is attainable. For Beloff regarded the
assurance of objectivity in the pursuit of historical knowledge as something like an antidote to his own pessimism about human progress. This
may have reflected the growing disenchantment with the state of Britain
that he certainly felt in the last decade of his life. Yet it was a view that
was not really in harmony with the rationalist element in his outlook and
his passionate belief in the possibility of persuading people by appeal to

reason and experience. Whilst he once described himself in the Lords as 'the last Tory', he was probably in fact much nearer to being 'the last Whig', a position he mischievously attributed to fellow historian Earl Russell when both were united in 1990 in opposing legislation to facilitate student loans.

What stands out in all Beloff's writing—historical or otherwise—is his fluency, clarity of presentation, and cogency in getting across the principal points he wants to make. And he attributed great importance to these qualities, as he makes abundantly clear in *An Intellectual in Politics* when he remarks that: 'The point of writing is to make one's knowledge and ideas accessible to others who may find what one has to say useful; much of narrow political science writing ignores this salient fact and will perish where Bagehot, Bryce and Bodley survive.' Since he could write so fluently and was a glutton for hard work, it is not surprising that he was so prolific. What is more, when Beloff was a young man learning how to become an historian, there was nothing unusual in a gifted scholar turning out short, well-written texts addressed to both students and the educated general reader: the age of academics writing in recondite language more or less only for each other had not yet arrived. Nevertheless, there was a price to be paid for Beloff's capacity to write so much. The quality of the output is variable: the work on Soviet foreign policy is impressively solid and thorough, the biography of Jefferson or the work on the rise of the modern state are just a shade lightweight. The two volumes of *Imperial Sunset* are perhaps Beloff's most carefully constructed and thoughtful pieces of historical writing, whilst some of the work on aspects of international affairs published in the 1960s sometimes suggests an author in too much of a hurry to move on to the next book. Yet these variations in quality are perhaps not really all that great. For the most striking feature of Beloff's *oeuvre* is that he establishes a characteristic style of writing right at the outset of his academic career and maintains it more or less unchanged for the rest of his life. There is thus not much development or change of approach in his work: it maintains throughout the same high standards of lucidity, care in the ordering and presentation of the facts, and a readiness to use the available evidence to ground wide-ranging and sometimes contentious conclusions. In addition it is characterised by many perceptive and sharp insights into the ironies and oddities of human experience and often enlivened by Beloff's acerbic comments on the follies and misfortunes of mankind. But Beloff the historian and writer on public affairs was notably more moderate and restrained than Beloff the journalist and active participant in political life. He is likely to be remembered longer for his achievements in the first of these roles than in the second. But reflecting on his life in 1992 he remarked, no doubt with reference to the university he helped to found: 'I now know how different is the feel of an institution if one is associated with its workings from the view that an academic obtains by studying it from the outside'. If the University of Buckingham continues to flourish in the years to come, then may be that will turn out to be the most enduring monument to his endeavours.

NEVIL JOHNSON
Nuffield College, Oxford

Note.   I am indebted to many people who knew Lord Beloff for their recollections of him and for valuable items of information. In particular I record my thanks to his son, the Honourable Michael Beloff, QC (President of Trinity College, Oxford), his brother Dr John Beloff, Baroness Carnegy of Lour, the late Baroness Young, Professor John Clarke (University of Buckingham), Dr Alistair Cooke, Ms Gillian Peele (Lady Margaret Hall, Oxford), Mr Robin Briggs (All Souls College, Oxford), Mr Robert Jackson, MP, and several other colleagues in the University of Oxford. I also want to record my appreciation of the help received from the staff of the library of Nuffield College, Oxford.

TOM BURNS

Tom Burns
1913–2001

I

TOM BURNS was born in London on the 13 January 1913. He was one of numerous children of a poor family of Irish origins. His early interest in learning seems to have found little support and understanding on the part of family members, except for his mother Hannah and, after her premature death, for an older sister, with whom he was to re-establish contact, several decades later, during a visit to Vancouver, Canada. He complemented his education, which took place in relatively unsupportive school environments, with frequent attendance at local libraries, where he nurtured his lifetime habit of extensive and voracious reading. By the time of his graduation from the University of Bristol in 1933 he had become an outstandingly well-informed and cultured young man.

A formative influence during Tom's early life was his acquaintance with Quaker groups and institutions. Without expressly associating himself with their beliefs and practices, he developed a deep respect for the Quakers, and an abiding commitment to pacifism. Prior to the outbreak of the Second World War he joined a Friends Ambulance Unit operating at the front during the Russian–Finnish war. When Britain entered the war he became a conscientious objector, serving in the army as a medical orderly and ambulance driver.

In 1941, Tom was wounded and taken prisoner by the Germans at Crete. The first entry in the collection of his essays entitled *Description, Explanation and Understanding*, published in 1995, is a cool narrative of

Proceedings of the British Academy, **120**, 43–62. © The British Academy 2003.

this experience. He was held in Germany as a prisoner of war for several months, until repatriated in 1943 as part of an exchange of wounded prisoners. In the second chapter he reflects on his Stalag experience, which marked him deeply. For years he would remain unwilling to attend films that depicted, however inadequately, prisoner of war camps, for he found himself troubled by the memories they evoked.

Tom's return to civilian life was not unproblematical, as he was deeply disturbed by the threat represented by the V2 attacks on London, where he lived, but his fortunes took a turn for the better when, in August 1944 he met Elizabeth Clark. The couple married on the 28 October in the same year, and by 1958 their family of four daughters (Catherine, Charlotte, Sarah, and Lucy) and one son (John) was complete.

After the end of the war, Tom joined the West Midland Group on Post-war Reconstruction and Planning in the capacity of research assistant, and began to develop and to practise his extraordinary professional gifts as an observer and analyst of social life 'on the ground'. In 1949 he became a research lecturer in the Department of Social Studies at the University of Edinburgh, where he pursued topics beyond those associated with planning. It was in this context that he became closely associated with Erving Goffman, who at the time was researching for his doctorate in the Shetland Islands and using Edinburgh as his academic base. Tom, Goffman, and the anthropologist James Littlejohn would often argue at length over their shared significant intellectual interests, which included a commitment to a mode of research emphasising close observation of natural social settings, whether based on locality or on working tasks.

The essay collection mentioned above elaborates extensively on that commitment in an original and penetrating manner—see in particular his inaugural lecture, 'Sociological explanation'. However, Tom preferred practising sociology rather than debating its nature or justifying its existence. One might say that, throughout his career, he preferred being a practitioner *of* sociology to being an apologist *for* it. While aware of sociology's persistently insecure status and low standing in the academic hierarchy, he refused to be distracted by the recurrent diatribes about the *crisis* of the discipline or the obsessive concern of sociologists and would-be sociologists (especially post-graduate students) with its 'foundational' problems and its epistemological status. Instead he remained committed to the task of advancing the discipline through original and significant scholarly achievements and through a serious commitment to high standards of education and training.

Nor did he share the tendency of other practitioners to associate themselves with this or that sociological school, identified chiefly by reference to one or the other of the discipline's 'founders'. Exegetical themes played a relatively minor role in his writings—except for his 1992 book on Erving Goffman, which, it could be said, resumed a conversation between the author and his subject which had begun in the 1950s, and had occasionally been carried forth into the ensuing decades.

Tom's extensive familiarity with the sociological tradition(s) was expressed in his teaching more than in his writings, where it was, rather than expressly displayed, presupposed or reflected. In any case, he could on occasion be rather iconoclastic in his treatment of 'classical' writers, particularly Max Weber. He certainly felt a deep affinity with this writer and admiration for his monumental contribution, and in a sense sought to emulate him in his own historically oriented research work. However he dissented from some aspects of Weber's seminal treatment of bureaucracy, which other contemporary scholars, according to Burns, accepted and celebrated too uncritically. Tom's own research on the French Revolution, in particular, suggested to him that Weber had overestimated the significance of the Prussian experience as a model for systems of public administration, and by the same token the relevance of juridical knowledge as the form of *savoir* appropriate to organisational structures at large.

Although Tom did not overlook the contribution made to his topics by Karl Marx, Emile Durkheim, and Max Weber in his teaching and writing, he did not subscribe to the utterly privileged status which that trio had acquired in the sociological canon. For one thing, he took Georg Simmel quite as seriously, and regretted that the corpus of his sociological writings was not more widely available and put to further use in research.

Furthermore, he found that some of his conceptual concerns, for instance with the notions of 'conduct', 'public order' or 'social organisation' were simply not thematised in the sociological canon. This led on the one hand to his greater reliance on some aspects of anthropological theory, on the other to his sustained engagement with historical materials, as in his last (and alas unfinished) work.

Tom kept himself well informed on contemporary sociological scholarship, both in his assiduous work in the library, and in his personal contacts with scholars on both sides of the Atlantic—and of the Channel. This last point deserves emphasis, for, although on the one hand Burns was aware and respectful of the leading role contemporary American sociologists were playing in the discipline, and was gratified by the recognition which he was receiving from some of the best of them, he was on the other hand a thoroughly *European* sociologist. Sometime in the 1960s he remarked, how unsatisfactory it was that, as things then stood, a British sociologist would have a good chance to meet a German, French, or Italian sociologist only while sojourning at Harvard.

Before express arrangements to this effect were made by European institutions, he did his best to remedy that condition, and more generally to become acquainted with his European contemporaries or to make use of their work before they became well known among his own co-nationals. He never assumed that only sociological writings in English, or already translated into English, were worth reading, and put to use his knowledge of French and German to remedy the ignorance of contributions in those languages common among his peers. Early on in its existence, the European Cultural Foundation (a Dutch institution) recognised and put to use Tom's intense interest in fostering the interaction between British and Continental social scientists.

But his efforts to, let us say, 'Europeanise' British sociology to some degree, were sustained also by his passion for travelling on the Continent, particularly in France and Italy, with Venice a favourite destination. During his repeated stays there (shared with his wife Elizabeth) his appreciation of the city was fostered both by his keen aesthetic sense and his knowledge of its history (he found the work of Frederic Lane particularly inspiring).

It must be said that Tom's views on contemporary sociologists could occasionally be quite dismissive—'he's shot his bolt' was a relatively frequent comment of his, and he sometimes professed himself baffled by the status achieved by some current 'stars'. Furthermore, his professional thinking was grounded also on writings from disciplines other than sociology—chiefly philosophy, which he had studied at Bristol, social anthropology, economics, and (later) history. His formal academic education had not been in sociology since the discipline barely existed in Britain at the time he was an undergraduate, and he had never done post-graduate studies. As already suggested, it had been accompanied and complemented by diverse and extensive reading, as well as by a sustained interest in the arts—chiefly literature, the theatre and music.

Furthermore, Tom's overall intellectual stance expressed a deep commitment to the moral values and the political priorities associated with the British labour tradition. This occasionally diminished his awareness of the significance of other public concerns: for instance, at first he criticised as a retreat from more significant and abiding problems the emphasis that some members of the sociology profession had begun to place on ecological themes in the 1980s, displacing somewhat traditional concerns such as equality and social justice. His early familiarity with and sympathy for the Quaker tradition never ceased to inform his public concerns, and to inspire his rejection of violence as a means of policy. He occasionally described the days when the USA and the USSR seemed about to go to war over Cuba as the darkest in his memory. All this gave a distinctively humane cast to Tom's thinking, his research and his teaching, without ever compromising his commitment to the highest standards of intellectual achievement.

II

Tom always wrote to a high literary standard, which reflected on the one hand his thorough familiarity with British and European literature, and on the other his keen sense for the social and moral significance of the way people express themselves verbally in 'real life'. His accounts of organisational life, whether in electronic firms or at the BBC, devote a great deal of attention to local speech codes, the expressive and ritual aspects of the way in which people address each other in a variety of contexts.

Tom Burns had an excellent ear for the nuances of verbal expression. His favourite data-gathering practice was a series of relatively unstructured interviews, which often came close to being two-way conversations, as is shown by a number of excerpts in his books. Generally the interviews were recorded on tape, but were *not* subsequently transcribed verbatim. Instead, Tom preferred to listen time and again to the tape itself, each time attuning himself to diverse aspects of the speech of his respondents, with special attention to delays, hesitations, rephrasings. In the process, he would constantly refer also to his own field notes.

An example of the many valuable insights he derived from this assiduous, meticulous attention to his field data was his observation that the content of a given verbal interaction between members of an organisation of unequal hierarchical status was often characterised as an order or instruction by the higher-placed member, and as advice by the lower-placed.

In sum, while Tom never described himself as a socio-linguist, his awareness of the speech dimension of interaction was highly sophisticated.

It expressed itself in two significant features of his work. In the first place, it tended to give a truly dialogical structure to the interview process. In 1977, the preface to his book on the BBC justified in the following terms this somewhat unconventional format of Tom's favourite research tool:

> How successful the procedure turns out to be depends ... on how non-threatening and intrinsically interesting the researcher can make his inquiries appear to the people he meets. It amounts, in other words, to a matter of engaging the people interviewed as willing co-operators in his inquiries, of involving them in the furtherance of the study. Hence, the constant need to make clear what I was up to, and what I was making of the information I had gathered so far.
>
> As a result, all the interpretative and explanatory ideas put forward in this book ... were discussed, developed, or amended during interviews or subsequently in talking to people who were or had been members of the Corporation.

In the second place, as suggested above, his great sensitivity to language may have inspired Tom to pay a great deal of attention to the literary dimension of his own writings, producing texts which are never either laborious or casual, and where the precision of the description and the sophistication of the interpretation are matched by the clarity of the prose.

The essay collection, *Description, Explanation and Understanding*, although it is selective and regrettably leaves out some rather significant publications, still enables the reader to understand why the lonely sociologist from Edinburgh, where he had few if any collaborators associated with the discipline (Goffman himself, in the Shetlands, had been researching toward a doctorate in anthropology), rapidly gained a remarkable standing in the discipline, signalled by the publication of very substantial essays in top journals. To mention only those included in the collection, in 1953 *The American Sociological Review* published 'Friends, Enemies and the Polite Fiction', in 1955 *Human Relations* published 'Cliques and Cabals', in 1961 *The Administrative Science Quarterly* published ' "Micro" politics: Mechanisms of Institutional Change'.

It was also in 1961 that Tom's masterpiece, *The Management of Innovation*, was published. This volume—one of the most significant sociology books of the second half of the twentieth century—had formally also another author, G. M. Stalker. However, the circumstances surrounding its genesis, and the content of prefatory materials associated with its later editions and several translations, clearly indicate a discrepancy. G. M. Stalker, who appears never to have pursued an academic career, had been associated with the original research project, and was meant to co-author the book, and to report its results. He had made a valuable contribution to what one would today call its 'data base' (according to Burns, Stalker was 'a superb interviewer'), but the book that came into existence and found its way to widespread acclaim had been conceived by Tom, and was totally his work.

As was the case with some of the essays that preceded it, *The Management of Innovation* dealt in the first instance with a significant empirical question: how the electronics firms which had operated in Scotland during the war had confronted the threats and opportunities which the return to peace represented for the industry. This was true to some extent everywhere, but perhaps particularly in Scotland. Most of those firms had been established there in the first instance, or had moved their plants from England in order to place them outside the range of German air attack. This as well as the fact that everywhere the electronics industry itself had been developed chiefly as an aspect of the war effort, confronted those firms with a special challenge—would they survive in the post-war environment, and if so, how?

Although the book demonstrates how conversant its author had become, in the course of his research, with a range of situational variables (including the technical nature of the electronics industry and the economic characteristics of its market), its focus was strictly sociological. Tom was chiefly interested in the organisational arrangements made (or not made) in the firms to deal with those variables, to allow or induce the people working in them to cooperate effectively. He was asking himself what effect those arrangements had had, or were having, on each firm's capacity to survive and to thrive.

The arrangements that mattered, his inquiries had determined, were much more complex and subtle than those conveyed by a given firm's organisation chart, or by the conventional distinction between 'line' personnel and 'staff' personnel. They had to do chiefly with the everyday practices of the firm—not just those evident in a plant's workplaces or in the titles assigned to its personnel, but also those suggested by the layout of its cafeteria or the way in which personnel grouped themselves within it and talked (or did not talk) with one another. It was Tom's close and perceptive observation of those practices which suggested some of his most valuable insights.

Let us mention one. In the firms he studied, knowledge and skills vital to the firm's success, especially those of a scientific and technical nature, were often vested in younger employees. To the extent that the firms' reward structure acknowledged this, it would necessarily place on the defensive more senior employees, who in most other industrial firms, considered themselves the firm's most significant resources and the main custodians of its future, and enjoyed titles and rewards to match. Early on in his inquiry, Tom had become aware of a significant phenomenon that had been relatively ignored in the existent sociological literature on industry. Such literature had emphasised the arrangements made by firms in order to acknowledge, and to reward with career success, the particular achievements of certain employees. It had paid but scant attention, however, to the fact that, by the same token, such arrangements acknowledged and penalised the failures of other employees.

In one of his most important essays, Tom had theorised both aspects of the phenomenon of differential rewards. He had suggested that each expressed itself in the spontaneous formation, within a firm, of two kinds of informal groupings with distinctive patterns of interaction (including, once more, verbal patterns). These were the *cliques,* assembling employees who had experienced, or were realistically anticipating, career success; and the *cabals* constituted by other employees, who instead had experienced, or were realistically anticipating, career failure.

The tensions embodied in this development of opposing internal groupings, and in the resultant 'micropolitical' relations, were intensified in electronic firms. Here, as indicated, the peculiar, irreplaceable contribution made by younger personnel in possession of strategic knowledge and skills had to be somehow validated, but this inevitably placed the more senior personnel under threat.

Firms would in various ways acknowledge and try to remedy and accommodate the tensions. But they could do so only up to a point; the inevitability of the threat persisted, for it reflected a broader phenomenon. A business such as electronics was, so to speak, condemned to innovation by the continually changing nature of its technical base and by the turbulence inherent in its markets. On this account, the organisational patterns appropriate to that business could no longer be those of firms operating in more stable environments, where a relatively high match between the age structure of the employee population and the distribution of the firm's rewards was one aspect among others of a well-established organisational model. Such a model, which Tom chose to label 'mechanical', reflected the presumption that, at any rate among white-collar, technically trained employees, more senior personnel possessed more valuable knowledge and skills than less senior personnel, and should be rewarded accordingly. In suitably organised electronics firms, which had adopted what Tom called an organic organisational model, such a presumption had to be abandoned, or at any rate strongly qualified.

Furthermore, within the organic model it ceased to be the case that the responsibility for monitoring the scientific, technical, and market environment of the firm, and for working out the required productive responses, should be left to its top managers, while the other personnel applied themselves to carrying out dutifully the policies knowledgeably laid down by their superiors. To survive, an electronics firm had to encourage all its technically trained personnel to keep abreast of current developments in electronic technology, of the new range of products they made possible, of the changing demands of potential customers, and of the strategies of competitors at home and abroad.

In other words, within an increasingly significant industry such as electronics, much conventional wisdom—including sociological wisdom—on the appropriate way to construct, to lead, to manage the organisational arrangements of firms, had to be surrendered or at any rate extensively revised and corrected. What made this necessary was, at bottom, the increasingly critical role played in such environments by sophisticated, science-based knowledge. This critical factor was continually being revised, left behind, and added to, and lent itself to intensive and sustained technical applications, both in the nature of the production processes and in the nature of the products themselves. But the organisational implications of that role were multiple and diverse, as the above examples show, and required a profound rethinking of the scope and method of the managerial aspects of industrial reality.

Thus *The Management of Innovation*, in contrasting what it termed the mechanical and the organic models of management, conceptualised a profound change in organisational philosophy which for some time had been at work in industrial practice but which had not been articulated as sharply and insightfully before. It made a distinctive contribution to the thinking of contemporary students (including those operating at the interface between social disciplines and industrial practice, particularly in business schools) on such problems as how to transfer knowledge and technology between firms or between branches of industry, or how to construct organisations capable of learning processes and thus capable of changing themselves. As the *Financial Times* stated on the occasion of a new edition of *The Management of Innovation,* 'Tom Burns . . . created a string of concepts which have had an increasingly powerful international influence . . . They have improved Western management practices immeasurably . . . and made millionaires of several famous American pundits who embroidered them.' Furthermore, Tom's masterpiece bore significantly on a growing range of important and visible aspects of contemporary society at large, such as the structure of educational and research institutions, and the phenomenon of mass consumption.

His sophisticated awareness of these multiple, ramifying connections made of him not only an outstandingly original scholar of organisations, but also a critical interpreter of a broader notion which, between the 1950s and the 1980s, informed much theorising about contemporary society—the notion of industrial society. (See in particular a review essay on the sociology of industry, published in 1962, and a successful reader, *Industrial Man*, published in 1969.) Another aspect of Tom's characteristic intellectual breadth, as we shall see, was his effort to determine what sense the notion of management itself acquired in contexts as different from industrial ones as hospitals and media organisations.

It is said of Thomas Jefferson that he is chiefly remembered for his two greatest achievements—writing the Declaration of Independence and founding the University of Virginia. Likewise, one could say that Tom's greatest achievements were on the one hand *The Management of Innovation*, and on the other the creation of the sociology department at Edinburgh University. The two were not unconnected, for it was presumably the first that led his University to appoint him Reader in Sociology in the Department of Social Administration and subsequently to put him in charge of establishing a department of that discipline.

Nearly forty years after its inception in 1964, the Edinburgh University Department of Sociology remains one of the strongest in the UK. It preserves the imprint of the inspired leadership of its founder, among other ways in the broad range of subjects it encompasses and in the commitment to supporting both teaching (under- and postgraduate) and research.

In establishing the department and putting it on the map, Tom took due advantage of intellectual and academic circumstances which were, at the time (and alas never again to the same extent) favourable to sociology. Acting promptly and energetically on the resultant commitment of his university to establish the discipline within its new Faculty of Social Sciences, he appointed as lecturers first a person who had already conducted research with him, then—over the subsequent years—a number of people from diverse academic backgrounds. With his collaborators, he embodied in the department's structure a strong commitment to undergraduate teaching—including a highly demanding four-year honours course— where quantitative subjects (such as demography) would be required for the degrees, alongside more conventional ones. Early on, the department undertook to teach for research degrees, availing itself of relatively extensive support from public funding bodies, but even its undergraduate programme acknowledged the vital importance of empirical work as an aspect of the intellectual identity of sociology. A number of methodological subjects were included in the curriculum, and each honours student was required to submit a piece of original empirical research.

Tom was head of department from 1964 to 1978, and from 1965 he also held the sociology chair. Over the years, the department became nationally and internationally known for the advanced research conducted there in a number of fields, ranging from industrial sociology to social stratification, the sociology of science, the sociology of the theatre, and of literature. It was thus, and remains, internally diverse, reflecting once more the breadth of interests characteristic of Tom Burns.

Tom undertook the responsibilities associated with the position of chair and department head in a highly personal style, and they engaged a great deal of his energy. There was nothing authoritarian to the man, but he liked to lead, as he was expected to do both by his senior colleagues in the university and by his junior ones in the department. His leadership thus took the form primarily of working hard at his job, and inducing his associates to see and to subscribe to the rationale for his preferences (concerning the curriculum, the selection of students, the selection of new members, or whatever). It was based on the recognition by his associates in the department (all at least one generation his junior) of the range and depth of his knowledge of the discipline as well as on his high and growing standing in the discipline at home and abroad. He invested considerable effort in securing for them the best working conditions and the best opportunities for professional development. The majority of those appointed to a lectureship at Edinburgh at Tom's initiative are currently holding chairs, or have ended their career while holding chairs, at Edinburgh or elsewhere.

Tom thus generated in his colleagues a strong feeling of commitment to the department, which as a result enjoyed for many years a continuity of composition, a sense of shared purpose, and an absence of internal dissent rather rare at the time among major sociology departments.

There is less information available on how he projected himself to his students. He seemed to be held in awe by them; but perhaps most of them were more aware of his sheer intellectual power and his mastery of whatever subjects he taught (including, in the early years of the department, the First Ordinary course, traditionally taught at Edinburgh by the most senior don) than they were of his intense concern for the students' intellectual and social welfare, and of the highly humane and respectful way in which he looked after them in his activity as department head.

The committed and most beloved father of his sizeable brood, Burns seemed to take a truly paternal, and thus in no way paternalistic, interest also in his students, beginning with the undergraduates. This was particularly evident in the context of the process whereby the department set examination papers and evaluated the students' performance in them. Furthermore, Tom took pride in their achievements, which were sometimes considerable. A number of students who left Edinburgh with first or advanced degrees went on to distinguished careers in sociology. Some of the students themselves, however, appear to have found him somewhat distant and forbidding, no matter how unjustified this judgement seemed to his departmental colleagues, who were well aware of how he understood, and discharged, his responsibilities to students and who benefited from the same attention to their own intellectual potentialities and requirements.

In the late 1960s, when he had begun to enjoy the eminence he deserved, Tom was asked to play a leading role in a massive effort then undertaken by Penguin Books to enter the academic market. He accepted, and planned and directed the Penguin Sociology series, which became one of the more significant components of that effort. His name figured on the series's masthead at the head of a distinguished editorial board. However the whole series was chiefly a product of his learning and enterprise, plus the keen sense he had been acquiring for the strengths of the discipline as an academic subject while building and directing the Edinburgh sociology department.

The main outcome of his collaboration with Penguin was a remarkable set of Sociology Readers, some of which were very well received both in Britain and in the United States, and went through several reprints. Among these were Tom's own *Industrial Man,* and *Sociology of Literature and Drama*, edited with his wife. Some expressly commissioned books also had a wide readership, demonstrating Tom's knack for identifying significant topics, as well as capable authors and editors (including some who had not previously made their mark). Unfortunately the success of Penguin Sociology was not shared by other components of the project as a whole, which was abandoned after a few years.

A man of considerable energy, Tom Burns, while building and leading the sociology department at Edinburgh, still found it possible to carry out serious research, to publish and to play a highly personal role in fostering the discipline. Early on, the uniquely effective way in which he would observe and explain the workings of organisations and, if so required, comment insightfully on how they could be improved, had led among other things to his being asked to act, formally or otherwise, as a consultant. Requests to this effect, originating from organisations as diverse as the BBC, the Shell and the British Petroleum corporations or the boards of hospitals, became more and more frequent after the publication of *The Management of Innovation*. Tom treated such requests (to which he could not always accede) chiefly as opportunities to enlarge and deepen his understanding of varieties of organisational experience, and to communicate some aspects of it to people active in, and sometimes in charge of, organisations. His consulting relationship with British Petroleum was particularly protracted, and is said to have made a serious impact on the corporation's organisational policies.

This may be said to reflect Tom's serious respect for what one might call the managerial class. He saw its activities principally as a critical aspect of a concern, shared with other participants in the units they managed—the concern to establish those units and to make them successful as the product and the frame of a sustained, effective collective effort. This does not mean that Tom could not be critical of the ways in which many British businesses were operated, but on the whole the concept of exploitation, like other concepts associated with the Marxian tradition, was not part of his own vocabulary. Perhaps this was because he researched chiefly organisations where the contraposition between 'bosses' on the one hand, and employees working at the coal face on the other, was not as visible and significant as in the favourite research sites of many other sociologists of industry.

Over the years, Tom's other projects were supported from two main sources. The first, particularly significant in the first phase of his research career, was a small set of Quaker foundations which, amongst their other commitments, undertook to support research. A good relationship with Quaker institutions was, as we have seen, a part of Tom's own biography, and greatly assisted his access to their support.

In the latter phase of his career, when Tom had gained national and international recognition as an outstandingly imaginative and productive researcher, public bodies expressly established in the UK to fund social research sought Tom's advice on their policies. They also occasionally supported his own research efforts, particularly on subjects not directly related to his prime interest in industrial organisations—such as the growing significance of life styles in creating collective identities, or the roots and significance of the student movement in the late 1960s.

It might be appropriate at this point to comment on one rather less positive aspect of Tom's distinguished career as a researcher, which was evident particularly in the phase leading up to his retirement. To use a typical Burnsian phrase, *there is a sense in which* the man's sociological imagination, his ability to identify significant but as yet inadequately explored and understood social developments was too good for his own good. This can be explained by constructing the following scenario from a few episodes in Tom's research career.

At any given time, his wide reading, his very diverse academic social contacts, his keen observation of ongoing facts on the ground, his sheer intellectual curiosity, would lead him to identify new themes for research. Once this happened—to summarise the typical sequence—Tom would promptly locate the relevant sources of information and assemble and analyse the existent literature on the phenomenon. He would then engage in sustained reflection and speculation on the causes and effects of it. Next, he would embody the results of the previous process in a research proposal, specifying the main hypotheses and indicating the appropriate research procedure. Typically, the proposal would commit Tom to being the project's principal investigator, though much of the actual research work might have to be conducted, under his guidance, by expressly hired researchers.

Tom would then submit his proposal to an appropriate funding body, typically in the form of a closely argued, elegantly written scholarly paper, complemented by a detailed statement of the project's research schedule, costs, and so on. Now, it happened a few times during Tom's research career that while the body in question deliberated on the proposal, its author's interest in the topic, without disappearing entirely, became less lively and compelling. He had meanwhile identified another theme for research, and was already focusing his intellectual effort on *that* topic.

At this point a positive decision by the body in question might be somewhat less welcome to Tom than one might have anticipated. He might in fact decide to entrust the actual conduct of the inquiry chiefly to the personnel expressly hired for it, playing a less active and involved role than that normally taken by the principal investigator. Later still, at the point where the data had been assembled and a primary analysis conducted by those personnel, Tom would find it psychologically difficult and intellectually unrewarding to take full charge of the final process and to do justice to its findings by writing a full-fledged report, possibly to be published as an essay or a book. In fact, on some occasions where the scenario described above was realised, Tom's inquiries, including some funded from outside sources, were never fully reported.

The causes of this may lie not just in his intellectual restlessness, but also in the difficulty he sometimes found in co-ordinating his efforts with those of others. Put in another way, this outstanding researcher of organisations was perhaps not at his best in organising research—even his own research, on topics of his own devising. This means that, imposing as it is, the intellectual legacy embodied in Tom's published writings is not as impressive as it might have been, had he been able to give a full account of his numerous research endeavours.

Tom's associates at Edinburgh would sometimes joke that, if you opened certain cupboards in the building (18 Buccleuch Place, where the department was located for most of its history) you would find yourself looking at skeletons. These cupboards contained masses of data assembled by Tom and his collaborators many years before (for the 'Pilton', or 'Housewife's Choice' projects for example), which had never been completely analysed, let alone reported on.

On occasion, this pattern had additional untoward consequences. Tom, as if stung by a sense that he had not fully acquitted himself of his obligations—toward his former collaborators, toward the funding body, toward the intellectual impulse itself which had motivated him to engage in a certain inquiry—would periodically seek to wind up a particular project by an intense bout of intellectual effort. However he did not always find himself able to accomplish this goal. The data had gone too cold, the intellectual processes themselves which had originally presided over the conception of the project had become difficult to reconstruct and to validate, the original methodology no longer seemed appropriate and the former associates involved in the project were no longer able or willing to collaborate.

In a few instances, there was a second consequence; the course of the inquiry itself, or its aftermath, would to an extent damage relations between Tom and his collaborators. A case in point is that of an inquiry into the causes of student unrest in the late 1960s. Here, Tom's creative interest in the subject did indeed bear fruit, in a remarkable essay, 'The Revolt of the Privileged', originally published in 1969 and now available in *Description, Explanation and Understanding*. However, the same essay had been used as a background paper for an application for funding which Tom had submitted to a public funding body and had been duly approved.

The proposal was for research teams to form at two British universities—the University of Edinburgh and a certain English one—and for each to conduct research, according to an agreed strategy, on the *other* university. The Scottish team was to be led by Tom himself, the other by the Professor of Sociology at the English university. It was a clever and promising scheme, but unfortunately the terms of collaboration and the respective responsibilities had not been sufficiently clarified. As a result, after some research efforts (and some funds) had been expended, the two principals began to disagree over their respective responsibilities, and the project had to be called off. It is impossible to determine what role was played in this story by Tom's inability to remain interested in his own interests, or by the fact that his true vocation (gloriously fulfilled) was that of a lone, hands-on researcher, not of a research organiser. It is difficult to dismiss the impression that both aspects played some role in the outcome.

On the other hand, neither aspect contributed to the serious complications, this time not of Tom's making, which befell a further research undertaking, that came nevertheless to a happy ending. The story is narrated in the preface to Tom's second great book *The BBC: Public Institution and Private World*. It begins in 1960–1, when Tom was invited by the Corporation to speak at two of its recurrent management conferences. The success of those presentations led to his being allowed to spend time at Broadcasting House and at the Television Centre, interviewing some twenty senior members of the staff.

This exercise became something of a pilot to a whole sequence of interviews, carried out in early 1963, and lasting between one and three hours each. It was understood that the outcome of this major research effort would be an extensive study of the Corporation, dealing with how members of staff form their working commitments and their career strategies, and with how these individual involvements merge (or conflict) with the social systems into which the organisation as a whole articulates itself in the pursuit of its institutional mission. It was also understood that no part of that study would be published without the consent (not necessarily the approval) of the Corporation.

Here lay the rub. When in due course Tom submitted to the corporation his 'working report', that consent was denied, for some key people in the Corporation felt that some of the findings were too sensitive, and could be damaging to the Corporation if made public. This was a bitter setback for the author, who knew he had produced a potentially very significant contribution both to his master theme, organisational life, and to the sociology of the media, but was prevented from making it known. As he was to write in 1995, he had been 'good enough to provide a gag for himself'. Furthermore, as he commented privately, he was also bound by his unwillingness, on moral and political grounds, to do anything that could conceivably damage one of the most important British public institutions.

About ten years after that aborted project, Tom was invited by the then Director General of the BBC to resume his study in order to ascertain what changes had occurred in the aspects of the Corporation's life he had previously studied. This led to a round of about sixty interviews, the collection of other relevant internal materials, and in due course to the completion of a report that encompassed the findings of both studies. Thus the report, and the subsequent book, have what could be called a 'longitudinal' dimension; although their main concern was with matters less subject to change over that period, they also addressed some changes which had occurred between the first and the second inquiry.

There was again some resistance to the publication of the book (not mentioned in the preface) on the part of Corporation officials, on the grounds that some of the findings, previously judged 'too hot', had meanwhile become out of date. (As Tom commented bitterly, 'heads you win, tails I lose'.) Fortunately the resistance was overcome, and in due course the book appeared as a volume in the series *Edinburgh Studies in Sociology,* that Burns had arranged to be published by Macmillan.

The series itself, it must be said, was not a great publishing success, and although the BBC book received considerable acclaim in Britain it was inadequately noticed in the US, where Macmillan had failed to find a partner publisher for an American edition. Understandably, this disappointed the author, who knew that to find the resonance it deserved the book had to appear in such an edition. This possibility was hampered by two considerations. In the first place, by the late 1970s the BBC apparently no longer enjoyed the standing it used to have as the senior broadcasting outfit in the English speaking world. Together with other things European and British, it was thought to have lost appeal as the theme of a book. In the second place—but this is more of an inference—Tom's new book could not be promoted as, so to speak, 'Son of' *The Management of Innovation,* a work which had been very well received by American academic audiences and made a serious impact on managerial circles. It had a different, more ambitious, more complex theme, and the argument it conducted did not lend itself to pragmatic applications.

Tom restated in the following terms what, *qua* organisations, the electronics firms he had studied years before and the BBC had in common:

> Organisations . . . are co-operative systems assembled out of the usable attrib-
> utes of people and are created and maintained to produce goods or services.
> But they are also places in which the people recruited into them compete for
> advancement. Thus, members of any business or non-business undertaking are
> at one and the same time co-operators in a common enterprise and rivals for
> the tangible rewards of successful competition with one another. The pyram-
> idal hierarchy of rank and authority familiar as representing the 'structure' of
> an organisation in fact represents both a control system and a career ladder.

The question was, how and to what extent this duality of aspects common to both types of organisation was inflected by their differences, and
thus what role the activity specifically intended to reconcile and moderate the resulting dilemmas—the activity of management, would play in
each type. With respect to the BBC, this was a particularly complex
question, as is suggested by the following considerations. The BBC was
a public, non-business organisation, intended to provide services, not to
produce a profit. The services intended were multiple (information, education, and entertainment) and not easily reconciled. It hosted a great
variety of participants, including a relatively large number identified as
'creative' personnel and/or specialists in particularly sophisticated,
demanding, and diverse fields. The environment in which it operated at
the time of the research was very different from that in which it had
been created: just think of the arrival of television and its continuous
technical developments (colour for instance), the unavoidable rivalry
with commercial television, the changes which had occurred since the
times of Reith in the BBC's relations with the government, parliament,
and political parties.

The challenge these changes posed for the organisation as a whole was
the main theme of Tom's study. It was not, in his view, adequately met.
He was particularly concerned by 'managerialism', that is by the increasingly disproportionate role played in the life of the BBC by its purely
organisational aspects and by the related political processes, as against
aspects more directly related to the participants' shared efforts to make
the organisation do its job. This trend is one that Tom noted with
concern also in the health service units he studied in and around
Edinburgh after finishing his research on the BBC.

In the second half of the 1970s Tom's health began to be undermined
by a condition, probably originating from an illness inadequately treated
during the war, which flared up again at unpredictable intervals. Up to
that point he had been a very vigorous man, and he resented its occasional debilitating effects. In the early 1980s, two years before the age at
which it would become compulsory, he decided to retire with the title of

Emeritus. By this time, he had moved with his wife to a suburb of Edinburgh. The children had all gone their separate ways, but the family remained very close.

This circumstance, together with Tom's apparent decision to distance himself from the academic environment he had so successfully created in the sociology department at Edinburgh, had one important consequence. Over the subsequent years he remained very active and creative as a scholar, but his assiduous frequenting of the Edinburgh University library became almost his only link with academic institutions. (This, one might say, spared him from witnessing at close quarters the onslaught of 'managerialism' on British universities in the 1980s and 1990s.) He was very proud, however, of his election to a Fellowship of the British Academy in 1982.

Throughout his remaining years, Tom remained highly committed to a massive and demanding scholarly project, from which he was distracted only for the time necessary for producing his excellent book on Erving Goffman. Regrettably, the project was still unfinished at the time he died, and the conditions in which he left his *Nachlass* make it difficult, for the time being, to describe its content and assess its import. The manuscript is currently in the hands of a prospective editor, an Australian scholar who had never met Burns but had long admired his work, and is working to convert it into publishable form. In the meanwhile, one can at best convey a tentative idea of what, in due course, may turn out to be another Tom Burns masterpiece.

It has been said that most sociologists work at one or another of three different levels: face to face interaction, organised units, and whole societies. Tom had gained his great reputation chiefly through studies located at the second level, though one of the strengths of these studies had been his awareness of the significance of interactions taking place at the first. He had of course discussed some of the societal determinants and effects of organisational life (while describing, for instance, the industrialisation process), but had not analysed societies at great length. In essence, he had been committed primarily to studying contemporary organisations, so that, while he was highly interested in change, the time span envisaged by his researches had perforce been relatively narrow. He gave notice of his intent to challenge the limitations of that commitment in an essay published in 1980: 'Sovereignty, interests and democracy in the modern state', the last reprinted in his essay collection. The title clearly indicates the societal scope and the much enlarged time frame of his thematic concerns; but the essay, while very significant in itself, is in fact a kind of promissory note, pointing to the massive research project he was to conduct over his last twenty years.

The project's theme was nothing less than the development of the major political and social institutions of Western societies. The study was to be narrative in form, and to begin with classical antiquity. Having taken notice of the recent (re)development within sociology of so-called comparative historical studies, Tom had made a decision to enter (and to challenge) that field. The decision had of course a corollary: the abandonment of the methodology of inquiry, based on extensive interviews and other forms of field work, which Tom had so extensively and successfully employed in his previous studies. The materials for analysis were now to be drawn from his reading of historical (or historical/sociological) literature, and up until the time of his death on 20 June 2001, Tom committed the greater part of his still very considerable intellectual energy to this activity. The other part was devoted to utilising those materials in drafting a book which, in two or three volumes, would take its story through to the twentieth century. The substance of the argument would be analytical; it would explore, this time, the varieties of institutional experience, with special regard to the institutions of public life, and a focus on the emergence of bureaucracy and of the more recent alternatives to it.

The writing process was clearly protracted, intense, and laborious. It produced a number of finished chapter drafts, and others left unfinished and sometimes overlapping. A glimpse at these materials (the editing of which has barely begun) suggests that this posthumous book of Tom's, different as it was from all its predecessors, will show that its author, in the last twenty years of a relatively long and very productive life, could still, as it were, 'stretch his wings', and perform most impressively a large and original scholarly mission.

GIANFRANCO POGGI
University of Trento

JOHN DESMOND CLARK   *E. J. Lofgren*

John Desmond Clark
1916–2002

FOR SIX DECADES, Professor John Desmond Clark played a leading role in archaeological research in sub-Saharan Africa. In the words of his former teacher, Grahame Clark, he did 'more than any other man to pull together the prehistory of the continent of Africa from the beginnings of human culture up to . . . recent times'. He was born in London on 10 April 1916, but the family moved to Turville in rural Buckinghamshire shortly afterwards. In later years Clark (1986) recalled how walks in the Chilterns with his father initiated his lifelong interest in the history and archaeology of the countryside, which was further nurtured by his teachers at Monkton Combe. It was at that school that his enthusiasm first turned towards Africa, with a short-lived interest in Egyptology. In 1934, Clark went up to Christ's College, Cambridge, where he read History before changing in his third year to Archaeology and Anthropology; his teachers included both Grahame Clark and Miles Burkitt, who contributed respectively to his concerns with environments and with artefact typology. During vacations in 1936 and 1937 he excavated under Mortimer Wheeler at Maiden Castle. It was at Cambridge that he met his future wife, Betty Baume, then reading Modern Languages at Newnham College. On graduating in 1937 he sought museum employment whilst undertaking volunteer work at the London Museum before obtaining an appointment in Livingstone, Northern Rhodesia (now Zambia).

A small museum had been established in Livingstone in 1930, mainly to house ethnographic specimens collected by administrative officers (Brelsford 1937); a few years later the collection was designated a

Proceedings of the British Academy, **120**, 65–79. © The British Academy 2003.

memorial to David Livingstone. In 1937, at the instigation of the Governor, Sir Hubert Young, an anthropological research organisation, the Rhodes–Livingstone Institute, was established and the David Livingstone Memorial Museum, by then housed in the building of the United Services Club, was placed under its control. Desmond Clark arrived in Livingstone in January 1938 to serve (at a total salary of £400 p.a.) both as Secretary to the Rhodes–Livingstone Institute and as Curator of the Museum, Godfrey Wilson being at that time the Institute's Director.

Livingstone in 1938 was a small and isolated town (Phillipson 1975). It had been the capital of Northern Rhodesia until 1935 when the Governor and Secretariat moved to the more centrally situated Lusaka. The six miles which separate Livingstone from the Victoria Falls were (and are) a major obstacle to tourist development. With the departure of the central administration, Livingstone became essentially a provincial administrative centre and a railway town on what was then the main line of entry from the south. In due course, the Rhodes–Livingstone Institute also moved its base to Lusaka where, long afterwards, it became the Institute of African Studies at the University of Zambia. The Museum, however, was formally separated from the Institute and remained in Livingstone, re-designated the Rhodes–Livingstone Museum with its own Board of Trustees. (When Northern Rhodesia became independent in 1964 as the Republic of Zambia, the Museum became known as the Livingstone Museum, and its Trustees as the National Museums Board.)

On arrival in Livingstone in 1938, Desmond Clark found himself in a huge territory about the archaeology of which very little was known. He was not, however, the first Cambridge graduate to take an interest in this field; Farquhar B. Macrae, an administrative officer in the central and eastern regions, had pioneered this study more than a decade previously (Macrae 1926; Macrae and Lancaster 1937). The presence of palaeolithic artefacts in the Zambezi gravels near the Victoria Falls had been recognised for many years (Lamplugh 1906; Armstrong and Jones 1936), and early human skeletal remains subsequently attributed to *Homo rhodesiensis,* discovered in 1921 during mining operations at Broken Hill, had been deposited (there being at that time no museum in Northern Rhodesia) at the Natural History Museum in London (Pycraft *et al.* 1928). Later Stone Age deposits had also been recognised at Mumbwa in the Kafue valley (Macrae 1926; Dart and del Grande 1931). Just how little was known overall is conveniently demonstrated by M. V. Brelsford's *Handbook of the David Livingstone Memorial Museum* (1937) which went to press a few weeks before Clark's arrival in Northern Rhodesia: discussion of archaeology occupies a total of seven pages (in the section headed 'Ethnological Collection'). Clark (1939), taking earlier discoveries as his starting point, summarised his aims in a twenty-seven-page pamphlet which provides a telling contrast with the Museum *Handbook*.

At Mumbwa, Clark conducted new excavations through deep stratified deposits which preserved a sequence from the Middle Stone Age onwards, paralleling the later stages of the Victoria Falls succession. The results, promptly published in the *Transactions of the Royal Society of South Africa* (Clark 1942), were particularly noteworthy on two counts: this was the first of many publications that was illustrated with Betty Clark's exceptionally accomplished drawings of stone artefacts, and because, almost alone of contemporary archaeological writings, it provided details of the pottery found in the more recent levels: such artefacts, now recognised as essential for the study of the archaeology of the past two millennia, were at that time generally ignored and discarded as 'kaffir rubbish'. Clark's research at Mumbwa was supported by a grant of £15. Subsequently, further investigations at the site (Savage 1983; Barham 2000) have provided much greater detail of a sequence now seen as extending over some 200,000–250,000 years.

Livingstone was a convenient base from which to investigate the Zambezi gravels, and Clark mapped these in considerable detail. Upstream of the Victoria Falls, gravels had been deposited at various heights as the Zambezi cut down through the Kalahari Sand to the underlying basalt. Downstream, the river flows through a zigzag series of gorges cut deep into the basalt, leaving gravels on the lips of the gorges as well as higher on the sides of the valley. Survey, surface collection and selective excavation enabled Clark to establish an outline typological sequence of stone artefacts and to link this with the processes whereby the river had cut both downwards through the sand and backwards along successive lines of Falls, leaving the gorges below. This research, essentially modelled on that of the Vaal terraces in South Africa (Sohnge *et al.* 1937), was not published until 1950 (Clark 1950a), although much of the fieldwork was undertaken between 1938 and 1940. Notwithstanding its prime importance in demonstrating the outline sequence of south-central African prehistory, it suffered from several inherent problems: it was carried out at a time when no reliable methods were available for establishing absolute ages, the artefacts were only very rarely recovered from primary contexts, and only occasionally were non-lithic materials associated. It was nonetheless clear that a long series of Acheulian-type industries was succeeded first by a phase characterised by core-axes, picks and other heavy-duty tools, and then by industries based on flakes struck from prepared cores; these artefacts became progressively smaller through successive phases of the Middle Stone Age before being replaced by backed microliths. It is not easy for younger prehistorians today to appreciate the fundamental importance of establishing this very basic framework in a huge area whose prehistory was previously unknown.

Broken Hill proved to be a long-lasting interest. The site of the original discovery had long-since been quarried away (Hrdlicka 1926). Clark was, however, able to reconstruct some of its circumstances and to examine the material preserved at the Natural History Museum. At the Broken Hill Mine itself, near the town now known as Kabwe, he located occurrences of artefacts which he believed to resemble those associated with the *Homo rhodesiensis* skull. The results of this work were published (Clark *et al.*) in 1947 and subsequently. In the absence of radiometric dating, the age of this material was seriously underestimated and an appreciation of its full significance had to await further discoveries towards the end of the twentieth century.

The Clarks were in Northern Rhodesia for less than three years before the outbreak of the Second World War. Desmond served with the East Africa Command, mainly in Somalia and Ethiopia, being subsequently attached to the British Military Administration. Betty remained in Livingstone with their son and daughter. This is not the place to record Desmond's military exploits; more relevant is the ability that he demonstrated, while in Somalia and Ethiopia between 1941 and 1946, to study and record the local Stone Age archaeology. The localities investigated were determined primarily by military considerations, and Clark did not on this occasion penetrate the low-lying Rift-Valley regions where abundant remains of early hominids have recently been discovered and where he himself was to work in later years. Like the earlier Zambezi valley investigation, that in the Horn was written up and published after the war (Clark 1954), the two projects having comprised Desmond's Ph.D. dissertation, submitted in five volumes at Cambridge under Burkitt's supervision in 1950. The extensive collections which he made were mostly divided between his own museum in Livingstone, the Coryndon Memorial Museum (now the National Museum of Kenya) in Nairobi, and the Cambridge University Museum of Archaeology and Anthropology. Although Clark was once again hindered by the impossibility of obtaining absolute age-determinations, an overall framework was constructed which, partly because of the scarcity of subsequent more detailed research, retains much value (cf. Brandt 1986).

Returning to Livingstone after the war, Clark turned his energies, with great effect, to expanding the infrastructure for archaeological investigations in Northern Rhodesia both administratively and through nurturing awareness locally as well as internationally. Recognising the limited prospects for museum expansion, in 1948 he founded a parallel organisation called, officially, the Commission for the Preservation of Natural and Historical Monuments and Relics or, more popularly and concisely, the National Monuments Commission, with himself as secretary. This body was established under a new ordinance which controlled archaeological research and provided a measure of protection for sites and artefacts; it had its own commissioners and government subvention, independent of the Rhodes–Livingstone Museum, even though its separation in terms of premises and personnel was less clearly defined. The manoeuvre achieved two useful purposes: it increased the support-base for Northern Rhodesian archaeology and provided a useful counter-balance of authority which avoided the conflicts of interest which may arise when a museum has sole authority to control research and export. (Several African countries have experienced such conflicts, but this has not prevented Zimbabwe's amalgamation of two formerly distinct organisations; in Zambia, however, the re-named National Museums Board and the National Heritage Conservation Commission have retained their separate identity.)

Thus reinforced, Clark expanded his researches in previously uninvestigated parts of Northern Rhodesia. He initiated excavations at Nachikufu and other rockshelters in the central and northern regions, recording the associated rock paintings. He promptly recognised that the Late Stone Age microlithic industries of these wooded plateaux were distinct both from those which he had previously studied at Mumbwa and in the Zambezi valley and from those already known even further to the south; the schematic paintings, also, presented a marked contrast with the well known naturalistic art beyond the Zambezi (Clark 1950b; Summers 1959).

It was during one of these reconnaissances, in 1953, that Clark made a discovery of the greatest importance. In the extreme north of Zambia, the small Kalambo river forms the border with Tanzania. Flowing westward to the southern extremity of Lake Tanganyika, it enters the Rift over a spectacular waterfall with an uninterrupted drop of 726 feet. Immediately above the Kalambo Falls, the river flows through a small lake basin and, in its banks, Clark found numerous well-preserved artefacts of Acheulian type, apparently in association with wood. Excavations were conducted at intervals until 1966, often on a large scale, revealing a stratified sequence from the Early Stone Age into recent times. Interpretation and publication of the resultant data proved to be a daunting task but was eventually completed (Clark 1969, 1974, 2001); an evaluation will be attempted below.

Clark's early years in Livingstone were ones of intellectual isolation. He has himself recorded (1990: 193) that, in 1938, 'there were only two or three professional archaeologists in the whole of the continent south of the Sahara, who . . . met only on rare occasions'. Fortunately, his contract of employment provided for overseas leave every three years; on these occasions the Clarks would rent a house near Cambridge in order to have the opportunity of writing while in contact with friends and colleagues.

The meetings of the PanAfrican Prehistory Congress, initiated by Louis Leakey in Nairobi in 1948 and held in Africa generally every four years thereafter, were particularly important in fostering contact and knowledge of research in other regions. As more posts were established within Africa, and archaeologists based elsewhere began to take an increasing interest in African matters, the meetings of the PanAfrican Congress have still retained their importance, becoming particularly valuable to the growing numbers of local scholars based in African countries with only limited opportunities for inter-regional travel. Clark attended all of the eleven meetings that were held during his lifetime.

In 1955 Desmond and Betty Clark organised the Third PanAfrican Congress in Livingstone (Clark and Cole 1957). Delegates came from all over the continent: a major achievement in those days of racial segregation was the organisation of accommodation for their African colleagues. In the absence of the Abbé Breuil, Louis Leakey presided; one of his duties was formally to open the Field Museum beside the Eastern Cataract of the Victoria Falls, which Clark had built over one of his excavations through the Zambezi gravel deposits. The Congress excursions took delegates to many parts of the territory up to a thousand miles from Livingstone, and into the then Belgian Congo, to see sites and excavations (Clark 1955; Mortelmans 1955).

At the same time, Clark was expanding archaeological capabilities and infrastructure in Northern Rhodesia. He greatly developed the Museum's buildings, collections, displays, and publications (Anon. 1951). He successively appointed to the Museum staff two young British archaeologists, Ray Inskeep and Brian Fagan, who pioneered the archaeological study of the last two thousand years, when the region saw the establishment of populations ancestral to modern African peoples. Additional colleagues were appointed to the Monuments Commission, where John and Lilian Hodges were followed by J. H. Chaplin.

It was at this stage in his career that Clark had to face the problem that, as the employee of a Northern Rhodesian organisation, he was expected to do most of his work in that territory. But African colonial borders—like those of the succeeding independent states—were arbitrary, bearing virtually no relevance to modern populations and none whatsoever to those of the remote past. In 1959 Clark was invited by a Portuguese diamond company to investigate the archaeology of northern Angola where open-cast mining in the valleys of the southern Congo tributaries had produced large exposures of artefact-bearing deposits. This was important and stimulating research, subsequently published (Clark 1963), but it did not fit well with a British colonial base.

This broadening of horizons now led Clark to attempt a work of synthesis, *The Prehistory of Southern Africa* (Clark 1959), one of a highly influential trilogy published by Penguin Books between 1954 and 1960. This book made Clark and his work much more widely known: he was appointed CBE in 1960 and elected to Fellowship of the British Academy in the following year. Shortly afterwards he accepted a Chair in Old World Archaeology at the University of California, Berkeley, a base he retained for the rest of his life.

Following his move to Berkeley, Clark proved a popular and inspiring teacher, and his research operations became truly pan-African, as was reflected in his work on the *Atlas of African Prehistory* (Clark 1967). In Malawi between 1965 and 1968 he undertook and co-ordinated palaeontological, archaeological and geological research on the Pleistocene lake beds of the Karonga region, while also facilitating investigations on sites of later periods by several of his students and by Keith Robinson who was then unable to continue his researches south of the Zambezi (Clark and Haynes 1970a, 1970b; Robinson and Sandelowski 1968). Subsequently, in 1970–3, Clark turned his attentions northwards to investigate the development of settled life, cultivation, and herding in the Sahara and the Sudanese Nile valley (Adamson *et al.* 1974). Particularly important were his excavations beside the Nile (Clark 1984, 1989) and at Adrar Bous in Niger (Clark *et al.* 1973). In 1974 he returned to Ethiopia after an absence of almost three decades. With students and colleagues, and concentrating in the southeastern regions, he investigated Middle and Late Stone Age sites and rock art, also seeking evidence relating to early farming practices (Clark and Williams 1978). Subsequently, he became increasingly involved with research on earlier periods of prehistory, turning his attention for the first time to regions beyond Africa: he undertook fieldwork in Syria (Clark 1967–8), India, and China.

At Berkeley, Clark found congenial colleagues, notably Sherwood L. Washburn and F. C. Clark Howell, with whom he developed close friendships and long-term collaboration. When Glynn Isaac (whose early death in 1985 was a sad loss both to Clark and to prehistoric studies worldwide) also joined the Berkeley Anthropology Department, there developed a school of African archaeology of unparalleled distinction. Its graduate students have gone on to hold important positions at many North American universities and in numerous African countries, notably Ethiopia, Kenya, Malawi, and Nigeria. The Department's decision, after Isaac's departure and death and his own retirement, not to continue this emphasis caused Clark sadness and disillusionment.

Glyn Daniel (1986: 422) saw fit to record that, in 1972, the Electors offered the Disney Chair of Archaeology at Cambridge to Desmond Clark in succession to his former teacher, Grahame Clark, but that the offer was declined, Daniel himself being subsequently elected. Desmond remained at Berkeley, taking formal but nominal retirement in 1986.

After retirement, Clark's attentions turned increasingly to Ethiopia where he undertook important work at the very early hominid sites of the Middle Awash region. This research, begun in 1982 following discovery by Taieb (1971) and earlier investigations co-ordinated by Kalb, was conducted in annual field seasons from 1990 onwards as a collaborative effort involving a large number of specialists. Clark was a major co-ordinator throughout, however, advancing age and failing eyesight gradually reduced his field participation. Although the importance of this work is clear, it has not been well served by the publications that have so far appeared. There have been a number of brief specialist preliminary papers (e.g. Asfaw *et al.* 1997; Clark 1987; Clark *et al.* 1994; Wolde Gabriel *et al.* 1994), but the one overview volume (de Heinzelin, Clark *et al.* 2000) is, frankly, disappointing in that it provides little comprehensive detail, particularly of the palaeontology, on a scale that would be commensurate with the effort and resources expended. It was unfortunate, too, that this research became enmeshed in professional rivalries and controversies with predecessors and contemporaries (cf. Kalb 2001) which caused much difficulty for the Ethiopian authorities (for an Ethiopian view of such matters, see Zelalem Assefa 1994).

In one of his autobiographical publications Clark (1990: 197) recalled his amazement that, in the 1940s, the Abbé Breuil claimed the ability to undertake typological classification of Acheulian artefacts by feel. Half a century later, with rapidly deteriorating eyesight, he developed the same ability himself in the Middle Awash (Dr Yonas Beyene *pers. comm.*).

Although Clark was primarily interested, particularly in his latter years, in the archaeology of early, so-called Stone Age, periods, he did not ignore more recent materials. Much of his work, notably in Zambia, Sudan, and Niger, was focused on evidence for early settled communities whose lifestyle was often, but not invariably, based on cultivation and/or herding. He took a strong interest in African traditional culture and technology, using his observations to aid his interpretation of archaeological materials. Little more than a decade after his synthesis of the archaeology of southern Africa, he produced a comparable work covering the entire continent (Clark 1970). It is instructive to compare them: the second work is based far more securely on recent fieldwork, much of it multidisciplinary. It frequently takes a worldwide view and, as befits a shorter and more general work, is less concerned with local variations on the overall theme. Both books strongly emphasise the earlier periods, before farming and permanent settlement, in marked contrast with more recent syntheses (Mitchell 2002 and Phillipson 1993 respectively).

Clark himself (1990: 189–90) recognised three phases in the study of African archaeology: a pioneer period before 1930, a formative period 1930–60, marked by 'the introduction of a more scientific approach to recovering, dating and interpreting the context and distribution of cultural remains', and a modern behavioural and actualistic period beginning *c.*1960. An outline of Clark's own career permits a somewhat different view. I suggest that Desmond Clark's research prior to 1946 belongs essentially to a pioneer period where sites were considered in isolation and often recorded or investigated simply because they had been discovered, often by chance. After the Second World War a markedly different strategy may be discerned, based on seeking sites and planning their investigation in order to answer specific questions or to fill gaps in the known distributions. For the first decade or so this process was greatly hindered by the effective absence of means to establish absolute chronologies and, as a consequence, inter-regional correlations. During the 1950s radiocarbon dating became available, to be followed by potassium-argon and other methods which respectively provided the first reliable age estimates for the last forty thousand years and for the period before one million years ago. The first results thus obtained generally indicated a far longer timespan than had previously been considered likely; several archaeologists, including Clark, initially regarded them with scepticism. It was, for example, some two decades after the first radiocarbon dates for the Zambian Later Stone Age were obtained that Clark fully accepted that this stage had begun significantly more than 20,000 years ago, as opposed to the 6,000 years previously estimated. Another source of misunderstanding was the lack of realisation that radiocarbon measurements before about 40,000 years ago must be regarded as minimum rather than absolute ages. Dates of *c.*60,000 years for the Kalambo Falls Acheulian were thus accepted in the 1960s as finite, whereas evidence more recently obtained has indicated a true antiquity four or five times as great. The third phase, for Clark, was marked by his move to Berkeley where his involvement with colleagues and students permitted his full participation in the international trend towards collaborative and multi-disciplinary research. In Africa, this period coincided with many countries' attainment of independence and the concomitant rising interest in local prehistory, and Clark was able to play his part in providing post-graduate training for young archaeologists from Africa. Despite his base in Berkeley, the controversies surrounding the rise and fall of the so-called New Archaeology effectively passed Clark by. He nonetheless deplored (1986: 188) what he saw as an increasing tendency to reconstruct prehistory on the basis of theory which was not based on firm primary evidence.

In later years, Clark sometimes found it hard to come to terms with changing economic fortunes and political priorities in post-colonial Africa. However, on his last visit to Zambia in 1995 he was gratified to be received with great warmth and affection by the Zambian staff of the institutions—National Museum and Monuments Commission—for whose foundation and development he had been largely responsible.

Clark's move to Berkeley had some effect on the flow of his publications. When he worked alone, he generally managed to publish his research reasonably promptly. When in the 1950s colleagues became available who were, in effect, research assistants, such as John and Lilian Hodges, publication fell behind. In Berkeley, early graduate students were able to work on much of this material and to publish it under Clark's supervision (e.g. Miller 1972). Clark's own fieldwork after 1960, however, presented greater difficulty: at Kalambo Falls, Adrar Bous and, to some extent, the Middle Awash, arrears of publication began to accumulate. Such was Clark's acknowledged eminence that he was inundated with invitations and requests for syntheses. The resultant papers and lectures were important and often highly influential, and Clark did not find it easy to decline such requests, although they took up a disproportionate amount of his time, at the expense of writing up his primary research. However, with help from numerous colleagues, virtually all Clark's outstanding research had been published at the time of his death. He was particularly pleased when the third and last volume of the Kalambo Falls report was published in 2001 by Cambridge University Press. This volume provides a convenient measure of Clark's achievement and of the changes in research strategy which took place during his career.

Clark discovered the Kalambo Falls site, as noted above, in 1953. Having confirmed the important presence of little-disturbed Acheulian deposits with associated wood, he organised the first season of large-scale excavation in 1956. It was an impressive undertaking, unparalleled in Africa at that time, separated by a thousand miles of largely unpaved road from his base in Livingstone. Fortunately, it took place at a time of economic optimism, in the early years of the Federation of Rhodesia and Nyasaland, and resources from Northern Rhodesia were supplemented by grants from the Wenner-Gren Foundation. Clark's collaborators in these early seasons were drawn mostly from southern and eastern Africa. Further research on the site took place over the period of his transfer to Berkeley, the team becoming increasingly international: large-scale excavations were conducted in 1959 and 1963, with more selective operations in 1964 and 1966. A complex and detailed stratigraphic sequence was established which Clark (1964) was able to link both with local environmental changes and with continent-wide developments. When, finally, this material was comprehensively published in 2001, the descriptions of the stone industries placed less emphasis on detailed metrical statistics than would have been expected in the 1960s, but more on the processes by which they had been made: typology as a prime concern had been replaced by technology and conceptualisation. The verbal descriptions are once again greatly enhanced by Betty Clark's magnificent drawings. There is, however, disappointingly little consideration of the uses to which these artefacts may have been put by their makers. Kalambo Falls, despite the total absence of hominid and faunal remains, is a key site, providing the best sequence yet known for the processes which marked the final demise of the Acheulian. When this sequence was first demonstrated, current interpretations of the radiocarbon dating evidence suggested that these processes had taken place over a remarkably short period of time. Now that it has been demonstrated that some 200,000 years were involved, appreciation of these changes is greatly facilitated. Volume III of the Kalambo Falls report contains description of the Early and

Middle Stone Age artefact assemblages by Clark, with help from others, specialist contributions by a number of former students and other colleagues, and a major but concise evaluation of the sequence in its Old World palaeolithic context, by Derek Roe.

Desmond Clark displayed great learning, prodigious energy and productivity, wide friendships and warm hospitality. He was elected a Fellow of the Society of Antiquaries in 1952 and a Fellow of the British Academy in 1961. He was a Fellow of the American Academy of Arts and Sciences, and of the National Academy of Science (USA). His Cambridge Sc.D. was awarded in 1975 and he held honorary doctorates at Witwatersrand and Cape Town Universities (1985), along with the Gold Medals of the Society of Antiquaries of London (1985) and the Archaeological Institute of America (1989). The British Academy awarded him the Grahame Clark Medal for Prehistory in 1997. He became a citizen of the United States of America in 1993. He died in Oakland, California, on 14 February 2002.

Desmond and Betty Clark worked together for more than sixty years; she survived him by two months. She and the late Frederick Sisii Wamulwange were probably the only people who could invariably read his handwriting. Desmond acknowledged his professional debt to Betty, describing her as his life-long collaborator: 'What I have been able to do in archaeology has been essentially a team effort by the two of us and, had it not been for her input, it would not have been possible to do half of what we have managed to do between us' (Clark 1986: 181).

DAVID W. PHILLIPSON
Fellow of the Academy

Note. I am grateful for the help and advice of Mr John Clark (son of the late Professor Clark), Mr Ray Inskeep (former colleague at the Rhodes–Livingstone Museum), Dr Laurel Phillipson (former graduate student at Berkeley) and Dr Yonas Beyene (collaborator in Ethiopia). For the photograph here reproduced I am indebted to Professor Edward J. Lofgren.

References

Adamson, D., Clark, J. D. and Williams, M. A. J. (1974), 'Barbed bone points from central Sudan and the age of the 'Early Khartoum' tradition', *Nature*, 249: 120–3.

Anon. (1951), 'The Rhodes–Livingstone Museum', *South African Museums Association Bulletin*, 5: 46–7.

Armstrong, A. L. and Jones, N. (1936), 'The antiquity of Man in Rhodesia as demonstrated by stone implements of the ancient Zambezi gravels south of Victoria Falls', *Journal of the Royal Anthropological Institute*, 66: 331–48.

Asfaw, B. *et al.* (1997), 'Fossil hominids, fauna and artifacts from Bouri, Middle Awash, Ethiopia', *American Journal of Physical Anthropology (Supplement)*, 24: 69.

Barham, L. (2000), *The Middle Stone Age of Zambia, South Central Africa* (Bristol).

Brandt, S. A. (1986), 'The Upper Pleistocene and early Holocene prehistory of the Horn of Africa', *African Archaeological Review*, 4: 41–82.

Brelsford, W. V. (1937), *Handbook of the David Livingstone Memorial Museum* (Livingstone).

Clark, J. D. (1939), *Stone Age Sites in Northern Rhodesia and the Possibilities of Future Research* (Livingstone).

—— (1942), 'Further excavations (1939) at the Mumbwa Caves, Northern Rhodesia', *Transactions of the Royal Society of South Africa*, 29: 133–201.

—— (1950a), *The Stone Age Cultures of Northern Rhodesia* (Cape Town).

—— (1950b), 'The newly discovered Nachikufu Culture of Northern Rhodesia and the possible origin of certain elements of the South African Smithfield Culture', *South African Archaeological Bulletin*, 5: 86–98.

—— (1954), *The Prehistoric Cultures of the Horn of Africa* (Cambridge).

—— (1955), *Excursion Handbook to Northern Rhodesia (Third PanAfrican Congress on Prehistory)* (Lusaka).

—— (1959), *The Prehistory of Southern Africa* (Harmondsworth).

—— (1963), *Prehistoric Cultures of Northeast Angola and their Significance in Tropical Africa* (Lisbon).

—— (1964), 'The influence of environment in inducing culture change at the Kalambo Falls prehistoric site', *South African Archaeological Bulletin*, 19: 93–101.

—— (1967), *Atlas of African Prehistory* (Chicago).

—— (1967–8), 'The Middle Acheulian occupation site at Latamne, northern Syria', *Quaternaria*, 9: 1–68 and 10: 1–71.

—— (1969), *Kalambo Falls Prehistoric Site, I: geology, palaeoecology and detailed stratigraphy of the excavations* (Cambridge).

—— (1970), *The Prehistory of Africa* (London).

—— (1974), *Kalambo Falls Prehistoric Site, II: the late prehistoric remains* (Cambridge).

—— (1984), 'Prehistoric cultural continuity and economic change in the central Sudan in the early Holocene', in J. D. Clark and S. Brandt (eds.), *From Hunters to Farmers* (Berkeley), pp. 113–26.

—— (1986), 'Archaeological retrospect 10', *Antiquity*, 60: 179–88.

—— (1987), 'Transitions: *Homo erectus* and the Acheulian—the Ethiopian sites of Gadeb and the Middle Awash', *Journal of Human Evolution*, 16: 809–26.

—— (1989), 'Shabona: an Early Khartoum settlement on the White Nile', in L. Krzyzaniak and M. Kobusiewicz (eds.), *Late Prehistory of the Nile Basin and the Sahara* (Poznan), pp. 387–410.

Anglicanism, attracted by a lively local church. His family mattered greatly to him. He was to speak of his grandparents as those whom at that time he loved best in the world. In adult life he found deep happiness in his marriage to Molly, whose death from cancer in 1978 was a severe loss. To his sons he was an excellent and caring father, sharing and encouraging their interests; to his grandchildren, simply 'great fun'. In old age he spoke of his brother John, a dozen years his junior, as his best friend, and the deaths of this beloved brother and of his sister, within a few months of each other and both from cancer, did much to precipitate his own decline into ill-health in the 1990s.

If his grandparents were a great Victorian influence on him, so too was Oxford. After education at Hymer's College, Hull, where he first learned German, Dickens went up to Magdalen on a scholarship in 1929. Here he benefited from two outstanding tutors: the legendary K. B. McFarlane in History, and the no less legendary, albeit in a different sphere, C. S. Lewis, in Political Thought. McFarlane's aegis was to cover Magdalen long after Dickens's undergraduate days, though his profound researches never issued, as did his pupil's, into intensely readable digests of his work. Dickens claimed to have been more influenced by Maurice Powicke's love of the Middle Ages, and thought that mixing with such medievalists had proved invaluable to his own development. McFarlane it was though who suggested the catholic recusants of Tudor Yorkshire as a suitable postgraduate research topic: a line of inquiry which was to bear unexpected fruit. From Lewis, Dickens must have learned something of his clarity of philosophical approach and felicity of style. There must also have been a congenial affinity in the Christianity of which both, in their different milieu, were such staunch defenders.

Surprisingly perhaps, Dickens's special subject in the History School was far removed from the English Reformation: he chose the Italian Renaissance. For a man greatly interested in the visual arts, this was less unlikely than first appears, and when in old age he made his unofficial office the room entitled 'Italy II' in the Institute of Historical Research, a wheel had turned full circle. A brilliant First in 1932 led to his election as a Fellow of Keble, a position he held, with an interruption for war service, until his return to Hull in 1949. At the age of twenty-two he found himself teaching sixteenth-century English history and mixing with older scholars, Victorians indeed, who addressed each other with extreme formality, like Watson and Holmes, and whose social code he found oppressive.

Life as a young don however allowed him plenty of time to travel widely on the Continent. His last pre-war visit to Berlin was in 1934, when, as he later said, 'Hindenberg's death broke the last connections with political decency'. Those were the days when the Kaiser's piano was on display in the Berliner Schloss, jacked up at an unlikely angle to cater for his withered arm, and to sit out in a street café on Unter den Linden was to be conscious of change for the worse. Accompanied on his foreign travels by Molly, also from Hull, whom he met at Oxford and married in 1936, he was aware of the storm clouds gathering: war he expected to come. During the few remaining pre-war years he teamed up with London doctors, including Haldane, to produce a propaganda warning about British under-preparedness for air raids. The war interrupted home life and scholarship; it allowed him, he said, some time to think, but not much to read books. Commissioned into the Royal Artillery, he found much of his time, as an academic, now devoted either to recruitment or to press censorship. Most significantly, as a German speaker, already conversant with German ideas and attitudes, he found himself in 1945 posted into Lübeck and tasked with producing a German-language newspaper on behalf of the Allied military government. As other young officers were to do, he culled most of his material from the BBC news. From this experience came his first published book, *Lübeck Diary* (1947). It was intended to help bring about a reconciliation with the Germans through a greater understanding of the ordinary people, and found in a hostile England a publisher in Victor Gollancz. The book did indeed aid Anglo-German relations—a German obituarist was to quote from it half a century later—and made him a sympathetic figure in Germany. His later contribution to establishing the German Historical Institute in London, and his honouring by the Federal Republic, can all be linked to that spell in the town-major's office.

Released unexpectedly promptly from war service, he returned to Oxford at the start of the Michaelmas term of 1945, but found it impossible to settle back into the old routine. The Victorians at Keble were dead or retired, and after the *Diary*'s publication he sought and found employment elsewhere. Even so, his lectures, already based on his York researches, were thought 'a goldmine'. 'I returned to my homeland (which I love) from 1949 to 1962, but I'm jolly glad I didn't stay longer', he wrote later. Thus, at the age of thirty-nine, he became G. F. Grant Professor of History at the University of Hull, later adding to his portfolio Dean of the Arts Faculty, Deputy Principal and Pro-Vice-Chancellor (1959). Colleagues and pupils from that period remember him with warmth and affection. His students were inspired by his lucid and amusing lectures, 'talking to us as if we were intelligent, listening to us as if we were interesting'. One recalled his bringing to a lecture the proofs of what must have been *Lollards and Protestants:* 'How thrilling! This was a man who wrote books!' After 'relishing the style and urbanity of his lectures', said another, 'no-one could have had a more caring supervisor . . . he was an enormous encourager'. This was not only a matter of personality, but of his seeking to broaden their experience: students were directed to classes where they could acquire an additional language, and taken on trips to churches and battlefields. Dickens had always a great interest in the visual arts, and a small gallery at his home in Cottingham, where he was then collecting seventeenth-century Flemish and Dutch paintings. This collection was later replaced by one of the early twentieth century, influenced by Hull's founding of its own art collection of this era, in which he and Molly became enthusiasts. He was indeed a competent draughtsman himself as well as an art collector. A gifted and generous man, his students were well aware of his generosity of time and spirit. So were his colleagues; even a tendency to return to his house and his research as soon as possible after 9 a.m. was forgiven: 'Such was his charm and generosity when one met him that the frustration that this practice sometimes evoked was soon dispelled.' He disarmingly gave even junior colleagues the impression of being the centre of his attention, and the warmth of his hospitality and many kindnesses were the abiding impressions. A brilliant raconteur with a fund of anecdotes, he enhanced the understanding of colleagues and students alike, yet carried his learning lightly with 'mischievous humour and engaging charm'.

Adapting to civilian life and to a northern university had actually taken some time. Perhaps it was the draining workload of Oxford and the style of his senior colleagues there which made him seem a little starchy at first, back in the North. Even at Oxford, where his teaching had been just as enthusiastically received, he had been noted as particularly point-device and formal, in dress at least, and notoriously attached to his army greatcoat. The change resulted, as it seemed, from his exchange year in America as Visiting Professor at Rochester University. Molly and their two sons Peter and Paul, by now aged twelve and seven, were received by Rochester with the same generous hospitality for which the family was already noted at home. Their presence was seen as fostering just the kind of cross-cultural understanding in which Dickens took such an interest in Europe. His time at Rochester gave him the opportunity to work in the Folger Library, producing several published articles, and resulted in his adding a course in American history to his repertoire on his return to Hull.

By the time *Lollards and Protestants* appeared in 1959, Dickens had been working on Yorkshire records for over twenty years, producing numerous articles and rescuing from oblivion a series of minor characters, including the Yorkshire priest of the Reformation era whom he was always to refer to as 'my friend Robert Parkyn'. Archival discoveries and his own natural inclination were directing him towards the study of the ordinary man, encouraging his unshakeable conviction that the Reformation was a grassroots movement, a view which bore its mature fruit in *The English Reformation* (1964). The deft use of original sources and the illumination of a general trend by an individual case study is already well in evidence in *Lollards and Protestants*.

In 1962 Dickens took what then seemed the momentous step of leaving Hull to take up a post at King's College, London. At Hull he had been surrounded by mediaevalists; now he had to work with an eminent group of Tudor historians: Bindoff, Collinson, Dugmore, Hurstfield, and Scarisbrick. He was only to spend five years at King's, but he remained in London for the rest of his life. Like other Northerners he was to find the intellectual stimulus of the capital too important to be forgone: 'In most walks of life—and most civilised pleasures—the stimulus here in London is tremendous, once one settles down', he later wrote. Once more a friend and mentor to younger colleagues, he was remembered as a wonderful lecturer, but less attuned to the seminar. Here barely a paragraph would have been read before his wealth of interest and knowledge led to a discourse on one thread of the argument, to be followed a paragraph later by a further interruption: the kindly fault of enthusiastic polymathy.

As an administrator, his natural charm and the management skills he had developed at Hull were brought to London and used to good effect. Avowedly preferring the rapier to the bludgeon, he could also deflect much with a sense of humour. Extremely courteous and quietly efficient, he was as willing to chat with secretaries as students about his times in Germany, or to discuss the art so readily available in London galleries but so little visited by his students. Here as at Hull he made friendships to endure.

London saw an end to his work in local archives. When he bought a house in Essex it was believed that he intended to work on the county archives, but was forestalled by the publication of another work on the Reformation in Essex. 'The failure', mourned a colleague, 'of the felicitous marriage between the Essex Record Office and Geoff Dickens is something we all have to regret.'

This was however the era of the publication of his best known work, *The English Reformation*. It is now difficult to recall with what acclaim and relief this classic was first received. Tutors who had deplored the confessionally partisan nature of the specialist works available to students suddenly found to hand an accessible and balanced analysis, based on wide research and presenting a period of political and social upheaval with accuracy and insight. It provoked a whole industry of Reformation scholarship which may in part have modified Dickens's thesis, but has not superseded it. 'He changed the landscape', said one former pupil; the book was 'quite simply regarded as the latest version of the Bible', according to another.

In fact, Dickens's interests seem to have been turning ever more certainly away from local history towards the Continental Reformation. He was certainly encouraged to do so by his appointment in 1967 as Director of the Institute of Historical Research, a post he held until his retirement in 1974, and his simultaneous responsibilities at the British Academy. The Director found himself in a new kind of prominence, with a pastoral role and a requirement for academic hospitality which could restrict academic output. He has been criticised for some of the textbooks and popular works of this period, but the demands on his time were formidable. There were the Institute's annual Anglo-American conference, and the editing of its *Bulletin,* a major task alone. At periodic Director's Conferences selected speakers would address an invited audience on a variety of topics. He gave one of Ford's Lectures at Oxford, and was Birkbeck Lecturer at Cambridge 1969–70, when his chosen topic of 'The Reformation and Martin Luther' showed plainly the developing direction of his thought. His work at the Institute would have been impossible without the support of his PPS, Cynthia Hawker, whose ability and efficiency made the huge administrative task feasible.

As if this were not enough, the British Academy, to whose fellowship he had been elected in 1966, appointed him in 1969 its Foreign Secretary. To the Anglo-American emphases of the Institute were thus added the European academic links in which he had long rejoiced. The roles tended to become homogeneous; he was inclined to spend time at committee meetings of the Institute in enthusiastic description of his latest European trip. He considered it a vital part of Western aid to the Eastern bloc nations to ensure that their academics were not left isolated, and took a prominent part in ensuring their continuing contact with Western thought. In 1968 he organised a boycott of an international conference in Moscow, so hurt was he by the Soviet invasion of Czechoslovakia which had abruptly put paid to the Prague Spring. He managed to visit nearly all the Eastern European states during his ten-year tenure of the foreign secretaryship: a level of activity on a par with royalty or the Pope.

Throughout this extremely busy time Dickens benefited inexpressibly from the support of his wife Molly, a constant companion at the compulsory social occasions which demand attendance from the eminent, and whose shrewd Northern sense and humour were a bulwark against the social pressures. Sadly, she did not long survive his formal retirement in 1977. Dickens referred to her death, from cancer, in 1978, as being 'like an amputation', which in the eyes of many friends curtailed the potential academic achievements of a now emptied retirement.

Dickens remained an active historian into his eighties, but became increasingly sidelined in the popular view by two major academic developments. One was his own ever-developing interest in the German Reformation; the other the rise of Reformation revisionism which will be discussed at length later in the memoir. The first made him increasingly popular on the Continent, where his definition of reformation as an 'urban event' struck a chord with a historical school ideologically delighted to reject the leadership of the princes. His deepening interest in Martin Luther and the personal and social aspects of Protestantism— themes which struck a chord with his own faith—led him ever deeper into European waters. Few English scholars had the linguistic skills to follow him, and most were inclined to ignore his work on *The Reformation and Historical Thought* (1985), with John Tonkin, and his later interest in *Erasmus the Reformer* (1994), with Whitney Jones.

Honours continued to pour in upon Dickens, even though his magisterial work was past. Unusually for a historian, he was made CMG in 1974, and honorary doctorates became a commonplace. He valued greatly the medal conferred in 1980 by the then Federal Republic of Germany for his work in establishing the German Historical Institute in London, back in 1968. Honorary vice-president of both the Royal Historical Society and the Historical Association, whose Medlicott medal he was awarded in 1985, he was for many years President of the Association's Central London branch, continuing as long as any intellectual activity was permitted him.

Before ill-health set in the mid-1990s, Dickens maintained a cultured home in London NW. Described as 'an unexpected combination of sumptuous display and asceticism', the sitting room painted a deep burgundy to highlight the gilt picture frames of his still considerable art collection (many paintings having been given to the University of Hull in memory of Molly), it was yet the home of a man who loved ice-cream and had only a couple of pots of Greek yoghurt in the fridge. He was puritanical about drink but loved food, and enjoyed the mild social life of Sunday lunch with good friends, his regular game of chess, and his love of music. He had his London club, the Athenaeum, at times entertaining guests there, in preference to large and amorphous social gatherings. He was a regular member of his local church, preaching occasionally but never becoming churchwarden. He was a member of their panel of visitors of the elderly, many of whom were considerably younger than himself. Still a great talker, his last few, semi-official, students remember with affection conversations, usually somewhat one-sided, in which they listened and learned about the wide range of Dickens's interests and experience.

In the mid 1990s his health declined rapidly. There began to be talk of a heart attack, of a possible hip operation. A series of bereavements affected him deeply. One by one, correspondents found their letters unanswered as he no longer remembered who they were. From his wine coloured flat he moved first to sheltered accommodation, which delighted him, as someone else would do the cooking, and finally to a nursing home. The Historical Association had to be abandoned as Dickens could no long grasp topics which had once been at his fingertips. His death on 31 July 2001, soon after his ninety-first birthday, was a merciful release for a spirit which a failing body had kept in chains.

There have been varied assessments of what he achieved, and sought to achieve, as a historian. He fitted no convenient pigeonhole, one writer on Reformation historiography being inclined to put him in a class of his own. It has proved easier to identify what he was not, and point out his methodological weaknesses. He has been criticised for being enamoured of his own thesis and therefore unable to accept any strength of Catholic feeling in England; for being too dismissive of the work of researchers into local Reformation history; for abandoning his real métier to dabble in the Continental Reformation; for producing no research students of his own calibre. Finally, his preference for writing accessible books has led to complaints of his having no real research plan, but being publisher-led.

There was a research plan and progression in Dickens's work, but dominated as it is for an English-speaking audience by the twin towers of *Lollards and Protestants* and *The English Reformation,* the progression is easily overlooked. His origins in local history are clear enough. When he was recommended by McFarlane to look at Elizabethan recusancy in

Yorkshire, use of diocesan records was in its infancy, the records having long been mouldering undisturbed in the diocesan registry. Today this kind of research is commonplace, and the records well catalogued. Then the only other interest shown in the registry archive was by Canon Purvis, first official archivist of the diocesan holdings, whose reorganising of the records and establishment of the Borthwick Institute during Dickens's absence on war service made his post-war task significantly easier. Dickens found the evidence in the Court Books about ordinary men and women invaluable.

It was a novelty, when history was largely a matter of politics, to consider the views of the common man or woman at all. Dickens became interested in the Pilgrimage of Grace because of the light its records also shed on the views of ordinary people, on both religion and politics. Working further backwards, he found that the Lollards examined by the church courts had their own story to tell. A series of articles came out of these Yorkshire researches, and the year at Rochester, permitting use of the Folger library, widened the range of his sixteenth-century papers. Always he sought to hold to his dictum that 'our business is getting at the common man or woman', in tension with another tenet, 'we must not get parochial in outlook as a result of our regional studies'—a comment with which he would temper the enthusiasm of later students for their own dark corner of the realm.

When it came to writing books rather than articles, there was always the advice given him by Sir Arthur Bryant: 'above all, when you take up the pen, resolve to be read by a lot of people'. As a result, he claimed, he had sought often to write 'teaching books', current textbooks in the post-war era being highly political and lacking in cultural or religious content. His involvement in adult education during his time at Hull probably contributed to this view. *Lübeck Diary* was certainly 'read by a lot of people', on the Continent as much as in the UK; *East Riding* was more of a tourist guide than a history. His essay on Thomas Cromwell in the *Teach Yourself* series probably issued from this reputation for readability, coming as it did when Elton's *Tudor revolution in government* was the academic rage. Undoubtedly however the two books which have stood the test of time as widely-read teaching books are *Lollards and Protestants* and *The English Reformation.*

Lollards and Protestants offered a fresh approach to English Reformation studies. Essentially the theme was the survival of a Wyclifite dissenting minority as a seedbed for popular Protestantism, ready to progress beyond the political changes instituted in the 1530s by the king in parliament. It expounded the interplay of forces in the Henrician reformation by making full use of his knowledge of local regional history. It is hard to remember, forty years later, the freshness then of his ideas of a 'diffuse but inveterate Lollardy revivified by contact with Continental Protestantism',[1] a claim now treated with some scepticism in the light of evident irreligion rather than vernacular bible reading. The Northern reputation for reactionary conservatism was one to which his own writing on Elizabethan recusancy had contributed. Using the material he had discovered in the diocesan court books, he now sought to explode that myth. In seeking to observe 'how the Reformation made its initial impacts upon a regional society',[2] he had found sources adequate to 'allow us to grasp the complex character of contemporary religion and trace some of the channels through which the new opinions were flowing'.[3] Lollardy, Lutheranism, and straightforward scepticism had all left their mark on the record. Gentlemen and merchants, as well as working class radicals, all played their part and were brought to life by Dickens, who had discovered afresh that 'the middle and lower orders of society had mental and even cultural lives, which included personal responses to religion'.[4] They ranged from the eccentric radicalism of Sir Francis Bigod and his circle to the deep conservative Catholicism of the priest Robert Parkyn. The pioneering use of will formulae to distinguish strands of belief has been honed, refined, rejected, and redefined since, but in 1959 it provided a novel insight into the reported views of ordinary will-makers, rather than the political orthodoxy of the traditional political textbook. It was groundbreaking work which, as his original introduction and subsequent preface to the second edition of 1982 made clear, needed the checks and balances of a similar depth of research into other local records. The clarion call was responded to enthusiastically in many and various ways, but has yet to produce a volume magisterially equal to *Lollards and Protestants*.

Lollards and Protestants, the culmination of twenty years' research in local archives, can be taken as marking the end of a first phase of Dickens's work. Perhaps those who expected him, once removed from Hull to London, to repeat the achievement in the Essex records, missed the shift in emphasis of his attention from the local to the national stage.

---

[1] A. G. Dickens, *Lollards and Protestants in the Diocese of York* (2nd edn., London, 1982), p. 243.
[2] Ibid., p. 1.
[3] Ibid., p. 7. `
[4] Ibid., preface to 2nd edn., p. v.

The prime achievement in this phase was his *English Reformation* of 1964. Any sixth-form student of Tudor history who has 'done' Dickens means this book, and it is some measure of his greatness that they will be expected to have 'done' it, and should be well capable of tackling his erudite but immensely readable prose, even in their teens. Its alternation of compelling narrative and detailed analysis contributes both to the general overview and the detailed evidence required to answer an examination question. Dickens possessed that attribute of great writers, the ability to write simply enough for the non-specialist reader, without being simplistic. 'One may still turn to him for the best concise account of many particular incidents in the tangled story of the English Reformation,'[5] not a tribute many forty-year-old books could still earn.

Dickens had three stated aims in this book: to give a fuller description of the background to familiar political events; to highlight the role played by the spread of Protestantism; and to depict the movement as it affected ordinary people, not just princes and prelates. He was therefore far more concerned to examine the character of Christian belief, both popular and sophisticated, than had been the previous norm. He did not expect the book to provide a definitive statement, but looked ahead to a more complete understanding, achievable after perhaps another twenty years of research by himself and others in Tudor diocesan records. Assessing his book twenty years later, he called it 'a book which should be regarded as an agenda, not a summa'.[6]

Other scholars indeed took up the challenge, in ways he had not anticipated. Dickens had painted a picture of degenerate late medieval religion, relieved by mysticism and irritated by Lollardy. He emphasised strongly a popular anticlericalism exacerbated by worldly prelates, decayed monasteries, and incompetent parish clergy. Thus a seedbed was prepared for the mission of the Continental reformers 'to steer Christianity back in line with biblical sources after many centuries of hierarchical manipulation'.[7] These ideas were adopted with enthusiasm by English reformers to whom he does full justice, who were anxious to press for fuller reform than the legislation of the 1530s had achieved, and only too ready to take the lead under Edward. Mary was unable to stem the change, because of its popular basis, and the Elizabethan

---

[5] R. Houlbrooke, 'Obituary, Professor A. G. Dickens', *Historical Research*, 75, no. 188 (2002), pp. 238–47.
[6] A. G. Dickens and J. Tonkin, *The Reformation in Historical Thought* (Oxford, 1985), p. 295.
[7] Ibid., p. 327.

rashly quoted Old Testament references to the wickedness of youth, he added, 'but "your young men shall dream dreams" '. It was never wise to seek to cross theological swords. A final note, following many ranging through Erasmus and the influence of the continental reformers, concluded: 'but a historian can only use credible and proximate sources i.e. Bible—not Tradition, always corruptible'. It summarised his historical methodology and his own Christian faith.

It was to Erasmus and the continental reformers that his last, and often overlooked, phase of work was to turn. Dickens had become aware, he said, of the international dimension of Protestantism while writing *The English Reformation,* and of how he needed to know much more about Lutheranism. Colleagues were inclined to deplore his abandonment of the field in which he was an acknowledged master, merely to become one of many in a foreign field. This shift of emphasis however marked the transition into his third field of active work, when by writing on German history he sought to counteract the ignorance of too many of those who wrote insular English history. His researches were thus complementary to his roles at the Institute and the Academy. Again, he chose to write for a wider audience by producing textbooks. Generations of students were grateful for his *Reformation and Society in Sixteenth Century Europe* (1966) with its partner, *The Counter Reformation* (1968), and his masterly little introduction to Martin Luther in the *Teach Yourself* series filled a lacuna in accessible writing on the German Reformation. In its focus on the man and his religion it again fulfilled his aim of bringing the common man and his non-political ideas to the fore, while the Thames and Hudson companion pieces revealed Dickens as the cultured Renaissance man himself in his wide artistic and religious knowledge.

The German Nation and Martin Luther, which had originated in the Birkbeck lectures, was the high point of this third phase of activity, to his readers if not to himself. His work made available to an English speaking readership the researches of German scholars, especially Bernd Moeller, and continued to operate on the principle of identifying and analysing intellectual and social forces behind the Reformation. As in England, this was a departure from the traditional approach, which, whilst retaining Luther as the hero, laid emphasis on the urban dynamic, with printing and preaching disseminating a true 'Reformation from below', not merely a political option of particularist princes. The German situation, with its multiplicity of petty princedoms and quasi-autonomous cities within the loose entity of the Empire, was indeed a much better exemplar of his thesis than was homogeneous England, with only London of a size and influence to warrant achieving an 'urban event'. To his understanding of the continental urban reformation Dickens's outstanding research student, the late Robert Scribner, then focusing on Erfurt, added significantly. Scribner's interest in the means of communication of the reformed faith to 'simple folk' complemented and developed Dickens's work. Equipped intellectually and linguistically to further such research, his potential development of such themes was cut short by his untimely death. In Scribner Dickens had at last owned a worthy successor.

Dickens's thesis remains valid for Germanic Reformation historians in its consideration of nationhood, and in his willingness to analyse complex elements rather than reduce them to convenient packages. His handling of Luther's theology was, as always, informed and balanced. He wrote about Protestantism from his own basis of faith, while remaining aware of the dangers of so doing: 'scholars of Christian persuasion . . . are no less likely to be hindered by youthful experiences and present loyalties from apprehending the peculiar qualities of Reformation religion',[8] he wrote later. His ability to empathise, and yet to view with detached judgement, contributed in no small part to the enduring quality of his work.

Criticised for not writing enough in retirement, Dickens was working for the rest of his productive life on two mammoth topics: the historiography of the Reformation, and the political and religious thought which precipitated it, as exemplified by Erasmus. From German history to (largely) German historiographers seemed an obvious and valuable progression. *The Reformation in Historical Thought* should have been a landmark in Reformation studies, charting the historiography of the reformation since the sixteenth century and providing dispassionate and balanced evaluations of a multiplicity of scholars. That was perhaps its disadvantage. In the search for evenness of tone in a collaborated volume, there was a tendency to the monotone. A far greater disadvantage was a species of sales resistance. The attempt to bring continental authors to the notice of an English speaking historical readership was dogged by lack of interest. Those who had barely heard of, and certainly never read, a German historian, were unlikely to read about him. Intended as a foil to Ferguson's *Renaissance in Historical Thought*, it failed to achieve that eminence.

---

[8] Dickens and Tonkin, *The Reformation in Historical Thought*, p. 328.

The book is perhaps more interesting for the light it shed on Dickens himself. He professed himself to be a great admirer of Ranke, praising him as 'the best equipped and most productive historian of the nineteenth century, much influenced but not engulfed by his conservative Prussian-Lutheran context'.[9] He was an outstanding scholar, covering social and economic, as well as local, themes, with outstanding moral force and dedication to his work. The carefulness of his methodology was second to none; his determination to show the past as it really was, the setting of the highest standards. Ranke, Dickens wrote, 'regarded the discovery of historical truth as a species of religious obligation'.[10] He placed culture next to church and state as the third great force in human affairs. Two of the volumes of his Reformation history contain elaborate analyses of the causes and early progress of reform, missing few of the factors prominent in modern debate. Dickens praises him for his handling of the cities, the proto-reformers, and the influences on Luther himself; for his discussion of Thomas Müntzer and the 1524–5 revolt; for his use of the popular pamphlets produced by the Reformation: all topics interesting to Dickens himself.

Interviewed by Scribner in 1990, Dickens was flattered to be compared with Ranke himself. The comparison, on Dickens's own showing, could scarcely have been more accurate. The aspects Dickens identified in Ranke as being of greatest worth are surely the outstanding aspects of his own methodology and style.

To that sense of style he owes much of his enduring readableness. 'We should be writing for an Anglo-American of *c.*2080 A.D.', he once advised a junior historian. 'I do wish I could persuade [x] to write deathless prose', he said of another. Interviewed, he expressed a strong dislike for the conversational style of writing for which he detected a vogue. Prose should be analytical. In his bigger books he had consciously sought a constant interchange between narrative and analysis. This was not the same as imposing a philosophy of history on one's writings. Each step should suggest the next, without losing touch with one's own earlier work. It was the job of a historian to tackle all aspects of the development of a country or region, a task which was being better done in his lifetime than before. Pressed for a definition, he saw himself as a kind of social historian, but thought that perhaps there should be a new name for his type of work.

---

[9] Dickens and Tonkin, *The Reformation in Historical Thought*, p. 150.
[10] Ibid., p. 168.

If one is to move on step by step, not losing touch with previous work, such a procession in Dickens's writing becomes plain. From local archives he moved to the national Reformation, and thence to the continental influences on it. After a closer analysis of the thought of Luther, he paused to overview the scene in company with other great historians. Finally, he became immersed in the thought which had paved the way for, and contributed to the impact of, the Protestant Reformation in the Germanic countries: that of Erasmus.

Dickens was aware of paddling at the edges of a pool where a massive scholarly edition of Erasmus's works was in progress. Once more he was seeking to be 'read by a lot of people', to make Erasmus accessible to an English literary public. *Erasmus the Reformer,* like *The Reformation in Historical Thought,* was a collaborative production: 'at the age of eighty-one, one *has* to think in terms of collaboration', he said. In some ways a better book than its predecessor in terms of its usefulness to British scholars, it applies again Dickens's twin principles of narrative and analysis to the various stages of Erasmus's life and works. The collaborative approach again leads to some unevenness of treatment and style, but *Erasmus* does succeed in making clear those areas in which Dickens's writings are usually strong: the roots of his thought, his Christian theology, its application to the ordinary person. The bible-based humanism expounded by Erasmus, like most calls for reform, was a godly back-to-basics. Disenchanted with scholastic theology, insisting on the concept of adiaphora in an increasingly polarised confessional world, deeply influencing Luther but later dissociating himself from Protestant reform, Erasmus is presented as a reformer but not a revolutionary. He deprecated Luther's approach to the faults of the sixteenth-century church, and his views won respect from other lines of thought. Zwingli was arguably the apostle of Erasmian evangelicalism, and some of his formulae for Christian living were adopted by Anabaptists. The complexities of his Christian humanism are manifest, and Methodism might stand for his fullest heir.

This last foray into religious thought showed Dickens following a dictum of his old tutor: 'higher up and further in'. Few specialists in English Reformation local studies felt called to the same heights, but leaving Moses on Pisgah were more likely to go further in to the promised land, engaging closely with the common man. On the Continent, Scribner must stand for his Joshua. At home, he lacked a true successor. Disciples of his own calibre were unlikely to be common, and he has been criticised for their scarcity. He was of course an impossible act to follow. There was little new to be said about Protestantism in Tudor England for another thirty years, while his work was tested against the findings of scholars of a different persuasion. Nor should such a Renaissance polymath be expected to have directed all his students into the same channel. If one went on to architecture and another into the church, are they not also heirs to Dickens's multi-faceted brilliance?

Dickens was above all a Christian, whose job was to use his God-given scholarly talents to the best of his ability. His strong faith comes through repeatedly in his work, not in a narrow confessionalism, but in a conservative Protestant faith not entirely removed from Erasmus himself. His *Lübeck Diary* concluded with a passionate call for reconciliation between erstwhile enemies as human beings, rather than indulging in indiscriminate group hatred. He thought this impossible to achieve 'without a sense of brotherhood in God, without that belief in the holiness of human personality expressed in the words, "Inasmuch as you have done it unto the least of these my brethren, ye have done it unto Me . . ." '.[11] Similarly, his epilogue to *The English Reformation* called for credal formularies to be clear, short, and simple, 'to bring men nearer in love to the real person of the Founder':

> As the best of [the reformers] sought in humility to recover the ever-living Word made Flesh, so we and our successors can continue the search in still greater humility . . . When they talk of God, or of the Son of God, fallen creatures and visible churches should at least be tentative.[12]

Not the most likely conclusion to a history book, but a mission statement from one whose moderate Protestantism, and deep and genuine faith, made a lasting impression on his friends. 'He strove to be the servant of the truth', concluded one, 'and hence the wide respect his writings always commanded.'

MARGARET CLARK

Note. This memoir would not have been possible without the assistance of many of Geoff Dickens's family, friends, and well-wishers. I must record my thanks in particular to Margaret Aston, Lucy Brown, Claire Cross, Patrick Collinson, Emma Dickens, Peter Dickens, Robert von Friedeburg, Barbara Harvey, Cynthia Hawker, Peter

[11] A. G. Dickens, *Lübeck Diary* (London, 1947), p. 347.
[12] A. Dickens, *The English Reformation* (paperback edn., London, 1967), p. 463.

Heath, Ralph Houlbrooke, John Newton, Vincent Orange, Martin Sheppard, David Sturdy, Brett Usher, Susan Wabuda, and June Walker.

Unattributed quotations are from personal correspondence in the author's possession.

EDMUND FRYDE

Edmund Boleslaw Fryde
1923–1999

EDMUND FRYDE liked to dwell on the quirks of fate. It was a game. He liked to explain how by some round-about chain of causation you, his friend, came to be where you were because of some long-past chance action on his part. Bonds, however far-fetched, were important. That Edmund himself, the gifted Jewish boy of cosmopolitan upbringing from Warsaw, should have spent over fifty years of his life in Aberystwyth, resigned to having been stranded there and, in his later years, increasingly content with his fate, was not to be predicted. The chain of events which led to this was a complicated one and—there were memories which brought pain—much of it he dwelt on rarely, but he took it for common knowledge among his friends.

The chain began with the sudden removal of the fifteen-year old Boleslaw from his Warsaw school to Bradfield College in 1938, a move which ensured that he survived the war. Then came historical research in a field chosen for him by another, which made a medievalist of him, and an appointment to lecture at Aberystwyth in a subject which was not his, economic history. And then came the succession of chances which brought about a sequence of shifts of interest, to constitutional history, to historiography, to Italian humanism, to Greek manuscripts, and lastly to a field which he found strangely sympathetic, that of learning and scholarship in Byzantium. To each area of interest he committed himself entirely, publishing important discoveries; in each he also gave rein to his gift for synthesis, for presenting the wide picture, one in which however the human presence invariably remained prominent.

Proceedings of the British Academy, **120**, 105–119. © The British Academy 2003.

Both Edmund's parents spent their youth in Czestochowa, at that time a Russian city of some 100,000 inhabitants. Its citizens could cross to Germany or Austria-Hungary with no more than a frontier-pass. Edmund's mother's family used to make annual visits to either Vienna or Breslau. His father's maternal grandfather, called Bursztynski, had been the official representative of the Jewish community in south-eastern Poland, and the first Jew allowed to settle in Czestochowa, in 1829. His son became a famous doctor. His grandsons emigrated to Russia and became distinguished civil servants. His daughter, however, at the age of sixteen, married a forty-nine year old bachelor, Henryk Fryde, Edmund's grandfather. Henryk Fryde, a self-educated man, had made himself rich by a franchise in vodka, and become owner of a village called Kraszewice, near Czestochowa, where he lived more in the style of the Polish landlords with whom he consorted than of a Jew. He sold his property in 1903 after a rising by the peasants and the burning of his house, and moved to town. His son Mieczyslaw was ten. Mieczyslaw studied mathematics and philosophy in Berlin in 1912–14. While there he joined the Russian Social Democratic Party. During the war he became a leader in the revolutionary socialist underground, first in Czestochowa, later in Warsaw and Lodz, organ-ising sabotage of German war factories. After the war, a brief period as a civil servant in the new Polish government came to an end when he was discovered at a secret meeting of socialists, and had to spend some months in prison. He then for a short while became a Privat-Dozent in mathematics at Warsaw university. But with the death of his professor, a victim of a bomb intended for the President (who was shot dead by an assassin minutes later), he realized that, as a Jew, now lacking patronage, he could not hope to advance his career in the subject of his first love. He had, by virtue of being in 1920 a regis-tered student in law, acquired by government decree a degree in law. He began to practise. In post-1919 Poland, when many wartime revo-lutionaries found themselves in government posts, his contacts in the socialist underground proved helpful. By 1928 he was legal adviser to the Polish Ministry of Finance; in 1936 he became also a legal adviser to the ministry of Foreign Affairs. At the same time, he pursued a private scholarly career, publishing widely on statistics, on the one hand, and, on the other, on public credit. After the Second World War, in which he served in the office of the Polish Prime Minister in Exile and later in the Inter-Allied Commission on War Crimes, he began an academic career in the USA (he was now known as

Matthew Fryde), teaching Economics and the History of Science at the universities of Columbia and Yeshiva.[1]

Edmund's mother, Salomea Ludwika (Sarah Louise) Rosenzweig, was the daughter of Nathan Rosenzweig, a rich timber merchant. The home was cultured and politically radical. The two elder brothers were recruited by the Social Democratic Party in 1915, betrayed, and imprisoned by the Germans from 1916 to 1918. Like Sarah, they remained radical, even idealistic, in the increasingly reactionary Poland of the inter-war years. Edward, the eldest, was a chemist and inventor, but, on principle, refused to take out patents. Very few of the large Rosenzweig family survived the Second World War. One cousin who as a child did survive, in the Warsaw Ghetto, then in hiding, and then in Bergen-Belsen, and was sent as an orphan to Palestine after liberation, became the novelist, Uri Orlev; his experience of the war underlies his novel translated into English in 1979 as *The Lead Soldiers*.

Sarah Rozenzweig had run away from home in 1911 in order to study Polish literature at Krakow University. She was a pretty and vivacious woman, passionately fond of art. She encouraged Edmund, her only child, to read widely in Polish literature, both prose and poetry. (In the 1980s a friend travelling with Edmund from Aberystwyth to London by train was, to his initial embarrassment, regaled with long and loud recitations from memory of Polish poetry.) She arranged for him to be taught French and German, and later English. When he came to school in England at the age of fifteen he could read both French and English with fair fluency, German less well. He studied the piano for eight years and used to play with pleasure. With his mother, he came to know museums and galleries. She loved to travel, and in her company during school vacations Edmund came to know many of the cities of Europe.

Boleslaw Edmund Fryde was born on 16 July 1923 and called Boleslaw (Bolek to family and friends). He enjoyed a happy, indulged, rather solitary childhood, living in an expensive apartment. He once, when he was twelve, on his way home from school, heard the noise of a mob and took refuge in the gateway of a nearby house; it was the closest he came to a pogrom. In 1932 he was sent to Mikolaj Rej Gymnasium, one of the best Warsaw schools. He was, by his own account, no more than an average pupil, not being pushed by his parents. He remembered

[1] A collection of tributes to Matthew M. Fryde first printed in *The Polish Review*, 10, no. 2 (1965), together with a bibliography of his work, was published as a pamphlet, *In memoriam Matthew M. Fryde* (New York, 1965).

two teachers in particular for their excellence, the classics master and the history master, Edward Bartel. Edmund enjoyed his Latin and Greek and acquired a taste for Greek literature which was to lie dormant for many years before it came to bring depth to his last book, when the transmission of the Greek classics came under his close attention. Above all, his time as a schoolboy was spent in reading. His father, a frequently remote figure in his life, had a large library, of six thousand books, and encouraged his son to make free use of it. Edmund remembered beginning to use it when he was eleven. His father would discuss books but would never direct his reading. Edmund recalled using the fourteenth edition of the Encyclopedia Britannica. Macaulay's *History of England* was there in five volumes in Polish translation. The first author he remembered reading in English was Oscar Wilde.

Edmund was never sure why he was sent to Bradfield College in 1938. His father once turned up unexpectedly at school and received permission to take his son to London for a weekend. Whilst reading an account of the Polish Enigma connection, after his father's death, he came across the name of a man he remembered coming to meet his father in his hotel room. He came to suspect that his father, a mathematician with a prodigious memory, may have been involved in intelligence work and that having a son at Bradfield was a cover for visits to London. It was his father's diplomatic passport that enabled him and his parents, on holiday in France at the beginning of September 1939, to enter Britain. Edmund did not find the teaching at Bradfield stimulating, but, compared with Polish schools, it was not anti-semitic; and it had a good library. And he could play chess in the back pew during chapel. It was there that Boleslaw became Edmund.

In January 1942 Edmund went up to an empty wartime Oxford, to Balliol College. He used to recall the particular early kindness of J. M. Thompson, of Magdalen College, his tutor for one term, and a later tutor, W. A. Pantin, of Oriel College. In the autumn of that same year came the event which most scarred his life. His mother, so loved by her son and neglected by her husband, took her own life. His greatest support at this difficult time came from William Peters, a contemporary at Balliol, who became his closest friend, and a constant friend for 57 years. Forty years after their first acquaintance, when William Peters was High Commissioner in Malawi, Edmund was his guest. This visit to Africa became a favourite subject of reminiscence in Edmund's later years.

Edmund sat his final examinations in June 1944 but was unable to take his degree until December and, encouraged by Goronwy Edwards, who had been his tutor for one term, Edmund began research. In his finals he had been placed only in the Second Class: as R. W. Southern explained in a letter 'his work was of First Class quality and he only failed to obtain the class which he deserved through a certain diffidence which hampered him in the examination'. To those who only knew Edmund in his maturity, the diffidence is hard to imagine. The subject of his research was one central to Goronwy Edwards's own interests: 'Edward III's war finances, 1337–41'. For better or worse, Edwards made of Edmund a medievalist; he also, as Edmund would recall, taught him the importance of writing clearly. With the help of a Polish government research scholarship and support from his father, Edmund was able to continue his research until 1947. During this period Edmund also, on the side, found employment calendaring some of the uncatalogued medieval Balliol archives; the high point in this work was his discovery of a deed of 1321 which named all the fellows of the college, providing the only point in medieval times at which the whole membership is known. On 31 July 1947 he was awarded his doctorate and on the same day appointed to a lectureship in Economic History at the University College of Wales, Aberystwyth.

Edmund used to say that R. F. Treharne had appointed him at Aberystwyth in the mistaken belief that he was an economic historian. Be that as it may, Edmund certainly became one, if only by virtue of having to lecture on economic history for twenty years. His knowledge acquired depth as a result of being invited by M. M. Postan to contribute a chapter on medieval public credit to the *Cambridge Economic History of Europe*. This invitation led to many years of intensive research in the Public Record Office. Economic history and especially financial history was moreover a subject Edmund had grown up with. His father's interests, even before he began to practise law, had embraced economics and history. During the 1920s and 1930s Mieczyslaw Fryde published widely on statistics and medieval economic history. Intellectually, Edmund owed much to his father. His father's obituarists describe the extraordinary range of Matthew Fryde's learning. Edmund himself regarded it as something exceptional, embracing creative and analytical abilities beyond his own; in comparison, he, Edmund, was 'a good squirrel', blessed, it has to be said, with a phenomenal memory. The shared interest of father and son in medieval finance found its monument in the chapter in volume III of *The Cambridge Economic History of Europe* (published in 1963), 'Public credit, with special reference to north-western Europe'. Of this joint contribution of father and son, E. M. Carus-Wilson wrote that it 'contains so much that is new that the volume is worth having for this alone';

while the chapter was described by Yves Renouard in a review in the *English Historical Review* as 'entirely novel in content' and 'a classic of the economic and financial history of the medieval West'.[2] It is the mastery of medieval finance and accounting that gives sinew to Edmund's work on medieval history.

The Clarendon Press expressed willingness to publish Edmund's thesis as a book, suitably trimmed and with some of the more specialized sections published as separate articles. Though some of these articles were published he became dissatisfied with the idea of the book and it was abandoned. In the early years after his appointment at Aberystwyth he published other articles on medieval financial and commercial history. The earliest of these on which he looked back with favour was 'Deposits of Hugh Despenser the Younger with Italian bankers' (1951), a piece of work which owed its origin to the kindness of Roger Ellis in offering transcripts of thirteenth- and fourteenth-century Italian documents he had made in the Public Record Office; several of these articles appeared in *Revue Belge de Philologie et d'Histoire*, a journal which, unlike some, allowed ample elbow room. Most of Edmund's articles in this field are collected in *Studies in Medieval Trade and Finance* (1983). A reviewer of this volume commented on the 'meticulous concern for documentation'.[3]

When Edmund was working for his thesis one inescapable character made his presence felt; later, when he came to do research on the Medici Bank, and again, when doing research on the discontents of peasants, this same character kept obtruding. The over-reaching William de la Pole, peerless in his financial skills as in his ruthlessness, 'the most influential merchant of the Middle Ages', could only be exorcised by a biography: *William de la Pole, Merchant and King's Banker, d. 1366*, written in the 1980s and published in 1988. It did not embody much new work; rather, it was a condensation of earlier articles on Edward III's finances, and material from the thesis, with particular focus on the chief protagonist. This volume was Edmund's farewell to high finance.

The Public Record Office became Edmund's home for long periods during vacations in these years. He acquired a formidable mastery of the *fonds*, and of palaeography and diplomatic. Indeed, in 1955 he came close to appointment as Reader in Diplomatic at Oxford (and was happy in later years to maintain that the right man had been chosen). He came to

---

[2] Review by Carus-Wilson in *Economica*, NS 32 (1965), 110; by Renouard in *English Historical Review*, 80 (1965), 114.
[3] *English Historical Review*, 101 (1986), 221.

know well a famous generation of Public Record Office staff. He remembered H. C. Johnson affectionately. C. A. F. Meekings became a friend for life. It was as a habitué of the PRO that he came to know V. H. Galbraith, one whom he used to hold in the highest esteem, for his scholarship and his radical and irreverent outlook, and to whom he felt particularly close. Through Galbraith he came to know May McKisack, pupil of Powicke, also later a source of much help and friendship.

Not that Edmund's teaching was restricted in these early years to economic history. He carried much of the burden of teaching in British medieval history, working closely in these years with R. F. Walker. During these early years he taught the man he looked back on as the ablest undergraduate of his teaching career, Gwyn A. Williams. In 1954 Edmund was invited by Sir Maurice Powicke to become assistant editor of the second edition of the Royal Historical Society *Handbook of British Chronology*—a recognition of his familiarity with medieval sources. The second edition appeared in 1961. Edmund's contribution to this edition is reflected by the words of Sir Maurice in a note added to the preface: '[Dr Fryde] is the actual editor of this second edition'. One of Edmund's proposals for the second edition was that the officers of state of the Commonwealth period should be included. This suggestion, however, met with a gentle rebuff from Sir Maurice: 'Her Majesty is our patron'. Among Edmund's fondest boasts was that it was he, a Polish Jew, when he became editor of the third edition, published in 1986, who ensured that these officials at last found recognition. The *Handbook* is a fundamental work of reference for British historians. Edmund's contribution to the second edition of the *Handbook*, and to the third (the sections for which he was responsible are detailed on p. ix), serve as an indication of his capacity for close, meticulous, and unobtrusive scholarship. It was while working on the *Handbook* that Edmund made his only incursion into Welsh history, editing the volume presented to Sir Goronwy Edwards, the *Book of Prests of the King's Wardrobe 1294–5* (1962), an edition of the financial and military records of Edward I's campaign to quell the last major Welsh rebellion against him.

Work on the *Handbook* extended Edmund's interests to new areas; in particular, as a result of revising the lists of medieval parliaments, to constitutional history. A consequence of this was his collaboration with Edward Miller in editing *Historical Studies of the English Parliament* in two volumes (1970), a most useful volume, highly intelligent in its choice of articles and in the quality of the introductory comment. In 1965, the year he agreed with the Cambridge University Press to edit these volumes with Miller, he also agreed to edit a similar collection of papers of 'Studies in institutional, social and economic history of late Antiquity and the early Middle Ages', but later under pressure of work withdrew from this agreement. Another proposal made by him about the same time was for an edition of select documents on 'the internal crisis of 1296–98 in England', a volume to be based mainly on the Memoranda Rolls and Ancient Correspondence in the Public Record Office (work subsequently in good part achieved in Michael Prestwich, *Documents illustrating the crisis of 1297–98 in England*, Camden Society, 4th Series, vol. 24).

In 1959 Edmund had begun to teach as a special subject 'English history 1485–1558 and its European background'. He had already, as a protégé of Goronwy Edwards, begun to work for the British committee for the revision of Potthast, *Repertorio delle Fonte storiche del Medio Evo*. In 1966 he first attended the Potthast General Assembly in Rome as British representative. He set about learning Italian and began to make regular visits to Italy, often twice a year. These visits stimulated his interest in Italian art and, as with any enthusiasm on his part, kindled a desire to teach on the subject. Treharne retired in 1966, to be succeeded in the chair by Fergus Johnston, a person altogether more indulgent to Edmund's wishes. Edmund began to lecture in a variety of new fields. One of them was History of Art, at first, on Italian art from Roman times to 1700. In later years, up till his retirement in 1990, he lectured on European (and British) art of many periods. These lectures were accompanied by slides drawn from an enormous and lovingly accumulated stock which included many made from Edmund's own photographs. The lectures had a devoted following. None gave Edmund greater pleasure. But although the subject lay close to his heart, Edmund always regarded himself as too much of an amateur, too lacking in technical expertise, to publish in this field. An article on Lorenzo de' Medici's patronage of art was the closest he came.

During 1966 Edmund married Natalie Davies, who had been his student. There followed a decade or so of frequent travel, many conferences and much contact with continental scholars. It was a period of fruitful collaboration. But then Natalie Fryde, now an established medieval historian, took her own path. In personal terms the marriage had not proved successful. A divorce came in 1981.

In 1969 Edmund had edited a revision of C. Oman's *The Great Revolt of 1381*, and the following year published an article 'Parliament and the Peasants' Revolt of 1381' (reprinted in *Studies*). His 1981 Historical Association pamphlet *The Great Revolt of 1381* incorporated his rounded view of the subject; it is an admirable example of his ability to embrace a complicated subject and represent it concisely and clearly. It was in 1969 that an invitation came from Edward Miller to contribute a chapter on 'Peasant rebellion and peasant discontents' to the *Cambridge Agrarian History of England and Wales*, vol. 3, *1348–1500*. This chapter, written jointly by Edmund and his wife Natalie, was not published until 1991. It had however provided the stimulus for what became a much more extended examination of the subject. Edmund began to think of a book-length treatment but because of the long delay in the appearance of the Cambridge volume that larger treatment had to bide its time. By then engrossed in Byzantine scholarship, he doubled back on his tracks in the early 1990s to write *Peasants and Landlords in Later Medieval England c. 1380–1525*. It is a work based on a number of detailed local studies, particularly in the west Midlands. It combines two of his strengths as a historian: on the one hand his financial acumen, and understanding of the strategies of landlords (such as the bishop of Worcester), on the other his human sympathy for the predicament of the peasants and the reasons for their occasional and sometimes violent protests.

An invitation in 1969 to write an article for the *Encyclopaedia Britannica* on 'Historiography and historical methodology' (published in the 15th edition in 1974) steered Edmund's interest in new directions. R. R. Davies had succeeded Johnston in the chair at Aberystwyth in 1976 and had initiated an innovative compulsory course in the history degree at Aberystwyth on 'History and the writing of history'; Edmund was an enthusiastic participant. Historiography also, inevitably, drew his interests to Italy. The encylopedia article was one he came to find unsatisfactory, but writing it had brought the growth of historical awareness to the centre of his interests, there to remain.

At this point in his career Edmund was not rooted to Aberystwyth. More than once he considered moving and applied for chairs elsewhere. But by the end of the 1970s any urge to move had waned. He may perhaps have come to sense what was clear to others: that in Aberystwyth he had come to be appreciated, within and without the university, as someone exceptional, and to be given an extraordinary degree of freedom in his department. He was moreover only beginning to discover how valuable to him was the National Library of Wales with respect to the new direction in which his scholarship was turning. In 1973 he was awarded a personal chair. It may have been a signal to him to enjoy his teaching and his research. With resignation or otherwise, he settled down. In 1988 he was elected FBA. He was deeply gratified by publication in 1996 of *Recognitions: Essays presented to Edmund Fryde*, edited by Colin

Richmond and Isobel Harvey. And about this volume he could not voice the complaint he made on the occasion of a surprise seventieth birthday party arranged for him: that he would have liked to have known in advance, in order to enjoy the pleasure of anticipation.

The germ of what became Edmund's governing interest in the last twenty years of his life was an invitation by A. G. Dickens, a close friend, to contribute a chapter on Lorenzo de' Medici to the volume *The Courts of Europe: Politics, Patronage and Royalty, 1400–1800* (1977) edited by Dickens. The article was 'Lorenzo de' Medici: high finance and the patronage of art and learning'. While Edmund's collection of papers, *Humanism and Renaissance Historiography* (1983), did not include this article, it did include three subsequent papers on Lorenzo: one 'A survey of the historiography and of the primary sources', one on his patronage of art, and one on his library. Lorenzo had moved to the centre of Edmund's interest. About this time indeed he contemplated writing a biography of Lorenzo. That half-formed ambition was however over-taken by the realisation of the significance of a discovery he had made. The article on Lorenzo's library, the most innovative of the volume, was the precursor of what became Edmund's next major work. While investi-gating the library, Edmund had come across the two inventories of Medici manuscripts made about 1508 by Fabio Vigili. The inventory of Greek manuscripts was slightly known but had not been used for a systematic reconstruction of the Medici library; the inventory of Latin manuscripts was barely known at all. Reconstruction of the library with the accompanying identification of manuscripts and the pursuit of trans-missions of texts became Edmund's chief preoccupation. The resulting work was eventually published in two volumes as *Greek Manuscripts in the Private Library of the Medici, 1468–1510* (Aberystwyth, 1996). A cor-responding work on the Latin manuscripts—manuscripts of less impor-tance—was set aside as a future project. The Medici Greek manuscripts, in 1494 probably about 600 in number, constituted one of the five most significant collections in the West at the time. By 1494 almost all the important ancient Greek authors were represented in the library; Aristotle in particular, by some eighty codices of text and commentary. The notable absences in the surviving collection appear in large part to be accounted for by depredations in the years 1494–1508 after the expulsion of the Medici from Florence.

Many scholars would have been more than content to have produced an annotated edition of Vigili's inventory, making such identifications as were possible. Perhaps Edmund as a young man might have been satisfied with such a work. By now he knew too much. He could not simply act the librarian. Many of these manuscripts played important roles in intellectual history; their significance demanded attention. Edmund's two volumes are discursive and to the general reader offer an engrossing exploration of many byways of intellectual life at this fascinating conjunction. They brought to light some unexpected discoveries: the explanation of the attribution of the unique text of the *Dionysiaca* of Nonnos of Panoplis; the likely source of the surviving tradition of Proclus's commentary on Euclid's Elements; and the identification of the manuscript used by William de Moerbeke for his translation of Aristotle's *De Anima*. But in opting for a broad canvas, Edmund sometimes slipped below the standards of meticulousness which characterized his early work. An appreciative notice of *Greek Manuscripts* by D. F. Jackson in *Scriptorium* has to correct a number of details (such as manuscript numbers), and offers besides some thirty additional or alternative identifications of items in the Vigili inventory.[4]

Edmund's interest in Italian humanism led to his frequenting Arnaldo Momigliano's Ancient History Seminar at the Warburg Institute and to a treasured friendship. He later came to feel that he owed to Momigliano a greater debt than to any other scholar. If Galbraith was the inspiration for his studies in medieval peasantry, Momigliano was for the studies in intellectual tradition. Edmund rejoiced at having left behind the study of the misdeeds of medieval tycoons—'cats fighting rats' was how he sometimes characterized the theme—a study to which he had been led by chance, for the study of the works of men who had sustained civilised values. His trajectory might be viewed as one which began with reaching an understanding of affairs of the powerful, a wholly cynical view, such as came naturally to his father; which then moved to an understanding of the plight of the downtrodden, something grounded in a sympathy held in common by both parents; and finally to an understanding of some of those who strived for things of spiritual value such as his mother had cherished.

A feature of the Medici Greek manuscripts is that the great majority of them originated in Byzantine scriptoria (as distinct from being copies commissioned from scribes living in Florence). Edmund's work on the Medici library drew him deeply into many areas of Byzantine scholarship. Some of his conclusions found a place in his two volumes on Lorenzo's Greek manuscripts. But his curiosity had been roused. His personal need to

---

[4] 'Fabio Vigili's inventory of Medici Greek manuscripts', *Scriptorium*, 52 (1998), 199–204.

satisfy curiosity about many of the questions brought to the surface during his work on the Medici library, and the inner compulsion to create order, led to his last completed book: *The early Palaeologan Renaissance (1261–c.1360)* (Leiden, 2000). This work, acknowledging Sir Steven Runciman's *Last Byzantine Renaissance* (1970) as its nearest predecessor, and following Runciman in its controversial use of the word 'renaissance' in this context, is a wide-ranging work of synthesis, one which is always ready to draw the background of scholarly achievement, whether intellectual, religious or political, and to indicate value, to bring people to life. Leslie Brubaker in a review welcoming the book as a good traditional overview, though one whose focus is resolutely on secular literature, calls it 'an old-fashioned book, with an intellectual framework that remains resolutely positivist', a view Edmund would not have taken amiss.[5]

Edmund was by all accounts an inspirational teacher. In the lecture theatre, as in conversation, he had a remarkable ability to bring characters to life. Martin Fitzpatrick, a colleague, who had been his student, describes him:

> He set us the highest of standards without ever making them intimidating. Above all, he taught that the best way to understand history was by going to the sources. Characteristically, his lectures used one key source, whether it was Clause 39 of Magna Carta, Edward III's statute of treason, a peasant's list of grievances, an apparently complicated balance sheet or a private letter. He would expound in detail their significance, and demonstrate their wider relevance. He blew the dust off documents and talked of them as if they had just been composed and of the characters involved as if he knew them from personal experience.

His lectures on subjects outside his specialities, subjects upon which he never wrote, were as gripping as any. Apart from art, these included eighteenth-century French history—Edmund was in essence a child of the Enlightenment—and nineteenth- and twentieth-century Russian history. The latter was, in effect, to a large degree, a branch of his own family history. Russian history, and the two World Wars, were of abiding interest; he kept up his reading to the end. Conversation with Edmund at all times was likely to slip into an impromptu lecture—as often as not a fascinating one. On Russia, and the World Wars, it might well begin: 'The published accounts are all wrong. My father told me . . .'. For most of his life, the purpose of Rudolf Hess's flight to Scotland came into this category. Edmund loved anecdotes, and had mastered the art of telling them. One

---

[5] *The Medieval Review* (2001).

of his gifts as a lecturer was to make history as alive as an anecdote. He would defend Herodotus against the charge of retailing anecdotes.

Behind the array of his friendships, Edmund was a lonely man, and behind the assertive protagonist, a vulnerable one. Family life was denied him; his marriage ended unhappily; he counted much on friends. Friendships of his early life at Aberystwyth had been largely within the university or ones which arose from his long periods in the Public Record Office. He kept in close touch with some former students. Later, as Italy, and, closer to home, the Warburg Institute, became his stamping ground, and above all the National Library of Wales—which became in effect his club—new friendships sprang up. Among the staff and readers of the National Library he found enduring ones. In his later years, he kept an open house. Many were they who had his front door key and were urged to make themselves at home in the house whether he was there or not. Visitors would be pressed to stay for meals, meals in which a place would always be found for delicacies which somehow conjured up what a Warsaw child of the 1930s might have delighted in from a superior delikatessen or patisserie. For many years there would also be the company of an amiable and intelligent Labrador, and later her stupid daughter. The death of the daughter brought to an end Edmund's going for walks; exercise was not something to be undertaken for its own sake.

Edmund could show startling impulsive generosity—to a friend in trouble, to a student in need—but could, in many ways, almost as though to put friendship to the test, make great demands of it. His friend, Colin Richmond, in an obituary, puts it in extreme terms: 'Edmund was an exasperating friend: at any time he was likely to turn into an enemy. It was not that he was unpredictable. Far from it. If—or rather when—he fell out with you, or made you fall out with him, it was because he would not compromise his devotion to a scholarly principle, his attachment to a person whom he considered worth supporting through thick and thin, or both' and 'the only terms on which one could be his friend were ones of complete capitulation.'[6] Edmund's friends, even those so blessed with the facility of abnegation as not to have experienced becoming enemies, will all recognise the man. Alun Davies, the historian, of Swansea, a dear friend of Edmund's, warning a colleague who had not yet met Edmund, put it differently: 'Beware of his bear-hug.' Reflecting on Edmund's life, Colin Richmond remarks: 'What saved him from despair was learning.

[6] *Renaisssance Studies*, 14 (2000), 396–8.

Edmund was immensely, hugely, almost monstrously learned', and, putting into words a thought that Edmund would never have brought himself to express, 'he doggedly clung to the idea that scholarship as well as art can, and does, make a man's life worthwhile, even and especially an unhappy man's life'—Edmund himself would merely say, from time to time: 'It keeps me out of trouble.' The scholarly activity seldom ceased. Richmond's experience of being met by Edmund at Aberystwyth station with a hug and the greeting 'You know, St Augustine was wrong about Original Sin' was typical. Such greetings were still commonplace in the last year of his life when, more or less immobilised, he was busy writing a book on the growth of historical awareness in fifteenth-century Italy. Martin Fitzpatrick sets the scene of the last years: 'One would open his front door, and see him down the tiled hallway, sitting at his table, working away surrounded by a nest of papers and bathed in the side light from his kitchen window. It was like a seventeenth-century Dutch interior'.

A provisional title of the uncompleted work was *From Petrarch to Politian: the Revival of a Sense of History in the early Italian Renaissance*. Five chapters were written, chapters which would have come in the middle of the book: 'Guarino Guarini: historical interests', two on Biondo, 'Pope Nicholas V and translators of Greek historians and geographers', and 'Florentine historiography in the later fifteenth century'. In the last weeks before his death on 17 November 1999 he was contemplating his chapter on Alberti. Petrarch, Valla, and Politian lay ahead. The writing of a chapter or article would bring Edmund's intense focus onto the matter in hand. His visitors would often be treated to a resumé upon entering the house. There would always, however, in relaxed moments, be in contemplation the work beyond the one on which he was engaged. The one which lay beyond his book on humanism and art in fifteenth-century Italy was to have been a collection of portraits of historians to whom—whether he had known them well personally or not—Edmund felt particularly close. Besides two Polish historians, these were to include Marc Bloch, Helen Cam, Galbraith and Momigliano.

For Edmund people were black or white. Or sometimes perhaps pied, in so far as a man might be 'a good historian but not a nice human being', or the reverse. (Those historians who were to have have appeared in his gallery of portraits were in all regards white.) Edmund loved the work of many painters and sculptors—his interest waned as one moved into the twentieth century—and had read deeply about them and was curious about their personal lives, but, always weighing them up as people as well as artists, would reluctantly admit that, while a few were, many were indeed not nice human beings. He moved in the past as he moved in the present, unable to view events and the people concerned in them without scrutinising what he saw as moral qualities. This comes out in his writing. In lectures, and in talk, it was a trait which gave instant life to the characters of history, even though at times the gift may have verged on that of the caricaturist. To the inexpert, at least, it was memorable history. Edmund was not a religious person, but he had the utmost respect for the religious. At the end of his life he often spoke of the humanity he found in some of the leaders and scholars of the Byzantine Church, comparing them favourably with those of Rome. Gibbon, on the other hand, also much in his mind during these years, was judged, for all his insight, to fall short, too lacking in human sympathy, blind to true devoutness.

Edmund liked to be involved. For much of his time at Aberystwyth he was active in the affairs of the College, as a member of the Senate, on the Finance Committee, the Library Committee, acting as secretary of the Staff House. He could be a fixer or he could be blunt and, willy nilly, could make enemies as freely as new friends. In the 1980s when the College, under government pressure, was closing department after department—Classics, Philosophy, languages—a stand was made for Music. Edmund was partisan. He moved in the Court of the College that the decision to close the department be overturned (the motion was carried but later nullified). The Principal, agitated, was driven to say: 'Professor Fryde. I have the impression that you wish to move a motion of no confidence in me.' 'No', answered Fryde, 'You quite misunderstand. We have far more important matters to discuss.'

DANIEL HUWS

Formerly of the National Library of Wales

Note. Two invaluable portraits of Edmund Fryde are provided by the address of Martin Fitzpatrick, 'Remembering Edmund Fryde', printed in *In memoriam Edmund Fryde*, for the funeral, and the obituary by Colin Richmond in *Renaissance Studies*. This memoir has also had the benefit of comment by Professor R. R. Davies, Dr Isobel Harvey and Dr N. G. Wilson. William Peters provided reminiscences of Edmund when a student at Balliol. In *Recognitions*, on pp. 1–8 there is an appreciation of Edmund Fryde by Daniel Huws, and on pp. 9–17 a bibliography of his writings by Dr Isobel Harvey. Use has been made of Edmund Fryde's surviving personal papers (which are to be donated to the National Library of Wales).

ALFRED GELL

J. Pembrey

Alfred Antony Francis Gell
1945–1997

ALFRED GELL died of cancer on 28 January 1997 at the age of fifty-one. He was at the height of his powers and widely regarded as one of the most interesting thinkers in the world in the field of the anthropology of art. He had been elected to the British Academy in 1995 and turned down a professorship (awarded posthumously) on a number of occasions at the London School of Economics, where he held a readership. The insightful obituaries of some of his colleagues, as well as his own frank, published remarks towards the end of his life give us an unusual opportunity to investigate the life of a highly creative and original scholar. His life and writings provide an interesting insight into the fashions and flows of one part of British thought in the later twentieth century.

In writing this obituary of Alfred Gell two major puzzles to be solved have emerged. One was, who was Alfred Gell? The second concerns how an academic works and creates something interesting and new. Neither is an easy task. At a general level, the probing of an inner personality and cognitive process is intrinsically almost impossible. As Gell himself wrote, 'the cognitive processes of any mind, especially over a whole biographical career, are inaccessible private experiences which leave only the most undecipherable traces'.[1] In relation to Gell himself I have certain disadvantages in addressing these questions. I did not know Gell at all personally. I have little overlap in terms of competence, his principal field being Melanesia,

---

[1] Alfred Gell, *Art and Agency: An Anthropological Theory* (Oxford, 1998), p. 236, henceforth cited as Gell, *Agency*.

Proceedings of the British Academy, **120**, 123–147. © The British Academy 2003.

though I do have an interest in his second fieldwork area among the Muria Gonds of Andhra Pradesh. Likewise I only have a partial overlap in terms of topic of concern, though I am interested in technology and recently in the history of art, and particularly in the ways in which artists and writers work. This, plus the objectivity of being an historian as well as an anthropologist, and someone outside his circle of close acquaintances, may give me certain compensating advantages.

The task is one of detection. There are various clues which, to use the approach of one of his favourite characters, Sherlock Holmes, allow us to reconstruct something about this interesting mind and person, particularly with the help of his own revealing comments made in the last few months of his life and published in the introduction to his posthumously published essays on the *Art of Anthropology* (Athlone Press, 1999).

Family and school

Gell was born on 12 June 1945. His real names, according to the obituary in the *Guardian* (4 February 1997) were Antony Francis, but at his public school he was renamed 'Alfred' by his friends, according to one of them. Gell describes himself on several occasions as of 'bourgeois' background and when describing why he felt hypocritical about aligning himself too closely with anti-colonialism referred to the fact 'my ancestors were all colonial officials, soldiers, and even missionaries and bishops.'[2]

His parents are the late Professor Philip (an eminent immunologist) and Mrs Susan Gell. One of their main influences on him was through an interest in art and drawing.

> Both my parents drew. My mother was a draughtswoman trained in the art of doing the drawings that go with archaeological expeditions and my father was an amateur artist, and so the materials were always present in our house. When I was a small child, I entertained myself by drawing mostly, as many small children do. I don't say I was a brilliant child artist but I would produce huge series of pictures. We had comics, and one week the comic started a big story about how some Vikings landed on a piece of rural Sussex . . . I was inspired to produce hundreds of pictures of Viking feats . . .'[3]

---

[2] Alfred Gell, *The Art of Anthropology; Essays and Diagrams* (London, 1999), edited by Eric Hirsch, henceforth referred to as Gell, *Art*.

[3] Gell, *Art*, pp. 26–7.

He wrote that 'for me the graphic channel of expression is as natural—in fact, more natural—than writing'.[4]

We gain other glimpses of his childhood interests in occasional asides in his essays; for example we hear of Alfred's reverence as an eleven-year-old for a matchstick model of Salisbury Cathedral. It was also at home and at school that he absorbed a love of music. It has been suggested in one of the obituaries that 'It is perhaps no coincidence that of all the musicians Alfred admired it was Schubert that he felt most passionate about. Schubert died at the age of thirty-one, a modest man during his brief life . . .'[5]

At Bryanston boarding school he met Stephen Hugh-Jones and Jonathan Oppenheimer, friends and students of anthropology, with whom he maintained close ties until his death. There Alfred developed his interest and skill in the practice of wit as a medium of social communication. He told Eric Hirsch in an interview that he became part of 'an intellectual elite founded on wit, the ability to make people laugh. . . . It was a form of mild verbal aggression, a sort of verbal competition, one-upmanship, the desire to be top dog. . . . I think I probably carried a lot of that sort of adolescent competition to, in some ways, be wittier than the next person into the academic work that I do.'[6]

Cambridge as an undergraduate

Gell read archaeology and anthropology at Trinity College, Cambridge. He gives a glimpse of his first year in the joint course and the way in which it strengthened his earlier interest in visual representations. '. . . [W]e did archaeology, anthropology and physical anthropology, as well. And of course both archaeology and physical anthropology involved drawing skulls and stones. The first book of anthropology that I studied was *Habitat, Economy and Society* . . . by Darryl Forde, and I copied out all the pictures in it.'[7]

A second major effect of Cambridge was to re-enforce his desire to impress by his wit.

---

[4] Gell, *Art*, pp. 8–9.
[5] Eric Hirsch, 'Obituary of Alfred Gell' in *American Anthropologist*, 101(1), 152, henceforth referred to as Hirsch, *Obituary*.
[6] Eric Hirsch in the foreword to Gell, *Art*, p. ix.
[7] Gell, *Art*, p. 27.

Gell himself is, in characteristic fashion, wryly modest about his achievement.

> I wrote my monograph on the Umedas in 1972–3. This was presented as a 'structural analysis' in the Leach/Lévi-Strauss mode, and seemed very fashionable when it came out, but only for a little while, because 'sixties structuralism' was already in decline. I like to believe that the attention *Metamorphosis of the Cassowaries* received from other anthropologists was due to its literary ingenuity rather than its theoretical message, which was really quite out of tune with the times.[14]

The fieldwork for this thesis was clearly very tough. Indeed Hirsch suggests that when Gell went down with malaria in New Guinea he 'felt he had come very close to death. From that time until his actual, tragic death from cancer some twenty-eight years later at the age of fifty-one, he had the sense of living on borrowed time.'[15] His only re-visit was to help with making a film about Umeda ritual, the 'Red Bowman'. Peter Loizos described this in a personal communication as a 'very solid, scholarly and valuable archival film' which is an important record and adjunct to the book.

The interlude: Australia and India

After completing his thesis Gell went to a lecturing position in Sussex, where he met his future wife, the fellow anthropologist Simeran. He was recruited to the Australian National University in 1974 with the help of Anthony Forge. During the next ten years he attempted to shift to a new theme for study and to a new ethnographic area.

'It was as at this time [the 1970s] that I conceived the idea of writing an anthropology of time, a project on which I squandered an inordinate amount of—time. The whole effort would have been wasted but for the fact that my manuscript, which had been rejected by Cambridge University Press in 1984, was eventually published in much revised form in 1992 as *The Anthropology of Time*.'[16] This was a book in which he asked how time impinged on peoples' consciousness, how societies dealt with time, whether time can be considered as a 'resource' to be saved or spent. He explored the theories of various authorities on time, from Durkheim to Bourdieu, and considered four main theoretical approaches. These were

[14] Gell, *Art*, p. 7.
[15] Hirsch, *Obituary*, p. 152.
[16] Gell, *Art*, pp. 7–8.

those of developmental psychology, symbolic anthropology, 'economic' theories of time in social geography, and phenomenological theories. He then presented his own model of social/cognitive time. It is a very clever work, but has never caught on among his fellow academics in the same way as his later work on art.

The widening of his ethnographic area occurred through the accident of marrying Simeran. Again his own wry account of what happened is revealing.

> Simeran went to do fieldwork in India among the Muria [Gonds of Madhya Pradesh, India, in 1977–8], and I went along as the spouse. . . . Not having any grant, I had nothing in particular to study, so I could choose myself. I must say, it was a very, very nice fieldwork indeed, not having any research grant, not having any research project. And so I collected material on the markets simply because the market was one of the most interesting social occasions which happened every week, and it was really wonderful. I loved the market, and I liked the traders and the hustle and bustle of it all—very beautiful it was, exotic.[17]

On the basis of his work he wrote several insightful essays. For example there was 'The Market Wheel: Symbolic Aspects of an Indian Tribal Market' which was heavily influenced by Geertz's famous essay on the 'Balinese cock fight'. And there was the essay which became the basis for his last public appearance. 'In 1977–8, when Simeran and I were visiting Jagdalpur during our first fieldwork. . . . We'd been hearing, in the village, stories about this great massacre and the death of the Raja of Bastar in 1966 . . . I was very intrigued from that moment onwards about the idea of a Raja of Bastar and his death and why it caused so much panic in the countryside as it did.'[18] So he worked up the material and gave it as the Frazer Lecture in Cambridge in November 1996. He describes its aim thus. 'So what I was really working towards, I suppose, was something like a Sahlinesian picture of history in which history is people replaying the categories which had been handed down to them from the distant past.'[19]

His other motive for writing and delivering this lecture is equally revealing about his views. As he put it,

> it also provides me with an opportunity to do something which I really like to do—which is to take the piss out of these development people, particularly in India, who think that the poor downtrodden tribals have got anything to

[17] Gell, *Art*, pp. 12–13.
[18] Gell, *Art*, p. 22.
[19] Gell, *Art*, p. 23.

thank them for. In India most of the petty government officials are pretty much corrupt. But they all nonetheless think that because they have got a bit of education that gives them the right to rip off ordinary country folk and despise them at the same time. They don't do it in the name of self-interest, which would be quite reasonable in my view. They do it in the name of 'development' and 'progress'. So I've always been very much against development and progress . . .[20]

He returned to India many times. He and Simeran were advisors for a BBC documentary on the Gonds, but refused to let their names be included in the credits of what is widely regarded as an intrusive unsatisfactory film. 'He leaves many friends and relatives there [in India].'[21]

The London School of Economics: phase two

Gell returned to the LSE as a reader in 1979. It clearly took him some years to return to his earlier enthusiasm, for he describes on several occasions how the years between 1977 and 1984 were his 'wilderness years'. He was still trying to sort out his ideas on time, uncertain of how to proceed further.

It is clear that the ambience of the LSE gave him tremendous support in relaunching his career. It was the ideal place for him to be. It had a lively 'seminar culture' which drew the best out of him. His colleagues were stimulating, especially Maurice Bloch with whom he shared certain interests in performance and language. Above all the department was extremely supportive. In many departments in the country he would have been forced to undertake the usual administrative tasks which weigh down most academics and often interfere with their creativity—chairing the department and faculty, senior examiner and so on. On the one or two occasions when Gell was asked to do this it became plain that he seemed temperamentally incapable of performing the task. Consequently he was spared almost all such tasks. He recognised that he was not playing his part in this way and this was one of the reasons he refused to be upgraded to a professorship. As Hirsch writes, 'Administrative burdens were tasks he greatly avoided and which explains why—with his consent—he was never promoted to a professorship during his lifetime.'[22]

---

[20] Gell, *Art*, p. 23.
[21] Hirsch, *Obituary*, p. 153.
[22] Hirsch, *Obituary*, p. 154.

His colleagues were also extremely tolerant of his tendency to take on a number of Ph.D. students whom neither he nor the department were really equipped to teach, largely because he could not say 'no'. Again, however, this was at considerable cost to others. He was a good teacher and inspiring lecturer, and this was obviously what he enjoyed most.

While the department provided the context, it is difficult to know exactly what brought him back to the subject to which he would make such a major contribution, the anthropology of art. Clearly one special book and moment was when, according to Hirsch, 'during 1984 Alfred read for the first time [E. H. Gombrich's] *The Sense of Order* (1979), which enabled him to see clearly the connection between the cognitive effects of patterned images and the potent cognitive processes informing them.'[23]

But this is only one small clue. In order to understand his progress and later work better we need to abandon the strictly chronological approach and consider several important themes and influences. We need to go to the under-ground rivers or, to change the metaphor, to see him reflected in other mirrors.

Some major influences on his thought

In tracing the major influences on Gell's academic development we notice three ways in which certain thinkers affected him. One was as a role model, someone to emulate or outdo in general. Secondly, he paid considerable attention to the way in which people wrote or otherwise communicated their ideas, their style and method of presentation. Thirdly, there was the content of their ideas, their methodology and substantive ideas.

The first major influence on Gell, the anthropologist Edmund Leach, shows all three types of influence mixed together. Gell's 'hero-worshipping' attitude at Cambridge has been mentioned, and he continues by assessing the influence as follows.

> The papers 'Rethinking anthropology', 'Genesis as myth' and 'The legitimation of Solomon', provided the model for my literary activity from the start. People complain about Leach's scratchy prose style; but I hear Leach's authentic and unforgettable drawl behind his printed words, and the whole text comes alive. Leach's style has the supreme virtue of allowing his wit, his sheer cleverness, to

---

[23] Hirsch, *Obituary*, p. 154.

emerge fully; the absence of shading, delicacy and embellishment only contribute to this central purpose. I, on the other hand, was more interested than Leach in prose as a literary medium.[24]

Writing of his essay on the Umeda dance, Gell suggested that

in a way [this article] is about the way I was introduced into anthropology by Edmund Leach, because one thing you'll notice with the mask analysis and the dance analysis is that they can be done on this rubber sheeting. Leach had this idea that you could put social structure on rubber sheeting and twist it around. Well, it's that idea basically. I think that idea (which comes in *Rethinking Anthropology*) had a very, very powerful long-term effect on me, so that whenever I come across bodies of data which do seem to be susceptible to being shown as a series of twistings and stretchings on rubber, I automatically do so.[25]

Gell's interest in prose style partly

came from my early and assiduous reading of Lévi-Strauss, a much more refined prose stylist than Leach. I still think that Lévi-Strauss is the greatest of anthropologists, and that he will never be overtaken, however long our discipline remains in existence—his only rival being Malinowski, a taste for whom I acquired only later. Lévi-Strauss' urbane and convoluted style inspired me greatly, and it is fair to say that at the outset of my career I wanted to produce 'Leachian' displays of hard-hitting anthropological wit, wrapped up in Lévi-Straussian gravitas and mellifluousness.[26]

Several of the essays in the final collection, as well as some of his shorter reviews give examples of what he was aiming at.

When he went to the LSE and during his fieldwork this structural influence was supplemented by another.

I also discovered phenomenology, or to be more precise, phenomenological social theory and psychological theory. My guides were Alfred Schutz and Maurice Merleau-Ponty, whose works I took with me to New Guinea when I went into the field in 1969. I made a very thorough study of Schutz's collected papers, and *The Phenomenology of Perception*, not least because I had little else to read and much time on my hands, immured in my mosquito-net. Exactly why I became interested in phenomenology is rather a puzzle to me.[27]

The next wave to break over anthropology, in the mid 1970s, when Gell was at the ANU, hardly affected him. He describes his negative atti-

---

[24] Gell, *Art*, p. 6.
[25] Gell, *Art*, p. 16.
[26] Gell, *Art*, p. 6.
[27] Gell, *Art*, p. 6.

tude in his characteristic way. 'Resurgent Marxism was in the air; but I had no left-wing leanings and I never believed that anthropology was a force to set the world to rights or undo the effects of colonialism.' Given his bourgeois and colonial ancestors, he could not feel himself to be a plausible anti-colonialist.

> I never had the slightest feeling that I could be 'engaged' or 'committed' or identify with the subjects of anthropology, if only because my middle-class income—even an academic salary—was so much greater, and cost me so much less sweat to obtain, than the incomes of Umedas or, later, Muria Gonds. I have never understood how bourgeois like myself can consider themselves the class allies of third world peasants, since it seems to me that we are all just walking, breathing examples of the results of their exploitation. All that people like me can do in the third world is watch and listen sympathetically, and maybe form a few personal relationships which, in the nature of things, are without significance so far as the wider historical relationships between nations are concerned. The business of bourgeois anthropologists like me is only to produce texts—or give seminars—directed towards a reception of other anthropologists and interested (metropolitan) parties.[28]

He then continues to explain what he read and who influenced him at this period. 'Because the anthropological Marxism of the 1970s repelled me, before I read Bourdieu and was reconciled, I was forced, more or less, to spend the decade interesting myself in non-anthropological studies, particularly philosophy and psychology.'[29] During the later 1970s and early 1980s 'The most important influence on my theoretical outlook during this period was Bourdieu. Only on the surface am I a Bourdieu critic. Actually, I read Bourdieu obsessively, and with unstinted admiration for his dialectical skill. I think of Bourdieu as just as much one of my masters as Leach, Lévi-Strauss, and the phenomenologists Schutz, Merleau-Ponty, and Husserl.'[30]

The final writer who influenced him both stylistically and in approach was a surprising one. He describes how in the early 1980s, as the background to writing his essay on 'The technology of enchantment and the enchantment of technology', he

> started to read Malinowski properly, especially *Coral Gardens* which I had not even opened before. I think that I became very much influenced by Malinowski stylistically, following this immersion, and that my writing became simpler and more expressive as a result . . . Malinowski was a supreme

[28] Gell, *Art*, p. 7.
[29] Gell, *Art*, p. 7.
[30] Gell, *Art*, p. 8.

literary stylist whose elegant texts (along with Evans-Pritchard's) should be imitated by every anthropological beginner.[31]

He was also influenced by Malinowski theoretically. As Hirsch explains

he was able to see how Malinowski's study of gardening magic could be interpreted as a form of social technology that works through means of enchantment. Alfred discerned resonances between these verbal icons of enchantment and material forms such as the Kula prowboards carved to have powerful and persuasive effects upon Kula competitors. Almost at once this provided an emancipation from semiotic structuralism.[32]

A final important strand was work in the history of art. We have already seen that the work of Ernst Gombrich proved to be a turning point in 1984 and there were others. For instance, in a personal communication Dr Gilbert Lewis remembered meeting Gell 'when I happened to be carrying a book in my hand (Edgar Wind's *Pagan Mysteries in the Renaissance*) which Alfred spotted immediately. It was one of his favourite books on the history of art, read more than once.'

Gell's interest in the history of art, his early love of drawing and painting, takes us to another deep influence, which was works of art themselves. Although he clearly liked the great masters, Titian especially, it was modern artists and particularly Duchamp about whom he explicitly wrote. He describes in relation to his essay 'Vogel's net: Traps as Artworks and Artworks as Traps', that this 'derives from an interest in Duchamp and conceptual art which I have maintained since the 1970s when I first studied Duchamp's notes for 'The Bride stripped Bare by Her Bachelors Even' as part of my 'Time' project. It has always seemed to me a pity that the anthropology of art has only joined forces with 'modern' art in the most stupid, reactionary way . . .'[33]

This love of Duchamp and what it meant to him is again usefully summarised by Hirsch.

At one level, Duchamp sought to challenge the prevailing Western aesthetic conventions of representation by famously exhibiting a urinal—a 'ready-made', as he called it. What attracted Alfred and countless others to Duchamp's masterpiece was the intentional complexity it embodied and its puzzling qualities: the actual choice of artifact among those possible, how it was physically displayed (i.e. in a manner so that it could not be used), its

[31] Gell, *Art*, p. 8.
[32] Hirsch, *Obituary*, p. 154.
[33] Gell, *Art*, p. 18.

arcane but potent signature ('R. Mutt'), and so on. It was through Duchamp's attempt to dissolve art as we know it that Alfred glimpsed the outlines of his theory: everything according to Duchamp could be art and Alfred rephrased this in anthropological terms as how it was possible that 'art' could be in anything.'[34]

His audience: seminar culture

Gell's work cannot be understood without considering the audience he was addressing. Here we come to a number of revealing passages where he describes what he was trying to do. In the introduction to his posthumous essays, Gell writes: 'All the essays collected in this volume began life as texts intended to be delivered out loud to audiences, mostly at seminars. They are not really essays for reading so much as scripts to be performed.' He then gives an amusing account of the abrasive yet sympathetic setting of an (ideal-type) British academic seminar.[35] He comments that:

> The point is that the seminar is a social occasion, a game, an exchange, an ordeal, an initiation. To one of a naturally social disposition, to hear a paper in a seminar is intrinsically much more interesting than to read the same paper in cold blood, because one's social proclivities are excited as well as one's strictly academic or intellectual interests. I confess to being a social animal of this type. Consequently, it is much more exciting for me to write a paper for presentation at a seminar than it is to write for an imaginary reader, as one does when writing a book. Books do not give anything like the feedback that one gets from seminars.[36]

We have seen the ways in which this skill and interest developed out of his experiences at school, Cambridge, and in the Firth and other seminars at the LSE. He wrote that

> while I never believed that I was better at 'anthropology' than my more intelligent age-mates, I always prided myself on giving better performances in the specific 'seminar' setting. So, since then, I have concentrated on working towards particular 'performances', rather than concentrating, as perhaps I should have done, on the development of anthropological theory in a more general sense. What I have always wanted to produce was the 'ideal' seminar paper for reading out loud (rather than some specific advance in anthropological knowledge).[37]

[34] Hirsch, *Obituary*, p. 154.
[35] Gell, *Art*, pp. 1–2.
[36] Gell, *Art*, p. 2.
[37] Gell, *Art*, pp. 5–6.

For those who never attended any of these occasions, it is reassuring to learn that he was largely successful. According to Hirsch his 'papers were a combination of wit, tightly reasoned argument, and creative iconoclasm that drew the listener in and enabled her/him to gain novel insights . . .'[38]

His method of exploring and communicating ideas; the visual dimension

Gell wore very thick spectacles for short-sightedness and read texts or examined objects with his face a few inches from the object of his attention. He also had other problems with his eyes in his middle life which nearly made him blind. He was reputedly saved from this by some of the earliest laser surgery performed in England. The curious nature of his eyes, the particular intensity of his seeing tiny objects when held close, all this seem to be connected both with his interests in visuality, his personality and his artistic abilities.

We have noted his parents' and his own interest in graphic and other representation. He wrote that the '*Metamorphosis of the Cassowaries* is dominated by this mode of expression, and is really an "art" book as much as a "ritual" book. The same could be said of my subsequent monograph on Polynesian tattooing.'[39] He furthermore described how he thought.

> When I write, I see pictures in my head and I write accordingly; the diagrams come first and the text later. There are many 'diagram based' papers in the present collection [Art of Anthropology]. Extensive use of pictures and diagrams is also part of effective seminar culture, since giving the audience something to look at, as well as to listen to, makes it far easier to ensure their concentration over the full hour.[40]

He deeply appreciated diagrams and visual representations in anthropology.

> When I was struggling during my first year as an undergraduate when I first tried to read *Les Structures Elémentaires de la Parente*, I seem to remember that the diagrams in Lévi-Strauss were one of the few bits that I could understand. . . . So I was always very diagram conscious, and I've always appreciated really good diagrams. For example, the diagrams in Robin Fox's book

---

[38] Hirsch, *Obituary*, p. 152.
[39] Gell, *Art*, p. 9.
[40] Gell, *Art*, p. 9.

> *Kinship and Marriage* are *superb* pieces of clear graphic expression.... The
> diagrams in Fortes are very interesting. There are innumerable diagrams in
> Leach's *Rethinking Anthropology*, many of which have a very, very clarifying
> effect on the text.[41]

He also had more theoretical reasons for this interest in non-textual
representations.

> It is said that 95 per cent of the information which we make use of is originally
> derived from visual sources. Yet anthropology as a business consists of the
> production of texts in propositional form. There is a basic contradiction here
> in the sense that anthropology is a very wordy business, yet the subject-matter
> of anthropology is—not always, but often—cognition or people's thought
> processes, or how people perceive and understand the world. If one wanted to
> know how X perceived and understood the world, one would have to know
> what they had seen and what they had made of what they had seen, rather than
> what they had thought in words and what they were prepared to express in
> propositional form.... When I am writing papers I generally start with an
> image, even in those papers which don't have any diagram as such. For exam-
> ple, the 'Swing's paper' starts with an image of somebody being swung. The fact
> that one constructs a paper out of a seam of life which is imaginable primarily
> as a visual image—or in the case of 'the language of the forest' as a move-
> ment—is significant.... I habitually think in terms of images, and of bringing
> images to things ...[42]

Discovery and originality

The *Guardian* obituary by Eric Hirsch is headed 'The art of discovery'.
This takes us to the heart of what is interesting about his life and work
for, according to those who knew him well, 'Alfred had a creativity, a fluidity and agility which we will remember ...'[43] Since creativity and the
conditions of discovering new things are so intriguing, yet so difficult
to investigate, how are we to proceed in this case? One way to approach
the matter is through someone else who may have influenced Gell. We
are told that 'Sherlock Holmes was one of Alfred's favourite literary
characters, and it is perhaps no accident that he deploys the method of a
sleuth searching for privileged zones of clarity in an opaque reality.'[44]

---

[41] Gell, *Art*, pp. 9–10.
[42] Gell, *Art*, pp. 10–11.
[43] Eric Hirsch, Suzanne Kuchler and Chris Pinney, 'Obituary of Alfred Gell', *Anthropology Today*, April 1997, 23, hereafter cited as *A.T. Obituary*.
[44] Hirsch, *Obituary*, p. 152.

The idea of approaching his creative art of discovery by analogy to the famous sleuth was developed by one of his Ph.D. students, Dr Chris Pinney at the Memorial Celebration of his life held at the LSE on 13 March 1997. Hirsch summarises his comparison.

> There are many points of similarity in their method 'for a mixture of imagination and reality' (as Holmes once put it), and a combination of breadth and the 'oblique uses of knowledge' characterized both their intellectual practices. Holmes's assertion that 'little things are infinitely the most important' would have gained Alfred's assent. Seeing Alfred peering at some object of illustration in a book recalls Holmes's voracious specialism; Holmes's knowledge of pipes . . . (etc.) were paralleled by Alfred's knowledge of tattoos, and of rat traps, giraffe traps, and fish traps along with an endless list of other recondite inhabitants of what Holmes called the 'brain-attic'. For Alfred, as also for Holmes, to a great mind nothing was trivial.[45]

The obsession with gathering vast amounts of apparently irrelevant materials in preparation for his task is delightfully described by Gell as follows.

> I'm interested in everything! I'm interested in the entire contents of the *Scientific American* every time it comes out. I read the ones about the sensory equipment of spiders and the ones about escalating health care costs in America, and so on and so forth. . . . I'm not more interested in one bit than I am in another and my interest in science and indeed the arts or anything else is simply that they provide a series of ingredients which can be combined—with luck—by means of pattern-building intuitions, to provide some kind of particular counter-intuitive, or apparently counter-intuitive solution to some kind of problem which can be stated in a fairly restricted sort of way.[46]

While he was interested in everything, it is clear that he also particularly hoarded specific materials. Thus from 1984 'he gathered together data—largely from published and archival sources—on artworks, both "primitive" and "modern"'.[47] How these and other materials were retained, whether in files or other ways, and what indexing and retrieval systems he developed we do not learn, unlike the case of Holmes whose system of files and his lack of enthusiasm at the boring task of filing is well described by Watson in 'The Five Orange Pips'.

The essence of creative discovery is to make counter-intuitive connections, to see hidden links and patterns which no-one has discovered

---

[45] Hirsch, *Obituary*, p. 153.
[46] Gell, *Art*, p. 24.
[47] *A.T. Obituary*, p. 23.

before. This was something which Gell (and Holmes) were well aware of and it is worth quoting passages where Gell explains what he was trying to do. 'Overall, what I'm interested in is producing something which is counter-intuitive—all that I ever wanted to do was to produce articles and papers which would make people sit up—and to do that the last thing that one wants really to be interested in is some Big Subject.'[48] This is what particularly excited him about Lévi-Strauss. 'What is interesting is what is counter-intuitive . . . So the pursuit of the counter-intuitive is always more interesting. Lévi-Strauss is a great master of the counter-intuitive. . . . [in relation to analysis of myths] Lévi-Strauss manages like a magician through manipulation of the data to turn what is apparently arbitrary into something which is very, very orderly.'[49]

This led Gell to claim that he was a post-modernist, before the term was invented, 'in the sense that I wasn't really interested in actually, as it were, "advancing the subject" in any particular way. All that I was interested in doing was producing a certain *frisson*, a certain artistic effect which could be achieved by taking a random collection of objects which could be made to fit together in an interesting way.' This, of course, reminds anthropologists of Lévi-Strauss's writings on the 'bricoleur' who mixes unlikely things together. One example among thousands in Gell's work would be in chapter 6 (on traps) in his *Essays*. '. . . what I want to be able to do is to produce an essay which allows me to combine Danto, the extraordinarily metropolitan New York Philosophy of Art Professor, with the Pygmy theory of why chimpanzees are too clever for their own good. It's the possibility of creating these conjunctions and unexpected connections that interest me.'[50]

This is why Gell loved conversations and seminars. 'Seminar culture obviously depends heavily on the pursuit of the counter-intuitive, in that it's saying the counter-intuitive proposition which is going to make people sit up and listen.'[51] It was an urge that did not just arise from a desire to discover. This desire to be subversive, to take the contrary, sometimes absurd, position was also, he claimed, something temperamental. 'I've always been on the side of the "language is not arbitrary" position. Well, first of all, because it is counter-intuitive. They're the underdogs, the people who say that language is not arbitrary. And of course, I'm a natural

---

[48] Gell, *Art*, p. 23.
[49] Gell, *Art*, p. 25.
[50] Gell, *Art*, pp. 24–5.
[51] Gell, *Art*, p. 25.

Contradictions and creativity

Several things stand out from the accounts. Firstly, like all creative workers, he was clearly filled with diametrical and opposing characteristics.
Some have been noted. As Chris Fuller noted in his obituary (*Independent*,
1 Feb. 1997, p. 18), '[I]n many ways he was a romantic, but he was also
adamantly rationalist'.[66] Hirsch writes that 'I was always struck by his
powerful intellectual capacities and insights and his equally powerful
refusal to develop a "Gellian" school or system of thought to rival some
of his other intellectually ambitious colleagues. The tendency is there in
his book *The Anthropology of Time* and in *Art and Agency*, but once the
exercise is complete, Alfred moves on to the next topic of interest, to the
next intellectual performance.' There was also a 'tension between the very
serious anthropological scholar and the man always intent on never taking
himself or his work too seriously'.[67]

Other contradictions could be noted. He was clearly rather shy and
inward looking, but loved performing in public in front of an audience.
He was an insider, who loved the collegial conviviality of being a member
of a group, yet he remained an outsider in some ways. As one colleague
put it, he was not a good team-player, at least in terms of routine teaching and administration. He was a self-confessed 'bourgeois', but was
clearly extremely happy sitting in a dusty Indian market-place and living
very simply.

He was a great lover of painting, music, and literature, and yet his
later work can almost be described as philistine in its dismissal of the content of art-works and concentration on their technical effects. This was
something which Hirsch *et al.* comment on.

> There was a central paradox at the core of Alfred's interest in art and its anthro-
> pology. On the one hand, he argued that anthropologists must assume a detach-
> ment from the artwork—to get away from the religiosity of picture-looking—
> through a process of what he called 'methodological philistinism'. On the other
> hand, he could still write about the intense pleasure he got from particular art-
> works, such as those by Titian and Duchamp.[68]

And it was something which he himself stressed. Of his essay on 'The
technology of enchantment' he wrote, 'I am not actually a Philistine, or a
promoter of philistinism, as some have apparently supposed. I merely

---

[66] Quoted in Gell, *Art*, p. ix.
[67] Quoted by Hirsch in Gell, *Art*, pp. ix–x.
[68] *A.T. Obituary*, p. 23.

advocate "methodological philistinism" as an analytic device, so as to wrest the anthropological study of artworks away from the soggy embrace of philosophical aesthetics."[69]

Another paradox was that while he was very interested in technology in the abstract, and in visual representations both as subjects to study and as ways of conveying ideas, he showed only a limited interest, as far as I know, in the areas where they intersect concretely, that is photography, films, video, computers etc. We do not hear of his photographic collections, his use of slides or video and so on. He was, however, very interested in aircraft technology and visited airbases with his son Rohan.

He was someone who spent much time writing about the importance of clarity and simplicity of style. But much of his work, admittedly some of it only in first draft, is not easy to follow and approximates more to the style of his beloved Lévi-Strauss or Bourdieu, rather than Malinowski or Evans-Pritchard whom he equally admired.

He clearly admired the tough and aggressive and 'punchy' Edmund Leach, but his own very gentle character makes his writing far less rebarbative than he would perhaps have liked.

He was someone who addressed very large themes, but usually approached them from particular details, seeing in Blake's famous phrase 'a world in a grain of sand', the characteristic of intellectual (and actual) myopia.

He was centrally obsessed with 'thought' and 'artistic' traps and entanglements, and how one could escape them. Yet for much of the central part of his life, the 'wilderness' years between the mid 1970s and 1980s he gives the impression of himself being entangled and trapped in systems of ideas which he found very difficult to escape from.

Like all of us he longed simultaneously for the applause and instant gratification, the *frisson* of a direct reaction from an audience, yet he also hoped for some kind of long-term immortality. He wanted people to admire and emulate him, but did not want to found a school. He was, in the famous metaphor, a fox (who knows many small things) rather than a hedgehog (who knows one big thing). Yet there was also something longer term behind the constant scurrying and searching which might well have become more apparent if his life had not been terminated so early.

He wisely cast his reading well outside the central area of British social anthropology, but there is little sign that he had a serious knowledge

---

[69] Gell, *Art*, pp. 16–17.

ERNEST GELLNER

Ernest André Gellner
1925–1995

ALTHOUGH ERNEST GELLNER had a successful academic career in Britain, becoming a member of the British Academy in 1974, his work was not properly understood. The fact that he was a brilliant polemicist, genuinely believing that there were devils at his back, tended to obscure his positive views. Of course, he had distinct reputations in different fields, notably as anthropologist, student of Islam, sociologist, theorist of nationalism, and philosopher. If this made him a latter day *philosophe*, seeking to understand modernity with whatever tools were to hand, little recognition was given to the presence of the metaphysic that lent unity and strength to all his work. As that metaphysic was based on the intense personal experience characteristic of a Central European exile of Jewish background, it is scarcely surprising that it centred on questions of identity.[1]

I

The infamous *Familiantengesetze* of 1726 and 1727 had limited the number of Jewish families in Bohemia, one consequence of which was the

[1] Gellner stressed this himself, early and late. See chapter three, 'Metamorphosis', *Thought and Change* (London, 1964) and his 'Reply to Critics', in J. A. Hall and I. C. Jarvie, eds., *The Social Philosophy of Ernest Gellner* (Amsterdam, 1996), p. 628. Note that Gellner referred to himself as an exile rather than an émigré in J. Davis, 'An Interview with Ernest Gellner', *Current Anthropology*, 32 (1991), 64.

Proceedings of the British Academy, **120**, 151–172. © The British Academy 2003.

movement of Jews to the countryside, beyond the reach of the limited powers of the early eighteenth-century state. Although these laws were not rescinded until 1848 (with full emancipation coming only in 1867), the *Toleranzpatent* of 1781 improved the life chances of Jews in cultural and educational terms. Reform Judaism took hold, and the most prominent strand of Jewish society initially sought to assimilate into the world of German liberalism. The emergence of national conflicts made matters much more complex.[2] The Germans of Bohemia were anti-semitic and ever more ethnically nationalist—particularly when they became a minority in the city that changed from Prag to Praha as rural Czechs moved in to man a booming industrial economy.[3] Relations were not much better with the Czechs. In 1846 a Bohemian Jew, Siegfried Kapper, wrote several poems in Czech calling upon his fellows to identify with Czech culture. This overture was dismissed by the Czech national writer, Karel Havlíček-Borovský, who insisted that 'anyone who wanted to be a Czech must cease to be a Jew'.[4] Despite this rebuff there were several more Jewish attempts to open links to the Young Czech movement, often as the result of nationalising pressures from Czech intellectuals. Many more chose to keep their heads down, often by processes of half-accommodation—learning Czech whilst making sure their children could function in German. A smaller number turned to Zionism, amongst them Max Brod, the novelist and the biographer of Kafka, and Hans Kohn, the first great theorist of nationalism. This Zionism had rather more to do with the search for identity than it did with encouraging active plans for emigration to Palestine because anti-semitism, though present, was not as vigorous as in Poland or Russia. This was a world, in a nutshell, in which identities were in flux—and always less inherited than gained as the result of choice or constraint. No wonder that it produced so many of the great theorists of nationalism.

Gellner's parents were secularised German speakers of Jewish background who moved to Prague in their youth. Rudolf was born in 1897, one of nine children—all of whom had Germanic names that

---

[2] H. Kieval, *The Making of Czech Jewry: National Conflict and Jewish Society in Bohemia, 1870–1918* (New York and Oxford, 1988) and *Languages of Community: The Jewish Experience in the Czech Lands* (Berkeley, 2000); S. Spector, *Prague Territories: National Conflict and Cultural Innovation in Franz Kafka's Fin de Siècle* (Berkeley, 2000).

[3] G. Cohen, *The Politics of Ethnic Survival: Germans in Prague, 1861–1918* (Princeton, 1981).

[4] E. Mendelsohn, *The Jews of East Central Europe between the World Wars* (Bloomington, 1987).

demonstrated their loyalty to the empire.[5] The family was poor, but culturally rich: the eldest sister Hedwig, who served as the organiser of the Zionist office in Prague before becoming a senior civil servant in Israel, read Schiller to the younger children at the kitchen table.[6] Gellner's mother, Anna Fantl, born in 1894, came from a less intellectual but slightly more economically secure background. But Perry Anderson's claim that the European intellectual exiles who came to Britain rather than to the United States at the end of the Second World War tended to the right in politics as the result of the loss of their estates or property has marginal relevance to Gellner.[7] There were tensions between the parents. Anna had Zionist views, whilst Rudolf, when held prisoner near Lake Baikal during the First World War, became a communist. But Rudolf's revolutionary enthusiasm soon faded, and the family became deeply loyal to Masaryk's new republic. For one thing, Jews were well treated in Czechoslovakia, albeit Masaryk's preference for political integration rather than total assimilation indicated both an element of personal unease and political calculation—namely, that of diminishing the size of the German population.[8] As ethnic tensions remained, the standard quip soon became that there were Czechs and Slovaks, but the only real Czechoslovaks were the Jews.[9] Interwar Prague was also exceptionally vibrant. The city had German and Czech universities, and it was home to Ukrainian and Russian émigrés and exiles, amongst them Roman Jakobsen, Rudolf Carnap and Albert Einstein.

Ernest Gellner was born on 9 December 1925. He was raised in the Dejvice quarter, a new middle class area far removed from more recognisably Jewish areas of the city. Gellner grew up speaking Czech to his sister and German to his parents because their efforts to learn Czech were never completely successful. Gellner remembered the meetings of many Czech intellectuals in the apartment, amongst them the sociologists Josef Navrátil,

---

[5] This point was made by Gellner in an interview recorded in J. Musil, 'The Prague Roots of Ernest Gellner's Thinking', in Hall and Jarvie, *The Social Philosophy of Ernest Gellner*, p. 31.

[6] Ernest Gellner's uncle Julius wrote a memoir (now in the possession of Susan Gellner) sometime in the 1970s dedicated to his grandson, Marc Gellner-Ward, entitled *England Receives Me as a Human Being* from which this information is drawn. Several of the brothers and sisters gained doctorates, and a full range of views was present in the family—from Zionism to Marxism, and with loyalties shown either to the German or the Czech nation

[7] Perry Anderson, 'Components of the National Culture', *New Left Review*, 50 (1968), Gellner admired this brilliant essay, but insisted—in his 'Reply to Critics', p. 624—that his insecure middle class background excluded him from the pattern described.

[8] Kieval, 'Masaryk and Czech Jewry', *Languages of Community*, chapter nine.

[9] Mendelson, *The Jews of East Central Europe*, p. 149.

the last director of the Masaryk Institute, and Karel Kupka, who worked in the Institut des Études Slaves in Paris, and who wrote several articles on Max Weber.[10] Gellner went to two schools in Prague. His primary school was at the edge of the park where one might meet the President on his rides if one was lucky.[11] The philosopher-president's portrait was hung in every class room, and his belief that democracy, though created in the West, was the inevitable wave of the future was deeply influential.[12] The school was Czech, and this led to a particular scene that Gellner would recount in later life. After the singing of a popular song, he put his hand up in class and said that he knew a different set of words, and then sang a German version. This was received with sufficient coldness that he never made the same mistake again. He then attended the Prague English Grammar School. There may have been calculation here on the part of his parents: one of Rudolf's sisters had married an Englishman, and this in the end did help the acquisition of visas to enter Britain.

Despite love of Prague and deep immersion in Czech culture, including his ability to play thirty Czech folk songs on the harmonica, national identity and personal security were not something to be taken for granted.[13] At the age of eleven Gellner would systematically miss out one word at random from the oath to Czechoslovakia taken as the flag was raised at his summer camp, less out of disloyalty than because he felt it too early to commit himself.[14] In the late 1930s fears that Prague would be bombed caused his mother to take the two children to Příbram, a small town in central Bohemia where her kin ran an ironmonger's shop. He later recalled President Beneš (whose actions he excoriated all his life) announcing that he had a plan to cope with the crisis, but subsequently resigning and flying off to Switzerland. 'In Czech, the word plan is the same as the final part of the word aeroplane, and the joke went around— yes, he had a plan, an aeroplane.'[15] Nonetheless, the family was in Prague when the Germans arrived in March 1939, and it was only with difficulty and considerable trauma that the dangerous journey across Europe into exile was made.

[10] Musil, 'The Prague Roots', p. 32.
[11] Gellner, 'Foreword' to Eva Schmidt-Hartmann's *Thomas G. Masaryk's Realism: Origins of a Czech Political Concept* (Munich, 1984), p. 7.
[12] 'The Price of Velvet: Thomas Masaryk and Václav Havel', *Budapest Review of Books*, 2 (1992).
[13] Gellner, 'Reply to Critics', pp. 624–5.
[14] Davis, 'An Interview with Ernest Gellner', *Current Anthropology*, p. 63.
[15] Gellner, 'Munich in Prague', *The National Interest*, 13 (1988), 118.

Gellner finished his secondary schooling at the St Albans's County School for Boys, a grammar school. He arrived at the age of seventeen as an Open Scholar at Balliol College, Oxford in the Michaelmas Term of 1943. He had decided to study Modern Greats, that is, the combined course in Philosophy, Politics, and Economics. His tutors, respectively in economics, philosophy and politics, were Thomas Balogh, A. D. Lindsay, the liberal anti-fascist and expositor of Hegel, and Frank Pakenham, the Catholic anti-fascist who later became Lord Longford. He made friends with Paul Stirling, who was to introduce him to social anthropology at the London School of Economics, and with John Hajnal, later to become a distinguished demographer and colleague at the London School of Economics, who later recalled Gellner saying repeatedly at the time that 'it was a disaster to be a Jew in modern Europe'.[16]

After just a year at Oxford Gellner joined the Czechoslovak Armoured Brigade, aged eighteen. He saw active service, including the experience of being under fire when the Brigade besieged Dunkirk, and took part in victory parades in Pilsen and in Prague. But Czechoslovakia had effectively been liberated by the Red Army. The four books he carried with him—George Orwell's *Animal Farm*, Arthur Koestler's *Darkness at Noon*, James Burnham's *The Managerial Revolution*, and Cyril Connolly's *The Unquiet Grave*—attest to his claim never to have held Marxist views.[17] His own earliest philosophical enthusiasm was for Schopenhauer, and he later described his early and avid interest in Sartre and Camus.[18] Doubtless, this interest in existentialism partially explains his attendance in Charles University for a term, for he was able to listen to the lectures of Jan Patočka (for which he did not in fact much care).[19] Still, he did not feel at home, despite having dreamt about Prague constantly during his first period of exile.[20] He was appalled at the manner of the expulsion of

[16] Interview with Hajnal, June, 1998. Hajnal suggested in that interview that this might have represented Jewish self-hatred, a trope described by S. L. Gilman, *Jewish Self-Hatred: Anti-Semitism and the Hidden Language of the Jews* (Baltimore and London, 1986) and by P. Mendes-Flohr, *Divided Passions: Jewish Intellectuals and the Experience of Modernity* (Detroit, 1991). No supporting evidence for this claim has come to my attention; general considerations, noted below, militate against it.

[17] Gellner cites the books in 'Return of a Native', *Political Quarterly*, 67 (1996), noting proudly that the books were left behind, as pioneering pinpricks in the Iron Curtain.

[18] 'Period Piece', in *The Spectator*, 37 (1975).

[19] Ernest Gellner, 'Reborn from Below: The Forgotten Beginnings of the Czech National Revival' (Review of Jan Patočka, *Co jsou Češi? Was Sind die Tschechen?*), *Times Literary Supplement*, 4702 (1993).

[20] Davis, 'An Interview with Ernest Gellner', p. 63.

the Sudeten Germans, even though he fully understood the motives behind this piece of ethnic cleansing. His later conviction that the fate of national minorities usually reduced to either expulsion or assimilation, was very probably rooted in his experience of the fate of both the Czech Jews and the Czech Germans. He was a witness to moral devastation and to a new occupation. In the fragments of a report entitled 'No Winter's Tale' that was never published, and that appears to be from the years 1946–8, Gellner described seeing Red Army officers billeted in the family home, which must have been traumatic no matter how detachedly he presented himself.[21] The text shows his partial contempt for the Czechs at that moment, noting the 'cheerful attempt by everyone to exculpate as many friends [from the charge of collaboration with the Nazis] as possible by any means at hand'. He was also shocked at his fellow Jews' complicity in their own fate, trying 'to solve the enigma of the passivity with which people, knowing what was in store for them, went to death with no attempt at resistance or escape, even the young and the vigorous'. He saw power changing hands both inside his own Brigade as well as the society at large, and came to feel that Czechoslovakia was in for as long a period of oppression as that which it had suffered at the hands of the Counter Reformation. There was significant and authentic local support for communism, and limited active opposition. The Czechs had no doubt that Germany would revive, and no faith that the West would protect them from that revival, quite naturally given their experience at Munich. This made them disposed to appease their own communists as the lesser evil, especially in light of the fact that they were expelling their own Germans. Gellner later placed part of the blame on the legacy of Masaryk, in so doing deploying Karl Popper's criticism of historicism. The Czechs had been taught to base their morals on historical evolution, and merely transferred their loyalties to communism once democracy failed: 'The truth is both ironic and bitter, but inescapable: Masaryk's philosophy of history did eventually lead to 1948.'[22] He went into exile again, not expecting to return.

---

[21] The allusion in the title is to the character in Shakespeare's 'The Winter's Tale' who believes that Bohemia has a coastline. (The allusion also provides the title for D. Sayer, *The Coasts of Bohemia: A Czech History* (Princeton, 1998)). Gellner's Papers are now housed in the London School of Economics. For permission to use them and to quote from them, my thanks go to Susan Gellner. It is worth noting that there is considerable overlap at key points between this piece and 'Return of a Native' written fifty years later.

[22] Gellner, 'The Price of Velvet', p. 122.

II

At first sight, he re-adapted to English society without great difficulty. He was a brilliant student, and benefited permanently from a close reading of Kant and from a more general absorption of the tradition of British empiricism, especially the writings of Hume and Russell. He was immediately attracted to Popper's *The Open Society and Its Enemies*, as is evident from the critical letter he wrote to Popper in August 1946—to which Popper sent an immediate and interesting reply.[23] In 1947 he obtained a first class degree and was *Proxime accessit* (runner-up) in the John Locke Scholarship in Mental Philosophy. These credentials allowed him to start his academic career at Edinburgh University as Assistant Lecturer in Philosophy. After two years he moved to the London School of Economics as an Assistant Lecturer in Sociology with special reference to Ethics. Further, he was still close to the Oxford philosophers by whom he had been educated, going regularly in the early 1950s to present papers. He was in correspondence with the then dominant figures in philosophy in Oxford, including Iris Murdoch, J. H. Urmson, Richard Hare, Isaiah Berlin, and Stuart Hampshire. Gilbert Ryle's letters from Magdalen College, Oxford make clear that he knew Gellner well, and it was in *Mind*, of which he was then the editor, that Gellner's first article appeared in 1951.[24]

Nonetheless, Gellner was in fact not at all at ease, the increasingly clear realisation of which eventually led him to rebel against the world he had joined.[25] Most immediately, the ethos of defusing great philosophical questions, treating them as mere puzzles that flowed from linguistic bewitchment, stemming from the philosophy of the later Ludwig Wittgenstein and from his proselytiser J. L. Austin particularly irritated Gellner. He gradually came to believe that Wittgenstein and Austin rested their philosophies of language on views of the nature of society that were unexamined and mistaken. Wittgenstein's *Philosophical Investigations* had argued that there was no escape from linguistic forms of life which

---

[23] Both letters will be available in a revised edition of I. C. Jarvie and S. Pralong (eds.), *Karl Popper's* The Open Society *after Fifty Years* (1st edn., London, 1999; rev. edn. forthcoming).

[24] Gellner, 'Maxims', *Mind*, 60 (1951).

[25] Many pages of jottings, often aphoristic in character, survive in the Gellner Papers, London School of Economics. These 'Notes', almost certainly from the mid 1950s until the early 1960s, show Gellner working out positions that he would thereafter hold. Some of the material was used in his first two books, *Words and Things: A Critical Account of Linguistic Philosophy and a Study in Ideology* and *Thought and Change*.

say for a moment that Gellner scorned or hated his Jewish background. But he was not religious, as was made apparent by critiques of varied arguments against belief made throughout his life.[34] Equally importantly, he made no attempt to hide his own background. He would have fought for Israel in 1948 had the war lasted longer, and thereafter said that he was prepared to die for Israel—albeit he always felt sure that the manner of its creation would lead to a 'tragic, perhaps insoluble confrontation with the Muslim world'.[35]

It took several years for Gellner to turn unease into attack, to take his stand against the hegemonic culture of the time—and in effect thereby to give up any real chance of being accepted within the world he had joined. Self-confidence seems to have come for at least three reasons. First, a successful second marriage to Susan Ryan and life with their four children seem to have provided an element of personal stability that had previously been lacking.[36] Secondly, he found something of a home as a doctoral student in anthropology at the London School of Economics, working on the Berbers of Morocco under the joint supervision of Paul Stirling and Raymond Firth. It is as well to say immediately that there was absolutely no split between the anthropologist and the philosopher. Indeed, an amusing strain within his fieldwork was the habit of asking questions about concepts derived from Wittgenstein to the tribesmen he was studying.[37] Differently put, fieldwork allowed him to work out exactly why Wittgenstein's assumptions were sociologically naive. Finally, he immersed himself in intellectual worlds outside Britain, most notably that of France—with particular connections to their philosophers of science and their North Africanists, and with a close personal tie to Raymond Aron whose work he much admired.

The end result was *Words and Things*, the attack on linguistic philosophy that made his name when Bertrand Russell sparked a debate—conducted at first in the correspondence columns of *The Times* but later

---

[34] A notable instance were comments addressed to L. Kolakowski's, *Religion*, in 'God, Man and Nature', *Sunday Times*, 28 Feb. 1982.

[35] Davis, 'Interview with Ernest Gellner', p. 67.

[36] The first marriage was to someone similar to himself, Laura Hertzstein, a Jewish exile from Germany who had lost all her family in the Holocaust, and was deeply traumatised as a consequence.

[37] He asked his tribesmen, for example, what they would do if confronted by twins when seeking to fill the last place in a posse. He records their amusement, and draws the moral that humans are often less concept-fodder than culturalist theories presume. For this story see, Gellner, *Saints of the Atlas* (London, 1969), p. 127. It is worth noting that the Gellner Papers contain a very large amount of material about Islam, including very extensive field notes.

becoming quite general—by criticising Gilbert Ryle's refusal to review the book in *Mind*. His attack had considerable impact, but the resentment created by his references to 'the narodniks of North Oxford' ensured that he was thereafter more or less excluded from the mainstream philosophical community. The book itself was always hard to read, and it is now dated. But this is not true of the sparkling essays about the philosophy of social science written at the same period in which Gellner spelt out an alternative to the idealism and relativism to which he was opposed.[38] At a general level, he was surely right to insist that concepts are not always, so to speak, foundational: meaning does not always make the world go round. To the contrary, concepts and values are quite often derived from other, more basic social processes: military victories and revolutions obviously have the capacity to change styles of thought, as too do changes in modes of production. More specifically, the insistence on the necessity and possibility for causal analysis in social and historical understanding rested on two sets of observations. On the one hand, belief systems were not seamless wonders, possessed of instructions as to how every facet of life should be lived.[39] The realisation that belief systems are loose and baggy monsters, replete with options, brings causal analysis back in since it becomes necessary to ask about the circumstances which lead to particular sections of a belief system gaining appeal for particular social actors. On the other hand, Gellner resolutely insisted that certain universal physical properties underlie the practice of social inquiry. We know about the nature of beliefs in adoption, say, precisely because we have a physical model of kinship at the back of our mind.[40]

There is a sense in which *Words and Things* was a distraction, a negative assault on error. Gellner's own position was spelt out in *Thought and Change*, a key work that contains the seeds of most of the books that followed.[41] Gellner's metaphysic is clearly expressed here in the form of a paradox. On the one hand, no philosophical position is truly grounded

---

[38] The two classic pieces are 'Concepts and Society', *Transactions of the Fifth World Congress of Sociology* (Washington, 1962) and 'The New Idealism'. These and related pieces were collected as *Cause and Meaning in the Social Sciences* (London, 1973).

[39] Gellner, *Legitimation of Belief* (London, 1975), p. 156.

[40] Gellner, 'Ideal Language and Kinship Structure', *Philosophy of Science*, 24 (1957). This article led to a prolonged debate, details of which can be found in I. C. Jarvie's complete bibliography of Gellner's writings, in Hall and Jarvie, *The Social Philosophy of Ernest Gellner*.

[41] An interesting appreciation of the impact of the book is offered by R. Szporluk, 'Thoughts about Change: Ernest Gellner and the History of Nationalism', in J. A. Hall, ed., *The State of the Nation: Ernest Gellner and the Theory of Nationalism* (Cambridge, 1998).

to appreciate the importance of the revolution of our time in large part because they feared the diminution of status created by the loss of their monopoly of literacy. Such figures were becoming an irrelevance to the real workings of society, mere cultural entertainers. An absolutely crucial part of Gellner's intellectual effort was involved at this point. The measure of certainty that could be found in modernity was small and spare. In this matter Gellner was a loyal follower of Max Weber's insistence that there is an opportunity cost to modernity, that science brings comforts at the cost of removing moral certainty. This adherence to 'the disenchantment thesis' lay behind his many attacks on spurious attempts to bring us in from the cold.[48] Of course, all this can be put in positive rather than negative terms. In effect Gellner was proposing a morality, that of a rather spare stoicism. On the one hand, we had to live with less given that atttempts to have the world make complete sense had led to such disaster. On the other hand, his deepest loyalties were to Kant, to a world in which we have to find our way precisely because it lacks any ultimate meaning or coherence.

III

Once Gellner had taken his stand, and articulated his basic position, he became extremely productive over the course of a long academic career.[49] The most important institutional base for this career was, from 1949 to 1984, the London School of Economics. Within the Sociology Department he was in turn assistant lecturer, lecturer, reader, and Professor of Sociology with Special Reference to Philosophy. The last slightly odd title was apparently designed to appease Morris Ginsberg, who belatedly came to recognise that Gellner did not share his evolutionist views, and who therefore opposed his promotion on the grounds that he was not a

---

[48] A particularly striking example is Gellner, 'The Re-Enchantment Industry, or, The Californian Way of Subjectivity', *Philosophy of the Social Sciences*, 5 (1975).

[49] This productivity was seen especially clearly in his essays, many of them written as that rare creature in British life, namely a public intellectual. These were collected in several volumes, including *Cause and Meaning in the Social Sciences*, *Contemporary Thought and Politics* (London, 1974), *The Devil in Modern Philosophy* (London, 1974), *Spectacles and Predicaments* (Cambridge, 1980), *Relativism and the Social Sciences* (Cambridge, 1985), *Culture Identity and Politics*, *Encounters with Nationalism* (Oxford, 1994), and *Anthropology and Politics* (Oxford, 1995).

real sociologist.[50] In 1979 Gellner changed departments, becoming Professor of Philosophy with special reference to Social Anthropology in the Department of Logic and Scientific Method. This move took place in reaction to the appointment of Donald MacRae to the Martin White Chair in Sociology.[51] The fact that this indicated a long-standing personal feud should not obscure the fact that Gellner benefited enormously from the London School of Economics. If the impact of the social anthropologists, particularly Firth and Schapera, and of Popper was constitutive, relations with Elie Kedourie, John Watkins, Imre Lakatos, Ronald Dore, John Hajnal, Tom Bottomore, I. M. Lewis, and many more left traces in his work.

Gellner finished his doctoral thesis in 1961, but it only appeared as *Saints of the Atlas* in 1969. It is without question a classic representative of the Malinowskian tradition of social anthropology. If the particular thesis of that book—that saints provided crucial mediation services allowing tribes to co-exist in relative harmony in a social world bereft of any overarching leviathan—was highly specialised, Gellner's later *Muslim Society* sought nothing less than to offer a general account of the workings of the classical heartland of Islam.[52] The core explanation of a cyclical movement characteristic of pre-modern Islam was derived from David Hume's *A Natural History of Religion* and Ibn Khaldun's fourteenth-century *Muqadimmah*. This element of his general sociology claimed that Islam was especially suited to modernity. Traditional societies faced with the power of the West were, he believed, deeply torn: to westernise was to spurn one's heritage, but to admire one's past was to condemn one's fellows to backwardness. The fact that the high tradition of Islam stressed discipline and literacy made it possible to avoid that choice, thereby allowing it to become, as noted, an ersatz Protestant ethic. Given the impact of Islam in recent years, it is scarcely surprising that Gellner's sociology of Islam received enormous attention, with fierce controversies developing about 'orientalism', the explanatory power of segmentation

[50] Davis, 'An Interview with Ernest Gellner', p. 67.
[51] Gellner, 'No School for Scandal' (Review of R. Dahrendorf, *LSE*), *Times Literary Supplement*, 4808 (1995). This is a fully fledged account of Gellner's own views of the character of the London School of Economics, as well as a barely disguised attack on MacRae.
[52] It is important to bear in mind that further fieldwork was more or less ruled out by the onset of osteoporosis from the late 1950s—a severe affliction he dealt with courageously by trying to pretend that it did not exist.

within Morocco, and about the very possibility of producing a single model for the core of a whole civilisation.[53]

Although Gellner had absorbed the spirit of nationalism in his youth, his insistence that most nationalist myth was false was massively enhanced by witnessing debates amongst Moroccan intellectuals in the late 1950s.[54] Still, he might not have been driven to attempt a general theory of nationalism but for his desire to refute the intellectualist interpretation put forward in Elie Kedourie's *Nationalism*.[55] If Gellner argued at all times both that nationalism was modern and the result of social structural change, there were significant changes in his explanatory account. *Thought and Change* made most of the role played by the native intelligentsia who, finding their mobility blocked at home despite their training in the metropole, had every reason to turn to nationalism. In contrast, the much longer treatment given in *Nations and Nationalism* concentrated in a far more abstract way on the manner in which the national principle was 'required' in order for industrial society to work.[56] Despite the brilliance of the account, and the great success of the book, the functionalism of the argument came in for much criticism.[57] Perhaps that was one reason for a final extended treatment of the subject that paid significantly more attention to historical and geographical variation.[58] But there was a second reason. When he began going regularly to the Soviet Union in the 1970s he was initially exhilarated to see how great was the explanatory power of his concepts when applied to the Soviet rather than the Austro-Hungarian empire. Those concepts suggested that some degree of national secession was inevitable—and that new nations would strive to be homogeneous, the hideous logic of which was to find your own state or join another (if they would let you in). In the last years of his life he

---

[53] His views about orientalism were first directed against B. Turner ('In Defence of Orientalism', *Sociology*, 14 (1980)) but this was followed by a dispute directly with the creator of the concept, Edward Said, that took place in the columns of the *Times Literary Supplement* following Gellner, 'The Mightier Pen? Edward Said and the Double Standards of Inside-Out Colonialism' (review of E. Said, *Culture and Imperialism*), *Times Literary Supplement*, 4690 (1993); the debate between Gellner and H. Munson on the applicability of the segmentary principle to Morocco is contained in Hall and Jarvie, *The Social Philosophy of Ernest Gellner*; the most important critique of the model as a whole is S. Zubaida, 'Is there a Muslim Society? Ernest Gellner's Sociology of Islam', *Economy and Society*, 24 (1995).

[54] Gellner, 'The Struggle for Morocco's Past', *Middle East Journal*, 15 (1961).

[55] E. Kedourie, *Nationalism* (London, 1960).

[56] Gellner, *Nations and Nationalism* (Oxford, 1983)

[57] See most of the papers in Hall, *The State of the Nation*, perhaps especially those by B. O'Leary and D. Laitin.

[58] Gellner, *Nationalism* (London, 1997).

was forced to think prescriptively rather than descriptively because he feared that the collapse of the Soviet Union might lead to as hideous a period of ethnic cleansing as had marked Europe from the late nineteenth to mid-twentieth century. The end result of these thoughts was an interpretation of the political theory of Malinowski, set in contrast to the views of Wittgenstein, which led Gellner to hope for some new combination of cultural autonomy and political centralisation.[59] The nobility of the attempt was perhaps not matched by the effectiveness of the solutions proposed. Fortunately, the collapse of the Soviet empire has not, to this point, resulted in catastrophes similar to those that marked Gellner's own life.

If the work on nationalism is in part a critique of one colleague at the London School of Economics, the treatment given to psychoanalysis in a sense spells out the basic view of another. *The Psychoanalytic Movement* is Gellner's most Popperian book in that it goes to great lengths to describe falsification-avoiding mechanisms at the core of the therapeutic encounter.[60] Gellner had in fact wanted to do fieldwork amongst the psychoanalysts, but his application had been refused. Still the book bears the marks of a sociologist in that its basic concern is less to confirm or debunk than to explain the astonishing success of an ideological enterprise. If one element of such success was the way in which psychoanalysis positions itself between causal reduction and meaningful analysis, another was the extent to which it could give pastoral care in a world bereft of much religious comfort. The book was very successful, and it marked something of a development in Gellner's views. For he here adds to the opposition he had noted between enlightenment and re-enchanters a vivid appreciation of the naturalistic tradition of thought derived from Nietzsche. By and large, the fact that our inner lives do, in Gellner's view, operate on the lines noted by Nietzsche makes the world of enlightenment at once more fragile and more important.

There is a sense in which *Legitimation of Belief*, which outlines his fully worked out philosophical position most thoroughly, represents his final coming to terms with the influence of Karl Popper.[61] The emphasis on open-mindedness in the world of Popper is attacked on the grounds that basic cognitive standards must be in place for criticism to have bite

[59] Gellner, *Language and Solitude: Wittgenstein, Malinowski and the Habsburg Dilemma* (Cambridge, 1998).
[60] Gellner, *The Psychoanalytic Movement, or, The Cunning of Unreason* (London, 1985).
[61] Gellner, *Legitimation of Belief*.

Early years in Vienna

Ernst Hans Josef Gombrich was born on 30 March 1909 in Vienna. His father Karl Gombrich was a lawyer and Vice-President of the Disciplinary Council of the Vienna bar and his mother, Leonie Hock, was a pianist. He had two older sisters. He described himself as coming from a 'typical middle-class family'. Clearly they were far from affluent, but the notion that the family was typically middle class has to be tempered by the the the reflection that his father was a close school friend of Hugo von Hoffmansthal, his mother was taught music theory at the conservatoire by Anton Bruckner and the piano by Leschetitzky, and lived in a social world which included close contact with the households of Schoenberg, Adolf Busch, Freud, and Mahler, whose sister was her pupil. The family was Jewish but under the influence of Siegfried Lipiner who had converted Mahler to a mystical Christianity, the family converted to Protestantism. Gombrich himself said that he had had no Jewish education, and while never denying his Jewish origins he seemed uninterested in them and said later that they would be of concern only to racists.

At the age of nine, during the famine in Vienna after the First World War he became acutely ill and undernourished; he was sent with his younger sister Lisbeth under a scheme run by the Save the Children organisation to Sweden to recover. There he lived for nine months with the family of a carpenter who specialised in making coffins. The family could hardly have been more different from his own in Vienna, where his father used to read Homer or translations of Indian poetry to the children, and then encouraged them to read the German classics. This was a family in which there was a concentration on *Bildung*; it replaced religion. Here music and literature, above all Goethe, were central. It was intellectually wide ranging and permeated by a strict ethic of restraint in social conduct and in language. Gombrich later remarked that this no doubt involved a certain snobbery—distinguishing one from the new-comers from the east and from the *nouveaux riches*—but it was a stance from which he would never disengage himself. The rejection of pretentiousness would find application in his rejection of high-flown language in the discussion of art.

On return from Sweden he had been sent to the Theresianum, a conservative but efficient gymnasium (his father had failed to put his name down for one of the more interesting schools) where, he recalls, he felt himself to be an outsider and was bullied; he was also bored as he clearly learned much faster than his classmates. For his school leaving examination he chose as the subjects for his viva German literature and physics (the interest in the sciences remained throught his life), and he wrote an extended paper on changing approaches to art from Winckelmann to his own time. He then went to Vienna University and enroled in the Institut für Kunstgeschichte and wrote his dissertation under Julius von Schlosser, the last of Schlosser's doctoral students.

Mantua

His dissertation, *Zum Werke Giulio Romanos*,[1] was on the sixteenth-century Palazzo Tè in Mantua, and some of the main themes of his subsequent intellectual concerns are already discernible. The study gives an account of the architectural peculiarities of this 'mannerist' building and of its internal pictorial decoration. At the time when Gombrich was writing, mannerism was a contentious issue: the forms in mid- to late-sixteenth-century architecture and painting were felt not to fit into the accepted progressive logic of European styles, the sequence of High Renaissance to Baroque; they were thought therefore to be either incoherent or to manifest some spiritual crisis. In the case of the Palazzo Tè Gombrich showed its deviations from standard architectural forms were consistent and deliberate and challenged the notion of a spiritual crisis. He could find no trace of this crisis in the correspondence in the Mantuan archives; on the contrary, what interested the patron, Federigo Gonzaga, were his horses, the hunt, triumphs and splendid festivals, which were also designed by his archtect-painter, Giulio Romano. Gombrich therefore looked for a different ground for the idiosyncracy.

He observed that the overall form of the building was dominated by the needs of the interior space and its large windows, rather than outwardly directed public rhetoric; the impression of the external architecture was one of ornament rather than a dramatic development of classical motifs. The incidental features like the dropped triglyphs and diplaced keystones, he suggested, should be read not as indications of collapse but of a building under construction and even, occasionally, of stone as not yet refined into architectural members. The underlying metaphor was of the play between nature and art; between determinate articulation and a sense of formlessness where either side could become

---

[1] This was published in two parts, *Jahrbuch der Kunsthistorischen Sammlungen in Wien,* NF 8 (1934) and NF 9 (1935).

this new means of aggression. A small book summarising their theories on caricature was published as a King Penguin in 1940, and essays on caricature recur through Gombrich's later work. He also completed a book on Aby Warburg based on his researches on the manuscripts, but it was not the kind of book that Warburg's associates, Gertrude Bing—later to become Director of the Institute—and Saxl had been hoping for. It was left unpublished until 1970 when it appeared, apparently only marginally revised, in the wake of the celebrations of Warburg's centenary.[3]

As enemy aliens the Gombrichs suffered real privation during the war, and were subject to absurd restrictions on movement. His war work involved monitoring German broadcasts for the BBC. This reinforced his sense that perception relied on anticipation, for under conditions of poor radio reception one required some assumptions about what kind of thing was being said to pick out the words. It was also during the war that he undertook the arduous task of putting Karl Popper's *Open Society and its Enemies* through the press. Although Popper was also from Vienna, they had only come to know each other in London just before the war. Popper then went to teach in New Zealand where he worked on *The Open Society*. He revised the text continually and because of the cost of postage sent his revisions on microfilm, making the task of updating it extremely arduous. (This is described in John Watkins's Memoir of Popper in the *Proceedings* of the British Academy, 94 (1997), 658.) The contact with Popper had an important impact on Gombrich; one sees him aligning his thought with that of the philosopher both in his general view of history, his antagonism to Plato as well as to Hegel and Marx, and in his notion that perception and not only science was structured by the process of testing hypotheses. After the war he returned to the Warburg Institute. The relations between Saxl, who was uninterested in theories of art, and Gombrich were never close although they clearly respected each other. Gombrich remarked to me on one occasion how he admired not only Saxl's learning but his lack of personal vanity and any proprietory attitude toward his scholarly discoveries which were exploited by others. On the other hand he felt aggrieved that he was only given a permanent post in 1948. His son Richard, later to be Boden Professor of Sanskrit at Oxford, had been born in 1937, and with the responsibilities of a young family he felt extremely vulnerable. The situation only became secure after the publication of the *Story of Art* in 1950. In 1956 he became

---

[3] *Aby Warburg. An Intellectual Biography* (London, 1970).

Durning Lawrence Professor of the History of Art at University College London and in 1959 Director of the Warburg Institute and Professor of the History of the Classical Tradition.

During the war he had been commissioned, on the strength of his world history for children, to write the *Story of Art* by Bela Horovitz, the owner of Phaidon Press, who gave him a small advance. Gombrich found it difficult with his other commitments and, embarrassed by constantly meeting the publisher on the street in Oxford, tried to give back the advance; Horovitz refused; 'I don't want your money, I want the book!' Eventually Gombrich wrote it, without access to a library, using for illustrations the volumes of the *Propyläen Kunstgeschichte*, which thanks to Ilse they had in their home. He dictated sections of text three times a week. This may have given the book its directness and economy. It does not tell one story but a series of overlapping stories, for Gombrich eschewed grand historical schemes. At the start of the book he said there was no such thing as art but only artists. He was virtually quoting his teacher Julius von Schlosser.[4] What Schlosser had meant was that although techniques, styles, symbols had continuous histories, art properly so called was something that occurred only episodically in the work of individuals, just as poetry occurred only episodically in the history of language. What was open to rational discussion, so Gombrich was implying, were the techniques, traditions, and purposes involved in image making; the question of what made the images a matter of art had no general answer, no continuous history and attempting to point to it led to vacuous gesturing. As an example of the sense of technique and purpose combined, one might take his account of Egyptian tomb art in which the aim is to provide the occupant with a substitute for the real world and the cycle of the seasons, not an invitation to the viewer to imagine the depicted subject; what concerned Gombrich was to reintegrate past images in their social practices. When it came to the twentieth century the problem was the isolation of images: they were seen simply in the context of art. The following passage on Giacometti might serve as an example of how he linked modern and earlier art:

> He is a sculptor who is fascinated by certain special problems of his calling and he asumes—rightly or wrongly—that we, too share his interest. This problem . . . was not invented by modern art. We remember that Michelangelo's idea of sculpture was to bring out the form that seems to slumber in the marble, to

---

[4] I am indebted for this observation to Werner Hofmann's obituary of Gombrich in *The Art Newspaper*, 120 (Dec. 2001).

for a volume on siege machines. We gain here a sense of the humanists and artists as part of a single social world. In the paper 'From the Revival of Letters to the Reform of the Arts: Niccolo Niccoli and Filippo Brunelleschi' (1967) which he contributed to the Festschrift for Rudolf Wittkower (republished in *The Heritage of Apelles,* 1976), he asked what enabled a very small movement involving both humanists and artists to become so successful within the city and then across Europe: on one side the correction of Latin spelling and reform of script from the spikey uneven Gothic to the rounded Carolingian—thought to be antique—and on the other the enhanced logicality of Brunelleschian architecture— thought to be derived from measuring Roman remains but really depend- ent on the Romanesque forms, in particular the Florentine Baptistery and SS Apostoli. What succeeded—in language as in architecture—was the enhanced regularity, elegance and coordination of forms. Another suc- cess story was the invention of the perspective construction; it enabled architects to show what would be visible and what occluded from any given point. It was a genuine discovery with practical implications even before its application to painting. The success, Gombrich implies, is in each case not a matter of mere fashion, although a sense of learned superiority would play its part, but of an objective achievement.

One of his most important papers on the early *quattrocento* is 'The Early Medici as Patrons of Art'(1960)[7] where he focused on the social dis- cretion of Cosimo de' Medici who—despite his wealth and being in effect the ruler of Florence—kept his subscription in public enterprises to a level that would not be disproportionate to that of his fellow citizens. He also observes how Vespasiano da Bisticci who wrote the lives of contem- poraries and was a friend of Cosimo speaks of his ecclesiastical commis- sions but not Donatello's bronze statues of David and Judith, suggesting that these private commissions might have been thought too grand for a nominally private citizen; in contrast to these, the ecclesiastical commis- sions were seriously intended by Cosimo the banker as public acknow- ledgement and restitution to be set against his sin of usury. (Gombrich observes that when Lorenzo de' Medici lists the outlay on such buildings he puts it together with charities and even the payment of taxes: anything that did not benefit the Medici themselves.)

---

[7] Originally published in E. F. Jacob, ed., *Italian Renaissance Studies* (London, 1960); repub- lished in *Norm and Form.*

A third group of Renaissance papers, written contemporaneously with some of these, focused on Leonardo, a figure in whom his own scientific, aesthetic, and psychological interests were to be most fully interrelated. The series begins in 1950 with 'Leonardo's Methods of Working out Compositions' in which he makes a fundamental distinction between Leonardo's drawing procedure and that of his predecessors: Leonardo allows a feedback from the suggestiveness of his marks on to the construction of his image, and this leads Gombrich to emphasise the painter's sense of his own creative power. In 1952 he wrote 'The Grotesque Heads' the first of two papers which later he republished under the heading 'Leonardo da Vinci's Method of Analysis and Permutation' in *The Heritage of Apelles* (1976).[8] He disposes of the notion that the grotesque heads were conceived as caricatures or physiognomic studies. He traces their development as a series of deliberate deviations from—or negations of—a norm, specifically the strong male 'nutcracker' face that even recurs in his doodles. Leonardo himself warned painters of the danger of compulsively repeating their own face in all the figures they depicted and Gombrich suggests that the grotesque heads were aimed at breaking away from his own obsessive image of himself.

The second of the Leonardo 'Analysis and Permutation' studies was 'The Form of Movement in Water and Air' (1969);[9] here he examined the drawings and the notes in which Leonardo analysed these movements, adapting Aristotelian physics and confronting the difficulties of its application. (After coming to England before the war he had compiled the index of the vast Richter edition of Leonardo's writings.) If Leonardo's thought often remains unresolvable, he makes the notes and drawings mutually informative and this enables him to explain in modern terms some of the scientific issues Leonardo faced. Gombrich then relates these hydraulic drawings to his great designs of the Flood, and suggests that Leonardo may have entertained the idea of a commission to paint a major work on the theme after seeing his old rival Michelangelo's Sistine ceiling; he follows Kenneth Clark's suggestion that Giulio Romano's Sala dei Giganti in Palazzo Tè, with its imagery of cataclysmic collapse, may carry echoes of such a project and Gombrich muses that Giulio Romano may have heard of it from Vasari.

---

[8] Originally published in Achille Marazza, ed., *Leonardo, Saggi e Ricerche* (Rome, 1954).
[9] First published in C. D. O'Malley, ed., *Leonardo's Legacy* (Berkeley and Los Angeles, 1969).

The cleaning controversy

The subject of Leonardo was to be drawn into the one major institutional controversy with which Gombrich became engaged. The cleaning of paintings in the National Gallery had been disquieting both art historians, painters, and other painting conservators. The response of the Gallery had been dismissive. The tone of the interchanges can be guaged from this sentence with which the very polite and circumspect editor, Benedict Nicolson, completed his editorial in Febuary 1962. 'All that one asks is that they [the National Gallery] should come forward without arrogance with clear answers to the actual criticisms being made, not answers to imaginary objections which no informed person would nowadays dream of raising.'[10]

There were two fundamental questions: first, was it the case that painters from the Renaissance onward had used glazes or tinted varnishes to control the tonal relations of pigments? Second, was it possible in cleaning a painting to know when you had come upon an original glaze of tinted varnish? The National Gallery at the time employed an extremely assured and persuasive restorer called Helmut Ruhemann, a sometime German Expressionist painter. He claimed that the restorers knew when they had reached the original paint surface (although the scientists MacLaren and Werner, defenders of the Gallery, had written at the time: 'it is difficult to make a chemical analysis of media used in glazes—or, indeed, of old varnishes.') and crucially, as explained by conservator Stephen Rees Jones in the same issue of the *Burlington Magazine*, varnishes were also used as a medium in painting so that the solvent which would attack an overall varnish would also attack the paint; there was not necessarily any clear borderline between them; Ruhemann also claimed that such tinted varnishes were not used in Renaissance painting. Gombrich and Kurz in two papers in the same issue of the *Burlington* demonstrated that from at least the sixteenth century such glazes had been widely discussed as they had been by Pliny in antiquity, whose comments were widely known. Ruhemann countered by saying that this was mere book knowledge and not derived from the paintings themselves. He went on—a trifle foolhardily—to challenge Gombrich's use of Leonardo's use of the term *sfumato* and cognate terms with regard to

---

[10] *Burlington Magazine,*104 (Feb. 1962).

softening the edges of forms.[11] Ruhemann's argument was discredited as was the defence of the Gallery Director at the time. The Gallery, however, never acknowledged any doubts and it remained unclear whether it was prepared to learn from its experience, something Gombrich remarked upon in what was probably his last contribution to the Burlington Magazine, a short letter in March 2001. He had written eloquently and temperately on the issue of cleaning in *Art and Illusion*: 'I venture to think that this issue is too frequently described as a conflict between the objective methods of science and the subjective impressions of artists and critics. The objective validity of the methods used in the laboratories of our great galleries is as little in doubt as the good faith of those that apply them. But it may well be argued that restorers, in their difficult and responsible work, should take account not only of the chemistry of pigments, but also of the psychology of perception . . . What we want of them is not to restore individual pigments to their pristine colour, but something infinitely more tricky and delicate—to preserve relationships. It is particularly the impression of light, as we know, that rests exclusively on gradients and not, as one might expect, on the objective brightness of colours.'[12]

Art and Illusion

Art and Illusion had been developed out of the Mellon Lectures given in Washington in 1956. There he set out to replace the theory of the necessary sequence of artistic styles which had dominated German art historical thought since the end of the nineteenth century through the work of Heinrich Wölfflin and Alois Riegl. Throughout Gombrich's work he contends with the ghostly figure of Riegl whose major books were published between 1893 and 1902. His responses to Riegl provide an overall sense of the thrust of his thinking. In Riegl's *Stilfragen*—of which Gombrich said that, despite his reservations, it was perhaps the greatest book written on ornament[13]—he had sought to trace the development of the Egyptian lotus motif in the acanthus and tendril design from ancient Egypt, through Greek art into medieval Asia Minor. What concerned

---

[11] Ruhemann's paper was in the *British Journal of Aesthetics*, 1 (1961), and Gombrich's reply 'Blurred Images and Unvarnished Truth' in 2 (1962).
[12] *Art and Illusion,* 2nd edn., p. 48.
[13] See Gombrich, *The Sense of Order*, p. 182.

Riegl was the continuity of this development seen as a matter of formal elaboration; he resisted the idea that the motif sustained itself because of symbolic meanings or changed by virtue of different techniques or references to different plants in nature. He saw the development as autonomous, springing from an aesthetic urgency which sought to elaborate and reintegrate its forms. This conception was then extended to representational art in the West in two major books, *Die Spätrömische Kunstindustrie* (1901) and *Holländische Gruppenrroträt* (1902). What made it possible for the development of a single decorative motif to serve as the model for the stylistic development of representational art in general was an extremely schematic sense of style: how one kind of perceptual coherence emerged as a revision of its antecdents, from the single figure isolated against its background to an overall optical effect; and later, from a unity which depended only on the relations between represented figures to unity which implicated the viewer within the imaginative order of the work. Gombrich's objection to Riegl's position (most fully argued in his paper on 'Kunstwissenschaft' in the *Atlantis Buch der Kunst* of 1952) is first of all that Riegl treated the development of styles as if they were like stages of natural growth rather than emerging from the contingencies of context or skill; and second, that he treated all the products of a given era as emanations of some central spirit. As he was to write later in his lecture *In Search of Cultural History*: 'It is one thing to see the interconnection of things, another to postulate that all aspects of a culture can be traced back to one key cause of which thay are the manifestation.' *Art and Illusion* sets out to replace these two assumptions and in the introduction he wrote: 'Both in the writings of Riegl himself and in those of his followers and interpreters, such as Worringer, Dvořák, and Sedlmayr, there is a wealth of challenging historical problems and suggestions, but I would assert that what is their greatest pride is in fact their fatal flaw: by throwing out the idea of skill they have not only surrendered vital evidence, they have made it impossible to realize their ambition, a valid psychology of stylistic change.'[14]

Gombrich, like Riegl, held that art was necessarily an historically developing enterprise, but it was not necesssary that it should take the course that it did. He set out to show how, within Western painting, those transformations of style came about. He asked the very simple question: why did the levels of lifelikeness found first in antiquity and then in

---

[14] *Art and Illusion*, p. 17.

Renaissance art develop so gradually. Could the painter not simply have looked at the world and copied it? His basic premiss, which was first given extended exposition in his essay 'Meditations on a Hobby Horse' (1951),[15] was that representation in painting was a species of substitution, as the child substitutes a stick for a horse she can imagine herself riding or a doll as a baby sibling she could throw on the floor. Crucially, representation does not start out by the intellectual feat of abstracting some form from the object it represents. The drunk who tips his hat to a lamp-post has not performed the feat of abstracting from it the essential form of a man. Representation starts with the spontaneous transference or projection onto a new object of what biologically or functionally interests us. This would not yet yield an account of representation as it figures within art, for this required discovering more precise controls of our propensities to project. The painter's process of discovery, so Gombrich argued, was conducted by having a provisional schema which he sets out to correct or modify in the direction of greater visual conviction and cogency. What counts as a schema may be a simplifying spatial armature—a simple diagram in relation to which more complicated shapes and details could be plotted as appear in some of the drawings in Villard de Honnecourt's album of the fourteenth century or in modern 'how to draw' books. But it may also be a motif upon which the artist can elaborate or, more problematically, some mental assumption or thought, like the assumption that a medieval cathedral will be Gothic and so have pointed windows, an assumption that led a nineteenth-century printmaker to give pointed windows to Chartres. The schema might even be thought of as a pictorial prototype, as Constable took compositions from Hobbema. We must interpret Gombrich's broad thesis of schema and correction as accommodating each of these, but then add his more specific thesis: that making comes before matching. According to this thesis, the artist looked at the object to be represented not just in the light of general anticipations gained from earlier paintings but with reference to material procedures, the system of marks like the diagrammatic shapes round which representations could be elaborated. In the work of pre-Renaissance art these diagrammatic schemata were fairly rigid, but—particularly from Leonardo onward he would seem to imply—the schema was more like a fluid procedure than a set of shapes; although even after Leonardo the egg-like oval as schema for a head and other geometric shapes recur in drawing.

[15] Republished in *Meditations on a Hobby Horse and Other Essays in the Theory of Art* (London, 1963).

denied can itself become expressive of values.'[19] It is true, however, that gaining mastery in coherently representing the visible world was central to Gombrich's conception of painting as an art. The other dimensions of achievement were dependent upon it.

Debates over *Art and Illusion*

One could hardly give an account of many of the insights in *Art and Illusion* without addressing the issue which has caused most subsequent controversy, that of his notion of illusion. At the start of the book Gombrich makes clear that the mind does not require simulacra to elicit recognition, for what determines recognition and what makes pictorial representation possible is that the mind seeks out patterns and relationships, not exact replications of prior experiences. We project a gestalt or interpretation onto the perceptual array. This is his background theory of perception. It is, however ambiguous: on one reading our perception projects onto its object and we have no recourse to the object itself; the projection saturates our experience of the object; but on the second reading we can modify our awareness of the object by other 'projections', by other responses to the object. The ambiguity, pointed out by Richard Wollheim in reviewing the book,[20] may have arisen because Gombrich structured his theory of perception on the basis of the perception of pictures (in a tradition which goes back through Helmholtz to Locke). In this account of perception, our eyes receive a two dimensional array onto which we project a three dimensional world but we do not see the two dimensional array in seeing that three dimensional world. More generally, we have no neutral uninterpreted access to the objects of perception. This seems to have been enforced by using, as examples, the duck-rabbit and Necker cube in which one way of seeing the figure effaces the other. The problem with these demonstrations is that they prove too much; not simply that we have no raw perception unmediated by a concept but that the projected concept—the triggered interpretation—absorbs the perception; seeing the duck prevents our seeing the rabbit. Yet when we see a landscape or a figure in the painted surface we do not lose our sense of the surface in which we see it. When this extreme reading is set aside the main thrust of the argument is that we project onto the shapes in the picture in

---

[19] *Meditations on a Hobby Horse*, p. 15.
[20] 'Reflections on *Art and Illusion*' in Richard Wollheim, *On Art and the Mind* (London, 1973).

a way which makes representational sense; unconsciously as well as consciously we select and neglect from what is present in order to make the situation before us intelligible.

There is a related problem, also raised by Wollheim, in Gombrich's seeming assimilation of the notion of naturalism to that of illusion. What Gombrich's main thesis would suggest is that naturalism in painting is relative to other painting and that when considered historically it is relative to the level of likeness of antecedents which the painter has both utilised and transcended. Illusion, on the other hand, while also triggering pictorial recognition which transcends our expectation, may not be a matter of relations to earlier works but simply something relative to our overall grasp of the painting in question, the dawning of unexpected vividness of the subject—something on which Gombrich sometimes comments with great subtlety. Both of these problems might be traced back to Gombrich's isolation of interest in illusion from the sense of the material surface and from formal order.

A second debate raised by *Art and Illusion* concerned the very nature of *likeness*. Nelson Goodman in his *Languages of Art* of 1968 sought to treat depiction on the model of language: pictures like words denoted objects. He did not deny the fact that resemblances might occur between pictures and what they pictured, but this was neither a necessary nor sufficient condition. He argued that the perspectivally constructed projection (which is taken to be a paradigmatic case of depiction by resemblance) would only yield the bundle of light rays corresponding to those delivered by the represented object if we looked at the picture through a peep hole; and this was hardly the normal way of looking at pictures. Furthermore, according to Goodman, the perspective construction itself did not even do this consistently. So likeness as exemplified by the perspective construction, could not, he maintained, be the basis of pictorial representation. In his paper 'Image and Code' (1978), published in *The Image and the Eye* (1982), Gombrich responded by distinguishing between plotting objective information about the world, irrespective of perceptual viewpoint or subjective experience, and representing such experience convincingly. In the case of the perspective construction we had both: a means of calculating what will be seen from a given position, what would be occluded and how size will diminish with distance and experience of how it would look. The perspective construction may imply a convention but it is not arbitrary, in the manner of the word-object relation; it yields true demonstrations of what we would see. Gombrich conceded that some images are harder to read than others, that they require as Goodman said,

Primitivism

The theme of *The Preference for the Primitive* (published posthumously in 2002) was the deliberate return from sophisticated styles of rhetoric and art to the simpler styles of earlier periods, a return motivated by rejection of the hollow display of virtuosity or sensuality in favour of simplicity and severity. It elaborates on the Spencer Trask Lectures given at Princeton in 1961; over the forty years Gombrich had gathered round his theme a wide range of texts, particularly from the eighteenth and nineteenth centuries, starting with the rebellious students of David, the 'Primitifs', who condemned current styles of painting as 'van Loo, Rococo, Pompadour', and followed by German Romantics like Wackenroder, Friedrich Schlegel, the Nazarenes, and later by Blake and the Pre-Raphaelites and Gauguin. (The book will be useful to students for gathering together—and translating—an array of nineteenth-century texts not easily accessible.) These rejections—like nineteenth-century medievalism more generally—took on by turns moral and religious and even nationalistic connotations. The search for moral or aesthetic simplicity had led to the high value set upon the art of the fourteenth and fifteenth centuries and the demotion of the High Renaissance and Baroque. This rejection of sophistication was seen to take an extreme form in the use of primitive masks by Picasso in the *Demoiselles* which Gombrich saw, in a standard art historical move, as the rejection of the meretricious virtuosity of Salon painting. Subsequently, in Surrealism and Art Brut the rejection took the form of a deliberate psychological regression, treating carnavalesque games as art. He clearly saw little value in these while he greatly admired Picasso and Klee. He saw such movements setting up an alternative to the traditional sense of painting—painting as progressively mastering the appearance of the visual world and controlling complex interacting variables. Gombrich's doubts about so much twentieth-century painting might be seen as putting a challenge to its sympathetic commentators to show how it possesses comparable complexities to the major art of the past. These essays, focusing on regressive as opposed to progressive changes, hardly form a free-standing book and need to be read as reflections on themes more fully articulated in his earlier work.

* * *

Gombrich retired as Director of the Warburg Institute in 1976. He had pioneered a much greater teaching role for the Institute, starting the two-year M.Phil. courses in cultural history which set numerous research students on their professional careers with much greater conceptual and technical scope than they would otherwise have had. As Director he was fortunate to have, as Registrar, Anne Marie Meyer, someone with a mind as fastidious and accurate as his own and deeply committed to the intellectual standards of the Institute, and as Librarian and Assistant to the Director the literary humanist Joe Trapp, who clearly took a great deal of the institutional burden and who succeeded him as Director. This made it possible for Gombrich to continue his own work, although he would complain angrily of the burdens of administration.

He was the recipient of innumerable honours in the last forty years of his life; he was made a CBE in 1966, knighted in 1972, and awarded an OM in 1988. He had been made a Fellow of the British Academy in 1960 and subsequently of many other academies; he was given the Erasmus Prize, the Goethe Prize, the Hegel Prize, the Wittgenstein Prize, received numerous honorary doctorates, and was made an honorary citizen of Mantua. In 1964 he reveived the W. H. Smith prize for Literature for his *Meditations on a Hobby Horse*. For his birthday at sixty in 1969 there was a concert at the Victoria and Albert Museum, presided over by John Pope-Hennessy, which included a new quartet dedicated to him by Joseph Horovitz. In 1994 he was presented with a Festschrift, *Sight and Insight*, by twenty art historians who had been formally or informally his students, and the papers could hardly have been more diverse in their topics and methods. He enjoyed his public recognition, crafting speeches of acceptance in which he defended his conception of the humanities, but he remained a very private man. It was when hunting for books in the stacks of the Warburg library or in conversation at home in Briardale Gardens that he was at his most genial and at ease. He and Ilse entertained students and visiting scholars with great warmth over many years. I have a particularly fond memory of sitting with Ernst over the translation of a German text which involved musical terms and metaphors; he referred the problem to Ilse, as she was the professional musician, and their conversation involved a small performance of hums and mimes as they agreed on the precise musical term we needed. Cared for as ever by Ilse, Ernst went on working through his final illness, revising chapters and making translations and they continued to entertain friends to tea, refusing to allow the discomforts of age to interfere with conversation. He died on 3 November 2001.

To be taught by Gombrich, whether in tutorials or seminars, was to be treated to an extraordinary range of suggestions, references and analogies for the subject in hand, as well as to brusque criticism. When engaged in argument he gave few concessions and many students—but not all— relished tales of his memorable put-downs. At the same time one was aware of his own anxiety about unchecked mistakes being left to breed confusion in the future. He saw the failure of intellectual clarity and care as in part responsible for the disastrous domination of Marxist and fascist ideologies, his response to the politics of the century being pessimistically conservative.

It is not easy to assess or summarise Gombrich's impact on the field of art history. Unlike Heinrich Wölfflin who was pre-eminent in the first quarter of the century and Erwin Panofsky in the second quarter, he did not proffer a method which others could follow. What he did was to toughen and vastly expand the conceptual awareness of those working in the field; one now had to ask whether a piece of work was engaging with a real, humanly significant question or merely with a self-regarding aca- demic game. From the point of view of method one might say that he made contingency dominant over systematicity while keeping up a run- ning battle against aesthetic relativism. Modes of achievement were his- torically variable but the achievements were nevertheless objective. For those of us fortunate enough to work with him he made accessible a more wide ranging and challenging tradition of humanist thought than we could otherwise have imagined.

MICHAEL PODRO
Fellow of the Academy

Note. In preparing this memoir I have been able to rely on J. B. Trapp, *Ernst Gombrich: A Bibliography* (London, 2000) and two memoirs: E. H. Gombrich, *A Lifelong Interest. Conversations on Art and Science with Didier Eribon* (London, 1991) and 'An Autobiographical Sketch' in E. H. Gombrich, *Topics of Our Time* (London, 1991). The text of four speeches at a memorial meeting held in February 2002 is being published by the Warburg Institute.

JEAN GOTTMANN   *H. S. Rossotti*

Jean Gottmann
1915–1994

Escape from Russia

JEAN GOTTMANN, who died on 28 February 1994 at the age of 78, was one of the most productive and creative scholars of his generation. He spanned two continents and several languages, almost uniquely making his mark in the French geographical world and in the Anglo-American one; no other geographer was simultaneously Fellow of the British Academy and Chevalier de la Légion d'Honneur. Even more unusual was that he was trilingual and tricultural. Born on 10 October 1915 into an affluent Jewish family of industrialists in Kharkov in the Ukraine, he lost both parents (Elie and Sonia-Fanny) in the revolutionary year 1917 when their home was robbed. A young widowed aunt came to rescue him and took him back to St Petersburg. They moved south through Moscow to Sebastopol in the Crimea where his aunt met and married Michel Berchin. The new family escaped via Constantinople and Marseille to Paris as part of the White Russian emigration to France. His uncle became art and music critic for an expatriate journal and brought up Jean in a rich cultural atmosphere of an extended family; visitors to the house included the historian Paul Milhiukov, Marc Chagall, and the Zionist leader V. Jabotinski. So, like so many émigré Russians of his generation, he grew up in a culture that was cosmopolitan yet francophone.

Proceedings of the British Academy, **120**, 201–215. © The British Academy 2003.

This brilliant and hard-working young man studied at the Lycées Montaigne and Saint-Louis, with Dr Elicio Colin, who had written about various French ports, as his geography master in the latter institution. He duly entered the Sorbonne, initially to read law, but soon found that his real love was geography. Like all other geographers in France at this time, he was required to devote part of his time to studying history. He also took a lively interest in philosophy, political science, and colonial affairs, especially appreciating the ideas of André Siegfried and of the geographer Emile-Félix Gautier. At the Institut de Géographie, numbers of staff and students were small. Emmanuel de Martonne, son-in-law of the great Paul Vidal de La Blache, taught all aspects of physical geography; Augustin Bernard specialised in colonial geography, especially of French North Africa; newcomer André Cholley occupied a chair of regional geography; and Albert Demangeon taught economic and political geography, having published influential books on *America and the Race for World Domination* (1921) and *The British Empire* (1923), and amassing evidence on the impact of the 'crash' of 1929 on the world economy. He also launched a devastating attack on the German practice of *Geopolitik* that he described in 1933 as 'simply a war-making machine'. De Martonne and Demangeon edited the influential *Annales de Géographie*, and Demangeon sat on the editorial committee of the controversial *Annales d'Histoire Sociale* that had been founded in 1929 by his historian friends at the University of Strasbourg, Lucien Febvre and Marc Bloch.

The late 1920s and early 1930s also saw the appearance of many of the volumes of the great *Géographie Universelle* that had been conceived in 1907 by Vidal de La Blache and Max Leclerc of the Armand Colin publishing house, but had been delayed by the events and dramatic territorial and economic outcomes of the Great War. De Martonne wrote two volumes on *Europe Centrale*, extending from the Rhine to the Black Sea, and had intimate knowledge of Germany, Czechoslovakia, and especially Romania, having presented three theses on Transylvania and the Carpathians. He had also served as official adviser on the delineation of Romania at the 1919 Peace Conference. Demangeon had inaugurated the *Géographie Universelle* in 1927 with two volumes on the British Isles, and on what would later be recognised as the Benelux countries. Together with Vidal's other favoured disciples (especially Lucien Gallois, Jules Sion, and Antoine Vacher) he had advised the French government during the First World War, drafting reports on strategically vulnerable sections of northern France as well as various other parts of Europe.

Following earlier contacts with the American geologist William Morris Davis and the physiographer Douglas W. Johnston, in the early 1920s many Vidalians published on European topics in the *Geographical Review*, the journal of the American Geographical Society based in New York. Its director from 1915 to 1935 was Isaiah Bowman who was well aware of the activities of the established geographers at the Sorbonne, and of their protégés. Foreign geographers, such as the Serb Jovan Cvijić (both geomorphologist and political geographer) and the Estonian Edgar Kant (a founding father of urban and quantitative geography), came to the Sorbonne to work with De Martonne or Demangeon. Without doubt, the Institut de Géographie was an exciting place to be between the wars, but its two leaders were very different personalities. Like several other scholars, including his friends Pierre Gourou and Jacques Weulersse, Gottmann was much more attracted to the open humanism of Demangeon than the cold science of De Martonne.

Gottmann received his *licence* (BA) in geography with history and continued with research for a *diplôme d'études supérieures* (equivalent of a masters degree by research) in 1934. In the previous year Demangeon had remarked that there were four over-arching themes that he wished his young researchers to consider: the densely-populated regions of the Far East, interactions between 'blacks' and 'whites', irrigation in arid lands, and the spread of urbanisation. He wanted Gottmann to focus on an urban issue, in particular the supply of foodstuffs to Paris, but the young man had an urge to travel and duly undertook his first period of fieldwork in the Levant, with a travel grant obtained with the assistance of Demangeon. His thesis was entitled 'La culture irriguée en Palestine' (Irrigated farming in Palestine) and was one of thirteen geography theses submitted in that year. However, it had the distinction of being published in abbreviated form in the *Annales de Géographie* in 1935. Amazingly, this was not Gottmann's first geographical publication, since he had already used his fluency in Russian to produce five short notes-cum-book reviews dealing with the second Soviet five-year plan, and recent developments in Turkestan, Uzbekistan, and Siberia. Apparently he wrote a number of journalistic pieces for French-language Jewish periodicals when he was only 16 and 17. During the remainder of the decade Gottmann's publications were mainly in the form of brief notes and reviews for the *Annales de Géographie* on Russian and Middle Eastern themes. Doubtless, these were undertaken at the request of Demangeon, co-editor of that journal, and of Elicio Colin who was responsible for collating the *Bibliographie Géographique Internationale*.

Assisting the Master

In 1937 Gottmann published his first English-language article that dealt with the extension of pioneer settlement in Palestine and appeared in the *Geographical Review*. This initiated what would be a life-long association with that journal, as Gottmann transmitted developments in Europe and the Middle East to American geographers, and wrote notes and articles in French on publications and research outcomes from English-speaking sections of the geographical community. This important pivotal position as a communicator on both sides of the Atlantic and his remarkable linguistic abilities offered opportunities for work to be recast for different audiences. Later in life, with his reputation firmly established, learned societies in many countries would be anxious to print the text of his keynote lectures, and this would have a similar effect on the pattern of his publications.

By 1937 Gottmann was working as a research assistant on various projects headed by Demangeon, who was especially concerned with agricultural issues during that decade. With the help of funds from the Rockefeller Foundation, a research centre for human geography was established at the Institut de Géographie and operated under the auspices of the Conseil Universitaire de la Recherche Sociale. In 1936 Demangeon launched no fewer than three investigations. The first of these dealt with foreign workers in French agriculture and was headed by Dr Georges Mauco, an established authority on international labour migration. That project would be fully completed, with a substantial volume appearing in 1939. The other two enquiries involved farm structures and rural housing; both were co-ordinated concurrently by the young Jean Gottmann. In addition, from 1936 to 1940 he helped Demangeon with contract research on the supply of foodstuffs and other raw materials into France, the compilation of detailed maps for the *Atlas de France*, being prepared for the Comité National de Géographie, and the compilation of publications on rural housing in France for the Exposition Internationale held in Paris in 1937. In addition, there were many editing and secretarial tasks to be handled for the *Annales de Géographie*. All this frenetic activity yielded an impressive array of reports, articles, book reviews and scholarly notes, predominantly in French but also in English.

On the negative side, however, Gottmann did not present himself for the rigorously competitive *agrégation* examination, in which success was obligatory in order to teach in a *lycée* or a university in France. Nor was he able at this time to proceed with work towards a *doctorat d'état* that would be required for the status of professor in a French university. (In fact, he would not be awarded a French research doctorate until 1970 when, at the age of 55, he presented copies of published work for examination rather than a single thesis.) During 1939 he continued with his rural enquiries but the outbreak of war and the German invasion of France in 1940 made life in Paris especially difficult for this talented Jewish intellectual. Neither project had reached completion but during 1939 Gottmann was able to synthesise the results of sample surveys into farm structures in much of western France. Despite Gottmann having received support from the Rothschilds, Demangeon advised his protégé to leave the city, encouraging him to move to Montpellier where his life-long friend, Jules Sion, was professor of geography. Demangeon's further advice was for Gottmann to consider quitting France if conditions became unbearable. On 25 July Demangeon died, leaving Gottmann with neither a master nor a protector. Together with Pierre Gourou, his fellow student from the Sorbonne, he wrote a lengthy and appreciative obituary. Indeed, Gottmann was doubly bereaved at this time since Sion had died a fortnight earlier on 8 July. In the depths of despair, Gottmann continued working at Montpellier on a part of the farm survey, having left the results of the rural housing enquiry in boxes in the basement of the Institut de Géographie in Paris. He would never see them again, and was only able to bring the material on farm structures in western France to publication in 1964.

Escape from France

As conditions for Jews worsened in France, Gottmann decided to leave Montpellier, escaping through the byways of Languedoc and Spain to Liverpool, reaching the USA on 7 December 1941, the very same day that Japan attacked the American fleet in Pearl Harbor. From the very start he was fascinated by the concentration of wealth and activity to be found in and around New York. Indeed, his major textbook on America would bear a picture of the magical skyline of Manhattan on its cover. Academic and personal contacts arranged by Demangeon and Henri Baulig, a specialist on North America who taught at Strasbourg, to some extent eased the way for this brilliant, cultivated and polyglot twenty-five-year-old. In addition, there were relatives in and around the city who could offer support. Because of his fragile health he could not enlist in the armed forces but was involved with the activities of the Construction Board for

Economic Warfare (1942–4). His detailed knowledge of the rural geography of western France was particularly valuable in the preparation for the Normandy landings. In 1944 he represented the provisional government of the French Republic in the French West Indies, from which he managed to write an article on the isles of Guadeloupe for the *Geographical Review* (1945).

Despite his potential for administrative or diplomatic work at the highest level, he retained his concern for academic research in a university setting. Indeed, for much of the middle period of his life he would hold a number of concurrent positions. In 1942, he started a twenty-three-year-long association with the Institute for Advanced Study at Princeton where he conversed, among others, with eminent physicists working on the Manhattan Project, and in the following year began a five-year position as lecturer and subsequently associate professor in the newly created Department of Geography at the Johns Hopkins University in Baltimore, where Isaiah Bowman (formerly of the American Geographical Society) had been President since 1935. Frequent train journeys through the discontinuously urbanised northeastern seaboard of the USA would, in due course, inspire Gottmann to produce his most monumental work.[1] Not surprisingly he began to write predominantly in English, with reviews, notes, and articles in the *Geographical Review* appearing on an astonishing variety of themes in the mid 1940s. Perhaps the most significant were his perceptive analysis of geographical research in France during wartime (1946) and his remarkable appraisal of Vauban (1944) as a military engineer, town planner, and regional surveyor during the seventeenth century, in which he argued convincingly that the art of territorial management, in the interests of wise government as well as defence, had many distinguished precedents in history.

Transatlantic transhumance

In 1945 Gottmann returned to France for a year to occupy a position as chargé de mission to advise the office of Pierre Mendès-France, Ministre de l'Economie Nationale. This involved many essentially geographical issues, such as evaluating sites for a new international airport on the

---

[1] Neil Smith's *American Empire* (Berkeley, 2003) shows that Bowman fired Gottmann for treating Johns Hopkins as a 'stopover between trains' (p. 267). The phrase was used by George Carter, Gottmann's head of department.

southern side of Paris that was duly constructed at Orly. Then followed a spell as director of studies in the research department for social affairs at the United Nations at Lake Success outside New York (1946–7). This enabled him to travel to Colombia and Venezuela and enhanced his knowledge of Central and Latin American affairs that would be put to good advantage in a future textbook. Thereafter he became research fellow of the Conseil National de la Recherche Scientifique (1948–51), while teaching for a semester each year at the Institut d'Etudes Politiques (1947–60) thanks to the intervention of his mentor André Siegfried (1875–1959) who taught there. In 1948 he went to Strasbourg to seek the advice of Henri Baulig on his early ideas for writing an urban geography of the north-eastern USA. Gottmann also served as visiting professor in numerous North American universities. It is hard to appreciate the rootlessness he must have experienced, living in different apartments or faculty clubs, month after month, year after year. As a political geographer—or more accurately, a spatially aware political scientist—Siegfried operated outside the confines of the Université de Paris (Sorbonne). Gottmann derived much inspiration from his senior colleague and some of his most influential work in political geography was written while he taught at the IEP.

He developed the concept of the compartmentalisation of the world (*cloisonnement politique du monde*); a division that arose through both material and cultural factors. Among the latter, he proposed that the most critically important could be isolated to produce what he called 'iconography', involving a sense of self image, spatial identity, and territorial belonging. More specifically, he identified a religious creed, a social viewpoint, and distinctive political memories (or a combination of all three) as central to this critical notion. (It is not too fanciful, perhaps, to see here an idea that Samuel Huntington developed so influentially, half a century later, in writing about the clash of civilisations.) These ideas appeared in articles, now increasingly written for political science journals, and also in *La Politique des Etats et leur Géographie* (1952) that distilled the messages of his seminars at the IEP. These embraced a thorough and rigorous review of 'geographical doctrines', past practices of political geography (including *Geopolitik*), frontiers, buffer zones, population distribution, and the resource needs of particular states. The book was published in a political science series, not a geography one, and was not reviewed in the *Annales de Géographie*. An English version was prepared but rejected by Gottmann, who let the idea drop as he turned to other things.

His energy continued unabated and in this phase of his life he edited an important international volume on *L'Aménagement de l'Espace: plan-ification régionale et géographie* (1952) that was presented to the XVIIth International Geographical Congress in Washington. Indeed, he chaired the commission on regional planning of the International Geographical Union between 1949 and 1952. In addition, at this time he wrote two very substantial textbooks for geography students on either side of the Atlantic: *L'Amérique* (1949), and *A Geography of Europe* (1950). These were not to the liking of all reviewers with, for example, Jan Broek remarking that Gottmann's coverage of North American physical geog-raphy had 'been cut to the bone if not further', while social geography and especially urban issues were overemphasised.[2] The *Europe* text is also remarkable for the large numbers of maps that were reproduced directly from the pages of the *Geographical Review*, admittedly with acknow-ledgement. Nonetheless, both books would go through several revisions and expansions, and be translated into different languages in subsequent years. In addition to a set of articles on port cities, perhaps stimulated by his impressions of New York and Baltimore and certainly advancing some of his early ideas on transactional economies, Gottmann continued to write about Israel and Palestine, a collection of his papers being brought together as *Etudes sur l'Etat d'Israël et le Moyen Orient* (1959). Such activity was all the more remarkable since he had experienced a seri-ous fall in the United Nations building in 1952 that broke his neck and required long periods of convalescence. Despite the physical pain from which he was never free, it may well have been that he found that these months of confinement to bed provided the opportunity to write and to revise his existing texts.

Although Gottmann displayed such productivity, he continued to operate on the margins of academic geography and did not receive the recognition that he undoubtedly deserved at this stage in his life from his fellow French academicians. Perhaps this was because he did not hold an *agrégation*—and was not considered 'one of us'—but more likely for other reasons: French geography at the time has been well described by André-Louis Sanguin as occupying a 'scientific and pedagogic ghetto'. The 'cos-mopolitanism and multiculturalism of Gottmann were light years away from the petit-bourgeois university milieu'. Besides, there was a political

---

[2] *Geographical Review*, 40 (1950), 336–7.

reason; the university establishment of influential geographers (e.g. Pierre George, Jean Dresch) in the post-war years was Communist or at least fellow-traveller in its leanings, and—with the Cold War deepening— heavily distrusted Gottmann's American connections. Certainly, Gottmann was still heavily immersed in American geography, and between 1952 and 1955 he worked on a detailed study of the State of Virginia at the request of Paul Mellon of the Old Dominion Foundation of Washington and with the active support of Abraham Flaxner, founder of the Institute for Advanced Studies. *Virginia at Mid-Century* (1955) was almost a French-style regional monograph set in North America. This 584-page account traced the social and economic processes at work in the past to produce the spatial characteristics of the state *circa* 1950.

As a work of geography, the book was filled with maps, but in several respects it differed from the painstaking one-man efforts that gave rise to *doctorats d'état* in France. Gottmann acknowledged the help of research assistants, minimised the quantity of academic references cited, and included a large number of photographs, none of which came from his own camera. The book was, indeed, an attractive and insightful representation of the state, rather than simply being a diligent, scholarly description. At a seminar in University College London in 1964, the distinguished British geographer, Henry Clifford Darby, FBA (1909–92) commented on Gottmann's various books and acknowledged the relative merits of *Virginia*, while insisting that its author appeared to be 'something of a showman' rather than a traditional scholar. Although Gottmann was anything other than brash in his speech, there was a measure of truth in Darby's appraisal and that may well have been echoed in the halls of the Sorbonne as well as in geography departments in Britain. Nonetheless, the text had an impact in the USA and would provide an opening for Gottmann to tackle a much greater theme; it would be revised and enlarged to reappear as *Virginia in our century* (1969). A further book on *Les marchés des matières premières* (1957), that he revised from earlier versions by the Vidalian Fernand Maurette, contained highly original sections on waste disposal, recycling, and mineral recovery.

The road to Megalopolis

Following the invitation of Robert Oppenheimer, director of the Twentieth Century Fund, Gottmann took the momentous decision in 1956 to become research director for metropolitan studies based in New York. In the following year he married Bernice Adelson, a journalist on *Life* magazine whom he had met during one of his many periods of convalescence. He occupied that post, with research assistants and appropriate financial resources, for five years (1956–61), and his massive 810-page study of *Megalopolis, the urbanised northeastern seaboard of the United States* was published in 1960. Gottmann was able to report to his ailing mentor Henri Baulig (1877–1962), who had been helpful in the darkest days of the early 1940s, that the project had finally reached completion. It was this remarkable volume that, above all, brought him international fame. Already presaged in an article of 1957 in *Economic Geography*, it was a *tour de force*. For the title, that had been suggested to him by Robert Oppenheimer as far back as 1950, Gottmann took an ancient Greek concept—and indeed an actual place name—that he knew well enough, for he had intensely studied Artistotle's work on the Greek *polis*. The direct borrowing was from Lewis Mumford, who had used the term so eloquently in his book *The Culture of Cities* (1938). There, it had become Mumford's symbol of what he termed the Insensate Metropolis: the vast sprawling post-industrial city, which Mumford saw in an apocalyptic way as presaging global war and the triumph of totalitarianism. Gottmann, who knew a great deal of those topics at first hand, used it in an altogether more neutral sense to describe what he saw as a new urban form: a 350-mile-strip of virtually continuous urbanisation on the eastern seaboard of the United States, from Boston to Washington (BOSWASH as it came to be known to generations of students).

A similar idea had been developed by the English geographer Professor Eva Taylor in the 1930s, in the then-celebrated concept of the 'coffin' of urbanisation from London to Liverpool and Leeds. In either case, the notion was metaphorical, even fanciful: as casual examination would have suggested but later research was to prove, the reality was very far from continuous urban sprawl. What did exist was a developing coalescence of urban fields or spheres of influence over surrounding areas of countryside: a functional, not a physical, urbanisation. Gottmann in practice conflated and thus confused the two concepts; and the book's achievement, considerable enough, was in evoking the operations of a highly complex urban region while never quite defining what in actuality it was. For this he was criticised somewhat roughly by some of the next generation of geographers, who had already espoused the new 'scientific' geography of exact measurement and model-building; this cut him to the quick, for in academic debate as in everyday social encounter he adopted an old-fashioned European courtesy.

The success of the book was due as much as anything to the timing of its appearance. In 1960, America was the symbol of the economic and social future, and Europeans in particular looked to it to understand what might happen to them in a few years' time. The popular academic literature of the time, including sociological classics like Riesman's *The Lonely Crowd* (1950) and Whyte's *The Organisation Man* (1956), was obsessed with the realities of life in the new automobile-oriented suburbia in which a whole generation of young Americans was growing up; Gottmann's book joined them, to become a classic in its turn, perhaps one of the few such by a geographer to reach a wide audience. But its success lay partly in its accessibility; and this stemmed from the fact that essentially it was a fairly traditional piece of first-rate French regional geography, with all the cultural and historical insights that implies, albeit applied to a highly untraditional kind of region.

That conclusion is fortified by the fact that Gottmann wisely made no attempt to join the revolution in geography that was then raging through the universities of the western world. He knew what he could do well, and he continued to do it, turning out polished essays, many of them derived from *Megalopolis* or developing the themes in it. His wisdom was sought on the American Committee on Resources and Man of the National Academy of Sciences that he joined in 1965. He began to lead an informal worldwide movement to study the phenomenon of the megalopolis, in which—for obvious reasons—he found particular support from Japanese geographers. Italian experts were also particularly interested in his ideas. He wrote a classic article for the *Geographical Review* in 1966, on the reasons for the skyscraper, which as a European he found a fascinating topic. In addition, he formed a close working relationship with the charismatic Greek planner Constantinos Doxiadis, lending his prestigious reputation to Doxiadis's science (or, as some would have it, alchemy) of Ekistics. His relationship with the American Geographical Society remained close, with the editor of the *Geographical Review*, Wilma Fairchild, finding him an invaluable authority on European matters.

The Oxford years

Meanwhile Gottmann had made yet another migration back to Europe, part of what he himself described as his 'Transatlantic transhumance'. In 1960 he accepted the position of Professor in the École des Hautes Études en Sciences Sociales in Paris (but not the Sorbonne), a title he was to retain as a *détaché* (on leave) basis until formal retirement in 1983. But in 1968 he was appointed to the Chair of Geography at the University of Oxford and to an associated Fellowship at Hertford College, which he occupied for the next fifteen years. The School of Geography had, of course, produced excellent scholars but by the mid 1960s it had become somewhat stale, with a rather elderly complement of academic staff, many of whom owed greater allegiance to their colleges than to their department or, indeed, their discipline. Gottmann's decision to move to Oxford was perhaps surprising. Undoubtedly the prestige of the university and the charm of the city attracted him, but arguably he did not appreciate the administrative characteristics of the institution, the unusually limited powers of the head of department (given the strength of the colleges in teaching matters), and the magnitude of the challenge ahead of him. Nonetheless, he was determined that there would be change and in the course of the next fifteen years worked to transform the School of Geography from an intellectual backwater into something of a powerhouse. As a thesis supervisor he was attentive, interested and inspiring, with a remarkable skill to set an individual's research into the wider context. He was accessible and hospitable, with his supervisory lunches at least once a term being particularly memorable. He attracted distinguished visitors to Oxford and promoted his vision of a graduate school of doctoral students, along North American lines. He succeeded in nurturing a new generation of research students, many of whom now occupy chairs of geography in Britain and the USA, and was able to appoint young staff to replace those who retired. It must have been a source of deep satisfaction that when he retired, one of his first appointments, Andrew Goudie, succeeded him.

Throughout the 1970s and 1980s, and even well into retirement, Gottmann and his wife continued to travel widely and to work prodigiously. Jean's output continued, much of it in the form of reviews of broad urban trends. His views on policies for spatial management were summarised in 1973 in *The Significance of Territory* that, unfortunately, was not widely known on either side of the Atlantic. Ten years later, he was presented with a handsome *Festschrift* edited by John Patten, who was just leaving academia for a political career that would take him to the position of Secretary of State for Education under Mrs Thatcher; it contains a full bibliography of his publications to that date. He became increasingly interested in the so-called quaternary sector of the economy, the producer services, directly stimulating the growth of studies in this area; he drew attention to the importance of university research as a trigger for innovative economic growth. In these areas he was a true pioneer, well ahead of his contemporaries. His contributions on these themes were not major pieces of empirical research but were designed to stimulate younger associates to follow new lines of inquiry—as indeed they did.

The volumes entitled *Megalopolis Revisited: twenty-five years later* (1987) and *Since Metropolis: the urban writings of Jean Gottmann* (1990, with Robert A. Harper) presented his later reflections on urbanisation and service economies, setting them in the context of his undoubted masterpiece. Despite the lingering effects of illnesses that had plagued him since youth, massively complicated by the accident at the United Nations in 1952, necessitating long spells in hospital and leaving him far less than completely mobile, he published down to the end, at the age of 78; in that very year, 1993, he published both in English and French. His scientific publications spanned exactly sixty years: among the longest of any twentieth-century geographer, but surpassed by W. R. Mead, FBA, whose first papers were published in 1939 and whose recent book, on Norway, appeared in 2002. A further monograph, on the distinguished Scandinavian traveller Pehr Kalm, was published in June 2003.

During the 1970s and 1980s Gottmann was showered with honours. His election into Fellowship of the British Academy came in 1977, three years after being made Chevalier de la Légion d'Honneur. He was elected into honorary membership of the American Geographical Society, the Royal Netherlands Geographical Society, the Société Géographique de Liège, the Società Geografica Italiana, and the American Academy of Arts and Sciences. He received honorary doctorates from the Universities of Liverpool, Southern Illinois, and Wisconsin. He was honoured by the Royal Geographical Society with the award of the Victoria Medal, in 1980, and by the Société de Géographie de Paris with the *Grand Prix*, in 1984. On that occasion, Professor Jacqueline Beaujeu-Garnier rightly hailed him in her address as a citizen of the world; justifiably so, since he had been made an honorary citizen of Yokohama and of Guadalajara. In his final years, he seemed particularly at home at various colloquia arranged by the Commission de Géographie Politique of the French Comité National de Géographie.

Jean Gottmann: a life reviewed

Jean Gottmann's life contained phases of great tragedy, including the murder of his parents in 1917 and the impact of Nazi regulations on French Jews in the early 1940s. However, his family connections and his sheer brilliance enabled him to fashion a new and influential life. The death of his master Demangeon in 1940 and of his friend and co-worker Constantinos Doxiadis in 1976 were major blows. His health was always poor and the severe accident in New York brought recurrent pain for the second half of his life. Students at Oxford were well aware of his physical disability and could not ignore the fact that he looked so ill at times. He proved to be something of an 'outsider'; perceived as a 'European' in the USA and UK, as an 'American' in France, as a 'political scientist' among geographers, and as a 'geographer' among political scientists and planners. His compendious textbooks, despite revision (and partly because of expansion), have not stood the test of time and now survive as monuments to an earlier encyclopaedic age. The notion of 'Megalopolis' has passed into common parlance among geographers and planners, to describe the northeastern USA and not the small town in the central Peloponnisos with an ugly lignite-burning power station. However, his path-breaking monograph is rarely taken from the shelves. Students at Oxford were not always in accord with their distinguished but stooping and apparently frail professor, so richly steeped in history and old-fashioned European culture, so quietly spoken and with an enduring foreign accent. Certainly the urban geography that Gottmann preached at Oxford was light years removed from the model building and quantification being developed at Cambridge and in Sweden and North America.

Like many prophets, he remained largely without honour in his own country until relatively late in life. It is a telling fact that the *Grand Prix* was awarded in Paris the year after he retired, coming almost as an afterthought by a grateful but perhaps also apologetic academic community. However, in the final ten years of his life, new trends emerged within academic geography. Cultural geography took on new guises and welcomed the rich humanism of Jean Gottmann, while political geography was no longer sullied by the *Geopolitik* of the 1930s that Demangeon had so roundly condemned. Jean Gottmann, with the constant support of his wife Bernice, came into his own. The tributes received in his latter years from around the world were richly deserved, since Jean Gottmann was one of the great human geographers of a generation reared in the classic school of French regional study. His achievement was to apply the insights and synthetic capacities of that school to illuminate the geography of the United States, his second adopted country. He came to Britain to make his third academic home, receiving there the highest academic accolade his hosts could confer upon him; altogether, a true academician.

HUGH CLOUT
Fellow of the Academy

PETER HALL
Fellow of the Academy

Note. A bibliography of publications by Jean Gottmann prior to 1983 is found in J. Patten (ed.), *The Expanding City: essays in honour of Professor Jean Gottmann* (London, 1983), with later items listed in A. Champion, 'Iona Jean Gottmann, 1915–1994', *Transactions, Institute of British Geographers*, NS 20 (1995), 117–21. A selection of Gottmann's urban essays is listed in J. Gottmann and R. A. Harper (eds.), *Since Megalopolis: the urban writings of Jean Gottmann* (Baltimore, Johns Hopkins University Press, 1990). R. J. Johnston has published an assessment of Gottmann's work as a political geographer: 'Jean Gottmann: French regional and political geographer extraordinaire', *Progress in Human Geography*, 20 (1996), 183–93. An earlier appreciation was by Robert E. Dickinson, *The Makers of Modern Geography* (London, 1969, pp. 246–9). In preparing this essay we have consulted these sources and appreciations published in various places by the late Jacqueline Beaujeu-Garnier, Paul Claval, the late Robert E. Dickinson, François Gay, Georges Prevelakis, André-Louis Sanguin, and Michael Wise. We are indebted to B. J. L. Berry, W. R. Mead, P. E. Ogden, M. Phlipponneau, H. C. Prince, and M. Williams for their recollections of Jean Gottmann.

OLIVER GURNEY

Oliver Robert Gurney
1911–2001

OLIVER ROBERT GURNEY'S LONG CAREER in Hittite studies spanned the greater part of the existence of this academic subject. He was born in London on 28 January 1911, only child of Robert Gurney D.Sc. and Sarah Gamzu née Garstang. The Gurneys from Norfolk came from the well-known group of Quaker families, including Barclays, Frys and Lloyds, who were so prominent in banking and other businesses in the eighteenth and nineteenth centuries. Indeed Gurneys were in partnership with Barclays in banking, and there is still a 'Gurney's Bank' in Norwich, but as Gurney liked later to point out when the question of his family's banking connections was being discussed, 'That Gurney went bankrupt'.

Nevertheless Gurney's father was a gentleman of private means, who had a lifelong and more than amateur commitment to zoology. His mother was the daughter of Walter Garstang, a Blackburn doctor with a strong interest in Hebrew, from which came her second name Gamzu ('and yet another'!) by which she was always known. Her brother was the archaeologist John Garstang, reader, then professor of archaeology at the University of Liverpool, whose career began in Egypt under Flinders Petrie and remained centred in that country, but later extended to Anatolia (Sakça Gözü, Mersin) and the Levant (Jericho). His Anatolian interests were fostered by his friendship with A. H. Sayce, whom he knew from Egypt. Gamzu shared keenly in her brother's interests and often accompanied him on excavations. This enthusiasm of his mother and uncle was to exercise a decisive influence on Gurney's life.

Proceedings of the British Academy, **120**, 219–240. © The British Academy 2003.

Gurney grew up at Ingham Old Hall, a large, rambling country house near Stalham in Norfolk. In 1924 he was sent to Eton, leaving in 1929. An early love and talent was music, and he was already a good enough pianist at school to give a performance broadcast on the BBC. He continued to play the piano for many years, until other commitments intruded on his time, leading him to give up and dispose of his piano. In 1928 his father moved to Oxford in pursuit of his zoological interests, buying Bayworth Corner, Boar's Hill, a pleasant and comfortable late Victorian house with a large garden and substantial tract of woodland. The Gurneys settled into Boar's Hill Oxford society, where family friends and neighbours included Gilbert Murray (next door), Sir Arthur Evans, and the Assyriologist Reginald Campbell Thompson. Gurney went up to New College to read Literae Humaniores, taking Honour Moderations in 1931 and Greats in 1933.

Already during his undergraduate days Gurney took part in his uncle Garstang's excavations, joining him at Jericho in 1931 for his first experience of archaeological life in the field. It was here that he happened to meet Sayce for the only time when the latter visited the excavations, remembered later by Gurney as 'a very old but still vigorous gentleman dressed in formal clerical garb with a dog-collar in the oppressive heat of the Jordan valley'. Gurney regarded Sayce as his 'spiritual ancestor' since he (Gurney) was to represent at Oxford that subject, Assyriology, first represented there by Sayce. Also it was Sayce who had first interested Garstang in Anatolia and the rediscovery of the Hittites, and had arranged for him to apply for permission to excavate at Boğazköy, already known as a source of Cuneiform tablets. In the event however, apparently as a result of the personal intervention of the German Kaiser, the Ottoman authorities awarded the permit to the German Assyriologist sponsored by the German Orient Society (Deutsche Orient Gesellschaft), Hugo Winckler, who commenced operations in 1906. Garstang paid an amicable visit to these excavations in May 1907 and actually witnessed the early discovery of the Hittite archives, recording for 21 May: '. . . lunch with Makridi Bey. Taken over lower temple and shown in a trench of excavation a myriad of fragments of tablets sticking in channel side. Their profusion was astounding. . . . Food beastly, bugs ghastly'. Garstang proceeded to prospect for a site and the following year opened his excavations at Sakça Gözü. In 1910 he published a topographical study of Anatolia and its Hittite monuments, *The Land of the Hittites*. He maintained this interest in the Hittites, especially after the decipherment of Hittite from 1915 onwards and during the publication and editions of the Hittite texts in the 1920s. In 1929 he published a new edition of his Hittite book, completely revised to include all the recent information drawn from the reading of the Hittite texts, under the title *The Hittite Empire*.

Thus it was that when the young Gurney during his classical degree became particularly interested in Homer, his uncle was able to direct his attention to the emerging field of Hittite studies and the possible background to Homer that might be found there. Garstang also urged that it was the right moment for a British scholar to master this field with a view to establishing the study in this country. So after taking his finals, Gurney arranged to begin the study of Akkadian, then taught in Oxford by Langdon, the Shillito Reader in Assyriology, as an introduction to the Cuneiform script, and a preliminary to embarking on Hittite. He studied with Langdon in 1933/4 and 1934/5, and in the latter session was able to make a beginning on Hittite with Dr Léonie Zuntz who was then in Oxford. With this preparation he was ready to head for the centre of Hittite studies in Berlin, the National Museum, where the Hittite tablets were sent for conservation and study. Curator of the tablets was Hans Ehelolf, who was also Professor of Hittitology at Berlin University and at that time principal epigraphist to the Boğazköy excavations.

Gurney spent the winter semester 1935–6 in Berlin studying Hittite with Ehelolf and attending also the Akkadian lectures of Erich Ebeling. His time there made him a fellow student with other future Hittitologists of distinction, including Sedat Alp from Turkey, later Professor of Hittite at Ankara University, and the young Heinrich Otten who became the official Boğazköy epigraphist after the war, and the doyen of Hittite studies in Germany. He also became friends with the Swiss Emil Forrer, whose controversial interpretations of Hittite texts had already provoked strong reaction from the Hittitological establishment in Germany.

This induction into Hittite left Gurney in a position to begin on a doctorate when he returned to Oxford. On Ehelolf's suggestion, he undertook the academic edition of an interesting group of recently published tablets containing parallel texts of prayers addressed by the Hittite king Mursili II to two different deities, the Sun Goddess of Arinna and the god Telipinus. These texts, showing a complicated recensional history which derived originally and in part from substantial Hittite re-working, were a tough assignment for a young scholar in the new discipline. An essential preliminary step was the creation of a personal reference dictionary of Hittite on file cards, based on a reading of all the Hittite texts published to that date, some thirty-six volumes of *Keilschrifttexte aus Boghazköi* and *Keilschrifturkunden aus Boghazköi* and others. (This work with continued to live in the spacious house at Bayworth Corner, which he inherited on his father's death.

In 1957 he married Diane Hope Grazebrook (née Esencourt). She was half French, and her parents had been friends and neighbours of the Gurneys in Norfolk, so she had known Gurney all her life. She took an interest in his academic activities and accompanied him on a number of extended visits to Turkey, where they travelled widely. As an accomplished draughtsman, she was often in demand to do archaeological drawing including much for Gurney's work. They shared a love of music and in particular opera, which they attended regularly, though Diane experienced some difficulty with Gurney's special favourite, Wagner. They had no children, but her daughter Caroline from her first marriage completed the family scene. In 1988 finding the upkeep of Bayworth Corner and its garden too much, the Gurneys moved to a smaller establishment, Fir Tree House in Steventon, where Oliver lived for the rest of his life.

The teaching of Akkadian at Oxford was much developed during Gurney's tenure, and he was also able to teach Hittite there. In 1948 Robert Hamilton was appointed Lecturer in Near Eastern Archaeology at Oxford, and the University tried to consolidate the field of Ancient Near Eastern Studies with the creation of a lecturership in Ancient Near Eastern History. Unfortunately this did not go through, but when Hamilton became keeper of the Ashmolean Museum in 1959, his vacant post was awarded to Peter Hulin, a former student of Gurney, thus effectively though not explicitly replacing Archaeology with History of the Ancient Near East. This was not altogether a helpful development, but it concentrated resources in the field of Assyriology and provided Gurney with an academic colleague.

The Akkadian syllabus, which Gurney inherited from Langdon, had been devised in 1928 and offered Akkadian only as a second language in the study of Hebrew. Gurney introduced a BA in Egyptology with Akkadian. When Hulin's appointment provided two teachers of the language, it seemed timely to upgrade Akkadian from second language to Hebrew and Egyptology to a subject of first choice. This was effected by offering the B.Phil. degree with options in Cuneiform Studies, Ancient History, and Hittite. Thus Gurney's special subject appeared on the University Examination Statutes for the first time. These courses on offer attracted a small but distinguished company of students over the years, a number of whom are now in prominent academic positions. In fact, Gurney's career in the post-war years coincided with an optimistic period of university expansion, and ended in retirement before the remorseless clamour for student numbers began to echo across campus.

His teaching was always thorough and enthusiastic, lightened by humour. Deeply involved in Akkadian and Hittite as he was, he communicated his pleasure in solving the problems and teasing out the meaning of the texts. The present writer early in his career in Hittite had the privilege of reading through the main Hittite texts with him and was always deeply impressed by the encyclopaedic knowledge of their content and background which he effortlessly and unselfconsciously displayed. Unlike many experts who have risen to dominant positions in their fields, he was always prepared to listen as well as speak, and throughout his life he remained unusually receptive of new ideas, which he would examine with rigour and, if they passed this scrutiny, adopt.

An interesting seminar grew out of his friendship with Leonard Palmer, then Professor of Comparative Philology. By the early 1960s the Hittite Hieroglyphic texts were becoming more accessible following the discovery of the great Karatepe bilingual and the publication of important studies based on it. At Palmer's suggestion, he and Gurney began to meet weekly to read through these texts to assess the progress that was being made, and in this they were joined by younger colleagues, Anna Morpurgo Davies, Gill Hart, and subsequently the present writer. In these memorable encounters, which continued for a number of years, the combined expertises of Palmer and Gurney served to set the subject on the move, with long-term fruitful results.

In his publications Gurney felt that his appointment to the Shillito Readership should direct his primary research allegiance towards Akkadian rather than Hittite. As it happened, circumstances combined to draw from him a good balance of both. In 1948 he was invited to publish the Middle Babylonian texts from Aqar Quf (Dur-Kurigalzu), and he spent the early months of that year in Baghdad (his only visit to Iraq) to copy them (Bibliography items 38 and 41). Yet two of his main contributions to Hittite studies appeared in the 1950s, his Penguin book *The Hittites* (1952) and his collaboration with Garstang, *The Geography of the Hittite Empire* (1959).

The Hittites (Bibliography item 2) was part of a Penguin series *Near Eastern and Western Asiatic Archaeologies*, published on the initiative and under the editorship of Professor (later Sir) Max Mallowan, which was to include a number of distinguished contributions. Gurney's volume was dedicated to Garstang, whose assistance is acknowledged in the foreword along with that of Albrecht Goetze and Sir John Miles. With mound of Sultantepe, north of Harran. It took a second season in 1952 to complete the clearance of this trove, and almost 600 tablets and fragments were recovered.

As it happened Gurney arrived in Ankara in 1951 with the purpose of conducting a geographical reconnaissance shortly after the first batch of Sultantepe tablets had arrived at Ankara Museum, so he was able to inspect them at once and make preliminary identifications and a catalogue. In 1952 he joined the Sultantepe excavations as epigraphist, and he wrote a preliminary report for *Anatolian Studies* of that year. In all he was to be preoccupied with Sultantepe for some thirteen years, which included many prolonged visits to Turkey for study and copying. Latterly he was often accompanied by his wife Diane, and when work was done, they would take the opportunity for Anatolian travel.

The tablet collection appears to have belonged to a scribal school of a temple and to have extended over three generations of scribes, and it comprised an important literary archive. Gurney's publication produced two volumes of tablet copies (I, with J. J. Finkelstein, 1957, and II, with P. Hulin, 1964, Occasional Publications of the British Institute of Archaeology at Ankara, nos. 3 and 7). He also published a series of editions of the most important texts, principally literary: the Eponym lists, the Poem of the Righteous Sufferer (with W. G. Lambert), the Cuthaean Legend of Naram-Sin, the unique folk tale the Poor Man of Nippur, a Letter of Gilgamesh, and the myth of Nergal and Ereshkigal. These articles made exciting contributions to *Anatolian Studies* for its first ten years (Bibliography items 40, 42, 43, 46, 48, 49, 52, see also items 44, 45, 47, 50, 51, 56, 60, 68, 71).

Gurney returned to Hittite studies in the early 1960s with the invitation to contribute the chapters on the Hittite Old and Middle Kingdoms to the revised *Cambridge Ancient History* (volume 2, part 1, chapters vi and xv (a)). The revised (second) edition was issued in separate fascicles as the individual contributors submitted, Gurney's being fascicles 11 (1965) and 44 (1966), and the volume itself (third edition) was published in 1973. But at this time the tectonic plates of Hittite history were on the move, and indeed a major earthquake occurred between the appearances of editions two and three. This related to the dating of the fragmentary Annals of Tudhaliya and his son Arnuwanda and a group of associated texts, principally the Indictments of Madduwatta and of Mita of Pahhuwa: the reattribution of these from Tudhaliya IV and Arnuwanda III (end of the Hittite Empire, *c*.1250–1210 BC) to Tudhaliya I and Arnuwanda I (early Empire period, *c*.1410–1370 BC) was beginning to be advocated. An associated but independent area of instability concerned the ancestry of the great king Suppiluliuma I.

Gurney's acute antennae picked up the preliminary tremors. Already in the second edition he considered the reattribution, acknowledging (fasc. 44, p. 20 n. 4) 'The credit for this observation belongs to Dr Edmund I. Gordon'. He is referring to a remarkable letter which he had received on 15 February 1965 from Gordon, a deeply eccentric scholar whose brilliance marched perilously close to the edge of sanity. This missive of fifty pages (dispatched in unnumbered and confused order) ranged over the fields of Hittite historical and geographical problems scattering extraordinary insights in wild confusion. A page selected at random reproduced as Figure 1 may give some impression of the style. (The only part of this document to find its way into print appeared in *Journal of Cuneiform Studies*, 21 (1967), pp. 70–88, where the reader feels overwhelmed by an unstoppable torrent of information. Sadly Gordon died soon thereafter.)

Important contributions arguing this redating in detail appeared from Otten (1969), Carruba (1969), and Houwink ten Cate (1970), and resisting it from Kammenhuber (1969), as recorded by Gurney in his Addenda to the bibliography (third edition, p. 812). Otherwise in the third edition Gurney was allowed to make minimal changes to incorporate this new information without unduly disturbing the text, and it may be stated that today this reinterpretation has won general acceptance.

The redating is very important, since it moves a group of historical sources previously thought to explain the terminal disintegration of the Hittite Empire *c.*1200 BC to an earlier period where they are now understood to illustrate a turbulent spell through which the Empire passed at an early stage. The implications for the *Cambridge Ancient History* revisions are worth noting. Gurney's prescience in the matter of the redating stands in contrast to the unfortunate position of Goetze, who in his second edition fascicle 37 (1965) cited the texts in question with their now superseded attribution and dating, and died in 1971 before being able to make the necessary revisions for the third edition.

Having completed these major publications, Gurney was able to return to the Kassite period texts from Ur, and these were supplemented with miscellaneous Ur texts of the Old and Late Babylonian periods. The volume appeared in 1974 (Bibliography item 6), soon followed by a volume of *Sumerian Literary Texts in the Ashmolean Museum* with S. N. Kramer (OECT V, 1976; Bibliography item 7). With these two volumes he discharged long-standing obligations to the British and Ashmolean

only in the pockets along the two north-south routes where they still survived
in name and memory until classical times; it is perhaps even possible that Arzawa's
reopening of her corridor to the East, forced most of the displaced Lukka of the
Zaballa area south into the overcrowded Pamphylia and western Trachea area, whence
they could do nothing else but soill over northeastwards into the Hittite territory
Then afterwards, Ḫattusilis having had his hands full of attacks from all sides,
Arzawa having finally cleared the Afyan "corridor" of Lukka, and then finding a
void in the LOWER LAND where the Lukka invasion of KUB XXI 6a will have wreaked
much havoc, so that Arzawa will then have come across the LOWER LAND as far as
Uda and Tuwahuwa, where they will finally have reached the outer limits of the
territory still under control of Ḫattusilis II.   Thus I XXXX find a possible
tion XXXXXXXXX from the victorious conquest of almost XXXXXXX "all the lands, and all
the mountains and all the rivers" of every corner of Anatolia, via KUB XXI 6a
in the beginning of Ḫattusilis II's reign (annals always seem to reflect the early
parts of reigns XXXXXXX anyway, especially if there were victories or even just
half-victories to write about), to the 'Ḫegur Pirwa' prologue in which the later
catastrophes of Ḫattusilis II's reign (and possibly part of his son's, Suppiluliuma'
father's, reign as well) were summarized by Ḫattusilis III at a later date. The
Lukka who had moved into Ussa and Pedassa and the LOWER LAND and the ḪULAYA RIVER
LAND will in the meanwhile have become Luwianized, and peaceable normal citizens,
with just a memory that they were once called Lukka, which therefore later caused
them to be called Lỹkannes and the region of the Lower Land + the Ḫulaya River Land
+ Ussa and Zallara altogether to be known as Lỹkaonia. The ones XXXXXXX who had
settled down in Walwaras and its 5 dependencies will also have become Luwianized,
as will those who had taken over the district of Walma, and by the time of Hattusilis
III they will have become little vassal-states of the Hittite realm. IT WILL BE ONLY
THOSE WHO WERE IN THE 'UNDERDEVELOPED' PAMPHYLIA AND WESTERN TRACHEA WHO WILL HAVE
BEEN CONTINUED TO BE CALLED LUKKA, perhaps only gradually becoming Luwianized, so
that the memory of that remained in Pamphylia (i.e., the tradition that they were
Achaeans who had lost their language, would have remained alive because they lost
whatever language it was that they originally spoke to become Luwianized last,
while presumably some groups that went into what was later called LỸKIA will also
have become Luwianized at an earlier date, presumably because the western Bronze
Age Luwians there too (presumably Talawa etc.) will have caused them to be assimilated; and it should be noted that in classical times, the Luwian-speaking people of
Lỹkia did not call themselves or their language Lỹkian but Trmmili, so that the
name Lỹkia for them may also have been a term given them by the last to Luwianize,
the pamphylians.   I just reminded myself that another piece of evidence connecting
Lukka with the north, particularly if I am right about Millawa(n)da being on the
Marmara coast, is that Strabo speaks of the arrival of the Milyai from the north,
and coming to Lỹkia.   (I May have something unclear in my mind on this, since I
have no copy of Strabo here to check it. There is also the business of Kaballia
and Milỹadike north of Lykia being all mixed up, the people of Kaballia, being themselves Maionians and kin to the Lydians.   THIS IS ALL A VERY PRELIMINARY THESIS,
BUT I THINK IT'S GENERALLY CORRECT, IF I HAVE A RIGHT TO DO SO MYSELF.

    Well tha about covers what I plan to through out; it's perhaps very ambitious
I don't know even whether you will be able to take it all but I think it's a reste-
ration that all fits together and makes sense.
    I have made only two carbon copies of this, one of which I will send to Profd.
Landsberger and Güterbock, so that I will have their comments and thinking, approval
or otherwise. I've always been on good terms personally with Prof.Goetze, but I
could never find the nerve to send him this, NOT YET ANYWAY, I appreciate knowing
that you have an open mind on the subject, and hope to hear from you soon. Unfert9
unately my typewriter won't make any more than 2 carbons, so I have but one copy
left for myself, and at some point soon, I'll be sending it (along with my 1961
papers, afte r you shall have returned them) to Prof. Sedat Alp who expressed an
interest.   I'll leave off on this now. I have so many other things to do, and I
must do some correspondence with colleagues whose recommendations I would like for
a fellowship for next year.   Sincerely yours,
                                               Edmund I. Gordon *Edmund I. Gordon*

Figure 1.   Fiftieth page of letter from E. I. Gordon to O. R. Gurney, dated 15 January 1965.

Museums. The preface and introduction to UET VII promised an academic edition of the texts copied and published by Gurney, which was delivered after his retirement. His Cuneiform copies in these two volumes like those in *The Sultantepe Tablets* were neat and precise, and he always maintained a subsequent interest in these, checking, collating, and correcting difficult and uncertain points.

Gurney was invited to give the British Academy's Schweich Lectures for 1976, and selected as an appropriate topic Hittite Religion, one of the features of their civilisation which had always attracted his interest. The choice again took him back to his first love, Hittite, and was generally a happy one in other respects, enabling him to expand and update the survey in his chapter 'Religion' in *The Hittites*, which had been written twenty-four years previously. The lectures were published in 1977 under the deceptively modest title *Some Aspects of Hittite Religion*. It is in fact a masterly survey of our current state of knowledge of all the main aspects of Hittite religion, and it is specially welcome as an English language publication in a specialist field as well as for its up-to-date bibliography. The lectures were delivered under three headings: the Pantheon, the Cult, and Magical Rituals. In the first Gurney was able to present the recent work associating the god lists in the treaties and the Hurrian *kalutis* (divine groupings listed for offerings) with the sculptural representations of the gods at the Hittite extramural sanctuary at Yazilikaya, and to supplement this with his own proposals. Under Cult, he drew attention to Hittite practices standing in the background to both the classical and the biblical worlds, and under Rituals to the interesting techniques for the transference of evil using either the scapegoat/carrier or the substitute, in both cases either human or animal, and again with parallels well beyond the Hittite world.

Gurney's career in post was a full and active one. In addition to his teaching and major publications, his Bibliography shows a steady stream of articles, in which his interests in Hittite dynastic history, geography and religion predominate. But his range was wide and embraced many Assyriological interests too. One special topic, which he pursued in several contributions (Bibliography items 58, 75, 80) and discussed with a number of specialists, was Babylonian music, specifically the tuning of the harp, an appropriate enough inquiry for such a lover of music. Nor should his very extensive number of reviews be passed over; these appeared regularly over the years until the early 1980s, usually short but always pertinent and incisive (see Bibliography, section D).

Over and above these many commitments Gurney gave outstanding
service to the British Institute of Archaeology at Ankara. After the war,
Garstang, who was again working at Mersin in 1946–7, lobbied tirelessly
with both the British and Turkish governments to open a British School
of Archaeology in Turkey. He wisely judged that this should be located in
the new capital Ankara rather than the old cosmopolitan city of Istanbul
where the other foreign schools were. His efforts were rewarded with success, and in January 1948 the Institute was officially opened in Ankara
with himself as first director. In London a Council of Management was
formed under his presidency, and in the first annual report covering 1948
and 1949, Gurney appears among the representative members (on behalf
of Oxford University), making him a founder member, and he remained
a member for the next 53 years, up to his death. The Institute inaugurated
its journal *Anatolian Studies* under the editorship of Gordon Childe, producing volume 1 in 1951, for which year Gurney was already named as
assistant editor. Childe was editor for the first five volumes but resigned
to go to Australia at the end of 1955, whereupon Gurney took over the
editorship. The first volume for which he was fully responsible as editor
was volume 6 (1956), planned as a *Festschrift* for Garstang, but sadly
turned into a memorial volume by Garstang's death in September of that
year. (In spite of evidently failing health, Garstang insisted on taking part
as Guest of Honour on a cruise in Greece and southern Turkey, accompanied by Gurney and his mother. Carried ashore for a visit to Mersin
he rallied sufficiently to give the company a lucid exposition of his
excavations there, after which he collapsed and died two days later at
Beirut.)

Gurney edited *Anatolian Studies* unaided up to 1997, an astonishing
forty-one volumes—missing only volume 30 (1980), which was dedicated to him in honour of his seventieth birthday, and was edited by
James Macqueen. Among the dedications and contributors to this volume, his friends and former students, a constant theme is their debt and
gratitude to him. Contributors to those forty-one volumes edited by him,
including the present writer, remember him as a meticulous and deeply
committed editor, interested in the whole range of Anatolian subjects
covered by the journal. His judicious touch saved many contributors
from error, and most of the articles which passed through his hands will
have benefited from lesser or greater editorial improvements. On the
practical side his relations with the printers over many years served to
restrain cost increases even over periods of high inflation. One occurrence that illustrates his devotion to the journal as well as his generally

stoical attitude to life was the occasion when he was taken to Moorfields Eye Hospital for an emergency operation for a detached retina. Afterwards he remarked cheerfully to me how conveniently it had all come about: he had been able to complete the galley proofs before going into hospital, and was sufficiently recovered in time to deal with the page proofs. He was himself a frequent contributor to the journal, in earlier years on the Sultantepe tablets, as already noted, and latterly on Hittite subjects (Bibliography items 70, 74, 76, 77, 78). On Mesopotamian subjects he most frequently contributed to *Iraq* (items 38, 53, 58, 59, 61, 62, 69, 75, 80).

Gurney's life after his retirement continued to be notably productive. He took the opportunity of his increased leisure to produce his edition of the *Middle Babylonian Legal and Economic Texts from Ur* (Bibliography item 9). For this purpose he schooled himself in the then rapidly advancing computer technology to typeset the entire volume himself: that is what lies behind the notice (reverse of title page) 'Typeset in Lasercomp Times at Oxford University Computing Service'. From then on he regularly used a word-processor and became adept at its intricacies. Similarly when he completed a further OECT (XI, 1989, Bibliography item 10), he typeset that volume too.

Nor did his services to the British Institute of Archaeology at Ankara flag with retirement. In addition to his editorship of the journal, he had been named in 1965 deputy chairman, a post which he filled under the chairmanships of Sir James Bowker and Sir Bernard Burrows. In 1982 in recognition of his long and distinguished service to the Institute, he was elected president which he remained until his death.

Under him the presidency was no figurehead role, and he concerned himself closely with the running of the institute, actively participating in meetings of the council of management, where as editor he was also responsible for publications, another job which he took seriously. When the council was discussing the production of an index to volumes 21–30 of *Anatolian Studies*, and voicing concerns at the likely cost, he immediately volunteered to do this himself for nothing, and using his newly gained mastery of the word-processor, do it he did. Again unlike many council members of learned societies he took a detailed interest in the accounts—too detailed, some harassed hon. treasurers may have felt. It was also as president that he penned the survey of fifty years of the British Institute of Archaeology at Ankara in Roger Matthews' fiftieth anniversary volume in 1998 (Bibliography item 26) as well as the retrospective chapter on Sultantepe and Harran.

By a happy coincidence the years of Gurney's retirement saw a dramatic harvest of new discoveries in the Hittite field, which had the effect of drawing him back into these studies. He followed each discovery closely and gave his own illuminating interpretations of the unfolding evidence in a series of articles (Bibliography items 19, 20, 25, 70, 74, 76, 77, 78). He was actively writing almost up to the end of his life, and as will be seen from the dates, at least three contributions were to appear posthumously (items 28, 29, 30). His continued areas of interest lay especially in Hittite dynastic affairs, and the new pieces of evidence for Hittite geography, in particular the way in which both of these topics impinge on the wide-ranging nexus of problems centering on the dating and attributions of the Tawagalawa letter. I myself have a voluminous file of letters from Gurney on these subjects throughout the 1990s, to which I would reply by telephone at weekends. This became quite a regular feature of our relationship, and indeed a continuing pleasure, and even now the feeling 'I must tell Oliver of this or that new discovery, he will be so interested' is very hard to shake off. It should perhaps be recorded that one point on which we were absolutely unable even after prolonged discussion to agree was the interpretation of a crucial passage in the Tawagalawa letter, which has such implications for so much of the thirteenth century BC Hittite history.

Oliver Gurney was a man of the greatest courtesy and integrity. A natural reserve might make him appear aloof at first, but behind that lay a warm and humorous personality. It must be admitted that these qualities were allied to a certain unworldliness. His refusal to think let alone speak ill of anyone could lead him to misjudge colleagues and others who did not adhere to his own high standards. When confronted as on occasion he was with academic impropriety, it could take a long time before he would bring himself to accept that something was wrong. He could sometimes show excessive loyalty to the unworthy, though in such cases he was seldom rewarded with any gratitude.

Mention has been made of Gurney's letter writing, which was indeed prodigious, and he belonged to a generation which very much believed in replying by return of post. He used to conduct many prolonged academic correspondences on subjects which interested him, but no topic was too small and no correspondent too inept to secure his full attention. This is no doubt connected with his persistence in pursuing problems through to their solutions. He did attract more than his fair share of cranks, though here his replies could be unexpectedly sharp from one so polite, but this was simply a reflection of his unflinching honesty.

Gurney found time in a sedentary academic life for physical activity. He was a keen tennis player until deteriorating eyesight led him to give up, and he played golf regularly almost to the end of his life. He enjoyed general good health, and a heart by-pass operation in 1993 gave him a number of years of active and productive life. He died after a short illness on 11 January 2001, some two weeks before his ninetieth birthday.

His distinction was duly recognized by honours. His presidency of the British Institute of Archaeology at Ankara, and the volume of Anatolian Studies dedicated to him have been recorded. He also served as member of Council for the British School of Archaeology in Iraq for many years.

He was elected Fellow of the British Academy in 1959. He became Foreign Member of the Royal Danish Academy of Science and Letters in 1976, and was awarded an Honorary Doctorate of Higher Letters in the University of Chicago in 1991. He was Fellow of Magdalen College, Oxford from 1963, and was also a Freeman in the City of Norwich.

J. D. HAWKINS
Fellow of the Academy

Note.   In writing this memoir I have been much assisted by conversations with Mrs Diane Gurney. For Gurney's academic career at Oxford I have drawn on the text of a lecture which he gave in November 1991 entitled 'A hundred years of Assyriology at Oxford'. For his war-time service with the Sudan Defence Force I was helped by conversations with Professor Edward Ullendorff and Professor David Williams, who both knew him there at that time.

Bibliography of O. R. Gurney

Abbreviations follow those of the *Chicago Hittite* and *Assyrian Dictionaries*.

A. Monographs
1. 1940. *Hittite Prayers of Mursili II* (*AAA* 27).
2. 1952. *The Hittites* (Penguin Books, 1952); rev. edn., 1954 (repr. 1961, 1962, 1964, 1966, 1969, 1973, 1975 (hardback), 1976; rev. edn., 1981, 1990). New rev. edn., The Folio Society (London, 1999).
   Translations: Italian, *Gli Ittiti* (Florence, 1957); German, *Die Hethiter* (Dresden, 1969, 2nd edn., 1981); Polish, *Hetyci* (Warsaw, 1970); Russian, *Chetty* (Moscow, 1987); Turkish *Hititler* (Ankara, 2001); Spanish, *Los Hititas* (Barcelona, n.d.).

3. 1957. *The Sultantepe Tablets*, volume 1 (with J. J. Finkelstein) (British Institute of Archaeology at Ankara, occasional publications no. 3; London).

4. 1959. *The Geography of the Hittite Empire* (with J. Garstang) (British Institute of Archaeology at Ankara, occasional publications no. 5; London).

5. 1964. *The Sultantepe Tablets* vol. 2 (with P. Hulin) (British Institute of Archaeology at Ankara, occasional publications no. 7; London).

6. 1974. *Middle Babylonian Legal Documents and Other Texts* (UET VII; British Museum Publications, London).

7. 1976. *Sumerian Literary Texts in the Ashmolean Museum* (with S. N. Kramer) (OECT V; Oxford).

8. 1977. *Some Aspects of Hittite Religion* (Schweich Lectures 1976; Oxford University Press).

9. 1983. *The Middle Babylonian Legal and Economic Texts from Ur* (British School of Archaeology in Iraq).

10. 1989. *Literary and Miscellaneous Texts in the Ashmolean Museum* (OECT XI; Oxford).

B. Contributions to composite volumes, Festschrifts etc.

11. 1953. 'A Hittite Divination Text' (in D. J. Wiseman, *The Alalakh Tablets* (British Institute of Archaeology at Ankara, occasional publications no. 2; London), pp. 116–18).

12. 1958. 'Hittite Kingship' (in S. H. Hooke (ed.), *Myth, Ritual and Kingship* (Oxford), pp.105–21).

13. 1965. 'Anatolia *c.*1750–1600 B.C.' (in *The Cambridge Ancient History*, rev. edn., vol. 2, ch. 6, fasc. 11 (Cambridge University Press); 3rd edn., 1973, pp. 228–55).

14. 1966. 'Anatolia *c.*1600–1380 B.C.' (in *The Cambridge Ancient History*, rev. edn., vol. 2, ch. 15 (a), fasc. 44 (Cambridge University Press); 3rd edn., 1973, pp. 659–83).

15. 1967. 'Boğazköy' (in D. Winton Thomas (ed.), *Archaeology and Old Testament Study* (Oxford), pp. 105–16).

16. 1974. 'Asia Minor, Religions of' (in *The Encyclopaedia Britannica* (15th edn., London, Chicago).

17. 1974. 'The Hittite Line of Kings and Chronology' (in K. Bittel *et al.* (eds.), *Anatolian Studies presented to H. G. Güterbock* (PIHANS, Leiden), pp. 105–11).

18. 1977. 'Inscribed cylinders and cylinder fragments in the Ashmolean Museum, Oxford' (in M. de J. Ellis (ed.), *Essays J. J. Finkelstein* (Hamden, Connecticut), pp. 93–100).

19. 1979. 'The Hittite Empire' (in M. T. Larsen (ed.), *Power and Propaganda* (Mesopotamia 7; Copenhagen), pp. 151–65).

20. 1979. 'The Anointing of Tudhaliya' (in O. Carruba (ed.), *Studia Mediterranea P. Meriggi dicata* (St. Med. I, Pavia, pp. 213–23).

21. 1981. 'The Babylonians and Hittites' (in M. Loewe and C. Blacker (ed.), *Divination and Oracles* (London), pp. 142–73).

22. 1982. 'A case of conjugal desertion' (in G. van Driel *et al.* (eds.), *Zikir Šumim* (Fs Kraus, Leiden), pp. 81–94).

23. 1982. 'Three contracts from Babylon' (in M. A. Dandamayev *et al.* (eds.), *Societies*

and Languages of the Ancient Near East (Studies Diakonoff, Warminster), pp. 120–8).

24. 1986. 'Hittite fragments in private collections' (in H. A. Hoffner and G. M. Beckman (eds.), *Kaniššuwar* (A.S. 23, Chicago), pp. 59–68).

25. 1992. 'Hittite Geography thirty years on' (in H. Otten *et al.* (eds.), *Hittite and other Anatolian and Ancient Near Eastern Studies in Honour of Sedat Alp* (Ankara), pp. 213–21).

26. 1998. 'Introduction: Fifty Years of the British Institute of Archaeology at Ankara' (in R. Matthews (ed.), *Ancient Anatolia. Fifty years' work by the British Institute of Archaeology at Ankara* (London), ch. 1, pp. 1–4); Sultantepe and Harran (ibid., ch. 15, pp. 163–76).

27. 2000. 'The Iconography of the Hasanlu Bowl' (in S. Graziani (ed.), *Studi sul Vicino Oriente Antico* (Memoria L. Cagni, Naples), pp. 417–20).

28. 2002. 'The Authorship of the Tawagalawa Letter' (in P. Taracha (ed.), *Silva Anatolica* (Fs Popko, Warsaw), pp. 133–41).

29. 2002. 'The Authorship of the Ulmi-Tešub Treaty' (in S. de Martino and F. Pecchioli Daddi (eds.), *Anatolia Antica* (Studi F. Imparati, Florence), pp. 339–44).

30. forthcoming. 'The Upper Land' (in G. M. Beckman, R. Beal, and G. McMahon (eds.), *Festschrift H. A. Hoffner* (Eisenbrauns), pp. 199–26).

C. Articles

31. 1935. 'Babylonian prophylactic figures and their rituals' (*AAA* 22, pp. 31–96).

32. 1935. 'A bilingual text concerning Etana' (*JRAS*, pp. 459–66).

33. 1936–37. 'A new fragment of the series ludlul bêl nîmeqi; an incantation of the Maqlû type; an invocation to the two Assyrian Ištars' (*AfO* 11, pp. 367–9).

34. 1937. 'Temple records from Umma' (*JRAS*, pp. 470–3).

35. 1937. 'Hittite paras = horse??' (PEQ 69, p. 194).

36. 1937. 'Note on Hittite Philology. Wappu' (*JRAS*, pp. 113–15).

37. 1948. 'Mita of Pahhuwa' (*AAA* 28, pp. 32–47).

38. 1949. 'Texts from Dur-Kurigalzu' (*Iraq* 11, pp. 131–49).

39. 1949. 'The Laws of Eshnunna' (with J. Miles, *Ar. Or.* 17, pp. 174–88).

40. 1952. 'The Sultantepe Tablets; a preliminary note' (*An. St.* 2, pp. 25–35).

41. 1953. 'Further texts from Dur-Kurigalzu' (*Sumer* 9, pp. 21–34).

42. 1953. 'The Sultantepe Tablets I. The Eponym Lists'; 'II. The tablet from room M2' (*An. St.* 3, pp. 15–21, 21–5).

43. 1954. 'The Sultantepe Tablets III. The Poem of the Righteous Sufferer' (with W. G. Lambert, *An. St.* 4, pp. 65–99).

44. 1954. 'Two fragments of the Epic of Gilgamesh from Sultantepe' (*JCS* 8, pp. 87–95).

45. 1954–56. 'The text of Enûma Eliš. New additions and variants' (*AfO* 17, pp. 353–6).

46. 1955. 'The Sultantepe Tablets IV. The Cuthaean Legend of Naram-Sin' (*An. St.* 5, pp. 93–113).

47. 1955. 'The Assyrian tablets from Sultantepe' (*Proceedings of the British Academy* 41, pp. 21–41).

48. 1956. 'The Sultantepe Tablets V. The Tale of the Poor Man of Nippur' (*An. St.* 6, pp. 145–64).

105. 1977. T. Jacobsen: *The Treasures of Darkness* (New Haven, 1976) (*TLS* 76, p. 734).

106. 1977. C. Burde: *Hethitische medizinische Texte* (*StBoT* 19; Wiesbaden, 1974) (*Bi. Or.* 34, p. 198 f.).

107. 1977. E. Neu and C. Rüster: *Keilschrifttexte aus Boghazköi* XXIII (Berlin, 1976) (*JRAS* 1977, p. 207).

108. 1977. E. Neu and C. Rüster: *Hethitische Keilschrift-Paläographie* II (StBoT 21; Wiesbaden, 1975) (*Bi. Or.* 34, p. 199 f.).

109. 1977. K. Bittel *et al.*: *Das Hethitische Felsheiligtum Yazilikaya* (Bo.-Ha. IX; Berlin, 1975) (*JRAS* 1977, p. 118 f.).

110. 1979. A. Kammenhuber: *Orakepraxis, Träume und Vorzeichenschau bei den Hethitern* (*THeth* 7; Heidelberg, 1976) (*OLZ* 74, pp. 537–40).

111. 1980. *Florilegium Anatolicum. Mélanges offerts à Emmanuel Laroche* (Paris, 1979) (*Bi. Or.* 37, p. 197 f.).

112. 1981. B. Lewis: *The Sargon Legend* (ASOR, Cambridge, Mass., 1980) (*Bi. Or.* 38, p. 348 f.).

113. 1982. S. Heinhold Krahmer *et al.*: *Probleme der Textdatierung in der Hethitologie* (*THeth* 9; Heidelberg, 1979) (*OLZ* 77, pp. 560–3).

114. 1982. E. Masson: *Le panthéon de Yazilikaya. Nouvelles lectures* (Paris, 1981) (with J. D. Hawkins, *Bi. Or.* 39, pp. 606–16).

115. 1983. H. J. Deighton: *The 'Weather-God' in Hittite Anatolia* (BAR, Oxford, 1982) (*JRAS* 1983, p. 281 f.).

NICHOLAS HAMMOND　　　　　　　　　*Bromhead*

Nicholas Geoffrey Lemprière Hammond
1907–2001

NICK HAMMOND stands in a class of his own among Fellows of the Academy. Others have been men of action, but few have been remembered as much for that as for their scholarship; others have been fêted abroad, but very few have attained the iconic status that he held in Greece; others have lived to see a son of theirs elected to the Fellowship, but very few indeed a daughter. What these achievements already hint at, the reality confirms: here was a personality of quite exceptional drive, a physique of the same robustness as his intellect, and a family life of unusual serenity. Hammond's whole career is a story of clearly focused motivation and unhesitating decisiveness, in his case (perhaps again unusually) coupled with a disposition of kindly bonhomie.

He was a son of the Church, born on 15 November 1907 at Ayr, where his father, the Revd James Vavasour Hammond, was the Episcopalian Rector of Holy Trinity Church. The Hammond family was not of Scottish but of Channel Island descent; but the Revd James Hammond had cemented the Scottish connection by marrying Dorothy May, the daughter of a Glasgow average adjustor in a shipping firm. The two had met while James Hammond was serving as a curate at St Mary's Episcopalian Cathedral. After their marriage came the move to Ayr, and the birth of their four children, of whom Nicholas was the second. It was to be his grandfather, Alfred May, who largely paid for the children's education: Nick was sent to a preparatory school in Ayr where his gifts, both intellectual and, when necessary, in physical self-defence particularly attracted note; then, after the First World War, he won a scholarship to Fettes

Proceedings of the British Academy, **120**, 243–259. © The British Academy 2003.

College, and his experience there was the root of a lifelong affection for the city of Edinburgh.

The family home remained in Ayr until the late 1920s; but the Channel Island link is deep enough to be of some interest in its own right. The 'Hamon' family could trace their residence in Jersey back to the time of the Conqueror, and the Revd J. V. Hammond had been the first member of his line to move permanently away from the island. His paternal grand-father had in his time become Bailiff of Jersey, the civil head of the island's community. The family were much intermarried with other noted Jersey families, and the Bailiff had married one of the Lemprières, of Breton origin: the wife's brother was to father the famous Mrs Langtry, the 'Jersey Lily'. The Lemprière family could also lay claim to the com-piler of a noted Classical Dictionary of 1788, and a tradition as histori-ans of the Channel Islands which went back even further. Nick's third given name commemorated all these links.

In 1926, Nick moved on as a Kitchener Scholar to Gonville and Caius College, Cambridge. By now he had acquired a clear destiny as a Classicist, and an equally clear reputation as a formidable sportsman: hockey (for which he became President of the University Club), rugby and tennis were among his accomplishments, but he also became Treasurer of the Union. Rather in the manner of earlier scholar–athletes like C. B. Fry, he achieved brilliant First Classes in both parts of the Classical Tripos, with a Distinction in History which seems to have settled the more precise path of his future career.

Already there were signs that, as an ancient historian, his approach was going to be of a distinctive kind. After graduating in 1929, he left for Greece on the first of that series of extended, long-distance, cross-country walking expeditions for which he soon became famous. Something had acted to direct his interests towards the mountainous north-western region of the country, Epirus, well away from the familiar seeding-grounds of Classical civilisation. For many weeks on end, he walked across this very rugged country, repeatedly crossing the modern frontier (not an ancient one) of Albania. He was to repeat this exercise annually, and by 1933 he had devoted a total of seven months to it. As a topographical historian, he was enrolling himself in a long-standing and characteristically British tra-dition, covering some three centuries: like his forerunners, he believed that personal autopsy not only was the key to understanding military and other history, but could also result in the discovery of important but hitherto unknown monuments. From the most distinguished of these, William Martin Leake, Nick adopted, along with the necessary recording of what he saw by means of notes, sketches and (in his case) photographs, the admirable practice of timing himself over each stretch of his walks—not that Nick's timings could be applied by ordinary mortals, at least of the jaded modern age. But the whole undertaking was to be revelatory: he rapidly added to his skills a confident handling of prehistoric archaeological material, an asset to which none of his predecessors could have aspired, and he had an excellent eye for the lie of the land. He reached, for example, the important historical finding (to be revealed presently in his first major publication)[1] that an army or a migratory people, seeking to move on southern Greece from the interior of Macedonia while avoiding the plains of Thessaly and Boeotia, must cross and then re-cross the main chain of the Pindus Mountains to do so. Many years later he was to summarise, in an entertaining paper, these experiences of the 1930s.[2]

It was during his second walking venture in 1930 that a telegram somehow reached him, summoning him back to Cambridge. It had been sent by Henry Thirkill, the Senior Tutor at Clare College. Clare at this time was a modest and (as we shall see) parsimonious college, which felt a need to make an appointment to a Research Fellowship in Classics: one of the dons at Caius had spoken highly to Thirkill of their graduate of a year previously. Nick made the laborious journey back to Cambridge and, after a one-to-one interview with Thirkill lasting only minutes, he was offered the position, with the implication that it could mature into a full Fellowship. Thus, some months before his twenty-third birthday, he could return to Greece in the knowledge that, barring accidents, his whole career was now secure. A request to be reimbursed for his considerable travel expenses was, however, brusquely turned down by Harrison, the Bursar.

So it was that he joined a small, all-male, celibate society which must have averaged twice his age. From the start, he was responsible for the entire Classical teaching of his 'side', for both parts of the Classical Tripos, with its heavy emphasis on the languages. Linguistically, Nick excelled: F. W. Walbank recalls attending an evening course in Modern Greek, given by Bertrand Hallward in 1930: on one occasion, Nick was brought in to demonstrate a fluency which already exceeded that of the teacher. He brought his typical vigour to all these duties; in return, he not

---

[1] 'Prehistoric Epirus and the Dorian Invasion', *Annual of the British School at Athens*, 32 (1931–2) (1934), 131–79.
[2] 'Travels in Epirus and South Albania before World War II', *The Ancient World*, 8 (1983), 13–45.

unnaturally assumed an entitlement to speak at the Governing Body. Learning with some dismay, before his first meeting, of the very low wages (even by Cambridge standards) paid to the College servants, he ventured to raise the issue under 'Any Other Business'. He was never to forget the Master's response, 'That's quite enough from you, young man'.

The Fellows nonetheless came to appreciate the qualities of their new recruit: proposals to promote him to a full Fellowship were thwarted for six years, on financial grounds, by the same Bursar; but in 1936, when the University itself appointed him to a Lectureship, the pressure to do so became irresistible. The publication in 1934 of the long paper already mentioned had helped to bring this about. Nick's nomination as Junior Proctor in 1939 was a confirmation of Clare's regard. Meanwhile, there was still sport, an aspect which Clare took at least as seriously as the academic: as a rugby hooker, the young Research Fellow was a regular member of the college first team until, at the onset of the Cuppers competition, the protests of other colleges forced his withdrawal.

Sport, too, had a hand in one of the two most decisive episodes of his whole life, both of which belong to the year 1938. It was while Hammond was taking a characteristically forceful part in a mixed hockey match, shouting exhortations to the triple blue Norman Yardley who was a member of his side, that he first met Margaret Townley, a final-year Newnham undergraduate who was also playing. They met again when Nick gave a talk to the Newnham Classical Society; and again when Margaret stayed with a friend whose father was, by coincidence, also a Minister (but a Presbyterian one) in Ayr. Margaret was the daughter of yet another Scot, the electrical engineer James Townley who, Paisley-born, had taken the road southwards and risen to be in charge of electricity supply for the LCC. Their wedding in 1938 was to inaugurate a marriage that lasted serenely for over 62 years.

The other event was portentous in a very different way. The War Office had begun to take its soundings, among academics particularly, of men who possessed special skills that could prove useful in the now imminent war. Their discovery that this supremely fit, thirty-year-old Classicist had fluent modern Greek, passable Albanian, and an unrivalled knowledge of the topography of northern Greece, was to bear richer fruit than they can have imagined. All too soon, he had to withdraw from further progress up the academic ladder, and from what was about to become his family circle (he was sent abroad just four weeks before the birth of his eldest child, Caroline, who would be more than four years old before he first set eyes on her).

Commissioned in the early summer of 1940, he was hastily trained in handling explosives, and flown out to Greece in June. His first mission was, transparently, at least in part of his own devising: to instigate a rising in Albania against the Italian occupation of the previous year. But at this precise moment, neither Italy nor Greece was yet at war: the Greek policy of strict neutrality required Hammond's immediate withdrawal before he could embroil anyone in his plan, though within days Italy was to join the Axis alliance. Instead, he was sent to Palestine, to pass on to special groups of trainees his new-found expertise in demolition and in wireless operating: some of the groups were composed of Zionist sympathisers with the Allied cause, among them names destined for fame in Israeli history (Moshe Dayan led the very first; another included Yigael Yadin). That October, Greece declared war on Italy and there followed the winter campaign in the Albanian frontier region, when the Greek army inflicted a resounding defeat on the Italian forces. Much as Nick would have relished joining them, he was not allowed to return to Greece until 15 March 1941, as a member of the Special Operations Executive. But this was the eve of the German invasion, and he was in time only to join in the forlorn retreat of the Greek and British forces.[3] From this experience, not for the last time, he was lucky to escape with his life: most notably at the end, on 31 May, when a German fighter machine-gunned the *caïque* in which he was escaping from Crete, killing two of his nine companions but then, providentially, wobbling and firing wide.

From now until early in 1943, Nick returned to his training duties. To his great satisfaction, his charges now included Greek volunteers who had escaped their country's occupation: from them he chose future comrades-in-arms, and it was from this time that his nickname, *Lochagós Vamvakopyrítis* ('Captain Gun-cotton') derived. All the while, clandestine operations in occupied Greece were being planned and indeed executed, at first by others: a striking success in the combined exploit of dynamiting the Gorgopotamos viaduct in November 1942 encouraged high hopes for the potential of British collaboration with the Greek Resistance forces. When the time came for Nick to be parachuted into Thessaly on a moonlit night in February 1943, he was to endure eighteen months of unbroken hardship, on hardly a day of which he was not in danger of death, by German action, by internecine fighting between rival guerilla forces, by accident, disease, injury, or betrayal. Protected only by a series

---

[3] See his 'Memories of a British Officer Serving in Special Operations Executive in Greece, 1941', *Balkan Studies*, 23 (1982), 127–55.

of ingenious disguises, he had prophetically anticipated one of them back at Clare in the 1930s, where he is recorded as having appeared at a masquerade of the College Dilettanti Society in the guise of 'a villainous Albanian bandit'.

Nick published several full accounts of his own part in these events:[4] their story in general has many times over been narrated, less often evaluated. From his own pages, negative sentiments emerge repeatedly, most often disillusionment with his Greek collaborators and impatience with the lack of understanding on the part of GHQ Cairo. To voice the exhilaration which many British participants derived from the unswerving courage of their Greek helpers, civilians and *Andartes* alike, he usually preferred to cite the comments of comrades such as Major R. R. Prentice and Captain H. A. Wickstead. A single root cause underlay these dissatisfactions: politics. Nick belonged to a generation for whom 'political' was a mildly pejorative epithet, more or less synonymous with 'left-wing'. It was galling for him to find that effective co-operation with the anti-German forces in Greece depended on the whims of two organisations, EAM and ELAS, which (as he rightly discerned) were already deeply infiltrated with Communism. For most of the British military, including it seems the staff at GHQ, this was not an obstacle: if these people would fight the enemy, they must be helped regardless. But Nick had a longer view of Greek affairs than they: he was appalled by the brutality of ELAS towards other Resistance groups, and by the designs which (again, rightly) he suspected that they held for seizing political control of Greece after the war, and he used every opportunity to alert his superiors to these aspects. He could not know of Stalin's undertaking to Churchill not to intervene in Greek affairs: still less that the promise would be honoured.

He leaves his readers with the impression that his was a voice crying in the wilderness; yet the facts encourage a more positive reading. For a start, GHQ was highly appreciative of Nick's personal contributions: at the very beginning of 1944, he was awarded the DSO and appointed liaison officer to all the ELAS units in northern Greece; twice mentioned in despatches and promoted Lieutenant-Colonel, in May he was appointed Acting Commander of the entire Allied Military Mission, a position that he later resigned on grounds of his differences with GHQ policy. Another positive factor was that Nick's 'apolitical' stance again and again paid

---

[4] See especially *Venture into Greece: with the Guerillas 1943–44* (London, 1983: Greek translated edition, 1984); 'The Allied Military Mission in Northwest Macedonia', *Balkan Studies*, 32 (1991), 107–44; *The Allied Military Mission and the Resistance in West Macedonia* (Thessaloniki, 1993).

dividends; the ELAS commanders and their political colleagues found that they were dealing with a man who was a hard negotiator, a fierce disciplinarian when necessary, and a shatteringly straight talker in their own language. This was not what they expected from their foreign helpers; repeatedly, the outcome was that concessions were made, in strategy, in collaboration, and even in subordination to the orders from British Headquarters, which perhaps no one else could have exacted. The farewell line from the able ELAS commander 'Kikitsas' to him, 'You're a good officer, but a bloody awful politician', which Nick quoted with relish and would have liked to reciprocate, conveys very much less than the whole truth. By the time that Nick was evacuated from Greece on 29 August, the war was running strongly in the Allies' favour; by 1 November the last German was to leave the Greek mainland, in a liberation that was largely free of additional bloodshed. Nick had by this time been repatriated and was recovering from the recurrent malaria which had been troubling even his iron constitution, though without ever incapacitating him for more than a day or two. In 1946, the new Greek Government honoured him with its highest distinction, the Grand Cross of the Order of the Phoenix.

Eventual demobilisation made it possible for him to resume his former positions in Cambridge, at the university and at his college. By now Thirkill, the former Senior Tutor, had become Master of Clare and he at once showed his confidence in Hammond by inviting him to become Senior Tutor. For the next seven years, Nick adopted the role of the 'College man' *par excellence*. He entered forcefully into College affairs and was soon, after Thirkill, its dominant personality. He evidently realised that Clare's pre-war image, as a place for 'men with nice instincts' (Thirkill's favourite phrase, which usually turned out to mean the sons of old Clare men), with its indifference to the academic performance of students and dons alike, and its emphasis on sport, would no longer quite do. One of his first steps was to invert the pattern of undergraduate residence, bringing the Freshmen into College at the expense of later years; other measures met with initial resistance, but he persuaded Thirkill successively that further Research Fellows must be admitted as he himself had once been; that the College should expand and, especially, that the number of research students should rise dramatically from the tiny handful present before the war; and that new undergraduate accommodation should be built.

All of these changes were rapidly assimilated: Nick, still in the prime of life, pursued them and everything else with his old vigour. One of his tutorial pupils recalls how Nick followed the then prevalent custom of entertaining at breakfast, in his case at 7.45 a.m. It was evident from the tutor's dress and brusque arrival that for him it was not the first, but at least the second engagement of the day, after a game of squash. More telling is an anecdote about his additional role as graduate tutor. A recent arrival from America had had the effrontery to decline an affiliation with Jesus College and, at the suggestion of his senior colleague Max Perutz, found his way through the unfamiliar streets to Clare. The Head Porter telephoned Mr Hammond to ask for an interview, somehow conveying by his tone of voice that he expected it to be a tiresome one. 'I'll see him at five to one' Nick stipulated, judging that lunch would give him an unimpeachable pretext for terminating the interview quickly. By the end of those five minutes, he had admitted James D. Watson, so giving the college, a decade later, the accolade of its first Nobel Laureate.

Many another Oxbridge college of those days had its 'good College man', often of sporting prowess, sometimes with a record of military distinction in one or the other world war, conservative in disposition, conscientious in all his duties—except that of conducting research. The remarkable thing about Hammond was how radically he diverged from this stereotype in the last and most important respect. Even before the war started, he had evidently decided on a new academic trajectory for himself, temporarily turning away from his early topographical studies and addressing instead some of the absolutely central issues of Greek history and historiography which he had encountered in his teaching. The first fruits of this change were already published or in press by the time he left for the war: the list of topics—the legislation of Solon, the two battles of Chaeronea, the composition of Thucydides' history and the sources for that of Diodorus Siculus[5]—give the skeleton of what was now, from 1945 onwards, to be fleshed out. To these and many like subjects, Nick brought his own distinctive qualities: a prodigious knowledge of the ancient sources and an unshakeable faith that, sometimes after due amendment, they (or the best of them) could be fully vindicated; a completely independent line of thought, derived from his own cogitations, which could not easily brook rival interpretations of the same material; a robust reliance on practical common sense; and that same unhesitating decisiveness which had stood him in such good stead in time of war.

---

[5] 'The Seisachtheia and the Nomothesia of Solon', *Journal of Hellenic Studies*, 60 (1940), 71–83, first given as a paper to the Cambridge Philological Society in 1938; 'The Two Battles of Chaeronea (338 BC and 86 BC)', *Klio*, 31 (1938), 186–218; 'The Composition of Thucydides' History', *Classical Quarterly*, 34 (1940), 146–52; 'The Sources of Diodorus Siculus', i and ii, ibid., 31 (1937), 79–91 and 32 (1938), 137–51.

These qualities he now went on to apply to one after another of the issues which most exercised the historians of the day. In succession there appeared, always in prominent journals, studies of the constitution of Lycurgus at Sparta;[6] of the chronology of the Pentecontaetia,[7] the early tyrannies[8] and the career of Miltiades;[9] more military studies, now including (after his amphibious experiences in the war) re-assessments of naval engagements such as Sybota[10] and Salamis.[11] The central place of these topics in contemporary syllabuses of ancient history meant that the attention of undergraduates would invariably be directed to these papers, if often (at Oxford anyway) as a challenge to their critical abilities. But the old interests in topography and archaeology had never been forgotten: his account of Classical houses at a remote site in Epirus, which he had seen more than twenty years earlier, was a typical presentation of primary archaeological evidence;[12] and two important new pieces of 1954 dealing with the Isthmus region (another part of Greece which he had come to know well), on the affiliations of the sanctuary at Perachora and on the north–south land route across the Isthmus, were to be cited for decades afterwards.[13]

In this same year, he surprised academic colleagues by accepting the Headmastership of Clifton College; yet it was not an uncharacteristic decision for someone of such breadth of experience, or as devoted as Nick was to the whole educational process. Here he remained until 1962, remembered as a forceful but genial Headmaster. His insistence on teaching the senior Classics forms himself bore detectable fruit in the quality of their 'A' level scripts in ancient history, as F. W. Walbank (marking them for the Examinations Board) could testify. He became a member of the Committee of the Headmasters' Conference; formed a new local affinity with Gloucestershire (for which he was later to serve

---

[6] 'The Lykurgan Reform at Sparta', *Journal of Hellenic Studies*, 70 (1950), 42–64.

[7] 'Studies in Greek Chronology of the Sixth and the Fifth Centuries BC', *Historia*, 4 (1955), 371–411.

[8] 'The Family of Orthagoras', *Classical Quarterly*, 6(2) (1956), 45–53.

[9] 'The Philaids in the Chersonese', *Classical Quarterly*, 6(2) (1956), 113–29.

[10] 'Naval Operations in the South Channel of Corcyra, 435–433', *Journal of Hellenic Studies*, 65 (1945), 26–37.

[11] 'The Battle of Salamis', *Journal of Hellenic Studies*, 76 (1956), 32–54, with 'A Correction', ibid., 77 (1957), 311; and 'On Salamis', *American Journal of Archaeology*, 64 (1960), 367–8.

[12] 'Hellenic Houses at Ammotopos', *Annual of the British School at Athens*, 48 (1953), 135–40.

[13] 'The Heraeum at Perachora and Corinthian Encroachment' and 'The Main Road from Boeotia to the Peloponnese Through the Northern Megarid', in *Annual of the British School at Athens*, 49 (1954), 93–103 and 103–22 respectively.

as Deputy-Lieutenant); and edited a volume of essays for the school's centenary.[14] But there is much evidence that he still felt the call of academic life: for one thing, his output of publications was not interrupted: he returned to the topic of Solon, this time from the aspect of his agrarian reforms[15] and now, in his fifties, set out (for the first time, apart from his youthful memoir of the Cambridge Classicist J. E. Sandys),[16] to consolidate his thought into books. In 1959, he began a long association with the Oxford University Press, who published his *A History of Greece to 322 BC*, a concise text-book which became prescribed reading at more than one level.

His next step, in moving to the H. O. Wills Chair of Greek at the University of Bristol, will have seemed to him as short in conceptual terms as it was in geographical: no pigeon-holing for him, whether as historian or as school-teacher. He embarked on yet another highly successful branch of his versatile career, building up the Bristol Department of Classics into one of the largest and best in the country. D. J. Blackman, who as Assistant Lecturer in 1964 was one of Nick's early appointments, remembers the immense popularity of the lectures, which now he could (was indeed required to) devote to literature as well as history. When Blackman left to pursue a career in politics Nick, who had drawn only strength from the variety of his own career, supported him warmly and in disregard of differences in their political views.

These years also saw his productivity rise to a new peak. There were major papers: notably one on the first Athenian Confederacy[17] and a second on the campaign of Marathon.[18] Most important of all, he now set out to distil thirty-five years of first-hand experience into his huge volumes *Epirus* (Oxford, 1967) and *A History of Macedonia* (Oxford: vol. i, 1972; vol. ii, with G. T. Griffith, 1979; vol. iii, with F. W. Walbank, 1988). On top of all this, he began an editorial engagement with new editions of two central works of reference, the *Oxford Classical Dictionary* of 1970, which was to hold the field for 26 years, and the early volumes of a new *Cambridge Ancient History* (vol. i (1970–3), vol. ii (1973–5), vol. iii.

---

[14] *Centenary Essays on Clifton College* (Bristol, 1962).

[15] 'Land Tenure in Athens and Solon's Seisachtheia', *Journal of Hellenic Studies*, 81 (1961), 76–98.

[16] *John Edwin Sandys* (Cambridge, 1932).

[17] 'The Origins and the Nature of the Athenian Alliance of 478/7 BC', *Journal of Hellenic Studies*, 87 (1967), 41–61.

[18] 'The Campaign and the Battle of Marathon', *Journal of Hellenic Studies*, 88 (1968), 13–57.

(1982–91) and vol. iv (1988)) which will certainly have a still longer life. In both, he was a substantial contributor as well as an energetic editor.

The consolidation of his work on northern Greece had involved engaging once more with its prehistory. A series of papers between 1967 and 1974 presented a new and visionary account of the early connections of the region, both northwards into the Balkans and the Russian steppe, and southwards to the Bronze Age heart-land of Greece, based on close study of prehistoric material culture and shaped by one over-riding conviction: he had become persuaded over the years that migrations, warlike or otherwise, had been the dominant agent of change in early Greece, and he was presently to publish a monograph, *Migrations and Invasions in Greece and Adjacent Areas* (Park Ridge, NJ, 1976) which synthesised his views on this issue. Three of the papers on the prehistory of northern Greece appeared as the first three chapters when, soon afterwards, the OUP produced a volume of his *Studies in Greek History* (Oxford, 1973). The rest were made up of his earlier articles of the late 1930s, 1950s, and 1960s previously listed, reissued in a revised form with, in some cases, a brisk response to the opponents who had emerged in the intervening years.

During his time at Bristol, besides acting as Pro-Vice-Chancellor from 1964 to 1966, he also found time to serve two institutions with whom he had long-standing associations, first as President of the Hellenic Society (1965–8), then as Chairman of the British School at Athens (1972–5). The latter was an especially fitting landmark in a connection which was to span seven decades: he had been the School's first Visiting Fellow in 1953, and his term of office as chairman was long remembered for the swift and genial discharge of its duties. His election to the British Academy came in 1968.

Soon after his retirement in 1973, he returned to live in Cambridge, where Clare very properly elected him Honorary Fellow in 1974. Now emerged perhaps the most surprising phase of his career in research; and it is not hard to identify the trigger which released it. In 1968, at a conference on ancient Macedonia, he had spoken on the early capital of the Macedonian kingdom, Aigai, where all its rulers save Alexander the Great had continued to be buried, long after it had lost its political status.[19] He proposed that Aigai had not been, as the learned consensus held, a place in the vicinity of ancient and modern Edessa, possibly forming no more than

---

[19] 'The Archaeological Background to the Macedonian Kingdom', later published in *Ancient Macedonia*, i (Thessaloniki, 1970), 53–67.

of Letters, to add to the Doctorates which he had earlier taken at Bristol (1965) and Cambridge (1974). Even this schedule was not intensive enough for him, interspersed as it was with visits to the Antipodes: he was Visiting Professor at the University of Auckland in 1980, at the University of Adelaide in 1984, and at Newcastle University, New South Wales in 1988, 1990, and (by now in his mid-eighties) in 1992. Audiences in each of these places had found that the stimulation of his lecturing style was as great as ever, and the word had been passed on.

But there was a third and deeper commitment, to Greece. His links with the Athens School had provided opportunities for periodical revisits over the intervening years, but what now took place was something stronger, an extended and emotional home-coming. In Greece, there were not a few people still alive who remembered at first hand his wartime exploits; and his reputation had received a further boost from his role in bringing about the discoveries at Vergina. Invitations to visit the University of Ioannina (as Leverhulme Professor in 1978) and the National Hellenic Research Foundation (1985) followed naturally enough; so too, in due course, did election as a Companion of the Society of Friends of the Greek People in 1993, and a further Honorary Doctorate from Ioannina in 1996. When the time came to celebrate his own eightieth birthday in 1987, it was to Athens that he brought his family, children, grandchildren, babies in arms and all. Everywhere he was fêted; but especially in northern Greece, where he would attend the series of Macedonian Congresses in Thessaloniki and later tour the villages where he had long ago dodged the German occupation forces. Later still, in the 1990s, when contemporary politics brought the issue of Macedonia to the forefront of Greek consciousness, his many publications on ancient Macedonia, and particularly his conviction on the currency of the Greek language there[25] were eagerly cited in support of the region's essential and long-standing Hellenism.

It is pleasant to record that in Albania, too, he was not forgotten: as early as 1971, he had been one of four British scholars unprecedentedly invited to a conference in Tirana on the ancient Illyrians. With only one weekly flight into the country, this visit extended to a fortnight's stay with, once again, some re-visiting of old haunts. Contemporary political relations made this a delicate mission, and the politically sensitive subject of the conference even more so: for the Albanians, the Illyrians were not

---

[25] Seen most notably in his paper 'Literary Evidence for Macedonian Speech', *Historia*, 43 (1994), 131–42 , repr. in *Collected Studies*, iv, 77–88.

only regarded as ancestors, but credited with a major territorial expansion into parts of Epirus which had generally been seen as Greek, in antiquity as today. Frank Walbank, who was also a member of the party, remembers more than anything else the tact and reticence that Hammond displayed in the face of such claims: Kikitsas's gibe of long ago, 'a bloody awful politician', once again stood refuted.

Only in his final decade, after a fall on the stairs of his house in Belvoir Terrace, was the physical pace of Hammond's life visibly abated. He and Margaret moved to a ground-floor flat off Chaucer Road, but he was still often to be seen in College, now walking with the aid of a stick, even if he could no longer act as chauffeur, on Wednesday evenings, for a colleague five years his senior. Now too came perhaps the heaviest blow to fall in his unusually serene life, when his daughter Caroline, whose distinction as a scholar of early Christianity had been recognised by her election to the Academy in 1994, died in the following year at the early age of 55: her husband and fellow-scholar Ernst Bammel, too, was to survive her by little more than a year. These were heavy losses, but Nick bore them with the same unshakeable calm as he had every physical or mental crisis. His continuing academic productivity was evidence of the unfailing happiness and support which he derived from Margaret and their four surviving children. Not long before his death, he completed the manuscripts of an edited translation of Aristotle's *Poetics* (since published by the Museum Tusculanum Press of the University of Copenhagen) and of a study of the tragedies of Aeschylus—not the first subjects to come to mind within his *oeuvre*, but in fact merely an extension of an earlier interest in Greek drama and especially dramatic production, on which he had periodically published since his Bristol days.[26]

His scholarly achievement, partly because it was utterly *sui generis*, is particularly difficult to evaluate. It was shaped by many untypical factors. His lifelong devotion to education, in every sense and at every level from the secondary onwards, gave it an unusual direction: until late in his life, much of his research had been driven by his teaching. His boldness in venturing into widely diverse branches of Classics,

---

[26] See 'Personal Freedom and its Limitations in the *Oresteia*', *Journal of Hellenic Studies*, 85 (1965), 42–55; 'The Conditions of Dramatic Production to the Death of Aeschylus', *Greek, Roman and Byzantine Studies*, 13 (1972), 387–450; 'Illustrations of Early Tragedy at Athens' (with Warren G. Moon), *American Journal of Archaeology*, 82 (1978), 331–50; 'Spectacle and Parody in Euripides' *Electra*', *Greek, Roman and Byzantine Studies*, 25 (1984), 51–61; 'More on Conditions of Production to the Death of Aeschylus', ibid., 29 (1988), 5–33.

together with his intensely personal view of the activity of research, is reflected in his own unclassifiable status; the fact that he had had no formal research supervisor of his own, nor was later in a position to attract a large following of research pupils, accentuated this. With little doubt, his best work was to be found in the fields where not only his exhaustive knowledge of the ancient sources, but also his personal virtues and experiences had full rein: the volume on Epirus, the trilogy on Macedonia and the best of his battle-reconstructions where he had walked over the landscape. Here the reader felt repeatedly in the presence of knowledge which none but the author possessed, and of a correspondingly sure judgement.

The same could hardly hold true for all his work: in his detailed reconstructions of central events in Greek political history, and especially in his source-criticism, there was more often a sense of the subjective and the arbitrary; of an orderly and definitive picture being offered where there was none to be had. At the same time, these qualities served him admirably as a writer of first-hand memoirs, and indeed of general historical works, where briskness and concision of style were at a premium. Supremely affable in his personal dealings, he was combative on paper, treating any dissident view as a direct challenge and hurrying into print to refute it. Of an earlier figure in Hellenic studies with whom Nick would never have dreamed of comparing himself, Arthur Evans, it was once written that 'He was always true to his principles, and always true, at the same time, to his own unconscious sense of the preeminent importance of the workings of his own mind.'[27] This judgement, which was that of Evans's own half-sister Joan, was not meant to disparage him: on the contrary, it was part of a tribute to, and an elaboration of, his essential integrity. Within limits, a parallel judgement could be applied to Hammond and his work. In his case, there is again no disparagement in saying that the greatness of the scholar could not quite match the greatness of the man.

By a happy piece of timing, Clare College organised a luncheon in his honour on 24 February 2001, attended by some 200 guests: among them were to be found representatives of the College entry of 1930, his first pupils, as well as current students of the class of 2000. Nick made a brisk, dignified response to the speeches. Exactly a month later, he was gone: pursuing one of his many enthusiasms, he was attending a concert in

---

[27] Joan Evans, *Time and Chance: Arthur Evans and his Forebears* (London, 1943), 351.

Jesus College with his wife and his daughter Alison when, on their way through the cloisters, he collapsed in their arms and died. It was an appropriate seal to his long life.

ANTHONY SNODGRASS
Fellow of the Academy

Note. In compiling this memoir, I have had the indispensable help, first and foremost of Nicholas Hammond's wife Margaret and his daughter Alison Skaer; then from F. W. Walbank, FBA, close friend and collaborator of his last twenty-five years; from Ernst Badian, FBA, Professor A. J. Graham and Dr David Blackman; and from John Northam, Timothy Smiley, FBA, and Gordon Wright, Fellows of Clare.

the official histories to completion should not be underestimated. He demonstrated qualities of persistence and patience which triumphed over what at times were serious efforts to persuade him to abandon the project altogether. He could occasionally be testy with those who failed to comprehend the hard realities in any situation—a fairly common occurrence in academic life, but that never affected the way in which he conducted business or thought about intellectual problems. It might be guessed that it was the results of both his historical output and his patience that eventually led to the offer of a knighthood which he felt he could accept.

Hinsley's second public career was carved out in academic life. Here there was a remarkable progression of apparent improbabilities: he became a Fellow of St John's College when he had no degree, not even a first degree, he fathered one of the most significant research schools of the twentieth century in international and diplomatic history without himself conducting basic research or proceeding to a Ph.D., and eventually he was to be elected Vice-Chancellor of the University of Cambridge when he had not yet actually been admitted to the Mastership of his College—an unheard of event, at least in modern times. The last of these was both a genuine improbability and a very wise move: Hinsley was always a highly competent, conservative in the true sense—occasionally parsimonious, and common-sensical administrator. It was probably as well for Cambridge that he was Vice-Chancellor during a particularly difficult period of straitened finances coming near the beginning of the long squeeze imposed by successive Cabinets on British universities during the last quarter of the twentieth century. He had some success in reducing costs within the University, but did not foresee how much worse the situation was going to become and that the University urgently needed to begin to raise funds from private sources.

The first two unlikelihoods, however, were the consequences of the war and the post-war educational emergency that arose as universities tried to cope with the arrival of a massive backlog of delayed student entry. A very large number of Hinsley's junior members of St John's College, Cambridge stretching from the 1940s to the 1970s are able to testify to the extraordinary personal relationship which they enjoyed with him either as undergraduate or graduate students or because he was their

---

1998). David Syrett (ed.), *The Battle of the Atlantic and Signals Intelligence: U-boats and trends, 1941–1945* (Aldershot, 1998). David Alvarez (ed.), *Allied and Axis Signals Intelligence in World War II* (London, 1999). See also the novel *Enigma* by Robert Harris (London, 1995).

tutor. He had an amazing memory for personal histories and in addition gave to each student his complete attention while they were at Cambridge. He never forgot any student he had taught or been tutor to and they never forgot their exposure to the way he thought about things and the often striking language and style of delivery he used to describe what he thought. They also never forgot the risk of personal annihilation which visiting him entailed. The threat came from showers of books which could and did fall from hopelessly overstressed and ancient shelves, themselves in evident danger of falling. He had the gift of total concentration on the person he was dealing with, whatever the circumstances, and was perfectly capable of forgetting that there were often other people waiting in his room during tutorial consultations. No one in more contemporary, privacy protecting, conditions would be likely to hear a fellow student asked, with evident interest and the usual slightly odd Hinslaic emphases, 'and what happened, my boy, *after* you set fire to the factory . . . ?' In short, he brought tremendous vigour and enthusiasm to every aspect of being a Cambridge don in his own time.

One important consequence of his vigour was the creation of the Centre for International Studies. Cambridge had never generated the kind of department of politics and/or international relations which became common in universities during the second half of the twentieth century. This meant that both teachers and students from several disciplines whose interests were essentially in the field of international relations broadly interpreted had no common place to pursue projects and exchange ideas. The connections between international history, international relations and international law would particularly benefit if some kind of common roof could be created. Hinsley, together with the eminent lawyer, Clive Parry, tried to arrange for this in a small way. They had no idea at the outset what was going to happen. The Centre was formed in 1975, existing under the wing of the History Faculty, and began to act as a central point for graduate students, interested dons and visiting fellows to exchange ideas and, a little later, to provide a home for a very small number of students taking a new one year M.Phil. degree in International Relations. Shortly afterwards the Chancellor of the University, Prince Philip, began to suggest that more work should be done in strategic studies, ideally by means of a separate Tripos. This suggestion was modified into a successful proposal that teaching in strategic studies should be funded by the Ministry of Defence and that a small cohort of talented senior officers should come to Cambridge each year to take the M.Phil. degree. This arrangement began in 1978 and at the same time, the think again. In *Power and the Pursuit of Peace*, Hinsley discusses efforts to achieve peaceful international relations both by philosophers and philanthropists, a unique account which takes up the first half of the book, and by the actual behaviour of governments up to and beyond the creation of the United Nations, which constitutes the second half. This is a book on a large scale, and it contains some of Hinsley's best writing: in particular the chapter on Kant in Part I, and the discussion of the causes of the Second World War in Part III. Partly because this structure enabled Hinsley to avoid complicated juxtapositions within single chapters, and partly because it contained straightforwardly useful information, students used to find the account of modern international relations in Parts II and III to be the most approachable, but parts of it have inevitably now become outdated. It is the discussion of international thought in the first half that has stood the test of time. Over and above that achievement, the book had another significance. The power of the interconnections that Hinsley created between the philosophical effort and the realities as they unfolded in international politics changed the way in which the subject of international relations in general was studied. It did not produce agreement about it—far from it—but it altered the intellectual basis of the discussion. It may be that his persistent refusal to acknowledge or use the quantitative techniques and methodological theories of political science limited the impact of his work, particularly overseas. But few scholars achieve such turning-points and Hinsley was one of them.

Hinsley's near passion for discussing the evolution of states, then the states' system, and his belief in the contemporary centrality of the state over the great issues of peace or war, or, as it became in his time, potential annihilation, can give the impression that he could only conceive of a state-centric world. He did so in the sense that what he observed about the world as he saw it and as it had been since the eighteenth century convinced him that it was indeed state dominated and controlled. He did not do so, however, as a general intellectual conviction. His most elegantly argued book, though also one of his more difficult discussions, *Sovereignty*, demonstrates this. Out of a finely wrought structure of tightly organised sentences the message clearly emerges that the man who wrote so powerfully about the significance of the fully sovereign state in modern international relations did not believe that sovereignty was inextricably bound up with the state, still less that it conferred upon states or the rulers of states special and overwhelming powers. It followed from the fact that 'for all men at all times, there has been no choice but to belong to a political community'[8] and that 'men will often in history have debated and quarrelled about who should rule and by what right.'[9] How they resolved that problem was subject to contemporary conditions and those conditions might produce the institutions of the state at some point and in fact did so, climaxing in the first half of the twentieth century. Even so, there were always limitations:

> At no time, in no society, has its identification with, or control over, the society been complete. Even under the regime of the state, the most powerful and effective of all the political institutions which societies have so far developed, and even under the rule of the most powerful of states, other institutions exist alongside it, men still speak of 'we' and 'they', and it is not uncommon for the society to limit the state by laying down fundamental rules by which it may or may not undertake certain tasks. . . . For while all societies, however, primitive, possess political institutions—we cannot say that every society must develop the state. Nor has every society yet developed it. We inhabit a world in which there still exist both stateless political societies and societies which are ruled by states. The distinction between the state and other political institutions is as decisive as is the distinction between a society and its political system.[10]

Similarly with nationalism: Hinsley is generally approving of the idea that nationalism is a state of mind in which

> political loyalty is felt to be owed to the nation [because i]t does not assume that when nationalism comes to exist where it did not exist before, it does so because men have discovered a political loyalty which they previously lacked. On the contrary, it implies that men have transferred to the nation the political loyalty which they previously gave to some other structure—that what has changed is not the quality of this loyalty but the object on which it is showered or the vehicle through which it is expressed.[11]

Here again, it is the machinery of change that has engaged Hinsley's attention rather than any one position in time.

It is worth drawing attention to these aspects of Hinsley's manner of thinking because they emphasise the way in which the consistency of his point of view allows his work to escape from any time-specific, issue-specific restriction. Except for the last chapters of *Power and the Pursuit of Peace*, which have been overtaken by events in specific instances, his work remains and will remain useful for building assessments of the very different conditions which are developing in the contemporary world.

---

[8] *Nationalism and the International System* (London, 1973), p. 11.
[9] *Sovereignty*, 2nd edn. (Cambridge, 1986), p. 27.
[10] *Sovereignty*, pp. 4–5.
[11] *Nationalism*, p. 11.

HARRY JOCELYN

Henry David Jocelyn
1933–2000

HENRY DAVID JOCELYN, the distinguished Australian Latinist, died on 22 October 2000 in Oxford. He was born on 22 August 1933 at Bega, a small town in southern New South Wales known for dairy farming, the first of four children of John Daniel Jocelyn and Phyllis Irene Jocelyn (née Burton), both native-born Australians. John Jocelyn was a police constable of the NSW Police Force, and Harry was born at home in a police residence attached to the court house and jail, where his father supervised low-risk prisoners. His mother was the daughter of another country policeman.

The family had colourful origins of a sort highly prized these days in Australia. John Jocelyn came from the Araluen and Majors Creek goldfields, where his family had settled in about 1860 after arriving from England in 1856. John's father too was Australian-born. From his mother's line Harry inherited a good deal of convict blood. Fifteen members of this side of the family, of both Irish and English origin, were convicts, traceable as far back as the First Fleet. They included a highway robber and a machine breaker, and several Irish patriots and petty thieves.

Harry (as he was always known) began school in Bega, but in the late war years his father became involved in an incident which was to work to his son's educational advantage. Bega, like many country towns of the time, was split on sectarian lines. The Jocelyn family were Protestants (despite Phyllis's strong Catholic links). Harry indeed had been admitted to the children's choir of St John's Church of England at a particularly early age because of his precocious reading ability. John Jocelyn accused

Proceedings of the British Academy, **120**, 277–299. © The British Academy 2003.

the local Catholic priest of running a crooked gambling establishment in his spare time, and refused to allocate him petrol coupons on the grounds that he was 'not performing an essential service'. Members of the Catholic Church organised a petition to have Jocelyn removed from Bega, and the Protestants for their part got up a petition to have him retained. The affair was investigated by the police authorities, and it was decided in the interests of local harmony that Jocelyn should be transferred to Sydney.

So it was that in late 1944 Harry found himself in Earlwood, in the western suburbs of Sydney. He briefly attended the Earlwood Primary School, and from there had the good fortune to move on to Canterbury Boys' High School in 1946. Canterbury, like various other state main-tained high schools scattered about Sydney at the time, was a selective school which drew bright boys from a wide catchment area. The school produced numerous academics, including classicists, as well as the odd politician. Its *alumni* include a Corresponding Fellow of the Academy (the late R. E. Emmerick). According to family tradition, Harry had since early childhood declared his intention of becoming a professor of Latin, after hearing of the exploits of a local worthy, Sir John Peden (1871–1946), who had gone on from Bega to take first-class honours in Latin at the University of Sydney (1892) and had taught briefly in the Department of Latin before becoming Challis Professor of Law. Peden was still active as President of the New South Wales Legislative Council when Harry was a boy in Bega, and was often spoken of locally. Anecdotes about Harry at this time stress his studiousness, and certainly later he paraded a lofty indifference to more typical Australian pursuits. Nevertheless, his brother Bill recalls being taken as a young boy by the fourteen-year old Harry to the Sydney Cricket Ground on the day in November 1947 when Bradman scored his hundredth hundred. At Canterbury Harry fell under the influence of Jack Gibbes, a Classics teacher of much learning and great enthusiasm. A man with prominent teeth and a craggy visage, Gibbes exuded eccentricity and enjoyed a reputation for a little stirring, qualities which appealed to the young Jocelyn. Harry was *dux* of the year throughout his time at Canterbury.

Jocelyn entered the University of Sydney in 1951, and graduated Bachelor of Arts in 1955, with first class honours and the University Medal in Greek and first class honours and the University Medal in Latin. University Medals are only rarely awarded, and it was a highly exceptional, perhaps unique, achievement that Jocelyn should have gained two in the same year.

The start of Jocelyn's long and eventful career as a controversialist can be traced back to his undergraduate days at Sydney. The pages of the student newspaper, *Honi Soit*, in this period are full of combative letters and articles under his name on a range of issues of the day, such as National Service training, religion, and the anti-communist hysteria during the McCarthy era.

In his first year as an undergraduate Jocelyn involved himself in a controversy which followed a public lecture on 'The University and religion' given by the Professor of Philosophy, John Anderson (1893–1962). Anderson was a notorious controversialist himself and several times the subject of questions in the state parliament after his public lectures, one of which began with an assertion that religion had no more place in education than a snake in Iceland. Anderson's criticism of the philosopher Whitehead for his theistic views provoked a furious response in *Honi Soit*. On 20 September 1951 Jocelyn entered the fray in an article entitled 'Belief in unbelief', in which he attacked one of Anderson's critics (a second-year student, Roderick Meagher, later to be a Judge of Appeal) and delivered some trenchant views on 'faith' and on the student Evangelical Union. The language reminds one of some of his later reviews, with one or two favourite words already in use. Typical attitudes are already apparent. 'Faith', he wrote, 'in the infallibility of one's beliefs betrays the doubt lurking beneath the theological verbiage and is merely a cover-up for the lack of evidence for them.' There is also a characteristic deployment of the outrageous: he admitted 'the possibility that unrepentant atheists, agnostics, and modernists roast in hell, while repentant murderers and thieves feast in heaven'. The affair rumbled on in the paper, with Jocelyn getting as good as he gave (a letter of 27 September refers to 'Mr Jocelyn's display of mental befuddlement') but constantly returning to the attack. Anderson seems to have been content to allow Jocelyn to speak on his behalf. The entry on Anderson in the *Australian Dictionary of Biography* (vol. 7) describes a character in many ways similar to Jocelyn himself.

Two years later, when a prominent Methodist clergyman, the Revd Alan Walker, brought the so-called Methodist 'Mission to the Nation' to Sydney University, Jocelyn was again moved to denounce Christian faith and to promote his own faith (in 'evidence'), in a piece entitled 'A rationalist looks at the Mission to the Nation' (17 September 1953). 'Perhaps the most objectionable feature of Mr Walker's apologetic', he said, 'is his emphasis on the need for faith. . . . We laugh at the faith of the gambler, but is it not for this very reason, that his hopes are not grounded on rational evidence?' 'The findings of astronomy', he went on, employing a clash of registers of a sort to which he often later resorted, 'would suggest that man is nothing more than a speck of sentient dung clinging to a recess of eternal and infinite space.' Alan Walker remained a sparring partner of Jocelyn's for a considerable time. A decade later, in the early 1960s when Jocelyn had returned from England, the pair took part in a public debate in the university on the subject of the historical Jesus. Walker's impassioned, faith-invoking peroration was countered by Jocelyn's parting shot, 'There is not enough evidence of the doings of Jesus to fill a respectable BA thesis.'

Australia was felt to be imperilled in the early 1950s, and National Service was compulsory. Students were drafted into the Sydney University Regiment and received training of a sort (described by Jocelyn in an article of the time as 'farcical') at Ingleburn, NSW. On 30 July 1953 we find Jocelyn publishing an attack (under the heading 'Does Army produce citizens or zombies?'), not so much on the institution of National Service itself, as on the notion that military training made one a good citizen. 'The army', he wrote, 'is incapable of teaching even civic morality, for murder and robbery are the chief subjects of the military curriculum. . . . Such a life is plainly the negation of citizenship and it is small wonder that the chief amusements of the soldier are the brothel and the tavern.' During the visit by the Queen soon after the Coronation, Jocelyn was deemed to be a 'security risk' because of his outspoken views on such matters, and he was accordingly placed in the back row of the guard of honour mounted by the Sydney University Regiment. Like several professors of Latin, he never learned to drive a car, and that failing he put down to his experiences as a trainee tank driver during National Service. A tank in his charge ran out of control, and he was henceforth classified as unfit for driving.

Jocelyn was not particularly political in later years,[1] though always ready to argue against someone else's position. He never voted in a British election, asserting that it was 'none of his business'. The writings of his in *Honi Soit* to which I have had access are for the most part not on political themes. An article of 26 March 1953, however, headed 'A Stalinoid speaks', objects in typical manner to another correspondent's 'belief in the possibility of defining clearly the black from the white in the present ideological confusion', and moves on to condemn the error of becoming 'hysterical and intolerant of everything savouring of communism' simply

---

[1] It was widely believed for some reason in Manchester University that he was a communist.

because of the crimes committed by individual communist officials. The article must have seemed outrageous at the time. It questions the methods adopted by the Western powers in the Cold War, appears to exonerate the traitor Fuchs, and suggests that the destruction wrought on innocent women and children in Korea 'gives us no ground for pride'.

Reading the pages of *Honi Soit* some fifty years on one is struck by the readiness of a student (Anderson's critic and Jocelyn's opponent) to take issue in direct terms with the Professor of Philosophy in print, by the strong language of the debate, and by Jocelyn's command at the age of eighteen of a form of invective which was to remain characteristic of him throughout his academic career. It has sometimes been said that in his reviews he was merely imitating Housman, but the style of his writings decades later is indistinguishable from that which he was already using in 1951.

When Jocelyn entered the University of Sydney the Professor of Latin was the Roman historian R. E. Smith (1910–78), who held the chair from 1946–53, before returning to England to the Chair of Ancient History at the University of Manchester (1953–74). Smith's influence on the course of Jocelyn's career was, many years later, to be profound. Smith was replaced by A. J. Dunston (1922–2000), who arrived from Reading in 1953 and maintained a lifelong connection with Jocelyn. A. H. McDonald (1908–79), Professor of 'Ancient World History', overlapped briefly with Jocelyn, who took History I in his first year. McDonald was in Sydney until 1951. It was probably G. P. Shipp (1900–80) who had the greatest influence on Jocelyn. Though he became Professor of Greek in 1954 and is known mainly for his writings on Greek language, Shipp was a member of the Latin department for half of the forty years he spent in the University. He had published (with A. B. Powe) a commentary on Livy book 22 in 1932, and, more significantly, a commentary on Terence's *Andria* in 1938 (second edition 1960), a work of modest scale which has many valuable observations on the language of comedy and on Latin usage in general. During Jocelyn's undergraduate years Shipp also published two important papers on the language of Plautus ('Greek in Plautus', *Wiener Studien*, 66 (1953), 'Plautine terms for Greek and Roman things', *Glotta,* 34, 1954–5). Jocelyn attended Shipp's class on Plautus, and decades later often spoke of Shipp's elucidation of this or that Plautine problem, including his decisive explanation of the odd expression *Athenis Atticis*. Neither Jocelyn nor this obituarist could remember what that explanation was, but agreed that it was decisive. Jocelyn had an abiding interest in Plautus, though unfortunately his commentary on the

Pseudolus was never completed. His edition of the tragedies of Ennius (see below) throughout displays the influence of Shipp's approach to the study of early Latin vocabulary. As recently as 1999 Jocelyn reverted to the subject of Shipp's first Plautine paper, in 'Code-switching in the Comoedia Palliata' (in *Rezeption und Identität*, ed. G. Vogt-Spira and B. Rommel).

After graduating Jocelyn was awarded the Cooper Travelling Scholarship in Classics by the University of Sydney, and he went in October 1955 to St John's College, Cambridge as an affiliated student. He graduated Bachelor of Arts in 1957, with starred first class honours in the second part of the Classical Tripos. At St John's he was a contemporary of F. R. D. Goodyear (1936–87). The pair saw eye to eye on most things, and shared certain characteristics. A long friendship ensued. Jocelyn was awarded the Sandys Studentship by the University of Cambridge in 1957 and the Craven Studentship in 1958. From 1957 to 1959 he was a scholar at the British School in Rome.

In the summer of 1957 Jocelyn began his Cambridge doctoral dissertation under the supervision of the Kennedy Professor of Latin, C. O. Brink (1907–94). He was to have a long and close friendship with Brink, whose obituary he wrote in this journal. In an obituary (in the Sicilian journal *Sileno*) of the Italian scholar Scevola Mariotti (1920–2000) which he completed shortly before his death, Jocelyn wrote revealingly of his early days as a research student. He was by late 1957 in Italy. As he puts it, 'what I wanted to do long remained unclear'. Otto Skutsch (1906–90), Professor of Latin at University College London, had advised him to read Mariotti's *Lezioni su Ennio* (1951), and he acquired a copy in a Roman bookshop. Soon afterwards he wrote to Mariotti and was invited to Urbino to meet him. The obituary contrasts the distaste Jocelyn felt for the attitudes he had encountered in Cambridge and at the British School with the appeal of Mariotti's approach to classical scholarship. 'Literary critics', he states, 'seemed to do no more than analyse their own feeling.' At the British School the prevailing atmosphere was 'odd', and marked by 'a certain hostility to letters, a wariness of history, . . . and a totally uncritical belief in the power of archaeology to answer serious questions about classical antiquity'. Mariotti, by contrast, in his first meeting with Jocelyn, 'made very clear his distaste for large judgement-laden literary syntheses and his fascination with apparently small problems capable of being defined and perhaps even solved. He emphasised . . . the need to study the authors who cite what we have of Ennius and the other early tragedians and to pay attention to the work of scholars who preceded Ribbeck and Vahlen.' Such talk, Jocelyn went on, gave special joy to 'one who had attended out of curiosity lectures by members of the Cambridge Faculty of English and listened with appalled disbelief to advocacy, sober and unsober, of the introduction of their approach to the Faculty of Classics'. The attitudes apparent here were those that governed the whole of Jocelyn's scholarly career. Literary criticism of the type which he felt to be 'judgement-laden', particularly if it were written in English and presented itself as a modern advance, he despised. His fine library contains few modern works written in English. His taste was for problems of detail, or, in a wider sense, for what he would call 'literary history'. He complied with Mariotti's exhortation to consult earlier scholarship when investigating any problem, and his articles are heavily burdened with citations of early editions. In conversation he would often pour scorn on modern scholars who were merely rediscovering what had been discovered long ago. His own work on fragments and his reviews of others' editions of fragmentary authors show a mastery of ancient grammatical writers and their methods of citation. Above all, Jocelyn's regard for Continental, including Italian, classical scholarship goes back to his days in Italy, though Brink and Skutsch were also influential. Jocelyn rarely attended conferences in England (though he made an exception of the Liverpool/Leeds Latin Seminar, which attracted numerous scholars from abroad), but was constantly performing at gatherings on the Continent. Between 1989 and 1995, for instance, he delivered a total of fifty-one papers, thirty-four in Italy and only four in Britain. He reserved his fiercest reviews for works written in English, whether by British or American scholars, and was usually somewhat milder when dealing with Italian works. Throughout his career Jocelyn visited Italy frequently, and maintained friendships with a number of Italian scholars in addition to Mariotti, including S. Timpanaro, A. La Penna, M. Geymonat, P. Gatti, G. Salanitro, and S. Prete. In Germany he was on friendly terms with E. Lefèvre at Freiburg, who published a tribute to him after his death,[2] G. Vogt-Spira at Greifswald, the ancient medical historian K.-D. Fischer in Mainz, and various scholars at the *Thesaurus Linguae Latinae* in Munich (see below).

Jocelyn's doctoral dissertation was submitted in 1961 and he took the degree in 1963. The revised dissertation was published in 1967 by Cambridge University Press as *The Tragedies of Ennius*, a work which has achieved the status of a classic and is cited as the standard edition of the

---

[2] In U. Auhagen (ed.), *Studien zu Plautus'* Epidicus (Tübingen, 2001), pp. 11–12 (with photograph).

fragments. The edition displays a formidable knowledge of the Greek sources of Ennius and a close attention to the contexts in which the fragments are cited by ancient authors. Each of the major fragments is introduced by a discursive essay which analyses the form of the citation and the metrical features of the fragment, and reviews in magisterial fashion earlier interpretations of the passage. Jocelyn then proceeds to a discussion of the phraseology of each of the verses. A marked feature of these linguistic discussions is the constant attempt to distinguish within the category 'Republican drama' between the language of comedy and that of contemporary tragic fragments. Some notable distinctions emerge. Jocelyn always sought if he could to elucidate the language of Republican authors by restricting himself to illustrative material from the Republic itself. This method is to be seen clearly in one of his latest papers, on Catullus ('The arrangement and the language of Catullus' so-called *polymetra*', in *Aspects of the Language of Latin Poetry* (1999) (*Proceedings of the British Academy*, 93)).

Jocelyn was not a writer of books. The edition of Ennius was the only book he wrote, though an annotated translation done in collaboration with B. P. Setchell of two seventeenth-century medical treatises, *Regnier de Graaf on the Human Reproductive Organs* (Supplement xvii, *Journal of Reproduction and Fertility* (1972)), is of book length (on which see below). Apart from these works, his publications comprise on a rough count fifty-six papers in books, conference proceedings and *Festschriften*, eighty-six articles in journals, and 131 reviews, many of them of article length. He also edited jointly with various others a collection of essays in honour of C. O. Brink (1989), selected papers of F. R. D. Goodyear (1992), and a notable volume in honour of John Pinsent (*Tria Lustra*, 1993). It is noticeable that, after the first decade or so of his writing career, during which he regularly contributed to the standard anglophone refereed journals, he turned increasingly to less prestigious journals run by his friends. After 1979 he contributed more than forty items to the *Liverpool Classical Monthly*, which had been founded by his friend Pinsent, and from the late 1980s more than a dozen papers to the Sicilian journal *Sileno*, which was edited by another friend, Salanitro. He fell into the habit of denouncing Anglo-Saxon refereed journals, asserting that the opinion of a learned editor (particularly if he were German or Italian) was worth more than the collective opinion of a committee of 'referees'. In the obituary of Mariotti referred to earlier Jocelyn noted with approval Mariotti's willingness to 'honour with a textual note the humble [journal] as much as the mighty'.

In 1960 Jocelyn was appointed to a lectureship in Latin at the University of Sydney. He was rapidly promoted, to a senior lectureship in 1964, a readership in 1966, and to a personal chair in 1970. In 1970 he was elected a Fellow of the Australian Academy of the Humanities, and he became a member of the council in 1972. He was not infrequently away from Sydney, and in the winter semester of 1967 he went as a visiting professor to the Department of Classics, Yale University.

In 1965 Jocelyn was back in Cambridge, on sabbatical leave from Sydney. He launched himself into controversy again, this time by means of a review published in *The Cambridge Review* (20 February 1965) of the Greek play of the year, Sophocles' *Oedipus tyrannus*. The review was signed only with the initials 'HDJ'. Jocelyn began with some strong remarks about the wooden acting ('The actors were clearly not told that they had some duty to give the audience their money's worth in entertainment . . . They achieved the gentility of a public school recitation'), then turned his attention to a favourite theme, the defective pronunciation of the ancient languages perpetrated by some products of the British public school system. A. H Robinson, a lecturer in Latin at Sydney during Jocelyn's student days, had been a notorious stickler for the reformed pronunciation of Latin, and his attitudes had rubbed off on Jocelyn. 'The enunciation of the Greek', Jocelyn wrote in his review, 'was a disgrace to a great centre of classical learning . . . the ludicrous practice of accenting Greek words as if they were Latin ones and shifting the accent when necessary to suit an imagined "ictus" of the verse offends both the philological conscience and the sensitive ear. . . . The actors of the Cambridge *Oidipous* emitted a meaningless gabble pausing for the most part only when they needed breath.'

The review greatly offended the Regius Professor of Greek, D. L. Page (1908–78), who wrote an irate letter to the magazine on 27 February, in which he affected not to know the identity of 'HDJ' (though he had taught Jocelyn a few years earlier). He described the reviewer's style as 'arrogant' and his spirit as 'uncharitable', and asserted that his 'statements [were] a mixture of the shallow and the ill-informed'. He exhorted the reader not to pay 'serious attention' to HDJ's 'diatribe on the pronunciation of Greek', claiming that 'none of us knows the answers'.

That was not the end of the affair. On 6 March there appeared a long letter from R. D. Dawe taking the side of Jocelyn against Page in no uncertain terms. Dawe defended a good deal of Jocelyn's invective, not least in the matter of pronunciation of Greek. 'The strange bleating noises', Dawe wrote, 'and the frequent stress on words corresponding neither with any metrical nor any accentual principle made the greater part of the play incomprehensible for many of us.' Jocelyn had his final say in a letter of the same day, in which, having noted the reactions to his review, he opined that the audiences of the play had 'got what they deserved'.

Jocelyn was not to remain long in the University of Sydney after his remarkably early elevation to a personal chair. By the end of 1973 he had moved to the Hulme Chair of Latin in the University of Manchester, a move which was to initiate a colourful period in the history of the subject in that institution. The circumstances of his appointment are somewhat obscure. At the time the Professor of Latin was G. B. Kerferd (1915–98), another Australian, but (perhaps significantly) a native of Melbourne. Kerferd, a Greek philosopher and not a Latinist, had held a senior lectureship in Manchester in the 1950s and from there had moved on to the Chair of Classics in Swansea. In 1967, following the retirement of the Hulme Professor of Latin, W. H. Semple (1900–81), he returned to Manchester as Professor of Latin. His professorial colleague was H. D. Westlake (1906–92), who held the Hulme Chair of Greek until his retirement in 1972. Kerferd's appointment, despite his lack of credentials in Latin, was justified on the grounds of administrative need, as the Department in Manchester was not flourishing and Kerferd had built up a reputation as a good organiser at Swansea. When Westlake retired, Kerferd (perhaps against his will) was moved sideways to the Chair of Greek, and the University set about finding a new Professor of Latin. At the time the University of Manchester did not advertise chairs. It was believed, in the words of the Vice-Chancellor, Sir William Mansfield Cooper (1903–92), as recorded in the Council Minutes for 15 July 1964, 'that in many cases it would be to the disadvantage of the University to advertise vacant chairs'. It is not known whether Jocelyn was the first person approached, but when he was it was undoubtedly through the influence of his old Sydney professor, R. E. Smith. Remarkably, Jocelyn was appointed from Australia without being summoned for interview.

At the time of his appointment Jocelyn's output numbered some fifteen articles, several reviews and the book on Ennius, and there were as well some items in press, including the translation of de Graaf. There was little sign in print at this time of the remarkable breadth of his interests. In this early period his research lay mainly in early Republican poetry and its reception and citation in the late Republic and beyond. Some of his best work dates from this period. I refer to two articles on 'Ancient scholarship and Virgil's use of Republican Latin poetry' (*Classical Quarterly*, 14 (1964), 15 (1965)), the 'The quotations of Republican drama in Priscian's treatise

De metris fabularum Terentii' (*Antichthon*, 1 (1967)), and particularly to weighty pieces on 'The poems of Quintus Ennius', in *Aufstieg und Niedegang der römischen Welt*, I. 2, and on 'Greek poetry in Cicero's prose writings' (*Yale Classical Studies*, 23 (1973)). Jocelyn always had an interest in the state religion of Rome, and his early article 'The Roman nobility and the religion of the Republican state' (*Journal of Religious History*, 4 (1966)) is something of a classic, though he himself was wont to disown it in later years.

The edition of de Graaf is little known among classicists, but regarded as important in some scientific circles. At the 190th meeting of the Society for Endocrinology held at the Royal College of Physicians in London in November 1999 a speaker singled the work out for high praise. As a piece of classical scholarship it is a minor masterpiece. The annotations comprise in part material of a physiological kind written by Setchell, and in part notes by Jocelyn on the Greek and Latin sexual terminology of de Graaf. Though Jocelyn's notes are short, he ranged widely, and always traced the terminology back to antiquity. The appearance of the work just at the time when Jocelyn arrived in Manchester was a foreshadowing of things to come.

Jocelyn fell out with Kerferd right from the start, and at the same time conceived a loathing for the University of Manchester which was never to fade. Local opinion had it that the old rivalry between Sydney and Melbourne was merely surfacing in another place, but that is no explanation of the prolonged discord that was about to begin. Jocelyn was put off by what he regarded as the pomposity and self importance of Manchester at that time. Scarcely had he arrived when he was summoned by his predecessor but one, Semple (a pupil of A. E. Housman), and advised that, as a 'Manchester Professor', he should equip himself at once with a hat and waistcoat. Jocelyn in return offered Semple an offprint of his magisterial paper on Ennius, but was rebuffed with the remark that there 'would be no time for that sort of thing henceforth'. Jocelyn alleged that Kerferd would stand about at street corners in Didsbury in the early morning, hoping to intercept him en route to the bus stop so that trifling matters of departmental administration could be discussed on the bus. He was forced to vary his route and time of departure. He would be dragged out of the library, he claimed, to settle some insignificant question to do with who should lecture in what room, and was being driven to distraction by the relentless persistence of his colleague. Virtually everything about the University annoyed him. There was, for example, the affair of the bells, in which he happened to score a minor success. Throughout the day and night during both term and vacation preset electric bells reverberated around the Faculty of Arts on the hour marking the theoretical start and finish of lectures. Visiting seminar speakers, unaware of the system, were often disconcerted. Many came to a full stop in mid-sentence, thinking that their time was up, though one outsider, 'speaking on Libanius at Libanian length',[3] soldiered on through several pealings to deliver the longest paper on record to the Manchester branch of the Classical Association. Jocelyn tabled a motion at the Faculty of Arts that 'the Dean should dismantle the bells and buzzers'. At a Faculty meeting an earnest debate took place, the matter went to a vote, and it was resolved that the bells should be silenced, with the Dean nevertheless insisting that he would not climb a ladder to do it himself.

Jocelyn's main complaint (surely a reasonable one) was that Kerferd, his immediate predecessor as Professor of Latin, was, against all academic precedent, still in post and taking an obtrusive interest in the teaching of Latin and in the administration of the Latin department. When Jocelyn arrived in Manchester he found a departmental structure in Classics which was somewhat confused, to say the least. On the surface before 1973 there had been a single Department of Latin and Greek. In the annual reports of Council to Court, to which departments were required to submit a statement of their activities for the year, Greek and Latin appear to have been treated as a unity until 1973, whereas the University Calendars fail to make the structure clear. The reality was probably somewhat different from the impression conveyed by the reports to Court. Senior Lecturers and Readers were permitted to lecture on one language only, and the Professors of Greek and Latin equally did not intrude into each other's territory. The consequence (on one interpretation) was that de facto there were two departments of Greek and Latin; and ancient history for its part was taught in the Department of History. This arrangement was formalised after February 1973, when the University's *Supplemental Charter and Statutes* came into force. The Senate minutes for 1 March 1973 reported that Senate would recommend that separate departments for Greek and Latin be created under Statute XIV (1) of the new Charter, and this recommendation was in due course implemented.

There were, though, complicating factors. First, Kerferd, noting, as others have noted before and since, that classicists were scattered across numerous departments of the University without ever coming into contact, had attempted to set up a 'School of Classical Studies' to embrace

---

[3] So David Bain, who was present.

in an informal union all the classicists in the University. The 'School' never became a concrete reality, except in the heading of the notepaper on which Kerferd wrote all his letters. Jocelyn took immediate exception to the word 'School', and soon after his arrival he circulated a statement that 'the Department of Latin has withdrawn from the School of Classical Studies, and the headmaster has been informed'. Secondly, there was an expectation on the ground that, though there were now formally two departments, the group of classicists would for the most part act as a unity. Jocelyn was having none of that. At the University of Sydney Greek and Latin had by long tradition been completely distinct, and Jocelyn set about replicating that arrangement in Manchester in line with the Senate's recommendation referred to above. He insisted that there should be two Departmental Boards (another creation of the new Charter), one for Latin and one for Greek, each with its own chairman and secretary, and that the Boards should meet separately. The result was that a meeting of the Greek Board would be followed on the same after-noon by a meeting of the Latin Board, the two meetings having much the same agenda and with much the same personnel present. Jocelyn quite properly took no interest in the Greek board, but Kerferd had a keen desire to be added to the Latin board.

A proposal to this effect was put to the Faculty of Arts by the secre-tary of the Latin board. Jocelyn heatedly opposed the motion at a faculty meeting, arguing that Kerferd had no right to inclusion, not because he had ceased to be Professor of Latin, but because there were doubts about his Latinity. The argument did not go down well with the embarrassed gathering sitting in the presence of the University's previous Professor of Latin, and the motion was carried by a large majority. This decision by the Faculty, which formalised an arrangement whereby a professor was virtually overseen by his predecessor, was to keep Jocelyn and Kerferd in close combat for the rest of Kerferd's tenure of the Greek chair. The Dean was urged by the meeting to use his 'good offices' to attempt to reconcile the pair, but it was to no avail.

As one of the authors of the edition of de Graaf referred to above and the sole author of the notes on sexual terminology therein Jocelyn could justly claim to have been the founder of the 'Manchester school' dedi-cated to the study of ancient obscenity which flourished particularly in the 1980s and eventually came to the attention of the national press.[4]

---

[4] See 'This England', *The New Statesman*, 7 Jan. 1983.

Again the influence of his old teacher G. P. Shipp can be detected. Shipp had long had an informal interest in such matters, and in 1977 had published (in *Antichthon*, 11) a short note in which he drew attention to several examples of the verb λαικάζω in Greek magical papyri from which the meaning of the word could be deduced. Jocelyn took the matter up himself in a long paper ('A Greek indecency and its students. λαικάζειν' (*Proceedings of the Cambridge Philological Society*, 206 (1980)) often described as 'magisterial', in which he produced some new evidence and offered a comprehensive discussion of ancient and later interpretations of the verb. Between 1980 and 1985 he published some eight papers on ancient sexual terminology, the majority of them in *Liverpool Classical Monthly*, of which one ('Eupla laxa landicosa', *LCM*, 5 (1980), 153), in homage to Housman's 'Praefanda', was written in Latin. Jocelyn was usually sceptical about the attempts of some literary critics to find sexual puns in unlikely places, and this scepticism is nicely exemplified in 'On some unnecessarily indecent interpretations of Catullus 2 and 3', in *American Journal of Philology*, 101 (1980). *Liverpool Classical Monthly*, as its title suggests, gave contributors the chance to publish their thoughts without the reflection imposed by more conventional forms of publication. Jocelyn, typically, welcomed this opportunity for instant controversy. He also managed at this time to cross swords with the editors of *Supplementum Epigraphicum Graecum* on a matter to do with obscenities, accusing them of 'prissiness' in not indexing examples of βινεῖν and πυγίζειν. An indignant response by the editors in *SEG*, 31 (1981), no. 362 asserted that the words had been omitted 'through carelessness and not because of the "prissiness of professional epigraphists"'. Thereafter *SEG* always indexed such words. Jocelyn's use of the quaint word 'indecency' for four-letter words and their equivalents in other languages was, incidentally, a typical stylistic quirk, of which there were numerous. He was, for example, unwilling in later years to call the poems of Catullus 'poems', but preferred to see them as 'items'. The plays of Plautus were always 'scripts', and the characters in them 'personages'. Another favourite was 'wind-bag', which was reserved for literary critics and anyone in a position of authority at Manchester.

Jocelyn made a big impact, for the good, in his long stay in Manchester. He managed to generate a scholarly atmosphere in unpromising surroundings (on one occasion he wrote of the 'Boeotian gloom' of the University, and on another declared that the place 'stank of Methodism') and, years before the Research Assessment Exercise was devised, to encourage with a marked generosity of spirit the research of those of his colleagues who were interested in such things. Long before every department in the country had to have its 'seminar', Jocelyn introduced at Manchester a remarkable seminar series which he entitled 'Topics in current research'. The series ran from January 1974 until the end of 1982. Speakers were required to submit a detailed summary of their papers, with bibliography, two weeks in advance, and then to endure a grilling, particularly from Jocelyn himself, at the end of the paper. Numerous memorable papers were delivered by a nice mixture of senior figures from various parts of the world, and younger scholars. Jocelyn had an eye for those who would make a name for themselves. Many papers foreshadowed significant publications. The second paper, for example, was delivered by A. K. Bowman on 14 March 1974, on the subject 'Latin writing tablets from Vindolanda'. Bowman's summary begins: 'The site of Vindolanda, a mile and a half south of Hadrian's Wall, has yielded . . . a collection of wooden writing-tablets far more extensive and important than any hitherto discovered'; twenty-eight years later a third volume of Vindolanda tablets is about to appear. Jocelyn himself read a number of papers over the years, starting with 'Interpolation and misattribution of parts in Plautus, *Pseudolus* 1052–1245' (1974), which dates from a time when he was actively writing the commentary on the *Pseudolus*. The seminar was wide-ranging. Notable contributors included G. Zuntz on the text and interpretation of a gold leaf from Valentia in southern Italy (1975), F. R. D. Goodyear on Tacitus and Virgil (1976), O. Skutsch on some problems in the *Annales* of Ennius (1976), C. R. Dodwell on the illustrated copies of Terence (1978), R. L. Hunter on the *Ecclesiazusai* and fourth century comedy (1978), K. M. Coleman on Statius, *Siluae*, IV. 7 (1978), J. A. Crook and J. G. Wolf on the Murecine tablets (1980) and D. C. Feeney on the speeches of the Virgilian Aeneas (1982). The winding up of the seminar in 1982 seems in retrospect to have marked a decline in Jocelyn's interest in the department, and he was in any case soon to fall ill (see below).

Many who participated in the seminar would probably agree that, long after the memories of their paper had receded, they retained a clear recollection of the hospitality that followed. Harry had married Margaret Jill Morton, herself a graduate in Latin of Sydney University, in Rome on 22 October 1958 while he was a scholar at the British School. Seminar speakers were splendidly entertained in the evening at the Jocelyn household in Didsbury along with a few members of the audience. The heated discussions of the paper were quickly forgotten, as Harry and Margaret were extremely hospitable. A choice Australian wine or two usually came forth, along with an Italian. Towards the end of the evening, however, Jocelyn would almost inevitably get worked up on some scholarly point.[5] Margaret, who appeared never to notice such outbursts, would withdraw unobtrusively to make the coffee as he pulled volume after volume from the bookshelves to demonstrate his point.

Jocelyn gave considerable attention to undergraduate teaching, and to the planning of the Latin courses. His own lectures on a wide range of Latin authors were always individually described in some detail before-hand and advertised on the notice board. He oversaw the construction of a Latin literature course which compelled students during their three years to read in the original language something of all the major literary genres (prose as well as verse), and introduced them to texts spanning the period from Plautus to the fourth century AD. Jocelyn firmly believed that students should be given what he called 'coverage' and he viewed as grossly self-indulgent those departments whose members taught only their 'research interests'. He showed a kindness towards and tolerance of students which contrasted with the more rigorous standards which he applied when dealing with academics. He was always much liked by the young.

Jocelyn was never as influential in Manchester academic politics as he might have been if he had acquired, at least in a metaphorical sense, the hat and waistcoat recommended by Semple. He was, however, a figure of standing in the eyes of several Vice-Chancellors, not least after he was elected to the Academy in 1982. His uncompromising public snipings on this or that matter of principle several times scored a direct hit. Perhaps most notably, he made his views felt about the University's decision to sell at auction in 1988 some alleged duplicate volumes from the John Rylands collection. The University house magazine *This Week* carried an article on 25 April 1988 under the tasteless heading 'Sale of the Century', which gloated over the fact that the sale had raised £1.6 m for a new 'research institute', and that a first edition of *Hypnerotomachia Poliphili* of 1499, which had belonged to a distinguished sixteenth-century collector, Jean Grolier, had sold for £170,000. Jocelyn wrote as follows on 9 May to the magazine: 'Your readers might have been given the names and the appointments of those who "made public protests against the sale and stirred up a brief flurry in the press". More importantly, they might have been told something about the controversy that surrounds the word

---

[5] According to David Bain, he would regularly thump the table in annoyance for the first time on the stroke of 11 p.m.

"duplicate" where early printed books are concerned. . . . The vulgar triumphalism of language like "sale of the century" must embarrass even some of those who think the sale justified.' The article in *This Week* had failed to point out that the opponents of the sale included the former librarian, the editor of the *Book Collector*, and probably one of the former Vice-Chancellors, who regarded the sale as a breach of faith.

Most of Jocelyn's voluminous publications were written in Manchester, and I here select a few significant items to bring out the diversity of his interests and the nature of his achievements.

Jocelyn was always at his most assured when dealing with questions to do with the editing of fragments, and some of his articles and reviews will be essential reading for any future editor of the texts in question. I single out here from many the formidable paper 'On editing the remains of Varro's *Antiquitates Rerum Diuinarum*' (*Rivista di filologia e de istruzione classica*, 108 (1980)), which is in fact a (largely favourable) review article.

He had a profound knowledge of Republican literature, and within that field his papers on Plautus, many of which foreshadow the edition of the *Pseudolus* which was never completed, bulk large. The paper 'Anti-Greek elements in Plautus' *Menaechmi*' (*Papers of the Liverpool Latin Seminar Fourth Volume*, 1984) has some typical elements. A mass of material to do with attitudes to Greeks in Roman comedy is assembled which is important on any count. There is also a general thesis, that the anti-Greek elements in the play do not merely reflect general Roman attitudes imported into the play by Plautus, but are meant to replace an Athenian attitude to western Greeks which had supposedly been present in the (lost) Greek original that Plautus was rendering into Latin. The thesis is somewhat speculative. It was a direct reaction against the arguments of a paper which had recently appeared, and in that it was not untypical. Jocelyn found it difficult to accept even the most convincing solution to a problem, and he would constantly come up with an alternative view of his own. In the process he would often deploy a vast range of evidence which was interesting in its own right, even if it did not establish decisively the alternative that he was advancing. Some other significant Plautine pieces include a series of three on the indirect tradition of the *Pseudolus*, a paper on language and characterisation ('Sprache, Schriftlichkeit und Charakterisierung in der römischen Komödie (Plautus *Pseudolus*, 41–73, 998–1014)', in G. Vogt-Spira, ed. *Beiträge zur mündlichen Kultur der Römer* (1993)) and, perhaps most importantly, 'The unpretty boy of Plautus' *Pseudolus* (767–789)', in E. Stärk and G. Vogt-Spira, eds *Dramatische Wäldchen. Festschrift für Eckard Lefèvre* words had. I once accused him of being overcritical of a distinguished book which he had reviewed, and he replied with just a trace of discomfort that his review had been 'favourable'. Some of his reviews were downright unfair, and on occasions he seemed to get it into his head against all reason that a book was bad. Several reviews prompted responses, either from the victim or from a supporter, and I have heard the odd rumour of threats of legal action.

In Manchester Jocelyn (like most of the rest of his colleagues) never had a research student in the conventional sense. Few undergraduates carried on, and in those days those who did were encouraged to move on to the superior facilities of Oxford or Cambridge. Nevertheless a number of younger scholars, such as Kathleen Coleman, Danuta Shanzer, Anna Chahoud, and Peter Kruschwitz, sought him out or came his way, and with these, as with his colleagues in Manchester, John Briscoe, David Bain, and myself, he was immensely generous both of his time and learning. It was an experience to submit a piece of work to him. The manuscript would come back defaced by abusive comments and expostulations, often written in bold black ink. Some of these comments would turn out to be irrelevant, but all were thought-provoking, and the paper inevitably had to be revised.

An obituary of Jocelyn by Frances Muecke which appeared in the *Sydney Morning Herald* on 28 November 2000 states that he 'believed that controversy was part of the life-blood of philology'. Perusing his articles and reviews one might indeed be tempted to come to such a conclusion, but I would not put it quite that way. He was incorrigibly provocative and counter-suggestible. Certainly the sentence with which he began a paper at a conference held in Manchester in 1993 on the development of Latin syntax reflected schoolboyish mischief-making rather than a philological method. Jocelyn, who spoke last at the two-day gathering, began with the words, 'I have listened without enlightenment to the papers so far delivered at this conference.' But the sentence had been composed and typed up three weeks before the conference took place. The secretary who typed it had left the paper lying in an out-tray exposed to public view, and there was not a member of the audience who was not anticipating the opening words. They brought the house down, much to Jocelyn's bewilderment.

Jocelyn was a character larger than life. He was warm hearted and amusing and extremely loyal to his friends, of whom there were many, and equally he inspired great affection and loyalty in those with whom he came into close contact. His savage reviews give a false impression of the man, and no one who knew him could ever take his outbursts very seriously. He was in fact easy to get on with. Whatever might have been thought of him in Manchester, he enjoyed and still enjoys a high reputation in classical circles in Italy and Germany. It may be some time before his achievements as one of the foremost Latin scholars of his time can be properly assessed, as his articles are scattered far and wide and in many cases difficult of access. A collection of some of his major pieces would reveal important contributions to the study of a very wide range of Latin authors, particularly but not exclusively of the Republic, and particularly in some of the less fashionable genres. If a text was in Latin, he was interested in it, whatever its content. Virgil perhaps alone of the major writers of verse did not elicit much interest from him, and that was because he was scornful of the deferential attitude of some British scholars to the poet. It is to be regretted that he did not finish the commentary on the *Pseudolus*, because hardly anyone is competent as he was to write a serious commentary on a play of Plautus. But he was well aware of what he was doing in confining himself to reviews and articles. About fifteen years ago he told me one day that Charles Brink had been urging him recently to stop doing reviews and articles and to get on with the commentary. He had replied that he intended to go on doing what interested him.

Jocelyn is survived by his widow, Margaret, and two sons, Luke and Edmund.

J. N. ADAMS,
Fellow of the Academy

Note. I am grateful to the following for help of one sort or another: David Bain, John Briscoe, Anna Chahoud, Kathleen Coleman, John Crook, John Croyston, Roger Dawe, Cynthia Dean, Lyle Eveille, Mario Geymonat, Bernard Gredley, Ellen Gredley, Nicholas Horsfall, Celia Jenkinson, Bill Jocelyn, Margaret Jocelyn, Vincent Knowles, Peter Kurschwitz, Guy Lee, Christopher Lowe, Joan Mackie, Bruce Marshall, Frances Muecke, Alanna Nobbs, Suzy Nunes (Reference Archivist, University of Sydney), James Peters (University/Medical Archivist, University of Manchester), Brian Pullan, Bob Sinclair, Christopher Stray.

with ambitions to become a librarian but, being told that that 'was not for the likes of for her', had left at thirteen to earn her living as a shop assistant. At least she had avoided 'going into service', which she would have considered a catastrophe. 'Never do other people's work for them!' had been her mother's advice, which she made a rule for life. But the Thomas family's support was strong and all through his schooldays Henry was to lunch with 'Granny Thomas' in the house in Donald Street near Roath Park where she lived with her widowed daughter, Bertha Prendergast, and the three Prendergast children.

Henry had therefore been born into an extended family, very firmly localised in one neighbourhood of Cardiff. It was to be his foundation and his springboard. After a few years in nearby rented accommodation, his parents (very much it would seem at his mother's instigation) made the momentous decision in 1928 to purchase, with the aid of a twenty-year mortgage of £500, their own house for £650. They settled in what was then still the village of Llanishen, on the northern edge of Cardiff, a twenty-minute bus-ride from Roath. In a world of limited communications (neither the Loyn, nor the Thomas families had telephones) this seemed to the rest of the family a step beyond civilisation. Granny Thomas, for example, was to visit the Llanishen house just once in twelve years. Money for the Loyns was always tight—his father never earned more than £4 a week—and of course they never owned a motorcar. His father smoked, but drank very little. His mother, Vi, managed the family finances with great caution. Henry was their first and only child. She seems to have suffered from post-natal depression after his birth and decided that thereafter there would be no further children. But his parents remained devoted to each other and to their son. Henry was brought up in the security of a happy home. Social life chiefly centred upon the large Loyn and Thomas families, but Henry also remembered evenings of Meccano and stamps, of card playing and chess with his father. His parents were not churchgoers. Vi was a true blue Tory and Henry believed that his father, despite some liberal sympathies, always voted Tory. It seems clear that their dearest wish was to enable their son to better himself and have opportunities that they had missed.

Schooling

With that background the five-year old Henry, already knowing his letters and able to read, joined the infants' class at Roath Park primary school in autumn 1927. Many of Henry's cousins had preceded him there and, once his parents had moved out to Llanishen during his second year at Roath Park, Henry took the bus there each day, going for his lunch to Granny Thomas's. Henry soon graduated to the more academic ('A') classes and in year 4 to the 'scholarship class', where the bright pupils were nurtured. Henry, who was quick at arithmetic and loved reading, was lucky in his teachers and in his fellow pupils. In his last year, when he was eleven, boys from Roath Park took the top four places in the city's annual scholarship exam for grammar school places (with Henry coming fourth) and another Roath boy in ninth place. The school's remarkable success was celebrated in the local press.

By entering Cardiff High School in September 1933, something that only one of his many cousins had achieved, Henry began to fulfil his parents' ambitions. There he found himself in a highly competitive Anglicising institution, which provided middle-class boys of the city with an education closely modelled upon English public schools, but without the boarding element. Henry was one of the youngest in his year and his progress was steady. Like his fellows, he lost his Cardiff accent and learnt how to keep out of trouble. He was relatively weak in Physics and Biology, but his interests in English, Latin, and Maths sustained him. He enjoyed playing cricket for the juniors, but disliked rugby, where his great height—he was already six feet by the age of fourteen—made him ungainly. His chief passion was chess. He was the school's best player from his second year and under the guidance of the classics master (Mr Michaels) he served both as secretary and captain of the chess club, organising matches with other schools from Cardiff, Newport, and Bridgend. In the sixth form he concentrated on English, History and (perhaps ill-advisedly) French. He might have done better to continue with Latin, but was reluctant to start Greek, which budding classicists were expected to take up at that stage. He joined the Air Squadron and played tennis, squash, and fives for the school. Though sharing his family's conservative political support for Baldwin, Chamberlain, and the appeasers, he had enough contact with several of the Jewish boys and teachers in the school to be aware of the shame of Munich and of the dangers of Fascism. In the Higher School Certificate in summer 1939 at the age of just seventeen he attained excellent grades in English and History and passed in French with oral proficiency. These results secured him a local scholarship to University College, Cardiff, but the decision was taken that he should rather stay on for a third sixth-form year in the High School and sit for Oxford scholarships in the winter. He became Deputy all. So, in October 1942, Henry resumed his course at University College, though initially the aim was just to cope physically. Almost all his school and college friends were now in uniform; Hilda had graduated in June and then married her Dutchman. Henry also had very little money; the £20 scholarship, though supplemented by his aunts and a kind neighbour, left little for paper, let alone for books. His doctor's orders were to do no more than two hours of academic work a day. His hope was to qualify for a Pass Degree, but in the event his results in June 1943 secured his entry into the final year of English Honours.

A holiday job was essential and Henry was delighted to secure one as a 'holiday master' in a Jewish boys' public school, Whittingeham, which had evacuated from Brighton to rural Carmarthenshire. Some pupils were unable to go home in the holidays, so Henry was paid £4 per week and his keep for relatively light duties supervising games and scouting, organising bird-watching, fishing, theatrical performances, and concerts. The countryside was a naturalist's paradise and Henry's skill at chess and bridge ensured his reappointment in both 1944 and 1945. By the time that he returned to College, he had had a brief holiday and still had £15 to supplement his scholarship. At College he found himself one of just twelve students studying for Honours English Language and Literature, though he also continued subsidiary Medieval History with Gwen Whale, whom Henry remembered as a poor lecturer but a marvellous tutor. As his health improved he began to get more involved with student societies, especially the Debating Society, which he recognised both as a key to learning to speak well and as a source of friends of different political persuasions. In his Finals in June 1945, he achieved first-class marks on his language papers (in Old English, Old Norse, and Middle English), where J. R. R. Tolkien was the external, but only good 2(i) marks on his literature papers. Nonetheless his 2(i) was the best English result in his year.

Until that time his expected career had been the Civil Service or school-teaching, but his health and continuing three-weekly treatments still excluded such employment. Since he had already taken subsidiary History, he found that his scholarship could be extended for a final Honours year of History to enable him to achieve a double degree. He chose to concentrate mainly upon medieval courses, thoroughly enjoying Stubbs's *Charters* with Gwen Whale and a special subject on the thirteenth-century Welsh church with Professor William Rees. He also studied Tudor economic history with Dorothy Marshall, whose friendly tutoring Henry greatly admired. In June 1945 he emerged from his finals (David C. Douglas was the external) with clear first class Honours in History to add to the 2(i) that he had previously attained in English. By any reckoning that result was a triumph over adversity and a testimony to Henry's ability to pace his efforts.

An academic future now beckoned. Henry was awarded a newly created University Research Studentship of £150 to embark on a two-year MA with a possibility of extending it to a doctorate, if a Fellowship could be obtained. On Henry's behalf, William Rees sought advice from Sir Frank Stenton concerning an early medieval topic that might be studied in Cardiff, with its more limited library resources than those of Oxbridge or London. Stenton suggested that work on the terminology of the Alfredian translations, particularly in relation to secular ranks and authority might be ideal for someone with Henry's combination of historical and philological gifts. The advice was warmly appreciated and created a sense of debt to Sir Frank—the greatest early medieval English historian of his age—that Henry retained throughout his life. This advice was perhaps particularly valued precisely because the start of his research had to be delayed while a greater opportunity presented itself.

Marriage and employment in Cardiff

By the autumn of 1945 those demobilised after the war were beginning to return to University. In the Cardiff History Department Gwen Whale's health was too fragile for an increased teaching load. Though there were not funds for a full post, William Rees was able to invite Henry to take on her teaching of the subsidiary class in European History at £100 per term. The job involved lectures to a large class, marking students' essays and holding seminars for groups of eight to ten students. He loved the work and by the spring of 1946 was able to start on his research. While a research student Henry was President of the Debating Society and he found some of his pupils among his committee, many of them older and more experienced than he. By June 1946 the pressures of student numbers led Cardiff to advertise an Assistant Lectureship in Medieval History. Such job opportunities do not often occur in life and Henry did not hesitate. He was appointed from a short list of two, and thus achieved some financial security for the first time in his life—and in his home city and home university to boot.

But the summer of 1946 had another life-changing event in store. Long before there had been any possibility of an academic post, Henry had committed himself to his usual summer holiday 'teaching' at

skills to resolve them.[4] What was especially impressive about this early
work was his ability to identify semantic shifts in the meaning of the
English and Latin words used to denote rank in the tenth and earlier
centuries, and his ability to subject Latin and Old English sources to a
sophisticated analysis. Two years later he was to show in an article in
History that he also had the ability to set these themes against a much
wider analysis of the development of English society.[5] In so doing, he
aligned himself very clearly with the school of J. H. Round, F. M.
Stenton, and F. L. Ganshof, which would allow no hint of feudalism
in the relations of thegns with the Anglo-Saxon king. He was, however, already exploring the concept of 'territorial lordship' to fill the
consequent vacuum.

For the first three years of their married life in Cardiff Henry and
Pat had rented a flat in 19 Llwyn-y-grant Road. The house belonged to
the mother of Max Ede, who had been Henry's mother's solicitor when
she had remortgaged the house in Llanishen. In return for keeping an
eye on the wellbeing of 'Granny Ede' (as they soon came to know her),
they enjoyed a low rent. They also had on their walls some of the pictures from the remarkable art collection kept in the house and gathered
by her son, the connoisseur and dealer, Stanley (Jim) Ede,[6] and they
were accepted as honorary members of the Ede family. Indeed three
generations of Edes were to become close friends of the Loyns and their
children. While Henry and Pat lived in the flat, their first son was born
(Richard, 1951), to Granny Ede's great delight. After her death in 1953
the Loyns initially moved back to his mother's in Llanishen before purchasing a Victorian house in Fidlas Road, Llanishen, with a large garden in June 1954 for £2,000. That was to remain their home until they
left Cardiff in 1977 and while they were there two further sons, John

---

[4] H. R. Loyn, 'The term *ealdorman* in the translations prepared in the time of King Alfred',
English Historical Review, 68 (1953), 513–25; H. R. Loyn, 'Gesiths and thegns from the seventh
to the tenth century', *English Historical Review*, 70 (1955), 529–49. Henry had given an initial
account of these researches at the Anglo-American conference of July 1952 and had been elated
at their reception by Stenton, Helen Cam, May McKisack, and others.
[5] H. R. Loyn, 'The king and the structure of society in late Anglo-Saxon England', *History*, 42
(1957), 87–100. This article was the first to show his gift for synthesis of a major theme in a
highly readable, yet scholarly, format.
[6] The collection included works by David Jones, Henri Gaudier-Brzeska, Ben Nicholson,
Christopher Wood, Paul Nash, and the Cornish primitive, Alfred Wallis; much of it was later
moved to his house in Kettle's Yard in Cambridge and given to that university. Stanley was a
figure of some controversy with an eye for an art bargain, buying in bulk the work of little
known artists.

(1954) and Christopher (1958) were to be born and raised. The joy of a happy and successful family, raised in the security of a good home with the support of a growing body of friends, who enjoyed the Loyns' hospitality, was to be a source of great pride and pleasure to Henry throughout his life. His family came first.

Following the publication of Henry's first articles in the *English Historical Review* in 1953 and 1955 and in *History* in 1957, he began to be much sought out, both as a reviewer and an author. From 1954 he reviewed an average of four books every year, initially just for *History* and the *English Historical Review*.[7] The overriding qualities of his reviews (as well as their quantity) reveal much of Henry's character. His reviews always convey the content of the book clearly; they are predominantly charitable (even where some would have thought charity inappropriate) and notably well written; they were also evidently produced on schedule. It must also have been in the mid- or later 1950s that Henry was approached by Asa Briggs to write the first volume in Longman's series on the social and economic history of England. The book was to be published in 1962.[8] In some respects Henry planned it to parallel Sir Frank Stenton's *Anglo-Saxon England*. Like Stenton, he included the reign of William the Conqueror, which made it possible to discuss evidence from the whole of Domesday Book. Henry's interpretation of the English social economy was also broadly Stentonian, particularly on such issues as the freedom of Anglo-Saxon peasant settlers, the origins of the manor or the scale of the Viking settlements.[9] It was therefore a deeply conservative book. It did not ignore the challenges to traditional interpretations that were, at that time, being advanced by Trevor Aston, Ralph Davis, Peter Sawyer, Eric John, and others. But rather than meeting them head on, it consistently sought to widen and to defuse the debate. He emphasised the evidence of the English language for the nature of both the Anglo-Saxon and the Scandinavian settlements. He gave pride of place to

[7] The reviews up until 1992 are listed in H. R. Loyn, *Society and Peoples: Studies in the History of England and Wales, c.600–1200* (Westfield Publications in Medieval Studies, 6, University of London, 1992), 462–73.

[8] H. R. Loyn, *Anglo-Saxon England and the Norman Conquest* (London, 1962), 472 pp. There were numerous subsequent impressions, a paperback version in 1970 and a revised second edition in 1991.

[9] Quite apart from his personal debt to Sir Frank in his initial research, it should be noted that Stenton's volume in the *Oxford History of England* had been published in 1943, the year that Henry had returned to his studies from Talgarth. It must have seemed a godsend to him then, and even more so in the summer of 1946 when he was first creating a set of lectures on early medieval English history without any years of research under his belt.

the Old English lawcodes in his account the growth of English lordship and of urban life in the tenth and eleventh centuries—a subject to which he would often return in later writings.[10] Despite its traditional conceptual framework, however, this was a work rich in new evidence for all its readers.

While this volume was at press in autumn 1961, Henry was promoted to senior lecturer. The timing suggests that Stanley Chrimes (who had been appointed to the chair of History in succession to William Rees in 1953) had taken the opportunity of the book's acceptance by Longmans to advance his colleague. Henry shared with Chrimes a deep interest in the development of English government and institutions. Meanwhile Henry was building up his activities outside the Department. His lecturing to branches of the Historical Association increased substantially in the 1960s. He also became in 1963, at the invitation of its secretary, Max Ede, one of the twenty members of Cardiff's 'Fortnightly Club' of leading citizens and academics, which met through the winter for coffee and conversation and an expert talk from one of its members.

The mid-1960s were a time of opportunity for historians of late Anglo-Saxon and Norman England. With the nine hundredth anniversary of the battle of Hastings approaching, British publishers vied with each other to secure new textbook accounts of the Norman Conquest. Henry's *The Norman Conquest* was commissioned for 'Hutchinson University Library' and provided a succinct and up-to-date textbook, which demonstrated his skill in synthesis. It was one of the best of that crop and among the first to be published. It met a need in the market and deservedly went to three editions.[11] It was therefore no surprise that Henry was immediately asked to assist with another volume created for the Hastings anniversary, namely to provide a brief account of *Norman England* to be illustrated by Alan Sorrell's superb reconstruction draw-

[10] Produced at much the same time and evidently as a by-product of it, was H. R. Loyn, 'Boroughs and mints' in the Festschrift for Sir Frank Stenton: *Anglo-Saxon Coins*, ed. R. H. M. Dolley (London, 1961), 122–35. The same year saw H. R. Loyn, 'The origin and early development of the Saxon borough, with special reference to Cricklade', *Wiltshire Archaeological and Natural History Magazine*, 62 (1961), 7–15. Some years later he added a chapter on 'Late Anglo-Saxon Stamford' to *The Making of Stamford*, ed. A. Rogers (Leicester, 1965), 15–31 and a study of 'Towns in late Anglo-Saxon England' to the Festschrift for Dorothy Whitelock: *England before the Conquest*, ed. K. Hughes and P. Clemoes (Cambridge, 1971), pp. 115–28.

[11] H. R. Loyn, *The Norman Conquest* (London, 1965), 212 pp.; 2nd edn., 1967; 3rd rev. edn., 1982. Henry's promotion to a readership followed in 1967.

ings. He enjoyed writing for a wider public and also collaborating closely with the artist.[12]

His next enterprise was a very different work, marking a venture into a new type of historical enquiry. In Cardiff Henry had not had access to any archive of early medieval manuscripts. He had never researched in the great repositories of Anglo-Saxon manuscripts: the British Library, the Bodleian, or Corpus Christi College, Cambridge. He was therefore delighted to be suggested by Dorothy Whitelock as a suitable editor for a volume in the expensive but prestigious series, *Early English Manuscripts in Facsimile*, which was to be devoted to BL, Cotton Nero A.1. This composite manuscript contained important texts of works of Archbishop Wulfstan II of York, some of them annotated in his own hand. These were bound up with a later collection of episcopal texts, possibly to be associated with the saintly Bishop Wulfstan II of Worcester. Henry's substantial introduction identified the component parts of the manuscript and its sources. He established its codicological and palaeographical details with exemplary clarity. He built on foundations laid by Karl Jost, Dorothy Bethurum, Dorothy Whitelock, and Neil Ker, but resolutely refused to push the evidence for the manuscript's coherence or its associations with either of the Wulfstans further than was warranted. As a result his work has continued to be a good starting point, and subsequent scholars have been able to find in the facsimiles some additional reasons for regarding the two parts as having been separate until the Reformation.[13]

It may be that his work on this manuscript helped to turn Henry's research interests more towards issues of governmental and institutional history. At all events when he edited—with his Cardiff modernist colleague, Harry Hearder—a festschrift in honour of Stanley Chrimes's retirement from the chair and Department of History, he contributed a notable opening chapter on the working of the late Anglo-Saxon hundred and its court.[14] He focused upon what he saw as the constructive role of

[12] H. R. Loyn with Alan Sorrell, *Norman Britain* (London, 1966), 48 pp. In 1977 Henry was to collaborate again with Alan Sorrell (and Richard Sorell) on *Medieval Britain* (London, 1977), 48 pp. The following year, also in popularising mode, he produced H. R. Loyn, *King Alfred the Great* (Oxford, 1967), 67 pp.

[13] R. Torkar, *Eine altenglische Übersetzung von Alcuins 'De virtutis et vitiis'* (Texte und Untersuchungen zur englischen Philologie, 7, Munich, 1981), pp. 168–85; P. Wormald, *The Making of English Law: King Alfred to the Twelfth Century*, I (Oxford, 1999), pp. 224–8.

[14] H. R. Loyn, 'The hundred in England in the tenth and eleventh centuries', in *British Government and Administration: Studies presented to S. B. Chrimes*, ed. H. Hearder and H. R. Loyn (Cardiff, 1974), 1–15.

governmental development. His interest was not in the problems of the
origins of the hundred and of private jurisdiction that had dominated the
founding fathers of legal and social history (Maitland, Chadwick, and
Vinogradoff). Rather he demonstrated how the vernacular lawcodes, charters, and writs showed the hundred to have operated within the new kingdom of England. The same sources, enhanced with some notable literary
reinforcement, underlay his analysis of the role of kinship in Anglo-Saxon
England.[15] He demonstrated how limited was the kin's role in disputes over
the inheritance of property in the tenth and eleventh centuries, at exactly
the same time as it had growing legal responsibilities in the maintenance of
law and order in relation to its members. Such nicely balanced paradoxes
and sympathy for the individuals portrayed in the sources were ever his
great strengths. Unlike some of his contemporaries, he did not seek illumination from the social sciences to elucidate the role of early medieval
kindreds, nor thankfully did he adopt sociological terminology. His
explanations were, therefore, jargon-free—though for some disturbingly
bland. The same virtues and the same limitations may be seen in the
paper he delivered to the *Regularis Concordia* millennial conference of
1973 on church and state in tenth- and eleventh-century England.[16] He
preferred to see the extension of reformed monasticism, of ecclesiastical
jurisdiction and of tithes as examples of royal and ecclesiastical 'co-
operation and support for God's acres' rather than as new burdens on the
labouring classes. And he made good use of his detailed knowledge of
BL Cotton Nero A.1 to illuminate Archbishop Wulfstan's pursuit of a
Carolingian ideal of monarchical authority, however divorced that model
may have been from the realities of Æthelred's England.

Within University College Henry had begun in the 1960s to play an
increasingly important role, culminating in his stint as Cardiff's 'Dean of
Students' from 1968 to 1970 (and again in 1975–6). This office, which
involved pastoral and disciplinary responsibility in non-academic matters, became of critical importance in 1969 when radical student challenges to political and institutional authority were spreading contagiously
through British universities from their origins in Paris and Berlin. Henry's

---

[15] H. R. Loyn, 'Kinship in Anglo-Saxon England', *Anglo-Saxon England*, iii (1974), 197–209.
There is a striking contrast with J. M. Wallace-Hadrill's view of the role of the kin in feud (deriv-
ing from a reading of Max Gluckman and Margaret Hasluck) in his 'Blood-feud of the Franks',
Bulletin of the John Rylands Library, 41 (1959), 459–87, reprinted in his *The Long-haired Kings*
(London, 1966), pp. 121–47.
[16] H. R. Loyn, 'Church and State in England in the tenth and eleventh centuries', *Tenth-Century
Studies*, ed. D. Parsons (Chichester, 1975), 94–102.

willingness to listen, his gift for friendship and his ability to persuade the college to grant student representation on key bodies defused any potential troubles. It must have been partly in recognition of this service that he was promoted to a personal chair in 1969. Within the Department of History he also had a growing role. Young lecturers, like David Bates, found Henry's interest in their teaching and first researches both practical and encouraging.[17] Typical of Henry's concern for a colleague was the volume of translated sources devoted to *The Reign of Charlemagne* that he published jointly with the ancient historian, John Percival. Henry had planned the volume in a new series (devised by Geoffrey Barrow and Edward Miller) which aimed to make the sources for the major issues of medieval history available to students, whose ignorance of Latin otherwise made the period a closed book.[18] This was Henry's only substantial publication devoted to a topic outside Britain, but the design for the book was very much his. Percival's interests in Roman estate management had already led him to the Carolingian *polyptiques*, so he welcomed the chance to investigate them further and undertook the bulk of the translations; Henry provided most of the commentaries and the introduction. It was a particularly effective collaboration and the book remains a wonderful tool for introducing undergraduates, coming afresh to the early Middle Ages, to a central figure.

In spring 1974, in advance of Stanley Chrimes's retirement, Henry's personal chair was converted into an established chair in Medieval History—a timely recognition of his scholarship.[19] But since the Headship of the Department was thereafter to be separated from the Chair of History, it surprised some colleagues when the first stint was given to Harry Hearder, who was no administrator. This outcome may have reflected the fact that the Principal, Bill Bevan, and Henry had little in common, although they had co-operated well when he was Dean of Students. In the early 1970s, however, there were compensations in other directions, particularly where Henry's gifts for good company and positive thinking were appreciated. He had become one of the University's two members of the

---

[17] Professor Ken Dowden, then a young classicist at Cardiff, has also told me of the encouragement that he drew from Henry's interest and conversation.

[18] *The Reign of Charlemagne*, ed. and trans. H. R. Loyn and J. Percival (London, 1975), liv + 176 pp.

[19] Harry Hearder had come to Cardiff as Professor of Modern History in 1967. Gwyn Williams from York was appointed to succeed Chrimes with effect from autumn 1974, but not to head the Department. Henry Loyn's inaugural lecture, entitled 'The Free Anglo-Saxon', was published in 1976 and is conveniently reprinted in his *Society and Peoples*, pp. 279–98.

Cardiff Rotary in 1970, and much enjoyed meeting city businessmen. He served a stint (1971–4) as Vice-President of the Society for Medieval Archaeology. In 1975 he became President both of the Glamorgan History Society and of the Cardiff branch of the Historical Association, after many years in its service. One year later he became the national President of the Historical Association. That three-year office involved council meetings in London, consultations at the headquarters in Kennington and (by then often chauffeured by Pat)[20] a phenomenal load of visiting and lecturing to local branches up and down the country. Henry loved and welcomed this work, and the Loyn years were later to be seen as a golden time in the HA. The regular stream of beautifully crafted textbooks also continued to flow from his pen. When Batsford sought a volume that would profit from the great public interest in the Vikings, aroused by exhibitions, excavations and films, Henry responded with a fine volume, covering the whole island of Britain. A notable offshoot of this book was his Dorothea Coke Memorial lecture on 'the Vikings in Wales' where he pulled together scattered fragments to present a convincing and thought-provoking picture.[21]

The Westfield years

In the light of the growing reputation both of such works and of his valued role in national bodies, it is not surprising that, when the Chair of Medieval History at Westfield College London became vacant (Christopher Brooke having returned to Cambridge in 1977), Henry was the chosen successor. Cardiff's loss was Westfield's gain. To some the Loyns' move to London from their beloved Cardiff seemed extraordinary, but it was well considered. They found a lovely house in Cunningham Hill Road, St Albans—very much Pat's home territory—whence, however, Henry had a simple daily train journey to Hampstead. Henry, moreover, believed in federal universities, so the move from a college of the University of Wales to one of the smaller colleges of the University of London posed no great problems. Westfield, formerly a women's college, still only had some 1200 students in 1977, of whom two thirds were in Arts

---

[20] The Loyns had had a car since 1960, but Henry never learnt to drive.
[21] H. R. Loyn, *The Vikings in Britain* (London, 1977), 176 pp; H. R. Loyn, *The Vikings in Wales* (Dorothea Coke Memorial Lecture, Viking Society for Northern Research, London, 1977), 24 pp.

subjects and two-thirds were women. It was a distinguished, somewhat conservative, and united college. Henry was made very welcome.

He threw himself into the opportunities that London presented, as well as the responsibilities it offered. He was elected a Fellow of the British Academy in 1979, and served on its Council from 1983 to 1986; he was also Vice-President of the Society of the Antiquaries of London from 1983–7 and much enjoyed the four meetings each year of its 'Hats' dining club. He was also President of the Society of Medieval Archaeology in 1983–6 and Vice-President of the Royal Historical Society in that same period. So committee meetings proliferated, where his calm and informed counsel was highly valued. But at that very time his responsibilities at Westfield were increasing. In 1980 at the request of the Principal, Bryan Thwaites, Henry became one of the college's two Vice-Principals, in which post he was renewed for a second three-year term in 1983, seeing into office the new Principal, John Varey (1984–89). When major surgery necessitated Varey's standing down for several months in 1986, Henry became the Acting Principal in his stead. Throughout these duties Henry remained Head of the History Department and he carefully nurtured History of Art as well. These were critical times for Westfield. The Thatcher government's financial cuts of the early and mid-1980s had brought increasing pressure upon a British university system, accustomed to decades of evolutionary growth. Within the University of London, the role of small colleges like Westfield, which had no space for expansion and occupied a site of prime real estate, was increasingly called into question. Its small Science Faculty had been removed, disastrously as it proved, just before government squeezing of the funding of Arts students made the whole college unviable. Henry had devoted himself to the defence of Westfield's independence, but when that battle was lost, he sought to ensure that the interests of Westfield staff and students might be retained through negotiations for a merger, first with King's College but then (after his retirement) with Queen Mary College.[22] What is striking is that throughout the whole agonising debates Henry inspired the loyalty and trust of both the academic staff and the administrators of the college to secure the best available deal. As John Varey declared in his valediction: 'Henry's calm strength of purpose in that critical period has placed all the college in his debt.'

---

[22] Earlier, in the late 1970s, ideas of a merger with Bedford had got nowhere; Henry's preference was for the King's College merger.

With such commitments some downturn in his publications might have been expected. The reverse was true. Invited by Professor A. L. Brown of Glasgow, Henry produced in 1984 the first volume (typically also the first to be published) of a series on 'The Governance of England'.[23] This was constitutional history by another name, since criticism of Stubbs's dominance of History syllabuses in Britain had made that term increasingly unfashionable since the 1960s. Henry adopted Stenton's date-limits of 500–1087 and boldly divided that period into two. He saw the reign of King Alfred (871–99) as the 'watershed' between an early period of 'tribal' kingship and a later one characterised by a single English monarchy, the rise of a 'territorial state' and of a powerful aristocracy. His account of tenth-century royal government, of the problems of the royal succession, of taxation, of rent and coinage, of boroughs, hundreds and tithings and of the vernacular records was both masterly and optimistic in its progressive faith. Above all it enthused students by directing them again and again to the sources. It was very much a teacher's book.

The year 1986 was the nine-hundredth anniversary of the production of Domesday Book, England's first public record. As the leading historian based in London who actually used Domesday Book extensively in his researches, Henry had naturally been consulted. Typically he had soon become deeply involved in planning the Domesday Exhibition in the Public Record Office and then in the preparation of the associated facsimile edition by Alecto Historical Editions. He advised on the contents, captions, and catalogue of the exhibition. He joined the Alecto Board, gave vital advice to the editors of several counties and wrote an opening chapter, which summed up current understanding of the survey's purpose and methodology. This introduced a volume of expert studies on aspects of the survey, whose authors Henry chose.[24] Henry continued to attend Board meetings regularly after his retirement, even

---

[23] H. R. Loyn, *The Governance of Anglo-Saxon England, 500–1087* (London, 1984), xvii + 222 pp. The same year saw the publication of two other innovative articles on neglected topics: H. R. Loyn, 'The conversion of the English to Christianity: some comments on the Celtic contribution', *Welsh Society and Nationhood*, ed. R. R. Davies *et al.* (Cardiff, 1984), 5–18 and 'Peter's Pence', *Friends of Lambeth Palace Library Annual Report for 1984* (1984), 10–20. These were reprinted in Loyn, *Society and Peoples*, pp. 20–44 and 241–58.

[24] H. R. Loyn, 'A general introduction to Domesday Book', *Domesday Book Studies*, ed. A. Williams & R. W. H. Erskine (London, 1987), pp. 1–21. Henry also gave the opening paper to the major Domesday conference of 1986, which was published as H. R. Loyn, 'The Beyond of Domesday Book', *Domesday Studies*, ed. J. C. Holt (London, 1987), 1–13.

contributing to the launch of the facsimile of *Little Domesday* in his final year. The extent of his passionate enthusiasm for Domesday issues was also signalled by the astounding number of lectures on Domesday Book—no less than forty—that he delivered in 1986 to Historical Association branches the length and breadth of the country. He never liked to turn down a request from a branch secretary of the organisation that had so enriched his life.[25] Yet that was a year in which he was also Acting Principal of Westfield, President of the Society for Medieval Archaeology, and Vice-President of both the Royal Historical Society and of the Antiquaries. Lecturing was indeed his life-blood.

It must nonetheless have been with some relief that in September 1986 he stepped down as Vice-Principal and handed over some teaching for a term to Professor Rosalind Hill. That was the nearest that Henry ever came to sabbatical leave, since Cardiff had had no regular system. It gave him a chance to develop the rethinking about William the Conqueror's reign that his year of immersion in Domesday had provoked and gives us the chance to gain something of the flavour of some of those forty lectures. He placed his study of Rayleigh in Essex, very appropriately, in the festschrift for R. Allen Brown, doyen of Anglo-Norman studies. This focused upon the fief of Sven, the son of Edward the Confessor's Norman favourite, Robert Fitz Wimarc, and one of the men 'who transformed an ancient monarchy into one of the most successful feudal states of medieval Europe'. His reflections on William's bishops were delivered to the Battle Conference and the fundamental question '1066: Should we have celebrated?' was addressed to the 1989 Anglo-American conference in London. His answer—a cautious but definite yes—was notable particularly for its characteristic refusal to identify modern nationalism with the Anglo-Saxon past.[26]

---

[25] In 1986 he was honoured by the award of the Historical Association's W. N. Medlicott Medal for services to history.

[26] H. R. Loyn, 'Rayleigh in Essex: its implications for the Norman settlement', *Studies in Medieval History presented to R. Allen Brown*, ed. C. Harper-Bill, C. Holdsworth, & J. L. Nelson (Woodbridge, 1989), pp. 235–40; H. R. Loyn, 'William's bishops: some further thoughts', *Anglo-Norman Studies*, 10 (1988 for 1987), 223–35; H. R. Loyn, '1066: Should we have celebrated?', *Bulletin of the Institute of Historical Research*, 63 (1990), 119–27. These papers were reprinted in *Society and Peoples*, pp. 339–49, 374–97, and 322–38.

Retirement

Retirement allowed Henry more time in St Albans. He enjoyed the progress of Martin Biddle's excavations near the cathedral searching for the dark-age transition from Romano-British to Anglo-Saxon Christianity. He played a growing role in the cathedral's Fabric Advisory Committee, becoming chairman in 1991. He and Pat were able to make several further visits to their son Richard in Australia, to see more of the antipodean wildlife and flora and to give lectures in leading universities there.[27] They also devoted more time to their lovely garden. Their tradition was to share the major chores, like the lawn-mowing, until Pat's brush with breast cancer for a time curtailed her activities. The flow of Henry's publications continued unabated with works that could be largely written in his own library and from a lifetime's experience of teaching. He was the editor of Thames and Hudson's encyclopaedia of *The Middle Ages*, choosing the items for inclusion, selecting the expert authors and writing many entries himself. Students and laymen were provided with succinct but up-to-date summaries of current knowledge on key individuals, events and themes of European history between *c.*400 and 1500.[28] Two years later he summed up, for the same publisher, his life's teaching on English history and English government between the tenth and the thirteenth century.[29]

Ever since his time in the Talgarth sanatorium in 1941–3 Henry had learned how to take care of his health. He avoided over-exertion and loved the walking (which kept him fit), regular food and plenty of sleep. In forty-one years of university teaching he had only missed two days through illness. Nonetheless the heaviest years at Westfield in the 1980s had taken their toll. A medical check-up in 1986 had revealed some diabetes. In the summer of 1989, after a strenuous day involving lawn-mowing and walking home after an FAC meeting, angina was diagnosed. That was controlled with tablets until the autumn of 1993, when he had a very successful quadruple heart by-pass. He was soon back home, recuperating in the sun and beginning to resume a normal life.

---

[27] Their first Australian trip had been in 1977 (when Henry had given 7 lectures in 6 universities in 9 days); another in 1984. Post-retirement visits followed in 1988, 1991, 1995–6, and 1998.
[28] *The Middle Ages: a Concise Encyclopaedia*, ed. H. R. Loyn (London, 1989); rev. edn., 1991. There were subsequent editions in Portuguese, Spanish, Polish, and Japanese.
[29] H. R. Loyn, *The Making of the English Nation* (London, 1991), 191 pp.

Indeed Pat and Henry took the decision to leave their beloved St Albans home and its half-acre garden and to return to Henry's roots in the Cardiff area.[30] In July 1994 they moved into a fine house in Clinton Road, Penarth with a compact garden. There he was able to resume close contacts with his alma mater, University College and with its History Department.[31] He continued to travel regularly up to London for meetings. These included the Medieval section of the British Academy, the Academy's committee for the Sylloge of the Coins of the British Isles (which he chaired from 1979 to 1993), the councils of the Selden Society and the English Place-Name Society, the Alecto Board and the Westfield Trust. Mostly these could be managed as day-trips, but sometimes he stayed overnight at the Athenaeum. As ever his interest was directed towards securing the promotion of outstanding younger scholars and helping projects towards publication. He also had one remaining book to write himself. At David Bates's request he produced for Longman's series on 'The Medieval World' a brief account of the English church from the beginnings of the tenth-century monastic reform movement to the mid-twelfth century.[32] Henry did not find it easy to write, having never been an ecclesiastical historian, but his ability to interest his readers remained with him to the end. That end, when it came, was unexpected. A diabetic crisis had led to heart failure and to his sudden death on 9 October 2000 at the age of seventy-eight.

The boy, who had been close to death from tubercle when just eighteen, had had a remarkable life. He had conveyed his enthusiasm for early medieval history and English culture to generations of Cardiff and London students. He had a wonderful gift for friendship and for bringing out the best in people. His sparkling eyes and mellifluous voice revealed the caring man, who wanted the best for all he met. Friends, like Peter and Dorothy Lewis, who had first been met on a family holiday in the Gower peninsula, found themselves joining the Loyns for family holidays for some fifteen years in succession. The Berner family, whom Henry and Pat first met in Norway in 1948, likewise maintained a continuing family friendship with them. Four generations of Edes have also interacted with the Loyn family at key stages. Henry was a devoted father to three sons. His and Pat's warm hospitality at their homes in Cardiff, St Albans, and

---

[30] The move brought them close to two of their sons' families.

[31] He gave the first lecture in the college's new Centre for the Study of Medieval Society and Culture and was made an Honorary Professor of the Centre.

[32] H. R. Loyn, *The English Church, 940–1154* (London, 2000), x + 174 pp.

HENRY PELLING

Henry Mathison Pelling
1920–1997

Quintessential Pelling

At the end of 1965, the *New Statesman* competition—quite a national institution in those days—asked for 'an extract from Alan Taylor's history of the years 1946–66'. Taylor's volume in the Oxford History of England, covering the period 1914–45, had been published earlier that year, to widespread public appreciation of its ability to make recent events into real history in a terse and provocative style that was often incautiously termed inimitable. Unabashed, another Oxford don, far less renowned than Taylor, claimed the first prize for his adroit parody:

> In January 1965 Sir Winston Churchill died. He was given a state funeral—a distinction reserved for royalty since the Duke of Wellington. He had saved his country twice—once by vigour, in 1940; once by sloth, in 1951–4, when England could have joined the Common Market. It was to no avail. With his death, the last vestige of national greatness disappeared.[1]

This was written by someone who evidently knew Taylor well enough to catch his prejudices as well as his intonation; and the pastiche was sustained to the end without a false note, like *1066 and All That*, using satire to etch images that were not wholly frivolous.

> Rhodesia declared independence. The Queen gave the governor a decoration. The Conservatives, if anything, were keener 'little Englanders' than the government.

[1] *New Statesman*, 17 Dec. 1965, p. 982, for both passages quoted.

Proceedings of the British Academy, **120**, 327–342. © The British Academy 2003.

> But there was not much in it. Still, there were the Beatles: if it had not been for them, no foreign schoolchild would ever have heard of England.

Henry Pelling took great pleasure in pocketing ten guineas for this contribution. It was a tangible reward, at 1965 prices, for all the homework he had put in. For this was not his only comment on Taylor's best-seller. The good-natured digs of the *New Statesman* were the distilled essence of a searching appraisal, published (unusually for that journal) as a review article in *Past and Present* a few months later. For many years his colleague at Oxford, Taylor found that he had ventured at his peril onto territory which Pelling had made his own, notably as a specialist on the history of the British labour movement. Hence a natural measure of professional reserve on Pelling's part: 'It is, I think, Mr Taylor's unwillingness to allow for the strength of social and political forces outside Whitehall and Westminster which constitutes the chief weakness of his book.' Though there might be general themes, such as the growth of state power, in Taylor's treatment, the 'staccato style of his narrative does not allow for a measured discussion of such matters'.[2]

What was long remembered of this review was not any frontal bombardment of Taylor's position but the sustained sniping on the flanks. Remarking 'that Mr Taylor himself, in reviewing other people's books, not infrequently regards factual errors as a criterion of general quality', Pelling opened up a finely calibrated small-arms barrage. 'Some [slips] of a larger size are due to Mr Taylor's unfamiliarity with economic and social history.' He was instructed accordingly. 'On electoral matters Mr Taylor is distinctly shaky.' The record was duly set straight. 'There are a lot of mistakes concerned with the Labour Party and its Members of Parliament.' Its social composition and constitutional arrangements were explicated. 'There are a number of mistakes in connection with the trade union levy.' This intractable topic had evidently provoked an exercise of historical imagination—'Mr Taylor manufactures an ingenious explanation of [an] imaginary fact'—which Pelling found it his duty to restrain and rebuke.

Yet it would be wrong to ignore the genuineness of the tributes to a book that Pelling well knew he could not have written himself. He reiterated that trivial errors of fact—'Too much importance should not be placed upon them'—were inevitable in such an enterprise, and were 'neither here nor there to those who read the book from cover to cover'. Pelling

---

[2] Henry Pelling, 'Taylor's England', *Past and Present*, 33 (April 1966), 149–58; all quotations in this and the next three paragraphs from this review article.

was not being ironical in calling for a second edition of the book—a corrected edition which would be 'not just a brilliant book, but also a reliable one—at any rate, if other reviewers take the trouble to point out the errors that they may find in their own departments of historical interest'. For users of the first edition, the listing of errata served as an obvious, useful public service rather than the inception of a private vendetta.

For Pelling, scholarship was more a collaborative process than a matter of competitive display. Not that he was unimpressed by the commercial success of the book, concluding with a Taylorian flourish that was virtually a rehearsal for the *New Statesman*: 'I shall not be surprised if the Clarendon Press, instead of financing learned books out of the sales of Bibles, begins to finance sales of Bibles out of the profits of Mr Taylor's volume.'

The episode was a classic clash between two fine historians: one a born writer with a gift for the striking phrase, his self-consciously radical public identity in tension with his schooling as a traditional diplomatic historian; the other a scholar with a distrust of hyperbole, his rather conservative mien belying his pioneering commitment to the study of history at the grassroots. Taylor's barbed riposte—'Mr. Pelling is a master of precision'—was subsequently blazoned on the jackets of Pelling's many books. These won the kind of esteem that mattered to him: the deep respect of his professional colleagues, primarily in Britain and the anglophone world and also notably in Japan. His oeuvre secured him a reputation as the foremost empirical labour historian of his generation.

Beginnings

Henry Pelling was born on 27 August 1920 at 4 Curzon Road, Prenton, Wirral, Cheshire. He had a brother John who continued to live in the area. Their father, Douglas Langley Pelling, was a Liverpool stockbroker; their mother, born Maud Mary Mathison, from whom Henry derived his middle name, was the daughter of a Birkenhead solicitor who was remembered in the family for having given F. E. Smith his first brief. Henry was sent to Birkenhead School at the age of six and stayed there for thirteen years till the summer of 1939. Meanwhile, at the end of 1938 he had journeyed to Cambridge to sit the entrance scholarship examinations and was elected to an open exhibition in Classics at St John's College, which was to provide him with not only an academic base but a home, on and off, over nearly sixty years. It seems that he

read Classics to please his parents, who envisaged young Henry following his grandfather into a legal career. When he matriculated at St John's
in October 1939, the Second World War had broken out a month previously, and his undergraduate studies were to be overshadowed ever more
heavily by wartime constraints. For two years he worked away with his
usual efficiency and dedication, with the reward that he was placed in
the First Class in Part I of the Classical Tripos in 1941.

At this point, as was normal at the time, Pelling's degree course was
interrupted when he was called up for military service. He was commissioned in the Royal Engineers in 1942 and served as a tank commander
in the Normandy campaign and the advance on Berlin, 1944–5. He never
talked much about his war service, though it was not a forbidden topic.
Late in life, asked about his holidays, he would drop into the conversation
characteristically dry and understated allusions: 'It was the first time I
had visited that part of Normandy since 1944.'

Pelling returned to Cambridge as an undergraduate in time for the
great freeze of the winter of 1946–7, when shortages and rationing
exceeded those of wartime. Robust ex-servicemen set their stamp upon
the college. These were clearly of another tribe than Pelling, who retained
vivid memories of conduct that he could barely fathom. Since open fires
were then the only means of heating ancient college rooms, as he would
explain in later years, undergraduates who had fecklessly gone through
their own coal ration were then driven to imposing on others. This
showed a shameless abandon that offended his sense of order and equity;
he accepted privations with a stoicism bordering on zeal. His political
commitments made him a strong supporter of the Labour Government
under Attlee, Bevin, and Cripps. Pelling was in many ways the epitome
of the age of austerity and perhaps thus its predestined historian.

It was when Pelling came back from the war that he made a decisive
change of direction, abandoning Classics in favour of modern history. He
gained First Class honours with distinction (a 'starred' First) in Part II
of the Historical Tripos in 1947. Under war conditions, he had qualified
for the BA in 1942; he took his Cambridge MA in 1947 (incorporated as
an Oxford MA in 1949). It was soon clear that he had found his vocation
as an historian, his interest in contemporary developments stimulated by
his war experiences. The elegance and precision of dead languages had
suited his style, and his own prose could often be lapidary; but he now
began research on the early history of the Labour Party.

Pelling had no obvious model or mentor. He consulted (Sir) M. M.
Postan, Professor of Economic History, about the idea of writing a his-

tory of the Communist Party; but in view of the anticipated difficulties over both sources and interpretation, Postan suggested research on the Independent Labour Party (ILP) instead. Pelling thus started with the plan of covering the ILP's history from its foundation in 1893 to its demise in 1932; the terminal date was successively cut off at 1918, then at 1906, finally at 1900, while the starting date was likewise pushed back to 1880, with the final title, 'The origins and early history of the Independent Labour Party, 1880–1900'. His research supervisor was the Professor of Political Science, (Sir) Denis Brogan, Fellow of Peterhouse. Here was a colourful, intuitive, extrovert polymath, who had indeed dashed off—on the hoof, under wartime conditions—a perceptive book, *The English People* (1943), but whose interests made him best known as a broadbrush interpreter of France and, above all, the USA through journalism and broadcasting. Pelling, with his usual courtesy, wrote: 'I had the good fortune to be supervised by Professor D. W. Brogan, and could draw upon his wide range of historical knowledge.'[3] But it is hard to think that Brogan had much specific input. The thesis was finished in an exemplary three years and awarded the Cambridge Ph.D. in 1950.

Pelling was undoubtedly drawn into the largely untilled field of labour history by his own political convictions, which he had no hesitation at this time in describing as socialist. Other notable labour historians of this generation were Marxist not only in allegiance but in methodology. For example, another Cambridge Ph.D. approved in 1950 was that by E. J. Hobsbawm of King's College, on 'Fabianism and the Fabians, 1884–1917'. But Pelling was an ethical, evolutionary socialist and, above all, an empiricist, determined that triumphalist myth-making should yield to exact scholarship.

The Origins of the Labour Party (1954), reshaped from Pelling's Ph.D. thesis, is a remarkable pioneering study of a subject typically enshrouded by polemic or myth. The variant socialist doctrines of the Fabians, the ILP and (perhaps best of all) the Marxist Social Democratic Federation are all spelt out with exemplary clarity and minute research into little-used archives. It is invaluable on then forgotten figures like H. H. Champion, and on obscure movements like John Trevor's Labour Churches. On the other hand, the emotional intensity of crusaders like Keir Hardie seemed rather less accessible. Half a century on, it remains a classic pioneering study, built to last.

---

[3] *The Origins of the Labour Party* (1954), p. vi.

MERVYN POPHAM

Mervyn Reddaway Popham
1927–2000

MERVYN POPHAM was a questioning, quiet person, driven by an uncompromising honesty to find the truth, and always ready to doubt accepted explanations or any theory-driven archaeology for which he could find no evidential basis. He was probably the most percipient archaeologist of the Late Bronze Age of Crete and the Aegean to have worked in the second half of the twentieth century, and became almost as important in the archaeology of the Early Iron Age, which succeeded the Bronze Age. In his archaeology he took an analytical–empirical approach to what he saw as fundamentally historical problems, reaching unprecedented peaks of intelligent, and commonsensical, refinement. He pondered long before making up his mind. He was expert at reading and hearing what is unsaid. It was a sensitivity and scepticism that existed equally strongly in his views of human motivation, and an asset that his friends, perhaps especially those who were Greek, appreciated. Once he had decided on an interpretation, however, whether to explain contemporary events or for the distant past, it was hard to induce him to change his mind. And so often he was right—as he would observe ('Didn't I say so?'), looking up with a half-grin as he heard of some new discovery in Crete that confirmed an *en passant* suggestion of his, or of apparently puzzling behaviour that, all the same, fitted his patterning of a person's character. He was as brave as he was decisive, qualities that characterise his scintillating contributions to the history of Knossos and the study of Late Minoan pottery—and achieved greatness in brilliant excavations of the highest forensic standards at Knossos, Palaikastro, and Lefkandi, sharing

Proceedings of the British Academy, **120**, 345–361. © The British Academy 2003.

direction usually with Hugh Sackett. For Popham digging was an ultimate test of mind, will, and concentration, the chance to release truths
that had been dormant for millennia. His approach was an artist's. For
those lucky enough to have worked with him at those sites, or to have
written a dissertation with him, he still seems present, asking questions or
pointing out overlooked evidence and always trying to place matters in a
larger context so as to elicit the likely truth. If gone, he still seems to be
shaping our lives, as he started to do when he arrived as the senior
Student at the British School at Athens in 1961, in 1963 becoming the
School's Assistant Director. We—a list that includes Mark Cameron,
Oliver Dickinson, Doniert Evely, Eleni Hatzaki, Roger Howell, Irene
Lemos, Martin Price, Cressida Ridley, Elizabeth Schofield, Ken Wardle,
Peter Warren, and Elisabeth and Geoffrey Waywell—came to see digging
as a philosophical paradigm. Our duty was to identify and create truth.
We were lucky to be digging whatever the particular spot was. Now we
had to make the most of the opportunity, and repay our debt to the
ancients whom we were trying to delineate.

Born on 14 July 1927, Mervyn Popham was the son of a West Country
engineer's fitter, as his birth certificate says, who had been an engineer
officer in the merchant navy in the First World War. His parents died in
1942 and 1943, when he was an adolescent. As a scholar at Exeter School,
he did well in classics and helped found the archaeology society. He was
also School Librarian, presaging one of his later duties in the post of
Assistant Director of the British School at Athens. National service was
in the Royal Navy in 1946–8, when he became an expert photographer—
a practical and artistic skill he exercised for the rest of his life. He then
went to St Andrew's (1948–52) and read classics, graduating with a second (and a medal for being best in General Ancient History in 1950). One
of those who taught him was Terence Bruce Mitford who kindled an
interest in epigraphy and took him as photographer on his excavations at
Kouklia (or Palaipaphos) in south-western Cyprus. When Hector Catling
visited in 1952, he found that among other members of the team besides
Popham were the young Franz-Georg Maier and Jörg Schäffer (Mitford
believed in re-establishing links with German archaeology), G. R. H.
('Mick') Wright, Angeliki Paschalidou (later Pieridou) and Mary Burn.
The year before, Popham had gone to Greece, and visited the British
School at Athens, for the first time.

    This first, working encounter with Cyprus must have been a factor in
his being posted there when he joined the Colonial Service in 1953, stay-

ing on the island until late 1959 (before Cyprus's independence in 1960). The experience did much to shape the rest of his life. He began as Assistant District Commissioner for Nicosia, and was then moved to the Secretariat, where he was when the Eoka emergency erupted in April 1955. Among his duties was visiting Eoka members in Nicosia prison sentenced to death. He was also present, I believe as secretary, at the meeting of the Executive Council when it was decided not to hang Nikos Sampson (later the short-lived puppet president of Cyprus whom the Greek junta installed in the attempted coup of 1974 that led to the Turkish invasion) for several convictions for murder—in view of the popular unrest that would result, Popham recalled. In 1958 he was given probably the most difficult posting in Cyprus, to be District Commissioner for the Troodos area, where the Eoka fighters used to hide. Of necessity, journeys were often by helicopter. Popham had the trauma of being in one that crashed, when he nearly died. He was pulled from the wreckage.

In Cyprus Popham came to form his apparently unsentimental ideas about Greeks, the people and their politics, based on his own experiences and observations. 'He was hard on us Greek girls', says his former pupil Irene Lemos, 'but that was because he cared. He had a theory that we had to be little Mrs Thatchers, and tough girls if we want to get on in the business. I said to him, "Yes, but you have to be proud of your Greek girls"', namely Eleni Hatzaki and herself. (That was in 1999, when Hatzaki became Curator at Knossos for the British School at Athens and Lemos was already a Lecturer at Edinburgh. But there were two others who did not last the course.) 'And the last time we met, he said, "I am proud"'. Fundamentally, he was always very fond of Greeks—even if, as one Greek colleague told me, 'he seemed still part of the British Empire, like many of you'—and liked the Greek readiness to adapt to the unexpected, and celebrate or create an occasion, recognising probably an openness in the culture that was not innate in himself. But equally he was sceptical of them, and quick to detect (and voice) unsaid motives and explanations: a quality that Greeks respect and practise in their relations with each other, but which can be misinterpreted by those not in the game. Cyprus shaped his attitudes and his politics, which were right wing in a Platonic sense of his valuing enlightened detached authority. 'The time in Cyprus must have been painful', his long-time colleague Hugh Sackett concludes. Similarly, I remember Popham later as sceptical of Lawrence Durrell, author of *Bitter Lemons* and Director of Public Relations for the colonial government, not for the quality of his writings but for his aura of sentimental liberalism, as it seemed to Popham. He learnt also as a civil servant the necessity of method and precision. Years later, when he would still answer the telephone with a clipped 'Popham here', it was easy to imagine the young member of the colonial administration in the Secretariat buildings in Nicosia.

Besides the driving energy of his intellect, another major impetus to his strong sense of self-discipline was his homosexuality, in the era when homosexual activity was still prosecutable and homosexuals had to be extremely careful. Some found, however, that they could sublimate their needs and desires, and cope with the desperate, continuous pressure of having to be untrue to themselves in public, by disciplined hard work. I think this applies to Popham. As Assistant Director at the British School at Athens in the mid-1960s, he was notable for the depth of sympathy, surely out of personal experience, that he felt for the anguish of the sexual entanglements of (some of) the students. While clearly quite aware of what might be going on in the hostel, he was not at all a prude. But, while tolerant of others, he abhorred shoddy behaviour, of any sort. He had no affection for the brazenness of gays in the late twentieth century. If he did from time to time treat men with an indulgence that he did not on the whole allow to women, he had many close women friends, especially among those with whom he worked. His male intimates included Takis Koukis, to whom he dedicated his first book.[1] Similar close alliances during the time in Cyprus would not be surprising, but things would have been difficult with the worsening security situation.

If Cyprus both revealed Popham's bravery and decisiveness and nurtured the sense of sadness and having suffered (but with no self-pity) that seemed so much part of his character, it also kept archaeology in his life, the more valuable perhaps as some sanity and detachment in the mess of the Eoka conflict. In 1955 he met again the newly arrived Hector Catling, the first Survey Officer of the island's Archaeological Survey, and his wife Elizabeth, and would often go on expeditions with them at the weekend (if the security situation permitted, on which Popham was briefed) to the island's many ancient sites, especially if they were of the Late Bronze Age. He read in the library of the Cyprus Museum, and stayed in close touch with Mitford and would photograph objects, especially inscriptions, for him in the Kouklia *apotheke* (storeroom) and check on its condition. His 'triumph', Catling recalls, was to re-identify the open air shrine at Rantidi near Kouklia, a spectacular site in the hills (above the new Aphrodite

---

[1] *The Last Days of the Palace of Knossos—Complete Vases of the Late Minoan IIIB Period*, Studies in Mediterranean Archaeology, 5 (Lund, 1964): 'TO MY FRIEND *T. K.*'.

Hills golf and leisure resort) with majestic views down to the sea across the foothills of south-western Cyprus. He visited the site during Mitford's last season at Kouklia.[2] Another epigraphical success was finding, in the village of Nikoklia two kilometres north of Kouklia, the inscription recording a Cypriot oath of allegiance to Tiberius on his accession in AD 14.[3] He also met the young Swedish archaeologist Paul Åström, who soon urged him to study and write up the Cypriot pottery known as Proto White Slip ware, dating to around 1600 BC. Popham's masterly essay[4] defined the pottery, and led to a further major essay on White Slip ware as a whole, including Proto White Slip, in the standard work of Cypriot archaeology, *The Swedish Cyprus Expedition*.[5] In 1998 at a conference in Nicosia on this pottery, Popham reviewed his work of 'some 25 years or so ago', admitting that he had originally hoped to write 'a synthesis of the main lines of development of White Slip', but 'not a D.Phil. thesis of the type which is inclined to go on for many years, adding detail to detail, and which sometimes never reaches an end'.[6]

With the impending independence of Cyprus, Popham had to decide whether to stay in the Colonial Service (as the Governor, Sir Hugh Foot, later Lord Caradon, urged), in which case he would eventually have reached the Foreign Office: he was offered the Secretaryship to the Governor of Malta. Or he could apply for the official bounty for termination of the post, and use it to change his career. That he decided to do. In 1959 he went to Oxford to read for the Diploma in Classical Archaeology, where he was taught by John Boardman and Dorothea Gray, and also David Lewis. During this time, he lodged with the Catlings at 381 Woodstock Road, who came to realise, Catling writes, that 'he

[2] 'Rantidi 1910 and 1955', in T. B. Mitford and O. Masson, *The Syllabic Inscriptions of Rantidi-Paphos*. Ausgrabungen in Alt-Paphos auf Cypern, 2 (Konstanz, 1984), pp. 3–11. For a new overview of Rantidi, see G. B. Bazemore, 'The Display and Viewing of the Syllabic Inscriptions of the Rantidi Sanctuary', in J. S. Smith (ed.), *Script and Seal Use on Cyprus in the Bronze and Iron Ages* (Boston, 2002), pp. 155–212.
[3] T. B. Mitford, 'A Cypriot Oath of Allegiance to Tiberius', *Journal of Roman Studies*, 50 (1960), 75–9.
[4] 'The Proto White Slip Pottery of Cyprus', in P. Åström and G. R. H. Wright, 'Two Bronze Age Tombs at Dhenia in Cyprus', *Opuscula Atheniensia*, 4 (1963), 277–97.
[5] 'White Slip Ware', in P. Åström, *The Swedish Cyprus Expedition, 4. 1C* (Lund, 1972), pp. 431–71; together with: 'A Note on the Relative Chronology of White Slip Ware', in P. Åström, *The Swedish Cyprus Expedition, 4. 1D* (Lund, 1972), pp. 699–705.
[6] 'Problems Encountered in the Preparation of the Section on White Slip Ware for *SCE* IV', in V. Karageorghis (ed.), *The White Slip Ware of Late Bronze Age Cyprus* (Wien, 2001), pp. 45–7. In this retrospective review Popham gives useful leads for further work on White Slip, including the possibility of creating a 'White Slip III' group for the very late White Slip bowls.

studies reveal an art historian's sharp, intuitive appreciation of style and its changes and development, which was enhanced by his ability to draw and photograph the pots and sherds himself, as well as having Petros Petrakis, the School's master-potmender, reconstitute them. If often much of the new creation was a plaster of Paris reconstruction, yet it was, and is, hard to fault Popham's decisive interpretations of how the originals would have been, so imbued was he in the creativity and style of the ancient Cretan potters and painters. He delighted in rounding off a reconstruction by painting the plastered part with the Minoan motifs that he knew had originally been there. Equally, he was driven by the historian's quest to understand the political and social changes that the pottery helped both to date and, as he saw it, to identify. He was incapable of viewing pottery, or any other of the Minoan achievements, in isolation from the circumstances that produced them. The debate on the history of Knossos in the fifteenth, fourteenth, and thirteenth centuries BC encouraged this approach, but here was a mindset that was innate in him and ruled his excavating as much as his study of what he, or others (and notably Sir Arthur Evans), had dug up. 'His view was, "If you want to be a pottery person, you have to be an excavator. And if you want to be an excavator, you have to be a pottery person"', says Hatzaki. History was the bond between all his studies. For Knossos and Late Minoan III Crete, the result was a sparkling series of precise pithy reports, often in reviews (and therefore in danger of being overlooked), of the evidence (usually with new, valuable nuggets of information) and the appropriate conclusions for discerning historians. Following the report on his first investigations into the Late Minoan III pottery of Knossos in the Stratigraphical Museum at Knossos in *On the Knossos Tablets*, his next gem of an essay was another short article with the typical title of 'The Palace at Knossos: a Matter of Definition and a Question of Fact'.[12] Many others like this continued to appear for the rest of his life.

Pottery studies were the core of his major review of the evidence for the date of the end of the Knossos Palace. *The Destruction of the Palace at Knossos. Pottery of the Late Minoan IIIA Period*[13] confirms, almost all scholars accept, the validity of the Evans–Mackenzie stratigraphical evidence for the event, while slightly adjusting the date of it from Evans's Late Minoan II to the time when the subsequent Late Minoan IIIA1 style of pottery was in general use and the first Late Minoan IIIA2 begininng

---

[12] *American Journal of Archaeology*, 68 (1964), 349–54.
[13] *Studies in Mediterranean Archaeology*, 12 (Göteborg, 1970).

to appear. This has the effect of placing the destruction sometime around 1375 BC, rather than Evans's 1400.

At the same time Popham was writing important articles on other aspects of Late Minoan pottery in the *Annual of the British School at Athens*, which remain—together with his subsequent articles on this pottery—basic reading for experts as much as for students. Particularly important is the judicious and authoritative conspectus he presents in 'Late Minoan Pottery, a Summary'.[14] In all of these accounts Popham shows himself well aware of the analytical approach of the Swedish scholar Arne Furumark towards the contemporary, and often closely similar, Late Helladic (or Mycenaean) pottery of the rest of Greece, and of the value of Furumark's approach in creating order—but he never follows such a *dirigiste* line as Furumark does. Two reasons suggest themselves. One may be that Popham's artistic sensibility and his empathy with the Minoan potter/painter forbade ultra-rigid demarcations. Styles did not change overnight. The other, connected reason may be his constant awareness of the often difficult to discern, but always present chronological value of pottery for dating archaeological levels and thus creating history. Both factors demand a sensitivity to the fluidity inherent in ceramic evidence—and make tight decisions all the harder. Equally, he encouraged others in the 1960s to study and publish pottery groups so that the subject would be better known—and more people would learn how to distinguish Late Minoan pottery from Late Helladic. Among these was Yannis Tzedakis, later Director of the Greek Archaeological Service, whose rescue excavations at Late Minoan sites in the town of Khania in west Crete opened a new chapter in the Bronze Age history of the island. Popham, of course, was quick to recognise their significance.[15] At Knossos he also set about the reorganisation of the many boxes of sherds that Evans had kept from his excavations in the early 1900s, in recognition of their value as primary evidence. Although this collection was known as the Stratigraphical Museum, it was in fact housed in dark unvisited corridors and cubby holes inside the ruins of the Minoan Palace. However, construction began in 1962 of a new building, on the site of the tennis court of Evans's Villa Ariadne, to house the sherds and other finds from Knossos. Here the material from Evans's excavations was arranged by students of the School, under Popham's general direction. He knew

[14] *BSA*, 62 (1967), 337–51.
[15] One early result was I. Tzedakis, 'L'atelier de céramique postpalatiale à Kydônia', *Bulletin de Correspondance Hellénique*, 93 (1969), 396–418.

abruptly and still mysteriously after an interview with Adolf Hitler in 1943. SR would have been delighted to learn that his son is now prime minister of Bulgaria. He had demonstrated that Tsars Boris I and II were culturally disoriented in Byzantium and knew perfectly well that Boris III came instead from one of the wild marriages of the dynasty of Saxe-Coburg-Gotha.

If he had had time enough and chance, SR would have been a model minor royal personage as a subsidiary career. His presence was handsome and his private life modest. He preferred to be host rather than guest. His 80th and 90th birthday parties in London were almost state occasions, when SR turned round from receiving, to bidding farewell to his guests— he developed what he called a 'liturgical stoop'. Through observation SR was critically aware of how such a person should patronise graciously, say a few well-chosen words, pretend not to hear political comment, neither fidget nor fall asleep during ceremonies and lectures, never forget a name and always write their own letters of thanks by hand.

SR extended his vivid sense of friendship from individuals to institutions, whole human organisms. The institutions reciprocated the attention he gave them. SR enjoyed the annual Runciman Awards of the Anglo-Hellenic League from 1990, and the Runciman Lectures at King's College London from 1991. He was patron, president, trustee, chairman, advisor or just friend of many bodies to whom he gave support, public and private, each with a network of old and new friends. I only know some. In Scotland, where his portrait in the Scottish National Portrait Gallery by Stephen Conroy of 1990 concludes a consistent iconography of enquiring elegance started by Cecil Beaton in the 1920s, SR served the Scottish National Museum of Antiquities (trustee, 1972–7), the Scottish Ballet (chairman of Friends, 1980–4) and the National Trust for Scotland (emeritus councillor, 1985–2000). In London there was the British Museum (trustee, 1960–7), the Victoria and Albert Museum (advisory councillor, 1957–71), but he was perhaps best pleased with the inauguration of a lift in the London Library (vice-president, 1974–2000). I do not know which office he held in the Tilling Society, but in the Great Church of Constantinople he was elevated to the princely office of Grand Orator in 1969. Among other bodies, SR was a supporter of the Mediterranean Studies Association, the Royal Historical Society (vice-president, 1967–2000), the Anglo-Hellenic League (chairman, 1951–67), the British Institute of Archaeology at Ankara (president, 1962–75, vice-president, 1975–2000), the Association Internationale des Etudes Byzantines (vice-president, 1966–2000), the

National Trust for Greece (chairman, 1977–84), the Society for the Promotion of Byzantine Studies (first president, 1983–2000), the St Catherine's Foundation, Mount Sinai, and the Friends of Mount Athos (first president, 1990–2000).

It was to Mount Athos that SR made his final and most astonishing journey, in July 2000, in his 98th year. It was to inaugurate the treasury and archives of the Holy Mountain, to which he had dedicated his Onassis Prize of 1997. They are housed in a fortified library, the Protaton Tower, which is a Byzantine version of Elshieshields Tower where SR kept his own papers in Dumfriesshire. The Patriarch of Constantinople did not come, having some trouble with the monks of Athos, but SR was pleased that the monastery of Vatopaidi gave him the guest-room used by the Prince of Wales. In an interview there he spoke of his first visit to Athos in 1937, but did not mention his return then, by bus to Thessaloniki when he assisted at the childbirth of a fellow passenger, in a thunderstorm. The scene is described in *A Travellers's Alphabet* under A for *Athos*. Z for *Zion* concludes: 'I shall bravely hope that what the saints of old have told us is true and that when my travels are ended I shall reach the New Jerusalem, Zion, city of our God.' But from the Holy Mountain in 2000 he was at first diverted. Through some wonder of flight and calendar he was taken from Athos on 2 July (OS) and delivered to the Athenaeum Club on 15 July, all within one day. In secular time Steven Runciman died on 1 November 2000 and was buried at Lochmaben according to the rites of the Church of Scotland.

ANTHONY BRYER
University of Birmingham

Note. Most of SR's historical works, of which this cannot be a bibliography, are referred to in the text.

I am primarily grateful to the Revd Dr Ann Shukman, literary executor of SR, for allowing me to sample and quote from her uncle's papers, which are being catalogued at Elshieshields. SR left his working library to the University of St Andrews. His collection of others' offprints is now in the Institute of Byzantine Studies, Queen's University of Belfast; his collection of paintings by Edward Lear in the National Gallery of Scotland; and of coins in the Barber Institute of Fine Arts, University of Birmingham. Apart from 242 papers in typescript, SR's main unpublished work is *Footnotes to a Long Life*, an unfinished typescript in seven chapters and prologue of autobiography to 1939. They are partial 'footnotes' to his *A Traveller's Alphabet. Partial Memoirs* (London, 1991). Notable series of letters include those from SR's mother to his father (1903–17); SR to his parents and sisters, SR to his brother Leslie (1925–46) and SR to Stewart Perowne (1952–62)—which are the most entertaining.

I am most grateful to Donald M. Nicol, FBA, for the loan of his letters from SR (1951–91). SR was a Gladstonian correspondent; his customised Christmas cards were glued together at home. Many, such as David Abulafia, have kept his letters. I first met SR in the House by Herod's Gate, Jerusalem, in 1942 and have letters since 1967.

I am also grateful to The British Council at Athens, Costa Carras, Lydia Carras, Malgorzata Dabrowska, William Davies, Nicholas Egon, Bernard Hamilton, Lord Jellicoe, Haris Kalligas, Charles King-Farlow, Peter Marshall, Faith Raven, Lord John Montagu Douglas Scott, and Henry Shukman, and many others.

SR on History include 'The Writing of History', *The Historical Association Jubilee Addresses* (London, 1956); and 'Medieval History and the Romantic Imagination', the Katja Reissner Lecture of the Royal Society of Literature, 13 December 1962. SR maintained that his most perceptive reviewer was Gore Vidal, *Reflections upon a sinking ship* (London, 1969), 154–9. It is a good review among many, but why did he choose it?

SR in Contexts of Place and on Friends include: Noel Annan, *The Dons: Mentors, Eccentrics and Geniuses* (London, 1999) on Cambridge and 'Dadie' Rylands, to whom SR later dedicated a moral fable, *Paradise Regained*, written in 1935 (privately printed, 1992) and a note in *Dadie Rylands* (privately printed, King's College, Cambridge, 2000); SR on Sir Charles Lambe in Oliver Warner, *Admiral of the Fleet* (London, 1969); SR on Edith Wharton, 'Mrs Wharton', *The Yale Review*, 77 (1988), 560–2; on SR in Jerusalem, J. Connell, *The House by Herod's Gate* (London, 1944); and on the Runcimans on Eigg (1922–66), Camille Dressler, *Eigg. The Story of an Island* (Edinburgh, 1998). A film, *Bridge to the East*, directed by Lydia Carras (Amaranthos, 1991), places SR in Elshieshields, Istanbul and Mistra.

Memoirs and Interviews with SR 1983–2000 include: Rachel Cullen, *The Times*, 7 July 1983; on Guy Burgess in Brian Penrose and Simon Freeman, *Conspiracy of Silence. The Secret Life of Anthony Blunt* (London, 1986) and Miranda Carter, *Anthony Blunt. His Lives* (London, 2001); David Plante, *The New Yorker*, Nov. 1986; Anastasios Sagos, *A Chronicle of The British Council Office in Athens*, typescript file, 1987; anonymous, *The Observer*, 3 May 1987; John Shirley, *The Observer*, 10 Feb. 1991; Malgorzata Dabrowska, unpublished interview, Nov. 1996; Sabbas Spentzas, *Kathimerini*, 14 Sept. 1997; James Owen, *The Spectator*, 15 Aug. 1998; Naim Attallah, *The Oldie*, Nov. 1998. Letter from SR, *The Daily Telegraph*, 25 Sept. 1999 on a passion for ducks, which SR shared with Lord Grey of Falloden from 1908–33, which may also be found a bibliographical home with G. M. Trevelyan.

Obituaries and subsequent Memoirs include: Philip Mansell and Tam Dalyell in *The Independent* and anonymous notices in *The Times* and *The Daily Telegraph*, 2 Nov. 2000; Patrick Bahners, in the *Frankfurter Allgemeine Zeitung* and Nigel Clive in *The Guardian*, 3 Nov. 2000; anonymous, *Annandale Herald*, 16 Nov. 2000; Desmond Seward, *The Art Newspaper*, 109, Dec. 2000; David Abulafia, *Mediterranean Studies*, 9 (2000), 1–16; Bishop Kallistos of Diokleia, Costa Carras, and Graham Speake, *Friends of Mount Athos Annual Report* (2000), 26–35; Konstantinos Angelides, *Pemptousia*, 4 (2000), 34–40; Anthony Bryer, *Anatolian Studies*, 50 (2000), v–vi, *Bulletin of British Byzantine Studies*, 27 (2001), 82–4, *Cornucopia*, 22 (2001), 37–8 and *History Today*, 51 (May 2001) 4–5; anonymous, *The Tilling Society Newsletter*, 36 (2001); anonymous, *National Art Collections Fund Quarterly*, Spring 2001; Lord

Jellicoe, *The Anglo-Hellenic Review*, 23 (2001); Giles Constable, *Times Literary Supplement*, 2 Feb. 2001; George Kalophonos, *AO*, Alexander Onassis Foundation, *Deltio*, 15 (2001); Charlotte Roueché, King's College London, Centre for Hellenic Studies, *Newsletter*, 12 (2001).

Commemorative Meetings. For a Memorial service, held in St Columba's Church of Scotland, Pont Street, London, on 25 Jan. 2001, Sir Peter Maxwell Davies composed '*Dove, Star-folded*', a string trio, noting that SR 'owned the small automatic organ which had belonged to King George III, with which the King, in his madness, had tried to teach caged finches to sing . . .' It is 'based on a Byzantine hymn . . . with a tangential flow of thought which I would like to think catches the essence of Steven's luminous thought processes and conversation. The end is calm and wrapt . . .' Subsequent services were held in King's College London on 1 Feb. 2001, in St Sophia, Moscow Road, London, on 28 May 2001, in Oxford on 1 Nov. 2001 and on Mount Athos in perpetuity. Commemorative meetings, to be published, were held at the Gennadius Library, Athens, on 12 Dec. 2000 (including Anthony Bryer, Costa Carras, Haris Kalligas, Katerina Krikos-Davis, and Angeliki Laiou); at the P. and A. Spentzas Foundation for Byzantine and Post-Byzantine Studies' Runciman Conference at Mistra, on 27–8 May 2001 (including Anthony Bryer, Costa Carras, Ann Shukman, and Speros Vryonis Jr.); *A Tribute to Sir Steven Runciman*, 3rd International Conference on *Crusades and Military Orders*, University of Zaragoza, on 19–25 July 2001 (including Bernard Hamilton and Luis Garcia-Guijarro Ramos).

Commemorative Publications: *Byzantine and Modern Greek Studies*. 4 (1978), ed. D. M. Nicol, was a *Festschrift* for SR. On 21–3 May 1993 Michael Angold assembled twenty-four Byzantinists at Glenesk to read papers on *Byzantine Cities* to SR for his 90th birthday (he was very patient). These have somehow developed into *Byzantine Style, Religion and Civilization*, ed. Elizabeth Jeffreys, essays in honour of SR, which will be published in 2004. The work of SR will be discussed and exhibited at the 21st International Congress of Byzantine Studies, London, in 2006.

DENIS SARGAN *London School of Economics*

John Denis Sargan
1924–1996

DENIS SARGAN was the leading British econometrician of his generation, playing a central role in establishing the technical basis for modern time-series econometric analysis. In a distinguished career spanning more than forty years as a teacher, researcher, and practitioner, particularly during the period that he was Professor of Econometrics at the LSE, Denis transformed both the role of econometrics in the analysis of macroeconomic time series, and the teaching of econometrics. He was Emeritus Professor of Econometrics at the London School of Economics when he died at his home in Theydon Bois, Essex, on Saturday 13 April 1996.

John Denis Sargan was born on 23 August 1924, in Doncaster, Yorkshire, where he spent his childhood. His paternal grandfather was a blacksmith and wheelwright, who also kept cattle on a small-holding in Conisburgh near Doncaster. Denis's father, Harry, was the youngest of eight surviving children, all brought up on the farm and smithy. Harry gained a place at the local grammar school—which was at Mexborough—but the family could not afford further education for him. As Harry had always had a great love of horses, and the corresponding ability to handle them, on the outbreak of war in 1914, he joined the Cavalry, in the Life Guards. When peace returned in 1918, Harry became a mounted policeman in Doncaster.

Denis's maternal grandfather was the organist and choirmaster of the parish church at Askern (a village near Doncaster), where he managed the Spa Baths. Denis's mother, Gertrude Porter, one of four children, was

Proceedings of the British Academy, **120**, 385–409. © The British Academy 2003.

musically gifted; she had voice training, and although she never took up a career in singing, she loved to sing in church.

While a mounted policeman was at least employed, the pay was meagre. Denis and his only sister (two years older than himself) were adequately fed, clothed and housed, but were brought up in a household where money had to be carefully budgeted. The mounted police were always on duty when horse racing took place in the neighbourhood of Doncaster: the big race there was (and still is) the St Leger, the oldest Classic, having been run at Town Moor for over two hundred years. Sometimes Denis and his sister would visit their father when he was on duty at the St Leger. Denis recalled later the colourful scenes, including a tipster, complete in fancy dress and featured head-dress calling himself 'Prince Monolulu'.

After a brief period at the nearby state infants' school, Denis attended the local Church of England primary school. Concerned at the state of children's health and well-being, the government had decreed that primary school children should each day receive half a pint of milk. Denis, with his fellow school children at six or seven years of age, appeared in a group photograph in the local paper. The children were sucking milk through straws from the small bottle each was holding: the caption under the photo read 'each enjoying his ha'porth of nourishment'. Denis's parents were very surprised when the teachers at the primary school told them that he was a boy of exceptional ability, particularly at mathematics. He won a place at Danum School (Doncaster Grammar School). His sister had also successfully obtained a place at the girl's grammar school, and the provision of uniforms for both children made a big hole in the family budget. However, his parents took this difficulty in their stride, and both children did well at school. The extended family of Denis's aunts, uncles, and their children kept in touch, with family meetings and parties in each other's homes, as well as visits to an aunt and uncle who were tenant farmers on the Castle Howard Estate. As a teenager at the start of the 1939–45 war, Denis, with his parents and sister, would cycle to his grandfather's farm at Conisburgh to help with the harvest.

At Doncaster Grammar School Denis flourished in all academic subjects: he read widely, and was a frequent borrower from the school and local libraries. There was an exceptionally good mathematics teacher, who greatly encouraged and fostered Denis's ability in that field. He was, and remained, interested in everything of an intellectual and cultural nature. He taught himself to play the piano, and derived much joy from this accomplishment throughout this life: even as a poor student later in Cambridge, he hired a piano to have in his rooms. He was never keen on sports, but the school both taught sports of various kinds and made the boys (it was a single-sex school) take part. They had to go for long runs, which Denis neither enjoyed nor excelled at. On one occasion, he was so slow that he was the last of the runners, and so far behind the boy in front of him, that an aged spectator (an old boy of the school) cheered Denis on, congratulating him for leading the whole field.

At the age of seventeen, Denis gained a State Scholarship for entrance to St John's College, Cambridge. Coincidentally, St John's was also the college of choice for Sir David Cox and Jim Durbin (of the Durbin–Watson test, *inter alia*), a surprising concordance of world-renowned statisticians. Denis read mathematics, but as it was wartime, he took his degree in two years, becoming a Senior Wrangler. His college years were a tremendous change, plunging Denis into new traditions, many of which he disliked. Naturally the war dominated life: he did not have much money, but there were few things to spend it on anyway. Even purchasing all the books he wanted was a problem, despite the severe restrictions on the quality of the paper on which any new editions were printed.

Immediately after his degree, like most of his generation, Denis was drafted into war work. Unusually for the military—given his mathematical abilities—Denis was assigned to a task for which his knowledge was useful. As a junior scientific officer, he was attached to the RAF and stationed for a considerable period in Haverfordwest, where he provided basic statistical advice on the testing of new weapons systems. Although technically a civilian and a quiet, shy person, he was welcomed in the officers' mess. There was a piano there and a squadron leader who had a musical dog which would 'sing' when the piano was played, usually by its master. Denis enjoyed piano playing with others there, and much later, during their days in Leeds, he and Joan Brown (Professor Arthur Brown's wife) often used to play duets. She was a good violinist, and their efforts provided a sight that Mary Sargan and Arthur Brown were delighted to watch, as well as listen to, since in difficult passages, whilst Denis became immersed in sight reading and interpreting his score, Joan would wiggle her toes in her sandals in time to the music.

At Haverfordwest, Denis's work also involved trips in RAF rescue launches and in submarines. He was a poor sailor and was much relieved when he had to go down in submarines, as there were no rough waves in the depths of the sea. When leave came round, he was sometimes given a lift by one of the pilots in their aircraft, which was a big help in getting the differences and the equilibrium were not, so the latter required co-integration between the levels. His analysis highlighted the role of real-wage resistance in wage bargains, interpreting the equilibrium correction—the deviation of real wages from a productivity trend—as a 'catch-up' mechanism for recouping losses incurred from unanticipated inflation. As the 1960s proceeded, this real-wage resistance was the rock on which many incomes policies foundered. It was typical of his modesty that it was not Denis Sargan, but Sir John Hicks, whose name became associated with that concept. There is no evidence that Hicks was aware of Denis's technical work, but still the latter's prior claim is beyond doubt. Denis's interest in wage-price inflation was reflected in his later work for the Ball Committee on Policy Optimization.

In his policy discussion, permanent and transitory effects were distinguished to ascertain which changes would persist and which fade out (such as devaluations). And he checked that his model adequately described the evidence by testing for various mis-specifications against the hypothesis that the residuals were white noise and independent of the instruments. Although not yet named, his model was an equilibrium-correction mechanism with explicit adjustment dynamics, embodying both derivative and proportional control, as in Bill Phillips's earlier work. At the time, and for many years afterwards, it was not known just how susceptible such 'equilibrium-correction models' were to shifts in the coefficients of intercepts and/or trends. Incomes polices, wage freezes and other related governmental interventions all induced such shifts, so over longer samples, the original specification will fail unless appropriate variables are added to characterise the changed process.

Although forty years have elapsed since Denis first worked on it, his Colston paper still merits rereading.

The London School of Economics

The LSE that Denis joined was home to at least three distinct approaches to economics, the first of which may have appeared rather antithetical to econometrics. In his 1932 *Essay on the Nature and Significance of Economic Science*, Lionel Robbins had claimed that economic theory provided general, formal explanations which were applicable always and everywhere that resource allocation mattered. Moreover, only theory (as distinct from studies of empirical reality) could provide a core understanding of economic activity and behaviour:

> Realistic studies may suggest the problem to be solved. They may test the range of applicability of the answer when it is forthcoming. They may suggest assumptions for further theoretical elaboration. But it is theory and theory alone that is capable of supplying the solution.' (Robbins, 1932, p. 120)

Since the assumptions of economics were 'self-evidently true' and the logic impeccable, the conclusions must be correct. However, such insights as economics delivered could not be given quantitative expression, since causes were non-uniform over both time and space. Robbins argued, therefore, that statistical relationships in economics would change when the world did, so the discipline could never boast 'statistical laws' like the natural sciences. Robbins's approach was sustained at the LSE by the work of Friedrich von Hayek. In principle, economic theory could indeed apply even when there were no quantitative laws, although such 'explanations' would be somewhat unsatisfactory—like predicting calm seas as the norm after a storm, to borrow from Keynes. Moreover, Robbins's positive argument for the power of economic theory explanations only becomes a negative one for econometrics on substantiating the claim that useful empirical regularities do not exist. Certainly, Dr Blank's nebulous demand function for herrings could only last the test of time if many factors other than price and income were included in the model, but such additional factors are not precluded a priori. When Terence Hutchinson launched his critical attack on Robbins in 1938, he made a similar argument and proposed instead a move towards 'positive economics'. Nevertheless, since Robbins was one of LSE's most eminent economists, the LSE might seem an unpromising location for an econometrician, particularly one with an interest in econometric methodology.

However, the post-war period saw a second movement at LSE, implementing the 'positivist' philosophical standpoint within economics. The LSE had a strong tradition in the philosophy of science with Karl Popper, continued by Imre Lakatos, so 'falsification' was already under discussion. The interested group in economics included Chris Archibald, Kurt Klappholz, and Richard Lipsey, all of whom published on economic methodology. The famous Phillips Curve was first presented and discussed at the Staff Seminar on Methodology, Measurement and Testing (M^2T). The appointment of an engineer–economist like Bill Phillips, who stressed empirical evidence, signalled that the mood was less inimical to econometric modelling than the heritage of Robbins might suggest. Indeed, important antecedents were already in place. Both Phillips and Rex Bergstrom (also then at LSE) considered models that were essentially equilibrium-adjustment mechanisms.

econometrics and hoped to publish in good journals. That work was now pretty much completed, he said, and he was happy to hand over to a younger generation. One can hardly imagine a more modest way of summing up such a distinguished career.

Denis is remembered with awe, as well as affection, for the insightful solutions he suggested after a few moments thought on many problems that students and colleagues had struggled with for weeks. He has left a splendid legacy of intellectual achievement, as well as cohorts of well-trained students, many of whom have continued to advance the discipline across, and beyond, the range of topics on which he left his mark.

When the history of econometrics in the second half of the twentieth century is written, Denis Sargan will undoubtedly figure as one of its most original and influential thinkers. The research agenda that he initiated has proved to be of tremendous scope, affecting almost every major area of the discipline; and, at a time when the half life of academic research is often measured in months, his scientific works show a remarkable durability, some of them (like the Colston paper and Walras–Bowley lecture) having the status of enduring classics. If Denis had lived longer, he would surely have been a leading candidate for a Nobel economics award. Since his passing, the world of econometric theory and its many applications has moved on. But many of the themes of his research programme persist in ongoing work and his technical results will surely continue to be used and cited for decades to come.

Denis's contribution to econometrics was enormous. His research accomplishments make him one of the architects of the edifice of theory, technique, and methodology that we collectively call econometrics. His memorial lies in this scientific work, in his impact on LSE econometrics, and in the achievements of the large number of students and fellow scientists to whom he devoted so much of his time and intellectual energy. Perhaps the greatest tribute to the life of Denis Sargan is that he is greatly missed by all who knew him.

DAVID F. HENDRY
Fellow of the Academy

PETER C. B. PHILLIPS
Yale University

Note. We are indebted to many individuals for their information and help. First and foremost, Mary Sargan filled in many of the details of Denis's early life and background. We have also drawn on reviews, obituaries, and memoirs written with, or by, Meghnad, Lord Desai, Neil Ericsson, Toni Espasa, Essie Maasoumi, Grayham Mizon, Hashem Pesaran, Peter Robinson, and Ken Wallis. Finally, we have drawn on the excellent histories of econometrics by Mary Morgan (*The History of Econometric Ideas* (Cambridge), 1990) and Qin Duo (*The Formation of Econometrics* (Oxford), 1993). In total, three special issues of econometrics journals have appeared in his memory. The first, in *Journal of Applied Econometrics*, 2001, on empirical macroeconometrics was prepared for and dedicated to him. The second, in *Econometric Reviews*, 2001, provided a biographical history of Denis Sargan's career, emphasised the breadth of his work in both theoretical and applied econometrics, listed the Ph.D. theses that he supervised, and printed several of his still unpublished papers which had nevertheless greatly influenced thinking at LSE. The third, in *Econometric Theory*, 2003, brings together two of Denis Sargan's essays on econometrics published for the first time, a laudation by Antoni Espasa, and three memorial essays written by David F. Hendry, Peter M. Robinson, and Peter C. B. Phillips respectively, offering an intellectual overview of some of his work.

RICHARD SOUTHERN   *Oxford Mail & Times*

Richard William Southern
1912–2001

RICHARD WILLIAM SOUTHERN, the medieval historian, was born on 8 February 1912 in Newcastle upon Tyne, as second son of Matthew Henry Southern and his wife Eleanor. The Southern family is easily traceable back in Northumberland to *c*.1700 (when the name could be spelt 'Sutheran' or 'Sutheren', forms still found in telephone directories). Its history from then on is a case study in slow urbanisation, as sons of tenant farmers from places within a thirty mile radius of Newcastle came into the city to earn livings in related trades—corn-dealing, butchery, confectionery, and timber. Timber had been the choice of the historian's father, Matthew Henry, who was seventeen when his own father died in 1888. Matthew Henry had then just qualified at Newcastle's School of Science and Art, and got a job at Newcastle's biggest firm of timber dealers, Clayton and Armstrong, on the north bank of the Tyne next to the Armstrong shipyard. In the next twenty years he rose to be depot foreman, so that at the age of thirty-seven (in 1908) he could marry, buy a house in Benwell (on the steep slope looking south over the shipyard), and hope in due course to be made a director. When this did not happen, and when in 1913 the depot moved, he put in a bid to rent part of the old site, bought secondhand machinery, and set up in business on his own.

The future historian, already called 'Dick', was by then two years old. He had a brother older by one year, Matthew Henry Junior ('Harry'). Born in the house at Benwell, the historian was destined to grow in academic distinction in step with his father's business. By the time his father died in 1947—when Dick was a Balliol don—the timber yard, now

Proceedings of the British Academy, **120**, 413–442. © The British Academy 2003.

controlled by Harry and a younger brother, Douglas, was outgrowing its predecessor's site, and in the 1960s—when Dick was professor—it was moved seven miles downstream to a bigger site on the semi-tidal mudflat known as the Jarrow Slake, a place which, by chance, had already lodged deep in Dick's historical imagination as the site of Bede's monastery.[1] When the directors took their professorial brother on a tour of the new sawmill his eyes kept wandering to the buildings a hundred yards away, and he insisted on taking them on a monastic guided tour afterwards. Finally, in 1985—when Dick was a knight, and his *Robert Grosseteste* was in press—it was the turn of the older firm, Clayton and Armstrong, to face an uncertain future, and 'M. H. Southern and Sons' bought up the business that had first employed their founder nearly a century before.

Besides two brothers Dick had a sister, Eleanor (born in 1914). All four received from their parents a strong cultural imprint. Their father had taken elocution lessons as a young man and kept a lifelong interest in acting, especially Shakespeare, and all four children would become fearless public speakers. Their mother, Elizabeth Eleanor, who came from another well-rooted Tyneside clan, the Sharps (and whom Dick was said to resemble physically), had inherited a gift for music. Three of Dick's uncles played violin or piano to professional standard.

When Dick was three years old the household moved up the hill to Fenham and bought a big house in leafy Moorside South, looking over the thousand acres of Newcastle's Town Moor. On the other side of the Moor was the Royal Grammar School. The three Southern boys would in due course be sent there, their sister to the Church High School next door. Dick entered the RGS at nine, as a junior. He enjoyed one carefree year, playing conkers, forgetting his school cap, and so on. But at the start of the next year he was woken with a jolt. He had been promoted two forms instead of one. So he was with older boys, and now had a form-master notorious for punishing boys with 'curfews': penal writings-out of lines from Gray's *Elegy*, a penalty Dick incurred at once for arriving without a health certificate. The biggest jolt of all was the arrival of a new headmaster: Dick's first glimpse of him stuck in his memory, as a menacing silhouette seen through a classroom door. He was Ebenezer Rhys Thomas, whose reign, lasting from 1922 to 1949, would increase fivefold the flow of boys from the RGS to Oxford and Cambridge. The newcomer's first act was to assemble all the boys and warn them they must

---

[1] See the opening of his essay on 'Bede', printed in *Medieval Humanism* (Oxford, 1970), 1. For full titles of Southern's publications until 1980 see the bibliography mentioned in n. 17 below.

work 'till it hurt', or be publicly shamed by receiving specially composed termly reports. Forty years later, undergraduates at St John's College, Oxford, were to get a talk suggestively reminiscent, and with a similar bracing effect on the institution.

As a headmaster, E. R. Thomas had two qualities, then rare in grammar schools. He laid emphasis on the social aspects of education, and had a gift for finding and keeping outstanding masters. The working week would be punctuated by debates and concerts, and against penny-pinching governors Thomas insisted that all boys eat lunch together. As for outstanding masters, the senior history master was Samuel Middlebrook (the 'Sammy' remembered with veneration by another Fellow of the Academy, Denys Hay, four years Dick's junior). Middlebrook was noted both for his crystal-clear exposition, and for an equally clear conviction of what history was all about: it was the story of liberty, and any boy who hinted it might be the story of anything else could expect correction. One of Dick's essays ventured an apologia for certain aspects of Laud's religious policy, and the script came back with a Middlebrook philippic on the back, ending 'Laud was a martinet!' (That Dick would, despite that, dedicate his last *magnum opus* to Laud's memory may or may not reflect the archbishop's unexorcised influence in the St John's presidential Lodgings.)[2]

A second history master, R. F. I. Bunn, came to join Middlebrook in 1925. Ex-Oxford, ex-Artists' Rifles, dressed in a double-breasted suit, with a handkerchief in his cuff—modes then unheard-of on Tyneside (and destined, years later, to win the heart of the daughter of the Cambridge medievalist, G. G. Coulton)—Bunn's effect on the thirteen-year-old Dick was (Dick's word) 'electrifying'. Bunn's complex mode of expression (a favourite phrase was 'so to speak') was such as to suggest there was always more implied in his words than showed on the surface, if you thought about it. The electrifying effect must have doubled in 1926 when the school's weekend camps began. These were largely the invention of Bunn and another of Thomas's prima donna appointments, Michael Roberts, a *stupor mundi* equally at ease teaching physics, mathematics, or English (he became a Faber poet), and incidentally a Communist Party official. For most summer-term weekends, Bunn and Roberts would take Dick and other boys to camp on the Northumbrian hills, where they would light fires, cook, and walk and talk with their

---

[2] *Scholastic Humanism*, vol. 1, viii. Full titles of writings published after 1980 will be found in the supplementary bibliography on pp. 441–2 below.

masters as equals. E. R. Thomas winked at occasional erosions of Monday's timetable.

For Dick, the walking and talking brought with it another and more menacing kind of erosion. Beyond living memory the Southerns had been regular members of the Church of England. For the Fenham Southerns, the parish church had been focus of, not just their Sunday worship, but also of their social activities, like music and plays. (The very far-sighted may see here a model for Dick's later view of twelfth-century humanism.) At fourteen, Dick had duly been sent to confirmation classes in Newcastle cathedral. But exposure to intellectual dare-devils older than himself, together with his voracious reading, were sowing doubts. For instance, H. G. Wells's *Outline of History* had exposed the chasm that divided the biblical account of the the world's origins from that given by modern science. Sixty-six years later, when he was eighty, Dick was to give a talk in Pusey House, Oxford, recalling the moment when religious doubt seized him, like an armed man. It was during a confirmation class in January 1927:

> The canon who was taking the class had got as far as the appearance of the rainbow after the Flood bringing with it an assurance that God would not again overwhelm the world with a deluge. My newly discovered critical sense was outraged. 'No, *no*, NO. This is nonsense!' I internally exclaimed. Of course it would have been better if I had said it out loud, for there is in fact an answer to this pert reaction. But anyhow I left the class and, much to my parents' sorrow, which I now regret more than anything in the whole incident, I never went back. I stopped saying my prayers, though I would sometimes start and then rather embarrassingly remember that I no longer did that sort of thing; and of course I never went to church.

Not, that is, until long after graduating.

At school, meanwhile, as that door closed, another opened. The defining moment this time came in one of his Tuesday essay-crises. He was reading for a Middlebrook essay and arrived at the sentence: 'Henry VII was the first businessman to sit upon the English throne'. Like Alice passing through the looking glass, Dick found himself suddenly in a new world. History had until then seemed a mere configuration of data to be remembered. But he had seen his father and uncles sitting up late with their accounts, trying to make ends meet; he knew about businessmen. Henry VII must be like that. Years later he would learn that the sentence was not true, but it was too late: the new world had opened. He sank himself with all the more devotion into its discovery, and when the time came for the Higher School Certificate examination he was able to put the outcome on paper. Or so we must suppose. For one of the examiners had been Kenneth Bell, history don at Balliol College, Oxford, and on reading Dick's papers Bell had taken a train to Newcastle, sought him out, and offered him a domus exhibition, spending the rest of the day overcoming Matthew Henry's opposition to so novel a prolongation of his son's education, and in the *South*. Dick would be headhunted again, but never with more consequence. He duly went up to Balliol in October 1929, at the then unusually young age of seventeen.

Here was another jolt. Dick's triumphant entry to Balliol did not at first bring contentment. There were two reasons. The more immediate—not uncommon with freshers coming from a broad schooling—was disappointment with the course. It all seemed to be about details of the English constitution, which was not the kind of thing Roberts and Bunn had discussed into the night. More than thirty years later, as Chichele Professor, Southern's early disenchantment would bear fruit in his initiative in changing the Oxford syllabus. But at the time the only fruit was the sour one of doubt whether he had picked the right course. To make things worse, he had to deal with the doubts on his own. At the freshers' dinner he and another seventeen-year-old historian, Geoffrey Nuttall, had met and struck up what proved a lifelong friendship. But Nuttall remembers that, while Dick would meet other Balliol freshers in his, Nuttall's, rooms, it was not often the other way round. With his family, meanwhile, Dick's relationship suggests another not-uncommon undergraduate preference: for keeping home and college separate. He would spend vacations mostly in the old way, trekking and reading, more often than not with his old schoolmaster, Bunn.

The second reason for Dick's undergraduate anxiety was on a broader stage. Within weeks of his entry to Oxford came the Wall Street crash. A Tynesider could not be insensitive to the resulting unemployment and poverty. Dick felt it the point of distraction from work, and thought of changing to the new PPE school. It promised to answer so many important questions in an Oxford where '-isms' about politics, philosophy, and economics were clamouring for the undergraduate soul, especially Roman Catholicism and Socialism. Although the former of these was espoused by the Balliol medieval tutor, F. F. ('Sligger') Urquhart, as more vocally by the Jesuits of Campion Hall, Dick's letters at the time show no trace of its having affected him. It was otherwise with Socialism. Dick read *The Manchester Guardian* ('the best paper by far') most days, and the *New Statesman* ('first-rate'), and attended socialist meetings; but he did not inhale (so to speak), thinking the Labour Party 'probably as challenge presented to faith by major scientific discoveries. When a friend later asked him what had brought him back to Christianity, Southern thought for a while and said 'Anselm, I suppose'. Both the answer and the hesitation are significant. Many influences were at work. Perhaps the safest answer to the question was one he gave in 1964 when it was sprung on him in the middle of a broadcast discussion with Michael Foot, and he just replied 'the study of history'.[14]

The erosion process was outwardly imperceptible until a particular date, 25 March 1937. In his Pusey House talk, Southern recalled the date as marking another of his unexpected experiences, changing everything. He had been in Cambridge, working in the library at Corpus Christi on a sermon-manuscript of Anselm's biographer, Eadmer. He felt no religious interest in Anselm or Eadmer, only absorption in their personalities. On the evening of 24 March he handed the manuscript back to the librarian and said he looked forward to seeing him in the morning. The librarian, normally friendly, became stern and said 'You will not!' He was Edwyn Hoskyns, a strong High Churchman, and he reminded the visitor that the next day was Good Friday, a time not for work but for reflection and repentance. Vexed, but at the same time ashamed at having forgotten what week it was, Southern found himself the next day stuck in Cambridge. To pass the time he went to sit in the nearby church of St Bene't's. A powerful sermon by a German anti-Nazi pastor was followed by the *Benedictus*, at the end of which come the words: 'to give light to them that sit in darkness and in the shadow of death, and to guide our feet into the way of peace'. The eighty-year-old Southern remembered: 'in that instant I found myself a Christian. Just like that. It happened without my stirring hand, foot, or mind.' He left the church not knowing what to do. Later, he was surprised that he had not gone back to tell Hoskyns, but he did not think of it then. Instinct pointed him to Newcastle. In the end, since he was about to be a Fellow of Balliol, he put himself under instruction by the Balliol chaplain, Tom Pym; and, fifteen months later, on 26 July 1938, he was confirmed in the bishop of Newcastle's chapel, in the company of others 'of about the age I would have been if I had not walked out ten years earlier'. After that, he recalled, he had never felt 'the slightest inclination or mental tendency' to be anything else than Christian.

---

[14] A transcript of the debate was printed under the title 'Looking at History' in *Dialogue with Doubt*, introduced by G. Moir (London), 9–28, with this exchange on p. 12.

The outbreak of war on 3 September 1939 did not at first interrupt Southern's tutoring. But half way through 1940 he decided to cross Broad Street and enlist in the local infantry regiment, the 'Ox and Bucks'. He was sent to its barracks at Cowley. For a time he was still able to dine in Balliol, going back afterwards to sleep in the barrack-room, an experience (he said) that gave him some idea of life in a Cistercian monastery. But by November, soldiering had become less academic. He wrote to Richard Hunt:

> The Army is not at all bad but it so happens that we have had a rather hard week. I manage to do a fair amount of reading, though it has got very scrappy lately, and I enjoy everything except the 'instruction' by the NCOs, which is unspeakable.

He was not put at this stage among the 'potential officers', for which in retrospect he was thankful, since, he wrote in another letter, he had come to share 'the habits and a lot of the prejudices of the platoon', which had above all given him an invigorating sense of collectivity:

> There was a lot of brutality and animalism among the men at Cowley, but no concentration on self; and one got a deep and unselective attachment to them, so that I was surprised at the pain of it and the breach there was in leaving them. Oh, how tedious it all was, and is; but it was not wasted time, and I shall never forget Johnny Toole and Schwarzberg and Thompson with whom I carried on disjointed discussions in the evenings.

By the time he wrote this the army had changed its mind, and made him an Officer Cadet after all. In February 1941 he was moved to the Officer Cadet Training Unit at Droitwich, and soon afterwards to another in Malvern, where his brother Douglas called on him from a unit nearby, and where he would relieve underemployment by slipping out to the Worcester Public Library.

Southern was commissioned on 26 April 1941 as second lieutenant in the Durham Light Infantry, and moved north to its depot (recently relocated from a barracks half a mile from his Fenham home) in the spectacular Brancepeth Castle, near Durham. Fell-walking had given him an exceptionally strong physique, and as a subaltern he so impressed his Commanding Officer (not least by insisting on getting up to do Physical Training with the Other Ranks) that he was short-listed for a commando regiment to fight in the Western Desert. The general who was to do the choosing arrived when he was at PT, and Southern was sent for, but the sight of Southern's thin, sweating, bare-legged, figure (so he later judged), saved his life. He was sent instead as platoon commander to the nearby

> I've never been so attracted by anything. . . . It's not just that I like the place,
> though I found it delightful; but somehow I believe in the future of medieval
> studies in America more than here. . . . But in the end . . . I can't come. There
> are just too many things on the other side that make it impossible.

Besides lectures and visits, Southern occasionally broadcast for the BBC,
twice in round-table debates on religion. A transcript of the debate with
Michael Foot shows listeners were not short-changed. At one point Foot
incautiously glorified the Renaissance, together with the Enlightenment
and French Revolution. Together, they had destroyed medieval superstition and barbarism. Southern's reply in the transcript runs: 'You must
allow me to say that what you have just been saying is such a jumble of
misapprehension and error that I find it difficult to know where to begin.'
He did begin, for all that, and summarised in a few eloquent sentences the
message to which, twenty years later, he planned to devote three volumes.
After the debate he thought it must all be over between him and Michael
Foot; mistakenly, for after Dick's death, Foot wrote to Sheila recalling his
sparring-partner with warmth and admiration.

The supervision of postgraduate students became formalised in the
1950s, and Southern was a natural draw. Here, too, he expected hard
work, less in measured hours than in the bruising struggles needed to
make sense of medieval evidence. There are professors around the world
today who recall the mutual comfort they had to give each other after
supervision with Southern. For all that, his graduates, like his undergraduates, knew they were learning what they could never have learnt elsewhere, and any confidence lost was recovered in group seminars, where
Southern—Galbraith's pupil in this, too—treated debate as the life-blood
of history, and believed 'you have to let them crawl all over you'. In the
end, all his graduates became grateful friends. The editors of a *Festschrift*
prepared for his seventieth birthday had to narrow its scope because, they
said, if all who would, could, and should contribute were to do so the
volume would be 'little less bulky than the Codex Amiatinus'.

In 1961 Southern was elected Chichele Professor of Modern History.[15]
He moved his study to All Souls, and his home to Sandfield Road,
Headington. The election had taken slightly longer than some had
expected, suggesting apprehension in some electors. If apprehension
there was, the key to it must lie in Southern's inaugural lecture, *The Shape*

---

[15] The association of this chair with medieval history was already understood, but was only
formalised in 1984 by a matching adjustment in its title.

and Substance of Academic History. For most listeners the lecture was a pellucid short history of the Oxford Modern History School. For initiates, it was a preliminary barrage in a campaign for change. Peter Brown was there, and perceived, behind Southern's words, a duel between the great ghosts of the Oxford history school:

> We got the message. Freeman lost out to Round. A school founded on the model of classical studies, based upon literary texts, had been taken over by German methods of archive-based scholarship. He said little more; but we heard him. By the end, we knew that he had sounded the death-knell of the Pipe Roll.

On the Faculty Board, the new professor deftly marshalled sympathisers for an amendment in course regulations, which went through in 1963. In appearance a technicality, in effect revolutionary, it dragged the noble lineage of Constitutional Documents down into a new middle class of 'options', to rub shoulders with an arriviste paper defined as 'a theme in general history (to be studied in depth)'. The final parenthesis re-echoes, almost audibly, the voices in a debate held forty years ago. In the end, as usual, the arriviste eclipsed the older lineage and laid out a new direction for Oxford's young historians into zones like late Antiquity, early Germanic Europe, and the Crusades, whose shared deficiency before then had been their lack of 'pipe rolls'.

In his first two years at All Souls, Southern finally brought to publication his twin project on Anselm, his edition of Eadmer's *Life*, and a biography, based on his 1959 Birkbeck lectures at Cambridge. Meanwhile he continued to work with Dom F. S. Schmitt on Anselm's *Memorials*, to be published by the Academy in 1969. Between lectures and reviews, he also started on his double volume (made double at his own suggestion to the publisher) for the Pelican History of the Church, and gave papers at conferences. Amid this apparent heterogeneity a single idea was beginning to emerge, and was destined to grow in clarity over the next forty years. It was expressed in his choice of title, and directly or indirectly in the contents, of his 1970 volume of reprinted essays, *Medieval Humanism and Other Studies*, dedicated to Galbraith. The dedication was particularly appropriate in the case of its most consequential essay, touched up from a paper given to the Ecclesiastical History Society in 1965. This essay, by a rigorous re-examination of the evidence à la Galbraith, undermined a belief held universally—including by himself in 1953—in a twelfth-century 'School of Chartres'. Southern's act of iconoclasm provoked a murmuring over much of the northern hemisphere, a

murmuring far from quiescent by 2000, when, in the first volume of his
Scholastic Humanism,[16] Southern repeated and amplified his earlier arguments, with an assurance one reviewer compared to that of Cyrano, dis-
posing of twenty swordsmen in an ambush, and went on (less in the
manner of Galbraith, now, more in that of Acton) to explain why the
question mattered. It was only by seeing the twelfth-century scholastics in
their single, Paris milieu, Southern explained, that we could appreciate
the unity of the scholastic enterprise, and hence its character.

In 1969 Southern became President of St John's College, Oxford. He
had refused earlier opportunities for headships, and his acceptance of St
John's was not given without hesitation. But as professor he had been
going home tired each evening to Headington. He missed undergraduates. His main professorial tasks were achieved. Great as his influence
was, as professor, it was not that of a supremo, such as might have made
it harder for another to fill his place while he was nearby. Again,
Southern's very approach to history, with its sensitivity to individuals and
their relationships, and the unpredictable patterns these relationships
form, found its natural soil in a college, especially in one like St John's,
where history was strong, and where its new-look variety was represented
by his former Balliol pupil, Keith Thomas. Not least, the move would
bring Sheila and home back into the heart of Oxford.

During his twelve-year presidency, St John's became acknowledged as
outstanding in its academic standards. (*Inter alia* it reached the top of the
'Norrington table', the device for comparing the Finals results of colleges.) One reason commonly agreed was the opening of the Thomas
White Building, a project Southern inherited and helped nurse to completion in 1975, and which drew gifted applicants by offering three years'
undergraduate residence. Another was the President's authority and character. His first presidential act, perhaps modelled on that of his former
headmaster, had been to gather the second- and third-year undergraduates in hall, and address them for a full hour in the presence of the dean,
senior tutor, and chaplain. As he walked round the hall, Southern spoke
of the history of the college, pausing under each portrait to explain its sit-
ter's distinction and observing, too, that the college's relative wealth
robbed slackers of any excuse for poor performance. His first remark to
Sheila on returning to the Lodgings was to tell her to start packing their
bags to go: the college would no longer want him as President. But they

---

[16] pp. 58–101, with all references.

did, and all the more so as they got used to seeing a light shining at the end of the Long Gallery, where they knew the President had contrived a study (shown in the portrait by Margaret Foreman now hanging in the college) and was himself working away. When Southern was knighted in 1974, the college as a whole felt honoured. The President himself remained as careful as before to remain accessible, especially to the vulnerable. A note he sent to freshers in 1976 marks the appropriate adjustment of tone:

> Dear Freshman,
> I have written this brief account of the College as an introduction for you. It's important that we should all know what the College does and what it stands for.
>   It's also important that we should all know one another and be able to talk frankly to one another.
>   As a beginning it will be a help—to me at least, since my eyes are better than my ears—if you will write your name (and initials or first name, whichever you prefer) clearly on the enclosed name-card and wear it at the Freshman's Dinner, when I hope we shall meet.   Yours sincerely,
>   [handwritten] R. W. Southern

Southern's deafness, serious by 1976, would become all but absolute by the 1980s. Its cause almost certainly lay in an overdosing with strepto-mycin in his treatment for TB. (In the 1950s, doctors had been unaware of the danger, and there were similar cases.) The cure had saved his life, but at this delayed cost. In his last years in the Lodgings there was still music he could hear, played on an illustrious successor to the gramophone of his youth, especially—remarkably enough, and a source of the deepest pleasure—the quartets that Beethoven wrote when he, Beethoven, was himself going deaf.

By the end of the academic year in 1981 Southern had become sixty-nine, and retired. Or rather, he left St John's, and looked forward to retir-ing one day when he had completed certain tasks he still saw ahead. Dick had often found his own private dreams wandering back north to Newcastle—'its sights, its smells, its people'—and he and Sheila also made a brief tour of rural retreats nearer Oxford. But in the end reality ruled. They knew he had to be near Oxford's libraries, and they settled in 40 St John Street. Although a mere three hundred yards from the college it felt, they said, like another world. Dick reconstructed a study on the top floor, and for the first time became expert in word-processing, while Sheila followed suit on the floor below, to translate Verbruggen's book on medieval war from Dutch, and to correct and prepare Dick's copy for the publishers. Below the industrial zone their ground-floor living room

they knew he could not hear the words. In the afternoons he would spend an hour or so, as he put it, 'tottering round the parks and admiring the clouds, which give me quite intense pleasure. They speak to me more clearly than anything for, as far as ears go, I'm now almost totally deaf.' At other times it was the trees he looked at, or, quite as often, people. Walking with a young colleague in the parks one day he paused to run his gaze round the human scene—a hockey match, a couple, a mother with a pram—and murmured almost to himself: 'as I get older, I come to love the human race more and more'.

Although he knew Chapman's Homer well, Southern did not need it to tell him that ghosts have to taste blood before they will speak. To a graduate who exclaimed at the difficulty of writing history well—a fact the youngster had just discovered—the ex-officer muttered in assent, 'it tears your guts out'. For Southern, the effort was that of the artist. His 1970 presidential lecture to the Royal Historical Society described the historian's goal as the creation of 'works of art', which he defined as works 'emotionally and intellectually satisfying, that combine a clear unity of conception with a vivacity of detail, and portray people whose actions are intelligible within the framework of their circumstances and character'. None of Southern's readers would deny his success in reaching the goal he defined thus. But many of them, because the result makes such easy reading, would not guess at the toll its achievement took on him. It was a toll which grew heavier as he got older; perversely, because he said, and not altogether playfully (his own *curriculum vitae* half-illustrates the rule), that academics should write their books not while teaching but in retirement, when they knew what they were going to know, and had time. But then—experience would have to add—because we are older, the toll is greater. Southern found it so. 'It really has been very hard work for the last six months, and I suddenly felt much older when it was finished,' he told Nuttall in 1989, on finishing the second Anselm book. But two more books—volumes I and II of *Scholastic Humanism*—were still to come; and as he worked on the second he still spoke of a third, if with a conviction that faded with his physical strength. As *The Heroic Age* went to press, Sheila and his close associates could see he was exhausted. He rested, sleeping at times, happily aware when *The Heroic Age* appeared in the New Year of 2001. But the energy was spent. On the evening of 7 February, members of his family were summoned, he received communion with them, and died around 2 a.m. next morning.

People with a logical turn of mind say that the history of the world can be summarised in a sentence. A précis of Southern's work made in that spirit would identify two characteristics, one housed inside the other, and both quite apart from the question of its quality as a work of art. The first is Southern's sympathy for a particular kind of medieval churchman, a kind who combined deep thought about faith with practical action. Anselm and Grosseteste are the obvious illustrations. But the same applies in different degrees to the other schoolmen he wrote about like Hugh of St Victor, Aquinas, or Eckhart. Indeed it applies to 'scholastic humanism' as a whole. That was its point. Faith was to be understood in the light of the world of flesh and blood; and so understood, it returned dividend in the form of principles for decisive action; whence the explosive vigour of twelfth- and thirteenth-century Europe. It is no accident that the two paragons of this double principle, Anselm and Grosseteste, should have devoted their own deepest thoughts to the mystery of the incarnation; that is, to ruminating, in their different ways (set out lucidly in Southern's biographies), on the question why, independently as it were of Scripture or Church authority, God *had* to become man, in order to be truly God. Once this—essentially incarnational—theme has been discerned as one running through all Southern's writings on the scholastics, it does not take rare powers of perception to see its consonance with Southern's own character, with its combination of searching thought and a capacity to command tanks and colleges.

This characteristic fits inside another, touching Southern's historical vision as a whole. Its genesis is traceable to those few seconds in his 'teens when he 'quarrelled' with his father about the Renaissance. The intuition that moved him to do so became a historical *fides quaerens intellectum*. By way of his undergraduate reading of well-chosen secondary authorities, and later directly of Anselm and his associates, Southern nursed this historical faith to maturity and, from the moment he began publishing, built up piece by piece what became an objectively persuasive portrait, accurately represented in his last, unfinished symphony, as the scholastic humanism which unified Europe. By creating this portrait, with a skill corresponding to his own ambitious canon of history as a work of art, Southern put his readers in more direct contact with these great medieval thinkers than they could otherwise have enjoyed. In doing so he broke a barrier of misrepresentation which the sixteenth-century Renaissance and its progeny had erected for their own purposes, and added 400 years to Europe's recognisable cultural ancestry. But it was not just a matter of addition. The addition entailed a readjustment of balance, through the rediscovery of a humanism whose root was in Christian faith, whose soil was the Church, and which is now better than ever recognisable as ancestor of our modern culture. What Southern achieved was in this sense to *un*make the Middle Ages, by restoring to the intimate acquaintance of our own time an ancestry estranged by that very term, as well as by the inveterate technical difficulties that lie behind it; an ancestry whose identification brings light into lost areas of ourselves.

Reflection on Southern's life work therefore leaves us with more than a sense of admiration, as for a cricketer who has scored a lot of runs. It leaves us with an example of the service a historian can perform for his contemporary world, as a truer self-perception seeps into the common consciousness by way of a lifetime of teaching and writing, spreading out through the world (all Southern's books were translated into one or more foreign language). For all our modern Information Technology, this process must necessarily be invisible and unmeasurable. But a consideration of the work of this particular life shows it can happen, and be as effectual in the world as are the slow and invisible movements of the earth's plates. The changes in perception I refer to were not of course Southern's achievement alone. People read his writings because there was a general apprehension that the pre-fifteenth-century ancestry of modern civilisation had been depreciated and misunderstood. And if Southern had died in the Western Desert, or of TB, a score of medievalists could be named who would have done a similar job, and indeed have done. For all his artist's individualism, Southern knew he was one of a fraternity, and, with a collegiate sense which went far beyond stone walls, rejoiced in being so; a fraternity of various ages, loosely-knit, to its inestimable advantage, spread over the globe, and united only in its wish and capacity to rediscover, in mutual co-operation and for the good of its fellow human beings, those lost and encrusted medieval perceptions. Among this fraternity Southern was nevertheless the one whose vision of scholastic humanism was most coherent and enduring, and hence gave his words most power. He was its poet.

ALEXANDER MURRAY
Fellow of the Academy

Note.   Of debts I owe to the Southern family the greatest, to the late Lady Southern, I regret being unable now to pay in print. Of others, I express special gratitude to Mr Douglas Southern, for acquainting me with family hisory, and to Dr Peter Southern, Literary Executor, for allowing me to quote from his father's unpublished writings. I am also grateful to the addressees of letters I have quoted or otherwise used: Dr G. F. Nuttall, Professor Giles Constable, and Sir Keith Thomas; and Dr R. T. Hunt, FRS, on behalf of his father, the late Dr R. W. Hunt; as to Professors the Earl Russell and P. R. L. Brown, for allowing me to quote from letters of their own. A whole constellation of Sir Richard's colleagues and friends have spoken or written to me about him or put relevant documents in my hands, rendering the obituary itself the work of a fraternity. I am glad to have this opportunity of thanking its members, namely (in addition to those just named, and many others whose help has been less specific but not less welcome): the Revd Professor Henry Chadwick, Sir Howard Colvin, Dr Andrew Fairbairn, Miss Barbara Harvey, Dr. William Hayes, Mrs Christopher Hill, Dr Maurice Keen, the Rt Revd Dr Eric W. Kemp, Mrs Jane McCarthy-Willis-Bund, Professor B. P. McGuire, Dr John Maddicott, Dr Brian Mains, Professor D. J. A. Matthew, Mrs Mary Moore, the Revd A. C. J. Phillips, Mr John Prestwich, Dr Marjorie Reeves, Professor D. A. F. M. Russell, Dr Lesley Smith, Professor R. M. Thomson, and Sister Benedicta Ward.

A bibliography of R. W. Southern's historical writings published since 1980[17]

1981:
'Richard William Hunt, 1908–1979', in *Proc. Brit. Acad.*, 67 (1981), 371–97.
1982:
'The Schools of Paris and the School of Chartres', in R. L. Benson and G. Constable, eds., *Renaissance and Renewal in the Twelfth Century* (Cambridge, MA, 1982), pp. 113–37.
1983:
'Anselm at Canterbury', *Anselm Studies*, 1 (New York & London), 7–22.
'Outlines of a National Church in the Thirteenth Century', in the *Annual Report* of the Friends of Lambeth Palace Library (London), 11–21.
1984:
Chapter 1: 'From Schools to University', in J. I. Catto, ed., *The History of the University of Oxford, I: The Early Oxford Schools* (Oxford), 1–36.
1985:
'Beryl Smalley and the place of the bible in medieval studies, 1927–84', in *The Bible in the Medieval World.* Studies in Church History: Subsidia, 4 (Oxford), 1–16.
'Peter of Blois and the Third Crusade', in H. Mayr-Harting and R. I. Moore, eds., *Studies in Medieval History presented to R. H. C. Davis* (London and Rio Grande), pp. 107–18.

---

[17] For a list of writings published between 1933 and 1980 see R. H. C. Davis and J. M. Wallace-Hadrill, eds., *The Writing of History in the Middle Ages. Essays presented to Richard William Southern* (Oxford, 1981), pp. 495–502.

The Monks of Canterbury and the Murder of Archbishop Becket. Lecture to the Friends of Canterbury Cathedral (The William Urry Memorial Trust) (Canterbury).

1986:

Robert Grosseteste. The Growth of an English Mind in Medieval Europe (Oxford, 1986).

'Beryl Smalley, 1905–1984', *Proc. Brit. Acad.,* 72 (1986), 455–71.

1987:

'The changing role of universities in medieval Europe', *Historical Research*, 60, no. 142, 133–46.

1989:

'Michael Wallace-Hadrill', [an address delivered on 8 February 1986] in *Addresses of All Souls College Oxford* (Oxford), pp. 199–205.

1990:

Saint Anselm. A Portrait in a Landscape (Cambridge).

1991:

'Intellectual development and local environment: the case of Robert Grosseteste', in R. G. Benson and E. W. Naylor, eds., *Essays in Honor of B. King* (Sewanee, Tennessee), pp. 1–22.

1992:

'The necessity for Two Peters of Blois', in L. Smith and B. Ward, eds., *Intellectual Life in the Middle Ages. Essays presented to Margaret Gibson* (London and Rio Grande), pp. 103–18.

'Anselm and the English religious tradition', in G. Russell, ed., *The English Religious Tradition and the Genius of Anglicanism* (Wantage), pp. 33–46.

Second edition of *Robert Grosseteste* (1986) with 'A last review', pp. xvii–lxvi.

1993:

'Lorenzio Minio [1907–1986]', in F. Santi, ed., *Luoghi cruciali in Dante. Ultimi saggi. Con un inedito su Boezio e la bibliografia delle opere.* Quaderni di Cultura Mediolatina, 6 (Spoleto), 3–8.

1994:

St Anselm at Canterbury. His Mission of Reconciliation. A lecture delivered in Canterbury Cathedral on 25 September 1993, on the 900th Anniversary of the Enthronement of St Anselm (Canterbury).

2000:

Scholastic Humanism and the Unification of Europe. Vol. 1: *The Foundations* (Oxford).

2001:

Scholastic Humanism and the Unification of Europe. Vol. 2: *The Heroic Age.* With notes and additions by L. Smith and B. Ward (Oxford).

Forthcoming 2004:

Biographical articles on 'Anselm of Canterbury', 'Peter of Blois', and 'Robert Grosseteste', in *The Oxford Dictionary of National Biography* (Oxford).

TOM WEBSTER   *Stanford University*

Thomas Bertram Lonsdale Webster
1905–1974

TOM WEBSTER was born on 3 July 1905. He grew up in London, and lived there for twenty years in middle and later life, when he was Professor of Greek in the University at University College, the scene of much of his most fruitful work. For seventeen years before that, he was Hulme Professor of Greek at Manchester, taking up his appointment at the age of twenty-six, as the University recalled with pride and affection when it made him, in 1965, an honorary Doctor of Letters. He began his academic career with eight years (mainly) at Oxford, as an undergraduate and then a young don at Christ Church, with a fruitful interlude at Leipzig; he ended it with six years at Stanford, as Professor of Classics and then Emeritus. At and after the end of the First World War he was a schoolboy at Charterhouse; during the Second World War he served as an officer in Military Intelligence. He died on 31 May 1974 after a terminal illness of some six weeks, active until then as ever.

A photograph taken at Stanford accompanies this memoir.[1] It shows the Emeritus Professor in his element, in a classroom. He looks much as many people knew him from early middle age onwards 'incredibly close to the man as he was in 1939', as one former pupil writes. If the image suggests a tall, spare figure with (in later years) a scholar's forward stoop, so much to the good. It gives the high domed forehead, the businesslike

[1] News and Publications Service, Stanford University, with grateful acknowledgement.

Proceedings of the British Academy, **120**, 445–467. © The British Academy 2003.

brows; a smile of engaging warmth, which could shade to an expression
of amused tolerance; the features had a range of negative aspects from
boredom to an episcopal air of disapproval when stirred to anger. One
sees the keenness of the eyes, not the pale blue that could seem by turns
bright or hard; only the abrupt fall away from the left shoulder hints at a
disability overcome with poise and courage, a lower left arm malformed
from birth. The Christ Church undergraduate was remembered by a contemporary as a good and competitive tennis player, and the talent survived on the squash court in the middle age of the Professor at University
College London.

The list of writings compiled by James Hooker for *Studies in Honour
of T. B. L. Webster* has 341 items, not counting newspaper articles,
unsigned reviews, and translations of his works into other languages. The
relentless energy that generated this work is not without parallel in other
scholars of our time; what is not always to be found in combination with
so active a record of publication is the intense and generous devotion to
promoting the work of others that is so well documented in prefaces,
footnotes, and in the personal recollections of colleagues and pupils of
whatever age, and from whatever place, over some fifty years. If just one
witness is to be quoted, it had best be the vivid and affectionate memoir
by John Betts at the beginning of the *Studies . . .* just mentioned.[2] That
voice speaks for many. Less directly felt, perhaps, but often of lasting
significance, was Tom Webster's effect on institutions in Manchester,
London, Stanford and elsewhere. The creative innovation that sustained
individual enterprise could also have its powerful effect on groups and
societies, even on those occasions when (as can happen) internal differences arose over policies or their implementation. In an *In Memoriam*
notice for the Joint Association of Classical Teachers, Charles Baty
remarked:

> It is common knowledge that he played a great part in the establishing of JACT;
> but perhaps only those who worked with him then know what he did by gain-
> ing the interest of influential supporters . . .; and it can now be said (what he
> did not like us to say at the time) that his own generous contributions in money
> helped us in days of difficulty and enabled us to expand. I do not myself think
> that JACT is quite what he originally had in mind in the days of its formation,

---

[2] J. H. Betts, J. T. Hooker and J. R. Green (eds.), *Studies in Honour of T. B. L. Webster*, vol. 1
(1986), vol. 2 (1988), Bristol Classical Press. The photograph that makes the frontispiece to each
of these volumes dates from *c.*1950; it is from one of a long series of unposed portraits of colleagues taken by Dr C. R. Bailey in University College London in (and for) the common room
of that period.

but he backed us whole-heartedly when we began to take shape, and I hope he was not displeased with the way in which we grew.[3]

Webster forebears and relations of different distances emerge from the reference books.[4] He would probably have deplored any incursion into family history, for like many (or even most) people of his generation and lifestyle, he politely kept the personal and the professional world apart.[5] There was a Thomas Webster, Vicar of Oakington and Rector of St Botolph's, Cambridge, at the time of his death in 1840, a graduate of Queens' College; his eldest son Thomas, born in 1810, had brothers who were doctors: he himself read mathematics at Trinity College and became secretary to the Institution of Civil Engineers; he developed an expertise on Patent Law, and after an interesting legal career of public engagement, involving among other matters the Liverpool and Mersey docks, he died in 1875, a QC and a Fellow of the Royal Society. Among his children were Richard Everard Webster, who was to become Lord Chief Justice of England, Viscount Alverstone; and Thomas Calthrop Webster (1840–1906) the grandfather of our TBLW, Rector of Rettendon, Essex. In these and in other related people, one sees an East Anglian family of the Victorian professional class, occupied with the Church, Medicine, the Law, with members of high public distinction and a fascinating variety of talents. TBLW's father, Thomas Lonsdale Webster, was Second Assistant Clerk of the House of Commons when his son was born in 1905; his wife Esther being the younger daughter of T. B. Dalton, again an East Anglian, of Fillingham, Lincolnshire; he rose to become Clerk and to be elevated at the age of fifty-four from CB to KCB, remembered for three successive editions, with W. E. Grey, of the parliamentarian's invaluable Erskine May. It might have been predicted, given generations of forebears at Charterhouse, that he would send his son there; less obvious, given family connections with Trinity, Queens', and other Cambridge colleges, that the son would break the mould and arrive one day as an undergraduate at Christ Church, Oxford. The young Tom was perhaps a little below form on entrance to the school, missing a Junior Scholarship; but he was

---

[3] *JACT Bulletin*, 36, Nov. 1974, p. 2, omitting a parenthesis.

[4] *DNB, Who's Who?, Who Was Who?*, Venn, *Alumni Cantabrigienses*.

[5] Compare John Bayley, *Iris* (1998), p. 14, beginning: 'There was a lot of privacy about in those days ...'; or (going back earlier) J. A. K. Thomson on Gilbert Murray, *Proc. Brit. Acad.*, 43 (1957) at p. 254 f., 'while he was one of the friendliest, he was one of the remotest of men ... His sympathy was unfailing and unwearied; he liked to give it and to get it. But he did not need it.'

Figure 2.   Göteborg, 1952.

to the Manchester Literary and Philosophical Society and appeared
subsequently in the Society's *Memoirs and Proceedings.*[21] Publications of
this kind, there and elsewhere, were to continue; they went on, over the
years; their interest here, setting aside such value as they have as contributions to knowledge, is that they show in a clear form the writer's enthusiasm for new material and for first-hand interpretation of it, as well as the
ability to deploy, from a splendid memory, backed by card-indexes of high
efficiency, the parallels that could transform an object into an object lesson. There is other significant work in the field of classical archaeology

---

[21] For instance, 'Greek vases in the Manchester Museum', *Mem. and Proc. Manchester Lit. and
Phil. Soc.*, 77 (1932–3), 1–7; 'Greek Vases in the Manchester School of Art', ibid. 78 (1933–4),
1–7; for more, see the list in Betts, Hooker and Green (above, n. 2).

from this period; but a major development is the appearance of studies in Sophocles, leading up to the book *An introduction to Sophocles*, first published by the Clarendon Press in 1936, and reproduced in a second edition with additional material by Methuen in 1969.

> It appeared to me [he writes] . . . that I could only interpret a passage to my own satisfaction by comparing it with other passages of the same kind. This necessitated my using the analytical and comparative method, and gave me the main divisions of this essay into thought, characters, plot, songs and style. But this procedure made it necessary to assume the order of Sophocles' plays and difficult to discuss his development. I therefore decided to begin with a chapter on the life of Sophocles and the chronology of his plays and end with a general account of his development.

More than thirty years later, the preface to the second edition expresses the hope that 'it still serves its modest purpose of providing a sort of comparative grammar of Sophoclean drama'. There is much in this that illuminates the method of the book and in large measure the great volume of work to follow. The base, as the author's own words tell us, is a close analytical reading of the text. It is presented with a conciseness and a wealth of primary documentation that challenges the closest attention, even as one may wish to delete and add. Additional Note N, for example, in under two pages, gives sets of line references for 'the chief motives in the surviving plays of Sophocles'. This, if it does nothing else, concentrates the mind powerfully. Likewise, on character-contrasts, in the course of an approach to Sophocles that was later to prove fruitful with Menander, the meat of the argument is presented schematically in just over a page (pp. 88–9). In the work on Menander too, the concentration on structure and design is evident; it is rescued from sheer formalism by a lively interest in the social and intellectual context of the writing, whether in the fifth century or the fourth, and by the concern that the narrative should lead to new insight.

In oral presentations and seminars the different elements of the argument could be more sharply separated. Michael Coffey makes the point in recalling the impact of the Professor of Greek on the undergraduates who met him on his return from war service in 1945, some of them also just demobilised, 'men of maturity, receptive to wide-ranging ideas, a powerful example to those of us who were young and immature, having had no break in our education'. The skill in linking ideas from different aspects of literature and life that was so conspicuous had its other side in the way in which 'he taught his pupils to distinguish between what is relatively certain and what is the bold imaginative suggestion that may editions appeared (respectively) in 1960 and 1970. The combination of innovative ingenuity and minimalist argumentation make some parts of this work hard reading, and there are tracks which no-one would now wish to retrace. The achievement remains considerable. On the appearance of the first set of studies, L. A. Post wrote 'This is the first book in English, I believe, that is devoted entirely to Menander and nothing else, except for editions, translations, or theses'; '. . . a book,' he concluded, 'that will be useful and necessary to scholars, but that might deter the less advanced student and obscure for him the pure genius of Menander by its sheer abundance of detail. It should be welcomed, then, not as scripture, but as learned and ingenious and intelligent commentary.'[29]

The powerful sense of forward movement that Tom Webster brought to his new appointment, however personal to him, was also evident elsewhere. It was evident nationally in the run-up to the Festival of Britain (he was a great enthusiast for it when it opened in 1951); and the colleges of London University, all with their own histories of wartime exile and damage of one kind and another, were alike regenerating and thinking, sometimes rather tentatively, of ways in which their departments might collaborate. The problems of joint action between institutions dispersed across a metropolis of ten million people or so have been known to be underestimated, sometimes by colleagues for whom another college is something a short walk, or a short bicycle ride away. A day used to be set aside for intercollegiate lectures, with sports in the afternoon for some.

It was in this context that a course by R. P. Winnington-Ingram was memorably parodied at a student party in a college not his own (the three principal parodists all later became Professors themselves);[30] some fifty attended T. B. L. Webster on 'Homeric Problems'. Other leading lights could be named; for younger colleagues, the foundation of the London Classical Society on the initiative of M. L. Clarke and Victor Ehrenberg gave regular occasions to meet and discuss papers in a way that was generally new to them. These developments are recalled here because they held within them seeds from which grew the Institute of Classical Studies, and—with the gift of the golden opportunity brought by Michael Ventris's decipherment of the Linear B script as Greek—the Institute's

---

[29] *American Journal of Philology*, 74 (1953), 107–9. See also Sandbach's acknowledgement to both books (once again this side idolatry), written some 20 years later in the Preface to A. W. Gomme and F. H. Sandbach, *Menander: a Commentary* (1973). My own debt to the two books is very great.

[30] This was, I think, not long before the publication of *Euripides and Dionysus* in 1948: he would have enjoyed the occasion.

first regular activity, the Mycenean seminar. It has met ever since. In all this Tom Webster's role, much though he credited to others, was cardinal. What made the initiative possible was a partnership between the two old-established national institutions, the Societies for the Promotion of Hellenic and Roman Studies, and the University of London. The societies had (and have) a wide membership, very high international prestige, and a fine library extending beyond texts and research materials to works of interest to an informed general public; the University's part was to provide new premises against the expiry of a long-running lease, and to enhance the academic side of the organisation with its own contributions to library resources and with its intercollegiate activities, reaching out meanwhile with seminars, publications, and facilities for visitors from home institutions and from overseas. The first Director was E. G. Turner (later Sir Eric); the inaugural meeting, held in University College, was addressed by one of the major figures of international scholarship, Bruno Snell, whose distinguished career as a classicist culminated in his Rectorship of Hamburg University. The official foundation date was 16 October 1953. Activities continued in the Societies' premises at 50 Bedford Square and in University College for a few years more, until the first stage of the vision was realised in the session 1957–8 with the move to a new building in Gordon Square shared with the Institute of Archaeology, a partnership which was to last for another thirty-nine years until the move in 1997 to more spacious accommodation with new partners in the University of London Senate House.[31]

The choice of Bruno Snell to give the inaugural lecture for the new institute was no accident. It was a token of the contacts made in pre-war years between scholars working in London and their continental colleagues, and now, in friendship, being resumed. Distinguished exiles—among them, Tom Webster could look to his colleagues Arnaldo Momigliano and Oswald Szemerényi in University College—made lasting contributions to the British classical scene; but the facility of both Websters in European languages (Madge Webster had happy recollections of times she spent in Sweden and in Vienna) made them congenial hosts and visitors alike. There came to London, among others, Gudmund Björck, Uvo Hölscher, Albin Lesky, Manu Leumann, and Karl Reinhardt; nor were English-speaking countries abroad overlooked, one of the furthest

---

[31] The story of the foundation of the Institute, of Tom Webster's part in it, and of later developments (in which he himself played a major role) is well told by John Barron, 'The vision thing: the founding of an Institute', *Bulletin of the Institute of Classical Studies*, 43 (1999), 27–39.

elsewhere. A younger generation with a marked inclination towards an interdisciplinary approach to classical studies and a special interest in the reception of Greek drama at times and in places away from its origins has given a new recognition to the value of all this labour and to the intellectual attitude that sustained it.[35]

The discoveries of the 1950s brought excitements of several kinds to the field of classical antiquity. Apart from the revelation that the Linear B tablets were written in Greek, we had a papyrus fragment of a historical tragedy that was presented as contemporary with Aeschylus (but was it Hellenistic after all?);[36] another that down-dated Aeschylus' *Supplices* to the 460s, some thirty years or so later than most people had supposed; and then the recovery of a complete play by Menander (less minor damage) in the shape of the *Dyskolos*—one could go on. Tom Webster's response to all this was manifold, and it is interestingly seen in his Presidential Address to the Classical Association in 1960, under the title 'First Things First'.[37] Amid all the excitement, he shows a concern, which he never lost, for the essential contacts, as he saw them, between the main achievements of the ancient world and the active interests of a modern non-specialist. This came at a time when the output of new specialist publications in all classical fields was increasing remarkably, as it has done since, and when the impulse to trace data and interpretations to their sources was fostered not only by a growing intensity of technical scholarship, but by more efficient means of international communication with libraries, archives, museums, and sites.

> Of course [he remarks] the specialist must pursue his special subject wherever it leads him . . . But the general practitioner (and we are all general practitioners over most of the field) is best served by the scholarship of his own time and perhaps of his own country. He will have been brought up on the scholarship of the preceding generation; the scholars of his own generation live in the same world that he does, are subject to the same influences, and face the same problems. New problems, new influences, as well as new techniques and new material, will appear in the scholarship of the next generation, which will be published when our hypothetical general practitioner is in his fifties. If he man-

---

[35] See for instance Pat Easterling and Edith Hall, *Greek and Roman Actors* (2002), xviii, with a quotation from an important review article by Hall entitled 'Theatrical Archaeology', *American Journal of Archaeology*, 101 (1997), 154–8.

[36] Strictly speaking its first appearance dates from 30 Sept. 1949, in a paper communicated to the British Academy by Edgar Lobel and published in *Proc. Brit. Acad.*, 35 (1949), 207–16; it is currently quoted as *Tragicorum Graecorum Fragmenta* [= *TrGF*] ii. 664.

[37] *Proceedings of the Classical Association*, 57 (1960), 9–20.

ages to keep up with this new scholarship, he will have a Nestorian view which includes three generations, and we should not ask for more.

The consolation for any readers of these words to whom scholarship is antiquarian rather than dynamic is present in the opening remark, as well as in the respect and support given over the years to colleagues and associates whose temperament led them to stay on the ground rather than to attempt flight. What is implied here is that while a grasp of primary evidence is essential, there is still some room for tolerance, according to the nature of the user, in deciding how far the term 'primary' extends; but essentially the view is that data are for solving problems and gaining insights and not simply for accumulation. Thus in *The Tragedies of Euripides* (1967), a book full of speculative hypotheses, the Introduction says that: 'This book is written in the belief that an attempt to describe all the tragedies of Euripides might be useful to students of ancient drama, both those who know Greek and the much larger number who study ancient drama in translation.' After brief remarks on translations, it goes on: 'Reconstructing lost plays is a dangerous business, and I have therefore thought it essential to give all the evidence (or at least to refer to places where the evidence can be found). Where the argument inevitably involves quotation of Greek, I have tried to make clear the points at issue.' An admirable objective; but the problem is not only that of Greek, but the unfamiliarity of many potential readers with the kind of arguments used in evaluating fragmentary evidence, among them the use of statistical methods, seriously discussed both before and since, for dating the development of Euripides' metrical style. The end of the book, reached after many intellectual adventures, seems worth quoting to show both its author's enchantment with his subject and the lack of illusion over its many intractabilities. He liked to fly with ideas, but was too good a scholar to press them, in the way some do, into doctrine.

> In so far as Euripides has a message [he writes] it is the play in its totality with all its metrical and musical varieties and gradations, all its range from beautiful fantasy to modern reality, all its differences between characters and within single characters, a flux of events and emotions in which nevertheless certain human qualities are always condemned and certain human qualities are praised without qualification, but except for them 'the lights are dim and the very stars wander'.

The decade of the 1960s, which this account has already invaded, was for Tom Webster one of high achievement and deep sadness. Teaching and research (always placed first) continued with intensity. There were sympathy and affection, and slightly amused tolerance if they failed to reach the very high standards which, as one of nature's aristocrats, he had set himself, and, as a convinced democrat, never despaired of finding adhered to by others.

Stanford, as it was planned to do, brought a fresh start and a new lifestyle. To a visitor it was not wholly clear if his host would appear dressed as a member of the Athenaeum or in jeans and in a blue top that must have seen many better days; but to have been surprised would only display ignorance of his acute sense of context; he was equally up to hosting a dinner party or offering a share of a home-made meal ('Will *oeufs florentines* do?') in his apartment. In California he could relax, as he perhaps never did quite so readily elsewhere; he enjoyed San Francisco; he was delighted by the humming-birds and other minor wildlife of the Stanford campus, and made excursions to different places with his sketchbook. It would be easy, from the outside, to sentimentalise this scene as one of idyllic retirement to the far West, if it were not one side of a deeply engaged life of teaching and research as a regular Professor in the Department of Classics, with an active relationship to senior and junior colleagues alike, who before long had him take his turn as Chairman. When not busy with all this, or with maintaining a correspondence in rapidly but neatly written pen or ballpoint with friends and colleagues in the United States and abroad, he could at times be found in the museum, labelling or cataloguing terracottas and other objects, some of them survivors from the earthquake of 1906—in fact continuing some work begun a few years before as a visitor. The *Introduction to Menander* published in 1974 was written while supervising a Stanford Ph.D. on the author; it had several articles and reviews as by-products; and, as ever, there was a diversity of other enterprises in hand, notably an attractive book for Batsford entitled *Athenian culture and society* (1973).

The spring of 1974 was not a happy time for the Classics at Stanford. At the end of March, Tom Webster was afraid that two of his colleagues and close friends would be axed and have to find posts elsewhere, as in fact happened.[40] Before long, he was himself struck down with what proved to be inoperable cancer. Visitors as the end came near included Otto Skutsch, who had been his colleague for a time in Manchester, and for seventeen years as Professor of Latin in University College London; Ron Mellor and William Berg were among regular visitors from Stanford, and they played him music till the last, when he found it hard to speak.

---

[40] TBLW to EWH, 27 Mar. 1974.

On 31 May 1974 he died. In a eulogy delivered at Stanford, Mark Edwards, who had known him in England, remarked how effectively his skilful guidance continued to function when transplanted to the different conditions of classical teaching in the United States.

> His enthusiasm and warmth [said Professor Edwards] affected any student anywhere who came into contact with him; and his immense knowledge somehow did not frighten or overwhelm the pupil, but only urged him on. I think this was partly because, for him, teaching and research always went closely together, so that one always felt *he* was learning too; it was very much this experience of shared excitement that made so many of his pupils keep in touch with him in later years.

The eulogy ended as follows:

> We must be glad that his long life of teaching and scholarship continued until only a few weeks before his death, and that he was spared the frustrations of old age, about which the Greeks were often eloquent. We must be thankful to him for his life, his work, the warmth of his friendship, his unending considerateness; but we may justly feel sadness for ourselves, who have lost an incomparable companion and friend. Plato used the same words about the death of his own teacher: ἀπέκλαον ἐμαυτόν—οὐ γὰρ δὴ ἐκεῖνόν γε, ἀλλὰ τὴν ἐμαυτοῦ τύχην, οἵου ἀνδρὸς ἑταίρου ἐστερημένος εἴην.

ERIC HANDLEY
Fellow of the Academy

Note. I am grateful to the Department of Classics at Stanford for visits there, and here particularly to Mark Edwards for a letter of 13 Sept. 1975 with a typescript of his eulogy, and to Ron Mellor for a very moving letter written on 1 June 1976. Without these and other personal communications acknowledged above, this Memoir would have been much harder to write; its finished version has benefited from comments by Peter W. H. Brown, Pat Easterling, Dick Green, and Carol Handley.

MARY WILKINSON

Elizabeth Mary Wilkinson
1909–2001

THE OUTSTANDING SCHOLAR of German humanism, Professor Elizabeth M. Wilkinson, died on 2 January 2001 at the age of 91. She was one of the greatest, and—across the whole spectrum of the humanities—one of the most highly regarded, scholars of German culture this country has produced, in particular because of her illuminating work, both historical and theoretical, on German Classicism, which did much to bring home its living significance. All who knew her were impressed by the depth and breadth of mind that she brought to bear on her work. As the large gathering of successive generations of her students and colleagues, convened at University College London on 16 March 2001, showed unambivalently, she will be fondly remembered as a teacher of genius who combined in a uniquely charismatic way sheer intellectual excitement, tender (and patient) regard for the development of individual students, and a passionate—sometimes fierce—dedication to the resolution of first-order problems. At a time when the term 'scholarship' is used more and more, even in university circles, in the debased sense of 'background knowledge', and is being replaced by 'research' (in the equally debased, journalistic sense of the mere elicitation of information), it is appropriate to celebrate the inspiring scholarly leadership she provided in post-war *Germanistik*, both in person and in print, by virtue of her clear articulation of the ethical, intellectual and therefore pedagogic importance of what it was she professed. In these days of intense intercultural engagement, the analysis of the position of non-German germanists that she offered to the Deutsche Akademie für Sprache und Dichtung, on

Proceedings of the British Academy, **120**, 471–489. © The British Academy 2003.

receiving the 1975 'Prize for Foreign *Germanistik*', seems, for example, uncannily prescient of our present condition:

> Every non-German germanist should, in my opinion, foster a stereoscopic approach. He should keep one eye firmly on the subject and try to approach the level of German *Germanisten*. The other eye he should keep on his countrymen and try, by whatever means, to bring home to them German culture in such a way that they assimilate what is other. If, later, he accepts the proposal of making available to a German public what originally was meant only for his fellow countrymen, then this should only be undertaken in the spirit of Goethe's 'repeated reflexion', of what he dubbed in the broadest sense of the term, 'World Literature'.[1]

This is the Mary Wilkinson of whom British germanists have every reason to be proud: unambiguously precise about highly complex matters, and uncompromisingly committed to a position once she had thought it through. She was unswervingly loyal to those who she believed shared her faith in the pedagogic and cultural value of what she liked to call 'perennial humanism', reformulated for the modern world in Weimar Classicism. Indeed her highly productive collaborations—not only with her partner of thirty-seven years, L. A. Willoughby, but also with younger colleagues (with George Wells, Kathleen Coburn, and Brian Rowley, for example)—are testimony to her conviction that scholarship is a shared, communal activity, one best practised in open debate and discussion. But she had no time in intellectual life for 'the Third Way', if what was meant by that was a diplomatic fudge. Her whole orientation was to identifying and tackling the conceptual problem rather than to finding a form of words which might obfuscate it—very much in the spirit of Goethe's saying, taken from his *Wilhelm Meister*:

> Truth, so it is said, is situated at the central point between two opposing views. Not at all! The problem lies between the two, that which is beyond our range of vision, eternally active life, contemplated in repose.[2]

Mary Wilkinson's heartfelt devotion to such intellectual virtues did not make her a predictably comfortable and reassuring interlocutor; but it was the mainspring of that lucid argumentation, high scholarly sophistication, and superb writing-style that she was able to sustain for fifty-odd years, and for which her colleagues honoured her. 'Altogether

---

[1] Elizabeth M. Wilkinson, 'Preis für Germanistik im Ausland: Dankrede', *Deutsche Akademie für Sprache und Dichtung: Jahrbuch* (1975), 18–23 (p. 22).
[2] *Johann Wolfgang von Goethe: Maxims and Reflections*, ed. Peter Hutchinson and trans. Elizabeth Stopp (London, 1998), p. 82. Henceforth referred to as *Maxims and Reflections*.

I am suspicious', she wrote in her tribute to Thomas Mann on his death in 1955, 'of the postulated dichotomy between abstractions and concretions, between theory and practice. The bearing they have on each other is incredibly close and fascinatingly complex.'[3] Her rare combination of theoretical rigour, long historical perspective, and astonishingly accurate aesthetic insight (*Anschauung*) ensure that, for many years to come, her work will be an exhilarating source of lively, scholarly education.

* * *

Mary Wilkinson was fond of reminding her audiences of her Yorkshire background. Born in Keighley on 17 September 1909, she considered the Brontës' moors (and, later, Jane Eyre's study of Schiller's 'crabbed but glorious Deutsch') formative influences on her life. But her aim was not simply to emphasise the Northerner's traditionally high evaluation of plain speaking (a trait which she believed had been powerfully reinforced by her attendance at Whalley Range High School in Manchester). Her yet more serious intent was to underline what she came to discover and artic- ulate as one of the foundational tenets of Weimar Classicism. 'Coming from a background which afforded little in the way of cultural experi- ences', as she put it in her Inaugural Lecture, delivered at University Col- lege London on 25 October 1962,[4] and though lacking the advantage of imbibing with her mother's milk and at her parents' knee those implicit criteria and standards which issue eventually in what we call taste, she was profoundly grateful to be in a position to authenticate Goethe's and Schiller's conviction that 'aesthetic education was to start far earlier than our encounters with art' (*Inaugural*, p. 24), 'in the indifferent and undif- ferentiated spheres of physical life . . . in our first apprehensions of shapes and spatial relations, our early preferences for performing one and the same natural act in this way rather than another' (p. 23). When she did eventually engage with art, her sensitivity to the delights of its different media, born of her early training in the physical-mental prehension of the significances presented to sense, led to a lifelong love of music (which at one point she intended to study on a scholarship to the Royal Academy) and, above all, to a passion for poetry which possessed her to the very

[3] 'Aesthetic Excursus on Thomas Mann's *Akribie*', *Germanic Review*, 31 (1956), 225–35 (225).
[4] *In Praise of Aesthetics* (London, 1963), p. 10. Henceforth referred to as *Inaugural*.

end. From her earliest childhood on, Keats, Shelley, Wordsworth, and Coleridge—to be joined in her youth by novelists such as D. H. Lawrence, Virginia Woolf, and, above all, Thomas Mann—informed, at the deepest level, her sense of what literature is and can be.

She came late to Goethe.[5] Prompted by motives 'far too unacademic to be recounted' (*Inaugural*, p. 12), she was, in her own words, 'deflected' away from her first loves of biology, history, and English into German— which she started from scratch in 1929—as an undergraduate at Bedford College, by her teacher, J. G. Robertson. He also tempted her back from a spell of school-teaching at Clapham High School and Southampton Grammar School, to undertake research, on an Amy Lady Tate Studentship (1937–9), under the supervision of another of those formidable women who have done so much to shape and establish German studies in this country, Edna Purdie. Her thesis on a comparatively unknown German figure of the eighteenth century, an uncle of the Romantic critics August Wilhelm and Friedrich Schlegel, entitled 'A critical Study of Johann Elias Schlegel's aesthetic and dramatic Theory', was accepted by the University of London for the degree of Ph.D. in 1943. The intense reflection on the fundamental principles involved in doing humanistic scholarship which work on her doctorate prompted issued in two precepts that were to inform her scholarly output for the rest of her life. On the one hand, the long and arduous coming-to-terms which she undertook, not just with the relevant secondary literature on her topic but with thinkers of the stature of Ernst Cassirer, J. M. Thorburn, Samuel Alexander, F. O. Nolte, and—above all—Susan Stebbing and Edward Bullough, her chief teachers in logic and aesthetics (*Inaugural*, pp. 25–6), gave rigorous intellectual expression to a characteristically conscientious concern with presenting to the critical reader the method, and the methodology, of research. It also yielded results that are truly significant, because they are illuminatingly set in the relevant theoretical and historical perspectives, without, as a consequence, either over- or under-estimation of their importance. The revised version of her thesis, *Johann Elias Schlegel: A German Pioneer in Aesthetics* (Oxford, 1945), awarded the Robertson Prize of the University of London (and reprinted in 1973 in Germany [Darmstadt], with a second Preface) emphatically marked the end of Mary Wilkinson's scholarly apprenticeship.

---

[5] 'Goethe's Poetry', *German Life and Letters* (henceforth referred to as *GLL*), 2 (1949), 316–29; re-published in Elizabeth M. Wilkinson and L. A. Willoughby, *Goethe: Poet and Thinker*, 2nd edn. (London, 1970), pp. 20–34; German version: *Goethe: Dichter und Denker* (Frankfurt, 1974).

Inspired by Susan Stebbing's answer to the question posed on the outbreak of the Second World War, of what she would now do—'carry on with my work'—Mary Wilkinson, after a spell of driving an ambulance in London, gave her first lectures, as a Temporary Assistant Lecturer, in Aberystwyth, where the German Department of University College London (which she joined in 1940) had been relocated. It was here that she embarked on a remarkable thirty-seven-year collaboration with her former teacher L. A. Willoughby, whom she had first met at a student party in 1931. Most of the profoundly insightful, epoch-making, post-war essays on Goethe which they wrote together, sometimes in collaboration, always in consultation, after 1946, were collected in what became a famous book, *Goethe: Poet and Thinker*, published in 1962, a year after her appointment to the Chair of German at University College London.

Her first study (1946) of Goethe's *Tasso*, as 'the Tragedy of the Poet'—like the second, published three years later with the characteristic sub-title, 'An Inquiry into Critical Method'—was soon re-published in Germany; and both established her international reputation for a compelling combination of astonishingly perceptive close-reading with revealing, authoritative historical and theoretical contextualisation.[6] Further essays on Goethe-as-thinker—'On the Varying Modes of Goethe's Thought' and the Henriette Hertz Trust Annual Lecture on a Master Mind, delivered to the British Academy on 11 July 1951, entitled 'Goethe's Concept of Form'—are masterly deployments of the high level of intellectual refinement to which she had trained herself in the preceding decade or so. But perhaps no essay of this period better exemplifies the quality of her scholarship than 'The Relation of Form and Meaning in Goethe's *Egmont*',[7] described by the distinguished American critic and

[6] 'Goethe's *Tasso*: The Tragedy of the Poet', *Publications of the English Goethe Society* (henceforth referred to as *PEGS*), NS, 15 (1946), 96–127; German version: 'Goethe: *Tasso*', in *Das Deutsche Drama vom Barock bis zur Gegenwart: Interpretationen*, ed. Benno von Wiese, 2 vols. (Düsseldorf, 1958), 1, pp. 193–214 and 486–89. '"Tasso—ein gesteigerter Werther" in the light of Goethe's Principle of 'Steigerung': An Inquiry into Critical Method', *Modern Language Review* (henceforth referred to as *MLR*), 44 (1949), 305–28; German version: '"Tasso—ein gesteigerter Werther' im Licht von Goethes Prinzip der Steigerung: Eine Untersuchung zur Frage der kritischen Methode', trans. Ernst Grumach, *Goethe: Neue Folge des Jahrbuchs der Goethe-Gesellschaft*, 13 (1951), 28–58. Both essays are reprinted in *Goethe: Poet and Thinker*, pp. 75–94 and 185–213.

[7] 'The Relation of Form and Meaning in Goethe's *Egmont*', *PEGS*, NS, 18 (1949), 149–82; German version: 'Sprachliche Feinstruktur in Goethe's 'Egmont': Zur Beziehung zwischen Gestalt und Gehalt', in *Begriffsbestimmung der Klassik und des Klassischen*, ed. Heinz Otto Burger, Wege der Forschung, 210 (Darmstadt, 1972), pp. 353–90. The essay is reprinted in *Goethe: Poet and Thinker*, pp. 55–74.

theoretician John Ellis as 'one of the most brilliant and sophisticated pieces of criticism ever written—on Goethe or any other figure'.[8] For here the fruit of the difficult apprenticeship to which she had dedicated herself—an apparently uncanny ability to read the mind of her author in a wholly original and convincing way—is at its most exemplary.

And it is entirely typical of Wilkinson's restless pursuit of truth that she so quickly came to question the conceptual adequacy of the theoretical underpinnings of this particular essay. Modification, in the face of both textual and contextual fact, of the regulative principles she had worked out in preparing her first book was her constant concern. So much is clear, for example, from the thorough, fundamental, book-reviews she undertook in the 1950s and 60s. Whether she was considering Agnes Arber's meticulous scrutiny of Goethe's science[9] or Barker Fairley's brilliant, if flawed, *Study of Goethe*;[10] Emil Staiger's theory of poetics[11] or F. O. Nolte's ground-breaking accounts of eighteenth-century criticism and aesthetics[12]—her preoccupation was with two theoretical problems about which she felt, a lack of clarity was hindering progress in understanding the cultural significance of German classicism: the Form–Content problem, and the question of aesthetic Illusion, as distinct from any other type. The re-thinking which this critical stance entailed, vis-à-vis her own work and that of others which she most respected, did not in any way hinder her productivity; indeed, as in the case of the Introduction to her immensely successful edition of Thomas Mann's *Tonio Kröger* (Oxford, 1944), it stimulated her to reflect on the pedagogic

---

[8] John M. Ellis, 'The Vexed Question of Egmont's Political Judgement', in *Tradition and Creation: Essays in Honour of Elizabeth M. Wilkinson*, ed. C. P. Magill, Brian A. Rowley, and Christopher J. Smith—henceforth referred to as *Tradition and Creation*—(Leeds, 1978), pp. 116–30 (p. 120). (This *Festschrift* contains an informative biographical introduction, and an excellent bibliography by Ann C. Weaver.)

[9] Review of Agnes Arber, *Goethe's Botany*; Maria Schindler and Eleanor C. Merry, *Pure Colour*; and L. A. Willoughby, *Unity and Continuity in Goethe*, PEGS, NS, 16 (1947), 120–4, and of Agnes Arber, *Goethe's Botany*, *MLR*, 43, 556–8.

[10] Review of Barker Fairley, *A Study of Goethe*, PEGS, NS, 17 (1948), 173–85.

[11] Review of Emil Staiger, *Grundbegriffe der Poetik*, *MLR*, 44 (1949), 433–7.

[12] Review of F. O. Nolte, Lessing's *Laokoon*, *MLR*, 37 (1942), 230–2, and of his *Art and Reality*, *MLR*, 39 (1944), 401–2. The former review is reprinted in Elizabeth M. Wilkinson and L. A. Willoughby, *Models of Wholeness: Some Attitudes to Language, Art and Life in the Age of Goethe*, ed. Jeremy Adler, Martin Swales and Ann Weaver, British and Irish Studies in German Language and Literature, 30 (Oxford, 2002), pp. 17–19. (See the editors' sensitively accurate Introduction to this companion-volume of *Goethe: Poet and Thinker*.) Henceforth referred to as *Models of Wholeness*.

benefits of inevitably problematic literary interpretation[13] and its rightful place in university education.[14] Moreover, precisely because she saw that such intellectual problems reflected vital issues of human existence, she relished opportunities to popularise her findings in such publications as *The Radio Times* and *The Listener*, and in BBC radio broadcasts during the Goethe anniversary celebrations in 1949.[15]

In her scholarly work proper the quest for a solution to the foxing question of how form '*as such* but an intellectual abstraction', in order to be aesthetic, yet *appears* to be 'inextricably interwoven with content'—as she formulated it in 1944[16]—took two, complementary, directions. On the one hand, she took a predominantly historical approach; on the other, a predominantly theoretical. Consciously and deliberately she tested the theoretical conclusions she had so far reached by applying them to problematic aspects of Thomas Mann,[17] of Coleridge,[18] and of Herder.[19] In her reading of *Joseph und seine Brüder* and *Doktor Faustus* (as of William Faulkner's story *The Bear*) she found welcome corroboration of what she was gleaning from abstract study of eighteenth-century Weimar aesthetic theory: that the 'content' (*Inhalt*) an artist uses to create his work is quite different from the 'content' (*Gehalt*) the work has in terms of significance; and that what is created is a 'semblance' (*Schein*), a frank illusion with no pretence to 'real' content.[20] The work, in collaboration with Kathleen

---

[13] See, for example, 'Group Work in the Interpretation of a Poem by Hölderlin', *GLL*, NS, 4 (1951), 248–60; German version: 'Gemeinschaftsarbeit bei der Textinterpretation eines Hölderlin-Gedichtes', trans. K. W. Maurer, *Studium Generale*, 5 (1952), 74–82.

[14] (With B. A. Rowley) 'Testing Candidates for a University Course in Language and Literature', *Modern Languages*, 42 (1961), 56–64.

[15] See, for example, 'Goethe's *Egmont* might have been written for us', *The Radio Times*, 22 April 1949, p. 4; 'Goethe's Art and Practice of Living', *The Listener*, 10 Nov. 1949, pp. 801–2.

[16] Review of Nolte's *Art and Reality*, 401; cf. *Models of Wholeness*, p. 19.

[17] See above, n. 3; and her speech to P. E. N. Club Memorial Meeting for Thomas Mann (5 Oct. 1955), *P. E. N. News*, 192 (1956), 27–32.

[18] See her transcriptions, translation, and annotation of German entries in *The Notebooks of Samuel Taylor Coleridge*, ed. Kathleen Coburn, vol. 1, *1794–1804* (London, 1957), two parts; vol. 2, *1804–1808* (New York, 1961), two parts; and 'Coleridge und Deutschland, 1794–1804: Zum ersten Band der Gesamtausgabe seiner *Notebooks*', in *Forschungsprobleme der vergleichenden Literaturgeschichte,* 2, ed. Fritz Ernst and Kurt Wais (Tübingen, 1958), pp. 7–23.

[19] (With L. A. Willoughby) 'Goethe to Herder, July 1722: Some Problems of Pedagogic Presentation', *GLL*, NS, 15 (1961), 110–22, and 'The Blind Man and The Poet: An Early Stage in Goethe's Quest for Form', in *German Studies presented to Walter Horace Bruford* (London, 1962), pp. 29–57; German version: 'Der Blinde und der Dichter: Der junge Goethe auf der Suche nach der Form', trans. Peter Hasler, *Goethe Jahrbuch*, 91 (1974), 33–57. Both essays are reprinted in *Models of Wholeness*, pp. 127–42 and 99–125 respectively.

[20] See above, n. 3, 230.

Coburn, on Coleridge's *Notebooks*, which she began in 1947, came to fruition over the next fifteen years or so. But the confirmation which Coleridge's reading of his German contemporaries provided of her own interpretations underpinned her sense of the fundamental rightness of the positions she had worked out. Furthermore, her explorations in collaboration with L. A. Willoughby of Herder's investigation of the psycho-physical foundations of a specifically aesthetic sense of form gave her an unshakeable conviction of having come at least close to discovering the truth of the matter. But, characteristically, she was under no illusion that she possessed the whole truth. She continued to test her historical findings in terms of the 'virtuous spiral' she saw at work in scholarship: the thought of the past and modern theorising dynamically related in reciprocal subordination, now the one, now the other gaining ascendancy (*Inaugural*, pp. 25–6). Like Herder, she 'never lost sight of structure when investigating genesis' (ibid., p. 17) or of genesis when investigating structure. By drawing on contemporary aesthetic theories (in particular, the work of Susanne K. Langer, itself indebted to the theorising of the German eighteenth century, mediated in part by Edward Bullough and J. M. Thorburn) she arrived at a more precisely formulated account of some of the central concepts of German classicism than was hitherto available—even to eighteenth-century thinkers themselves. In principle, such progressive refinement is open-ended: as current theory develops, so historical insight may grow. In short, by a skilful interplay of history and theory, she arrived at an understanding of Weimar aesthetics, which is open to further re-thinking in the light of whatever 'postmodern' consciousness is yet to come, once brought to bear on emerging historical knowledge.

The upshot of Mary Wilkinson's scholarly reflection during this middle period of her career was a powerful theory, rooted in her mastery of key texts of the late eighteenth- and early nineteenth-century debate on the role of the aesthetic. It was Goethe's and Schiller's shared conviction that objectification of the inner life is the distinctive function of all art: 'the poet', as Herder had it in opposition to Lessing, 'should express feelings'.[21] 'Feeling' in the eighteenth century had a much wider meaning than it has today, encompassing what T. S. Eliot called 'felt-thought', the whole continuum from tactile sensation to thought—i.e. thought not yet reduced to the either-or categories of discursive language and, thus,

---

[21] See 'Schiller's Concept of *Schein* in the Light of Recent Aesthetics', *German Quarterly*, 28 (1955), 219–27 (225).

highly ambivalent. A work of art, like any other aesthetic phenomenon, articulates such feeling by providing, for our contemplation, an analogue of the felt-life within, something which can be achieved only if this analogue—this 'semblance' (*Schein*)—exhibits the same sensuous-abstract quality as the felt-thought it is designed to express. Where this illusion is achieved the direct benefit for our minds is twofold. On the one hand we gain in self-awareness, and self-control. On the other, aesthetic insight is knowledge and, like any form of freshly acquired knowledge, enables us to conceive the world with a new tool. Commonly shared but dimly apprehended feelings become, through aesthetic experience, no less shared but now articulated 'convictions' or 'attitudes'—*Gesinnungen*—upon which we act and base our reasoning, but to which (for the reason that they are still in part tethered to sensation) we find it impossible to give adequate intellectual expression. Such sensuous-abstract schemata permit us to 'see into the life of things'. *Gehalt*—'content' in the sense of 'import'—is that aspect of our felt-life that the work of art 'contains' for us. Feeling, Susanne Langer argues, has distinctive patterns; it exhibits what she calls a 'morphology':[22] the structure of the inner life is an organic, developmental one in which thinking-feeling-bodily sensation are interfused. And it is in constant interaction with the external world: we internalise ideas and impressions—what Goethe and Schiller called *Stoff* ('content' in the sense of 'material')—by aligning them with the felt, dynamic, patterns at work within us. Because of different life-experiences the felt-life of one individual will, to a lesser or greater extent, differ from that of another. But, because we share the same, or at least a similar, natural, cultural, or social environment, the overlap will be considerable. The more fundamental and encompassing the felt-thought an aesthetic object articulates, the more 'universal' its appeal will be, the greater its significance. If what is within us is to be projected outwards on to it, the aesthetic phenomenon must exhibit the same organic structure as the morphology of our inner life; it must, as Schiller argued, evince 'manifest freedom' (*Freiheit in der Erscheinung*): it must appear to be both self-regulating and self-regulated. In order to achieve this, peculiarly aesthetic, illusion, the relations established in the aesthetic object must inhere in the medium used, so that its aesthetic order does not appear to be imposed from outside, but *seems* rather to be immanent in the object itself.

---

[22] Susanne K. Langer, *Philosophy in a New Key: A Study in the Symbolism of Reason, Rite, and Art* (New York, 1961), pp. 92 and 202.

anchored in the grammatical, rhetorical, logical, and aesthetic, detail of her text, Wilkinson succeeded in re-presenting Schiller's arguments in a mode which caught the interest of her contemporaries, at home and abroad: a German book-version of the Introduction, Glossary and Appendices to their joint edition appeared in 1977.[28]

After producing, with L. A. Willoughby, a masterful, short, account of the logic of Schiller's conception of 'wholeness' in human life,[29] Mary Wilkinson felt she had done for the moment all she could to explicate Schiller's thought, and turned back to Goethe, and his *Faust*. Like her work on Schiller, the development of what was announced in 1973 to be a theory of *Faust* as 'Tragedy in the Diachronic Mode' had a long history.[30] An early article on the traditional theological material built into the First Part of the play was deeply unfashionable on its first appearance in the 1950s heyday of New Criticism, with its exclusive interest in what the Germans call *werkimmanente Interpretation* ('reading restricted to the work in itself'); and it likewise seemed to owe its new-found popularity in the 1970s to the swing in fashion to the other extreme, that of 'tradition-hunting' for its own sake.[31] Given the pervasive advocacy on all sides today for 'literary (and cultural) theory', it might seem that Wilkinson's three great essays on *Faust* of 1957, 1971, and 1973 are poised to enjoy another bout of fashionable acceptance.[32] But her interest in theory is a predominantly practical one; she held, with Goethe, that 'theory in and of itself is of no use' (*Maxims and Reflections*, p. 70), and that its chief value lies in raising sensibility to the level of clear, and therefore, *applicable*, principles. It would be difficult to find better illustrations of Wilkinson's typically practical theorising than her three *Faust* studies.

---

[28] *Schillers Ästhetische Erziehung des Menschen: Eine Einführung* (Munich, 1977).

[29] ' "The Whole Man" in Schiller's Theory of Culture and Society: On the Virtue of a Plurality of Models', in *Essays in German Language, Culture and Society*, ed. Siegbert S. Prawer, R. Hinton Thomas, and Leonard Forster (London, 1969), pp. 177–210. Repr. in *Models of Wholeness*, pp. 233–68.

[30] See 'Goethe's *Faust*: Tragedy in the Diachronic Mode', *PEGS*, NS, 42, (1973), 116–74 (136–44).

[31] 'The Theological Basis of Faust's Credo', *GLL*, NS, 10 (1957), 229–39; German version: 'Theologischer Stoff und dichterischer Gehalt in Fausts sogenanntem Credo', in *Goethe und die Tradition*, ed. Hans Reiss, Wissenschaftliche Paperbacks, Literaturwissenschaft, 19 (Frankfurt, 1972), pp. 242–58, repr. in *Aufsätze zu Goethes 'Faust I'*, ed. Werner Keller, Wege der Forschung, 145 (Darmstadt, 1974), pp. 551–71. Cf. above, n. 30, 139–41.

[32] The second of these three articles is: 'Faust in der Logosszene—Willkürlicher Übersetzer oder geschulter Exeget? Wie, zu welchem Ende—und für wen—schreibt man heutzutage einen Kommentar?', in *Dichtung, Sprache, Gesellschaft: Akten des IV. Internationalen Germanistenkongresses 1970 in Princeton*, ed. Victor Lange and Hans-Gert Roloff (Frankfurt, 1971), pp. 115–24.

Her argument, *in nuce*, is that, at all levels of the text, *Faust* invites a double response: on the one hand, to the 'synchronic' dimension of the (illusory) 'presence' which it shares with all other fictional works; and, on the other, to a 'diachronic' dimension, deliberately contrived by Goethe, that opens up to the reader's/spectator's critical contemplation the perennially recurrent structures of Western modes of feeling, thinking, doing, and being. Her concern is to account for a salient fact of the text, noted by successive commentators: namely, that whether *Faust* is dealing with theology or economics, with the dramaturgy of the theatre or poetological semiotics, its astonishing wealth of material is always redolent of the whole length of Western history. In arguing that Goethe is out to trace the ramifications of those constituent forms of our shared cultural inheritance, recurring, in a non-successive, ahistorical, pattern, Wilkinson affirms the relevance of the greatest text in the German language to a generation which sees itself as inhabiting a postmodern age which seeks in such works as Jostein Gaarder's *Sophie's World* or Richard Tarnas's *Passion of the Western Mind* orientation in the otherwise bewildering welter of cultural forms that have come down to us.

The intellectual excitement generated in and by Mary Wilkinson's writings also accompanied her into the classroom. In crucial ways she was the perfect teacher at both undergraduate and postgraduate level (and was proud of the Diploma in Education she was awarded at Oxford in 1933). Her instruction in translation from German into English was a model of how to instil the difficult discipline of giving due weight to grammatical, lexical, logical, and rhetorical values in interpreting written (and oral) language. Her view of grammar, for instance, as a repository of age-old human thought, always to be respected, if not always adhered to, was a liberation to a generation of students disoriented by the 'alternate' grammars which flourished in the wake of the Chomsky revolution. In seminars and lectures the back-and-forth of genuine exchange—she also put her own positions to the test in class—engaged head and heart alike, in order, as she had it, 'to set the feeling expressed in art before the eye of the mind'. Her continued reflections in print on the pedagogic value of language and literature as a university subject were the precipitate of her own teaching experience.[33] Even her negative comments (perhaps in part

---

[33] 'Vox Collegii', *New Phineas*, 22, n. 2 (1963), 2–5; 'On Being Seen and Not Heard', Presidential Address to the Modern Language Association (3 Jan. 1964), *Modern Languages*, 45 (1964), 4–13; 'On Teaching Prescribed Texts: Further to the "Form-Content" Problem', *Modern Languages*, 55 (1974), 105–16.

and Thomas Mann, her personal taste did not in any way dictate her appointment-policy as Head of Department: she engaged distinguished teachers and researchers in the medieval period, in the nineteenth and twentieth centuries, as well as in her own field of specialisation—many of whom went on to occupy Chairs of German at home and abroad. But perhaps her most memorable, and enduring, administrative contribution was to the English Goethe Society, which she served in various capacities from 1945 on: most notably as Editor (1953–71), as President (1974–85), and as Vice-President (from 1986 until her death).

Mary Wilkinson's helpfulness to, and patience with, younger colleagues helped ensure that her sense of the human importance of scholarship as the open-ended and inherently difficult process of apprehending, at all levels, the interrelation of multifaceted cultural phenomena, was passed on to succeeding generations. She never forgot to acknowledge her own formative influences, and she impressed upon others the need to see the work of the individual scholar as a contribution to a group-effort, both past and present. The motto, 'Ist Fortzusetzen' ('To Be Continued')—taken from the end of Goethe's *Wilhelm Meisters Wanderjahre* of 1829, which its editors have given to the newly published collection of some of her and Willoughby's finest essays, *Models of Wholeness*—nicely captures her view of scholarship as provisional and dependent on the scholarly community for further development. In a 1968 article on *Wilhelm Meister* she and Willoughby offered their findings to others, since 'we ourselves are unlikely to put [these raw materials] to either of the uses mentioned in our sub-title'.[35] And six years later they provided, explicit for the further consideration of other scholars, a sketch of the largely untold story of the filiation of Weimar Classicism down through the Russian Formalists to French (and American) Structuralists, emphasising the consequent damaging distortion caused by such a lack of historical perspective.[36] Amongst much else, this paper alone has stimulated a research project, supported by an AHRB Large Research Grant, in the Department of German and the Centre for Intercultural Studies at the University of Glasgow investigating the intellectual background of Ernst Cassirer's theory of culture with

---

[35] 'Having and Being, or Bourgeois versus Nobility: Notes for a Chapter on Social and Cultural History or for a Commentary on *Wilhelm Meister*', GLL, NS, 22 (1968), 101–5 (101); reprinted in *Models of Wholeness*, pp. 227–32 (p. 227).

[36] 'Missing Links or Whatever Happened to Weimar Classicism?', in '*Erfahrung und Überlieferung': Festschrift for C. P. Magill*, ed. Hinrich Siefken and Alan Robinson, Trivium Special Publications, 1 (Cardiff, 1974), pp. 57–74.

reference to Weimar Classicism and subsequent German cultural theorists. Indeed, Wilkinson's impact on *Germanistik* has been immense: work by Jeremy Adler, Paul Bishop, Ilse Graham, Martin Swales, Hans R. Vaget, and David Wellbery—to mention but a few, distinguished examples—would be unthinkable without her. Moreover, partly because of her work on Coleridge, her writing has resonated far beyond the confines of German Studies. Lore Metzger's acknowledgement, in a study of English Romantic poetry, of her indebtedness to Wilkinson's 'exemplary scholarship' is indicative of broad influence which has continued unabated.[37]

To those who knew her, Mary Wilkinson was an inspiring, and occasionally daunting, presence on the academic stage, on account of both her warm, and magnetic, personality, which evinced an incredible liveliness of spirit well into late old age, and her indomitable character, which enabled her to wage a successful battle against cancer from her late fifties on. After her retirement from her Chair in 1976 she continued to work, giving lectures to the Conference of University Teachers of German ('The "Scandal" of Literature', in 1980) and to the English Goethe Society (her Presidential Address entitled 'Perception as Process: Goethe's Treatment of "Auf dem See"—with an Excursus on Emblematics', in 1976 and her valedictory address, 'To Estonia, With Love: Reflections on the Name and Nature of Scholarship by a Rank Outsider', in 1989); chairing the special joint meeting of CUTG and EGS in 1982 at Queen Mary College, London to mark the one hundred and fiftieth anniversary of Goethe's death, in connection with which she broadcast on both Radio 3 and German radio. She also edited a collection of essays by various hands, celebrating the 1982 Goethe-Year, to which she contributed a piece of her own, 'Sexual Attitudes in Goethe's Life and Works'. She had been refining the lecture version of this since the late 1960s, during which time, no doubt because of its theme—and the fact that she drew on a *Playboy* translation of Goethe's poem, 'The Diary'—it had gained almost mythical status. The printed version, like the radio broadcasts on the same topic, revealed its central topic to be, by contrast, Goethe's theory and practice of Renunciation (*Entsagung*).[38]

---

[37] Lore Metzger, *One Foot In Eden: Modes of Pastoral in Romantic Poetry* (Chapel Hill, 1986), pp. xiv–xv and 11–12; cf. Morag Harris, *Emily Dickinson in Time* (London, 1999) and *The Garden of Language and the Loaded Gun: Linguistic Transformations in Romantic Aesthetics* (New York, 2002), passim.

[38] *Goethe Revisited: Lectures delivered in sundry places and on various dates to mark the 150th anniversary of Goethe's death* (New York, 1983; London, 1984), pp. 171–84.

writings, he was honest, fair, reasonable and moderate. There was a hesi-
tancy in his speech, and he was conciliatory, but none of this came from
timidity or lack of self-confidence. He had a dry sense of humour and a
dislike of humbug.

Early life, 1916–1938

The Wilsons had come over from Scotland in the seventeenth century and
had been farmers in County Antrim with land holdings of 30–40 acres
typical of Ulster. The Ellisons, Tom's mother's family, were similar, but
from County Down. Tom's father dealt in grain and had a grocery business, while continuing with the farm. Eventually Tom inherited it, passing
it at once to his children, who sold it on his advice. Tom's parents were
Methodists. The family went to church twice on Sundays, and his father
read them part of the Bible every evening. They lived in Belfast which, in
the early 1920s, was torn by civil strife. As a child he was in a tram caught
in a fusillade of bullets from the IRA. The terrorists on both sides often
picked on respected persons, who had taken no part in the violence, to be
shot, and Tom's father was at risk. Decent families on both sides tried to
shelter those on the other believed to be in danger, and Tom's family sheltered some Catholics who were old friends. After 1923, when civil war
developed in the South, the energies of the IRA were diverted there and
Belfast became peaceful, apart from sporadic outbreaks.

Just before he was six, Tom was forced to spend a year in bed as treatment for a suspected tubercular hip, followed by a year on crutches. He
learned to read, and was read to a great deal by his father, but his schooling was delayed. After a church school, he went to Methodist College
('Methody'), a large co-educational grammar school, strong at rugger,
which Tom was not allowed to play because of his leg. The school was not
especially religious, despite its name. Tom did best in history and English,
but described his school career as 'undistinguished' (despite winning
prizes and being made a prefect). At all events, it enabled him to proceed
to a four-year Honours degree (along Scottish lines) at Queen's
University. Tom chose to read economics from the second year because
he was concerned by the unemployment and poverty caused by the 1930s
depression. Not being allowed to specialise entirely in that, he combined
it with economic history and political science, but regretted not having
stayed with straight history, where there was a strong department. The
lecturer in economic history had lost interest in it, and Tom found it very

boring, especially Clapham's great volumes. The professor of economics was H. O. Meredith, a Cambridge first in classics and economics, who had been a Fellow of King's slightly senior to Pigou, and an Apostle and friend of E. M. Forster. Why he had gone to Queen's University Belfast just before the First World War Tom never discovered. From him, Tom learned much about Keynes's *Treatise* and also, as soon as it came out, *The General Theory*, for this was a part of economics in which Meredith's interest was well maintained. Otherwise, he occupied himself in translating Euripides into blank verse. In his finals, Tom did well in theory, with John Hicks as his external examiner, but not in economic history or political science. So he got a top second, not a first, despite having previously won prizes and a gold medal. There was then no chance of winning a studentship for post-graduate work.

His four years at Queen's had transformed Tom from a schoolboy into a young man with expertise, energy, and growing self-confidence. Besides his success in academic economics, he shone in other activities. After failing in sport at school, he became a leader of opinion at Queen's, an editor of *The New Northman*, an active participant in debates at the Literary and Scientific Society—the 'Literific'—and a chosen delegate to a debate at the University of Glasgow (where he had to oppose Conor Cruse O'Brien), and to the Zimmern Summer School of International Relations at Geneva (both of these in 1937). Then, in 1938, as representative of the churches of Northern Ireland, he attended a world youth peace conference at New York. Tom was at this time a socialist and anti-Unionist, as his writings for the New Northman show. However, his experiences at these meetings shook his faith, guiding him towards the eclecticism referred to above. Queen's was avowedly non-sectarian, and several of Tom's friends were Catholics, but for him a new and unpleasant aspect of that religion was revealed by the Vatican's support of the Franco regime in Spain, as well as by the vituperation he met when he accompanied a Labour candidate canvassing in the poorer Catholic streets of Belfast. The New York conference's proceedings and resolutions were, he came to realise, entirely controlled by the communists, with no effective input from any other of the numerous delegations. The hard face of reality made him less confident of youthful ideals, but he became more confident of his own ability to go beyond them.

requirements in the knowledge that they would inevitably be cut down—an early lesson in 'public choice'.

Early in 1942 the chance came for another move—to the Prime Minister's Statistical Branch under Lord Cherwell (the Prof), who, as well as being Churchill's scientific adviser, had a brief to record and comment on the strength and state of readiness of the armed forces in the various theatres of war, on shipping, manpower, munitions production, and other aspects of the war economy. The Branch was quite small, consisting at any one time of half-a-dozen economists, one scientist, Cherwell's private secretary (John Clarke) and some chartists and typists. Roy Harrod had been responsible for recruiting the economists, and remained as the Branch's nominal chief until he resigned in mid-1942, when Donald MacDougall took his place. In fact, MacDougall had become Cherwell's right-hand man since Harrod had recruited him at the outset. The work was governed by Churchill's desire for independent advice on the conduct of the war effort (but excluding military strategy), and in particular its quantitative aspects. Cherwell and MacDougall both had a flair for seeing what was quantitatively important and could handle and manipulate figures with ease. One kind of output of the Branch consisted of volumes of charts recording the progress of the war from many different aspects, of which Churchill (and Roosevelt) was an avid reader. Another kind of output consisted of succinct minutes to Churchill (averaging about one a day) on any matter where his intervention might improve the war effort. They could originate with a question from Churchill, or an idea of Cherwell's, or of a member of the Branch. The main task of the members of the Branch was obtaining the information both for the charts and for the minutes. Whereas the charts could be routinised, for the minutes it was often necessary to persuade departments to provide facts which, they were aware, could be used to criticise their own actions. It required a tremendous investment in tact and perseverance to develop and maintain good relations. Tom's talents in 'networking' were put to good use and strengthened, as also was his ability to sift the important and sensible from the welter of available information. Each member of the Branch had his speciality, and Tom's was manpower planning; but he also worked on post-war employment policy (leading to the famous 1944 White Paper) and on the reform of social insurance (following the Beveridge report of 1942). He returned to both topics after the war. He remained in the Branch until the war in Europe was over and Churchill was defeated in the 1945 summer election, when the Branch was disbanded. His success there can be gauged from two events. Just three members of the Branch accompanied Cherwell to the Potsdam Conference in July 1945: MacDougall, Clarke and Tom. Just three members of the Branch were decorated at the end, of which Tom was one, receiving the OBE.

In later years Tom expressed dissatisfaction with his war career. This was not because his work was uninteresting or unimportant, nor even because he was less exposed to danger as a civilian than as a member of the armed forces. On the contrary, he knew that he had made a more important contribution than a great many servicemen, and had been in greater danger in London in the blitz. What he regretted was not having shared the experiences of so many of his generation. His initial self-satisfaction with his OBE turned to self-reproach 'when I thought about the thousands of men who had given life and limb to the struggle against the Axis with their sacrifices unacknowledged and often unobserved, whereas I had been sitting in comfort in Whitehall'. Tom's modesty is abundantly displayed. He hardly ever talked about his wartime role. Nor about an experience resulting from his restless dissatisfaction. With the Normandy invasion imminent in the Spring of 1944, and Churchill pre-occupied with it, work in the Branch died down. Tom made contact with a shipowner working in the Ministry of Transport through Dorothy, also working there, to see if he could get into the Merchant Navy to play a part in the landings. After getting (reluctant) permission from Cherwell, he was taken on as part of the larger crew required for a Thames estuary tug which towed parts of the Mulberry harbours across the Channel. Two other members of the Branch (Charles Kennedy and Jack Parkinson) were allowed to join him.

On the disbandment of the Branch, Tom went to the Economic Section of the Cabinet Office, then headed by James Meade. He found the work there more academic than in the Branch, and himself less in sym-pathy with it. One hot topic was the control of nationalised industries, with Meade and Fleming advocating marginal cost pricing even where this involved making losses. Tom wrote an article, published in the *Economic Journal* (55, 1945), criticising their views. He looked around for alternative employment and found an *embarras de richesses,* with offers from Queen's University, Belfast, Manchester (John Jewkes), Bristol, the LSE (Lionel Robbins), and Cambridge (Richard Stone), amongst seven. The LSE was the most tempting, and Tom later felt it would have been better for his development as an economist than his final choice which was a Fellowship at University College, Oxford (as successor to Harold Wilson). However, at that stage he had had enough of London and longed for the country.

made a big difference. He followed up the subject later by an unpublished paper with C. V. Brown on 'Price competition under oligopoly' (1969) and, finally, by a survey 'The microeconomic foundations of microeconomic policy' in his collection of essays *Inflation, Unemployment, and the Market* (Clarendon Press, Oxford, 1984). The closely related topic of competition policy was examined in two reviews of British experience (Department of Trade and Industry, *International Conference on Monopolies, Mergers and Restrictive Practices* (HMSO, 1971), and in a Danish publication). Tom also edited, with Andrews, a collection of articles that had appeared in *Oxford Economic Papers* entitled *Oxford Studies in the Price Mechanism* (Clarendon Press, Oxford, 1951), of which the most famous was one by Hall and Hitch which originated the idea of the kinked demand curve under oligopoly.

Oxford Economic Papers, which had been occasional pre-war, became a regular journal from 1949, with Tom as editor. He had a heavy burden of tutorials, initially twenty hours a week, and became, successively, domestic and estates bursar of his college. Despite all this he found time to edit *Ulster under Home Rule* (Oxford University Press, 1955), to write a book on inflation (see below), and to have published a dozen journal articles and two chapters in different books before leaving Oxford in 1958.

One of his concerns was monetary policy and inflation, and here, as often, he swam against the tide of fashion. This was that changes in short-term interest rates were not a good way of influencing domestic demand for a variety of reasons: it was dangerous to put them high (say 10 per cent or more), and small changes had little effect; their effects were on industrial investment and housing, which was undesirable; they were unquantifiable and so unsuitable for the fine tuning of the economy then in vogue; and higher rates would increase the cost of servicing the national debt, including that held by foreigners. The Bank of England largely accepted these views, and monetary policy relied on persuading the bank cartel to restrict advances and on controls on hire-purchase. By contrast, in an article in *Oxford Economic Papers* in 1957 and in evidence to the Radcliffe Committee on the Working of the Monetary System in 1958, Tom proposed a revival of the old Currency School doctrine that there should be statutory limits to the fiduciary issue (he proposed a growing limit). He argued that the velocity of circulation of the note issue varied less than that of more widely defined stocks of money, and that limits of this kind would constrain the government to keep inflation within reasonable bounds, and would reassure foreign opinion. This proposal (which had support from Lord Robbins and E. V. Morgan) was given short shrift by the Radcliffe Committee and derided by Tom's colleague, Charles Kennedy, who likened it to asking the doctor to treat the rise of the column of mercury in the thermometer instead of the causes of the rise of temperature in the patient—a misunderstanding, to put it mildly, of the argument. Tom also argued the case for a more active monetary policy against another colleague, Dick Ross, who had served in the Economic Section, in *Bulletin of the Oxford University Institute of Statistics,* 19 (1957), and in an unpublished address on wage inflation given to several audiences, including one at the Bank of England in 1957. He stressed the need to reduce demand and accept some increase in the then very low rates of unemployment (below 2 per cent). He was sceptical of 'sermons and appeals to the trade union leaders for moderation in their demands'. All this, and more, came together in a book on *Inflation* (Blackwell, 1961) completed after leaving Oxford, but mainly written there. It was one of the first post-war books on the subject and attracted an unfavourable review from Friedman, lukewarm from Robertson, but enthusiastic from *The Banker.* It was to take about 20 years before the wheel of fashion in Britain would turn round to, and beyond, Tom's position.

Glasgow, 1958–1984

In 1958 Tom was appointed to the Adam Smith Chair of Political Economy at the University of Glasgow, where he remained, rejecting invitations to move elsewhere, until he retired. He felt that 'Political Economy' suited him. He wanted a change from Oxford, expected to find more time for his own writing and research, and welcomed the opportunity provided by his position as head of department to shape the courses. He succeeded A. L. Macfie, who was an expert on the history of economic thought, and who had been in the teaching tradition which followed through the classical writers Smith, Ricardo, Mill, and so on. While courses on the history of economic thought were retained, the main course was modernised. Tom's department was responsible for single-year courses in economics taken by about 1,200 students of accountancy, law, engineering and science, as well as for the last two years in the four-year honours course in economics, with about a hundred students. Following tradition, Tom gave lectures to the large audiences of the one-year courses, although he did not enjoy doing so. He decided to abolish signing-in attendance at these lectures, but when he announced this he was disconcerted by the students' way of welcoming this reform by drumming their feet. Tom introduced a requirement that his lecturers should speak for only half the time, the rest being used for discussion with the class, assisted by an additional member of staff. This suffered, at least initially, from the reluctance of Scottish students to speak. Tom's friendly and informal relations with the staff of the department, his enjoyment in discussing a wide range of topics with them, his many contacts outside Glasgow which enabled him to invite interesting and famous economists to give lectures and seminars, and which he was ready to use when graduates or staff wanted to move elsewhere, are all well remembered. His arrival appeared to many as a breath of fresh air. He believed in 'horses for courses'. Although continually writing articles and books himself, that was not essential for everyone—administration and teaching were honourable activities in which excellence could be achieved. He thought the Scottish general degree was probably more useful in later life for many students than the narrower honours degree courses insisted on in English universities.

The department Tom inherited was a lively one, benefiting from close relations with the applied economics research department headed by Alec Cairncross. As it was a time of great expansion post-Robbins, Tom confronted the problem of recruiting more staff. He succeeded in attracting a number from outside Scotland, including a future Permanent Secretary in the Treasury (Gus O'Donnell) and an American from Berkeley (Diane Dawson). He also instigated the appointment of Alec Nove to a new chair with responsibility both for Soviet economic studies, in which he was an acknowledged authority, and for the administration of work on development economics. Tom had long maintained an interest in the former, and his interest in the latter began in 1962 with a term as Nuffield Visiting Professor at the University of Ibadan in Nigeria, and continued with several visits to Kenya, following an arrangement under which economists from Glasgow were seconded for a term to the University of Nairobi.

A major occasion in Tom's tenure of the Adam Smith Chair came in 1976 with the bicentenary of the publication of *The Wealth of Nations*. A new edition of Smith's works was prepared and published by Oxford University Press, accompanied by a substantial volume of *Essays on Adam Smith* (Clarendon Press, Oxford, 1975) edited by Andrew Skinner and Tom. A conference to which over two hundred guests were invited was organised and the papers presented there published in another volume, *The Market and the State* (Clarendon Press, Oxford, 1976) with the same editors. Tom played the major part in making the invitations (net-working again) and in planning the papers for this second volume. The first volume was more Skinner's responsibility, as he was expert on the subject. An accident also threw on his shoulders much of the 'nuts and bolts' organisation, as Tom suffered a heart attack just beforehand. He was a great hill walker, and had accompanied a group of much younger persons up a long and very steep slope from the glen of Balquhidder. He had to be assisted down and taken to hospital. He recovered sufficiently to appear at the conference, but his paper for the second volume was read for him by Malcolm MacLennan. This paper, on 'Sympathy and Self-Interest', explored the proper role of sympathy and benevolence in market transactions, making the point that an efficient functioning of the market as a device for coordinating and informing economic activity required that those on each side of a transaction put aside the interests of the other—what Wicksteed called 'non-tuism'. Each side could be acting benevolently towards *other* persons, but market signals would be confused if they did so vis-à-vis each other. Much the same considerations applied to the behaviour of different units in a socialised economy, and even to different departments within a government. However, the larger the unit, the greater both the need and the ability to take a broader view of social interests, and in all cases there had to be a framework of rules within which behaviour was constrained. He made other interesting points, and this essay shows Tom as a political economist at his best. The volumes and the whole conference demonstrated the depth and durability of Smith's contributions to the social sciences. There were favourable reviews in the *Economic Journal* and the *New York Review of Books.*

Dorothy had shown the first signs of multiple sclerosis in 1952. In 1966 she had a severe attack. Her mobility then slowly declined and she had to use a wheelchair, although never completely confined to it. Before 1966 she looked after home and children and did some extra-mural teaching and voluntary work, but in that year she obtained a full-time lectureship at Glasgow University in social administration, which she held to retirement in 1982. She had published a short comparison of welfare provision in the USA, Canada, and the UK. ('America and the Welfare State', *Planning,* 26, 1960), and then became interested in Sweden, leading to her book *The Welfare State in Sweden* (Heinemann, 1979). Tom, whose earlier concern with the Beveridge Report has already been noted, became a director and later chairman of the Scottish Mutual Assurance Society, and wrote a number of articles and contributions to books on the welfare state. He edited *Pensions, Inflation and Growth* (Heinemann,

1974). This was a comparative study of state provision for the elderly in six continental European countries by four different authors (the chapter on Sweden by Dorothy), with an introduction and a substantial comparative analysis including the UK and the USA by Tom, the whole representing a major research project. He and Dorothy together wrote *The Political Economy of the Welfare State* (Allen & Unwin, 1982), a succinct but comprehensive description and analysis of the British system, with useful international comparisons. Together they organised a workshop at University College, Oxford in 1989 from which emerged a volume of essays on *The State and Social Welfare* (Longman, 1991), devoted to discussion of the principles underlying state provision of social benefits. His last published collaboration with Dorothy was 'Social Justice and the Reform of Social Security' in *Social Policy Administration*, 29 (1995), a critique of the Report of the Commission on Social Justice, set up by the Leader of the Opposition, John Smith.

In the early 1960s planning was attracting renewed interest in Britain with the setting up of the National Development Office in London and the attempt to increase the rate of economic growth. Tom wrote several papers and then a book on *Planning and Growth* (Macmillan, 1964). He also became involved in regional planning and development as vice-chairman of the Committee of Inquiry into the Scottish Economy appointed by the Scottish Council (Development and Industry), chaired by Sir John Toothill, whose Report was published in 1961. Subsequently he served on an advisory panel of academic economists consulted by the Scottish Office. In 1963 he was invited by the Prime Minister of Northern Ireland, Terence O'Neill, to prepare a development programme for the province. Tom had always maintained his interest in Ulster affairs. In rather more than a year of part-time work, and with the assistance of Jack Parkinson, a war-time colleague who had also been at Glasgow and was now a professor at Queen's University, Belfast, he produced what became known as the 'Wilson Plan', (Government of Northern Ireland, *Economic Development in Northern Ireland,* Cmd. 479, HMSO, 1965). It was not a comprehensive economic plan, for Tom was sceptical of planning, but rather a five year plan for public investment, designed to bring the infrastructure nearer to standards in the rest of the UK, and to improve training, thereby, with some financial assistance from the government, to encourage more private investment in the province. It was followed by some years of relative prosperity, and a reduction in unemployment, but hopes were dashed by the outbreak of the 'troubles' in 1969. Both Tom and Jack Parkinson supervised the production of a second development programme for the years 1970–5, published in 1970, but it was overtaken by events.

Other studies of regional policy and fiscal federalism included *Financial Assistance with Regional Development* (Fredericton, NB, 1964), for the Atlantic Provinces Research Board of Canada; 'The Regional Multiplier—A Critique', *Oxford Economic Papers,* 20 (1968); a chapter on 'Economic Sovereignty' in John Vaizey (ed.) *Economic Sovereignty and Regional Policy* (Gill and Macmillan, 1975); 'Devolution and Public Finance', *The Three Banks Review,* No. 112 (1976); a chapter on 'Regional Policy and the National Interest' in D. Maclennan and John Parr (eds.) *Regional Policy* (Martin Robertson, 1979); and 'Issues Posed by Fiscal Transfers in the European Community', *The World Economy,* 3 (1980).

His last foray into local finance concerned the poll tax, and exemplified his concern to express his view of the truth without fear or favour. Towards the end of 1984 he was invited by William Waldegrave, a Minister at the Department of the Environment, to be one of four assessors (the others being Lord Rothschild, (Lord) Hoffman and (Sir) Christopher Foster) of a project to reform local government. Although initially the project appeared to be wide in scope, it was narrowed to local government *finance*, then (and still) in an unsatisfactory state. At the first meeting of the group in early 1985 an elaborate scheme was tabled for which no papers had been circulated in advance. This proposed a combination of domestic rates with a *small* poll tax, to secure some contribution from non-ratepayers. As there was little time to digest the scheme, and as the poll-tax element was small, little objection was expressed. However, after further consultation within the government, the proposal became one of completely substituting the poll-tax for domestic rates. Tom received further departmental papers, but he was not informed by the Department of the Environment of the Chancellor's (Lawson's) opposition to the scheme, nor given a paper by Hoffman critical of it, nor was any further meeting of the assessors called. Hoffman resigned on becoming a judge, and Tom considered resigning, but decided to write to Rothschild asking for another meeting. This was held in August 1985 with Baker and Waldegrave, senior civil servants of the department, Rothschild and Foster. At this meeting, Tom's was a lone voice in opposition to the poll-tax. He subsequently published his views in the *Economic Journal,* 101 (1991). The poll-tax was introduced with disastrous effects on the popularity of the government, proved difficult to collect, and has since been abandoned.

By the late 1960s monetarist doctrines were beginning their revival, although it was not until the 1980s that they would achieve their maximum power in the UK. They received attention in official circles largely as a result of borrowings from the IMF in 1968, when, as a *quid pro quo*, the IMF required that limits should be placed on domestic credit expansion. In academic circles there was Friedman's article in the *American Economic Review* of 1968, and Friedman expounded his views at a conference of economists in Sheffield in 1971, following which Harrod was the first respondent and Tom the second. Having argued the importance of the quantity of money in the 1950s, Tom now felt compelled to criticise those who seemed to think that little else mattered in the fight against inflation. His Keynes Lecture at the British Academy in 1975 had much to say about the problems of wage-push, and his contribution to a symposium on inflation in the *Scottish Journal of Political Economy* in 1976 criticised the concept of the natural rate of unemployment in monetarist theory. In *Inflation, Unemployment and the Market* (Clarendon Press, Oxford, 1984), which brought together some earlier articles (together with a useful bibliography of his writings), he added two substantial new essays which criticised monetarism and provided a balanced and eclectic analysis of macroeconomic policies and their effects on unemployment and inflation.

Dennis Robertson and Maynard Keynes were two economists for whose work he maintained an abiding interest and admiration. He felt that Robertson's method of analysing the determinants of the rate of interest through the supply and demand for loanable funds was preferable to Keynes's liquidity preference theory, and contributed a paper on 'Robertson, Money and Monetarism' to a meeting of the History of Economics Society at Harvard, which was published in the *Journal of Economic Literature*, 18 (1980). In the same year he attended a Keynes Seminar at the University of Kent, giving a paper, published in A. P. Thirlwall (ed.), *Keynes as a Policy Adviser* (Macmillan, 1982), on Keynes's policy recommendations, especially regarding domestic stabilisation and the famous White Paper of 1944. The myth had taken hold that Keynes had had to water down his proposals for running budget deficits in recessions, but the truth was, he pointed out, that Keynes's more cautious views had prevailed against more radical ones. Keynes thought the 'ordinary budget' should be balanced at all times and that countercyclical variations should be confined to the 'capital budget', which included, however, social security. Keynes also thought that unemployment could probably not be kept below about five per cent. Tom was anxious that

Keynes should not be regarded as an all-out expansionist whose policies were responsible for post-war inflation, although he accepted that Keynes stressed the desirability of low interest rates, and believed that in the medium to long run investment opportunities would be exhausted.

Towards the end of his tenure at Glasgow, Tom was awarded several distinctions: Fellow of the British Academy in 1976; Honorary Fellow of the London School of Economics in 1979; Fellow of the Royal Society of Edinburgh in 1980; and an Honorary Degree by Stirling University in 1981.

Bristol, 1984–2001

Tom retired from the Adam Smith Chair in 1982. He and Dorothy had lived at No. 8 Professors' Square, one of the large houses built in the 1860s when the university had occupied its greenfield site on the (then) western edge of the city. These houses were ultimately taken over as administrative offices, but there was no immediate demand for Tom's house, and so they remained there until 1984, when they found a flat at Bristol in which Dorothy could move about and which was also close to a daughter. Tom knew the head of the economics department at the University of Bristol, which was a further advantage. During their stay at Glasgow, they had bought a cottage just outside Callander, closer to Tom's beloved mountains and glens, and with a garden which they filled with flowers. This they retained, going up every summer, reviving old friendships and revisiting the places they loved. Many friends as well as family were invited to stay in the cottage when they were away. They had built up a collection of paintings, and Tom was a skilful painter himself. Most of these could still be displayed in the smaller Bristol flat or the cottage.

Tom continued to be very active. He had been energetic throughout his life, and this was sustained almost to his last days. Several of his post-Glasgow publications as well as the poll-tax episode have been mentioned. Two books, each requiring a substantial research effort, occupied much of his time, the first on Ulster and the second on Churchill and the Prof.

Ulster: Conflict and Consent (Blackwell, 1989), was perhaps his finest book. It rested on his virtues: his ability to understand, and set out fairly, conflicting viewpoints; his ability to assemble the important and relevant facts; and his no-nonsense approach. It gave enough Irish history to enable one to understand Republican grievances, but also to puncture the myth that Ireland is, or ever has been, one nation, despite its being one island. It discussed the most important issues: demography, religion, political parties, discriminatory policies in employment, housing and education, and the problems of maintaining law and order. There is probably no better introduction for those who really want to understand the Ulster tragedy, and there was probably no-one better qualified to write it.

Churchill and the Prof (Cassell, 1995) was Tom's last book, but, remarkably since he was seventy-nine when it was published, among his best. His work in the Prime Minister's Statistical Branch during the last three years of the war has been described. This had given him first-hand knowledge of some of the Prof's (Lord Cherwell's) work for Churchill, but there was much more, both on scientific matters and on strategic concerns. The bomber offensive against Germany is one of the most controversial of the issues discussed. The Prof was a strong proponent of the bombing of German cities, but this has since been condemned as both brutal and futile, and as consuming a disproportionate share of the war effort. Tom showed that the share was not, in fact, as large as some (e.g. A. J. P. Taylor) had seemingly implied, and that, while the critics were right to point out that German war production rose despite the bombs, and German morale was not broken, the bombing nonetheless had serious effects on war output and led to its collapse after January 1945. There were other important gains: the Germans never resorted to chemical or biological warfare, they concentrated their aircraft production effort on producing fighters to ward off the attacks and neglected their own bombers, and, perhaps most important of all, a million men and a very large number of guns were kept to defend Germany and so not available for the Russian front. However, while these arguments could be used to justify the bombing offensive during most of the war, and while selective bombing of the transport system (for example) made sense until nearly its end, Tom concluded that it was hard to find any adequate defence for the severity of the attack on Dresden in February 1945. Once more, Tom's careful and balanced assessment of the arguments shows his concern for the truth and refusal to accept fashionable opinion.

In 1998 Dorothy died, thus ending over fifty years of a happy marriage which had produced a son, two daughters, and eight grandchildren. She and Tom had surmounted her multiple sclerosis with characteristic humour and stoicism. Tom went up every summer to the cottage near Callander (now driven by his children so that he had the use of his own car there), and still worked away on a book. This was an assessment of the current state of macroeconomic theory in the light of post-war experience, which had, so it seemed, discredited one theory after another, leaving 'pragmatism' alone on the field. He died on 27 July before this could be finished on his last visit to the cottage in 2001, and his ashes lie with those of Dorothy in the cemetery of Balquhidder, not far from the grave of Rob Roy.

M. FG. SCOTT
Fellow of the Academy

Note.   My main debt is to Tom's unpublished short autobiography. All Fellows of the British Academy should be persuaded to write one. I must also thank the following for suggestions, amendments to an earlier draft and encouragement: Max Gaskin, Mary Gregory, Bryan Hopkin, Gavin McCrone, Chrissy MacSwan, C. J. Martin, Gus O'Donnell, Sarah Orr, Jack Parkinson, Alan Peacock, George Richardson, Andrew Skinner, and Tom's three children: John, Moya, and Margaret. They are not responsible for errors that may remain.

DAVID WORSWICK

George David Norman Worswick
1916–2001

DAVID WORSWICK was born on 18 August 1916, in Chiswick, London. He came from an academic background in as much as his father, who had graduated in mathematics from Liverpool University, was a lecturer in the subject at Regent Polytechnic College (of which he subsequently became Director of Education), whilst his mother had studied History and English at Manchester University. David attended school at St Paul's and, although an unexpected straightening of circumstances following the death of his father cut short a longer stay there, he was nevertheless able to make his way via an Open Scholarship to New College, Oxford; with additional Scholarship support he was able to finance his studies in mathematics there, which he began in 1934. He graduated with First Class Honours in 1937. Funding was available to enable him to extend his study over a further year and he chose to use this opportunity to work for the Diploma in Economics and Political Science. Henry Phelps Brown was an influential teacher. Like others of his generation part of his motivation to take up the study of social science was a concern for the experience of unemployment in the 1930s; this motivation—and the lessons that he learnt from study of the period—was to remain with him throughout his life. In 1982 he contributed a paper, 'Unemployment in Inter-war Britain' (jointly written with Paul Ormerod) to the *Journal of Political Economy* (vol. 90, no. 2, April) in which he criticised the view that the unemployment of the 1930s was driven by changes in real wages.

Proceedings of the British Academy, **120**, 515–524. © The British Academy 2003.

scope for macroeconomic policy. He gave a lecture in the University of Glasgow on the theme: 'Has mass unemployment come to stay?'

Other involvements

If in his retirement David had more time to devote to his personal research and to service for the profession and the subject in the wider sense, as well as for government; these had always been with him in greater or lesser quantity. One way or the other he worked a great deal for the government, and for his university and he also managed to publish quite a lot. David had great clarity of mind and a lot of plain common sense as well economic intuition and he could write well in the literary sense (though definitely not in the literal one: his handwriting was below the class of doctors' prescriptions!). He could listen to others and whilst of strong opinions on some subjects himself he did not allow this to impair his dealings with others. These qualities recommended him to numerous others who needed a job done, especially one with economic content.

Early in his time at Magdalen he sat on a number of committees and working parties—a tripartite working party on the lace industry was the first of these in 1946, involving much time in Nottingham, and this was followed somewhat later by membership of a committee on purchase tax and another on tax-paid stocks (in 1951 and 1952 respectively). He was also an expert witness for the Registrar of Restrictive Trade Practices, though most of his cases were withdrawn before coming to court and the only one in which he was involved as a 'live' witness in the court room was lost. The University of Oxford took advantage of his talents in a number of ways: first as Chairman of the Board of the Faculty of Social Studies from 1948, then as an examiner for the PPE degree in 1949–51 and as Senior Tutor for the College from 1955 on. In addition he pre-invented what subsequently came to be known as the 'Norrington tables': these list by college the results obtained by Oxford students in their finals, were published in the *Oxford Magazine* and were always much referred to. He discontinued their compilation in 1963, just before going to the National Institute: subsequently a similar compilation was produced on the instance of Sir Arthur Norrington, by whose name the presentation was consequently known. David in addition prepared tables listing the scholarship awards obtained by men in Oxford and Cambridge colleges (this was mostly published in the *Times Educational Supplement*); this was possibly one reason why he was drafted onto a committee to review admissions in the light of the creation of the UCCA system. Also during these years he undertook a mission for UNCTAD to Turkey, which for various reasons beyond David's control proved a failure, though he was able shortly afterwards to spend some time at the UNECE in Geneva, which he found congenial. With Phyllis Deane from Cambridge he also attempted to build a Ph.D. programme for Argentinian economists—the programme stopped short, though, with some classes imparted by British academics in Argentina and failed to move to the second stage where the students would have come to the UK to complete a dissertation. A major achievement of David's at this time was to organise and edit, with Peter Ady, the publication of the first regular textbook to cover the applied economics of British economic policy, a volume in which some twenty economists, mostly from Oxford, were involved. The success of the first volume, named *The British Economy, 1945–50*, led to a second version, *The British Economy in the 1950s*, before there became available a number of rival texts and many other sources of information on the subject.

At the National Institute David found his time for external activities somewhat more limited, but he was a founding member of the Social Science Council for five years, and was president of Section F of the British Association in 1972. He also served on the government's Committee on Policy Optimization in 1978 and previously (1967) had served on a committee for the Building Societies' Association, to investigate their reserves and liquidity. For quite some time (1982–90) he served on City University's Council.

Honours

In a life of dedication to economics and the analysis of economic policy, it was not surprising that David came by several honours. In 1975 he received a D.Sc. from City University and was elected a Fellow of the Academy in 1979—and from 1986/7 to 1988/9 he served as Chairman of its Section 9. In 1981 he was awarded the CBE.

Other things in life

If David lived a full life in a professional sense, he complemented it with a lively and fulfilling domestic life. He married Sylvia Walsh in 1940 and had three children—Eleanor, Rosalind, and Richard. Their Oxford house was a home from home for many a student. David never owned a car, preferring to ride a bike or walk (a firm fixture in the family calendar was a walking holiday in the Lake District every year); he played a vigorous game of squash and could also play tennis. From the age of about thirty he suffered from severe hearing deficiency ('otosclerosis'), which could be alleviated by the use of a hearing aid. The latter, some swore, could also be used as a tactical weapon as it was inclined to burst into a whistle and splutter phase just when someone was repeating something particularly inane or pompous and had an immediately disconcerting effect. However this may be, David did confess to using the power to turn the aid off occasionally; more to the point, he never complained about his problem. Together with his wife David shared a broadly 'left' view of life, with a long membership of the Labour Party, and in the early days an active one. He had a gentle sense of humour, an enjoyment of the simple things in life ('Match of the Day' was a case in point) and a sense of self-deprecation that highlighted his lack of pomposity. He represented, not only the intellectual commitment of a generation of British economists, but also just about all the best features of a man in public life in Britain in his time. David Worswick died on 18 May 2001.

MICHAEL ARTIS
Fellow of the Academy

FRANCES A. YATES   *Bassano & Vandyk*

Frances Amelia Yates
1899–1981

WHEN FRANCES YATES was elected to the Fellowship in July 1967 her qualities as intellectual historian, long appreciated internationally but within a restricted circle, had begun to be recognised as widely as they deserved. This was in large part the result of the two books she had recently published. *Giordano Bruno and the Hermetic Tradition* of 1964 and *The Art of Memory* of 1966 were then the latest in a series of studies notable for adventurous argument and scope of learning. Though they had been long maturing, the rate at which they had finally been produced and had followed each other into print was remarkable; *Bruno* had actually been written in well under a year—with time out for holidays and an important Oxford lecture—and *Memory* in about the same time. Remarkable also is that she was already in her sixty-fifth year when the first was published and in her sixty-seventh when the second appeared. Both have had a lasting effect on the study of the European Renaissance.

Neither the success of these two books and of the round half-dozen that followed nor the controversy which parts of them engendered was a surprise either to those who knew Frances Yates, or quite to herself. In her teens she had made up her mind that she would succeed as a writer and had begun reading hard.[1] Her innate tendency to self-deprecation, reflecting the genuine personal modesty and diffidence which made her

---

[1] Diary entry quoted by J. N. Hillgarth, in Frances A. Yates, *Ideas and Ideals in the North European Renaissance: Collected Essays*, 3 (London, 1984), pp. 276–7. There is a list of her writings in this volume, pp. 323–36.

Proceedings of the British Academy, **120**, 527–554. © The British Academy 2003.

characterise her work as only a beginning, did not impair a conviction of her fundamental rightness. This was a function of her candour and independence of mind, as well as of a certain stubbornness, concealing vulnerability. In the end, however, she could hardly disguise from herself that she had fulfiled her ambition. Basing herself on a huge acquaintance with primary sources, verbal and visual, she wrote vividly and readably. Despite her moments of self-doubt, especially at beginnings, she never lacked intellectual courage. Always prepared to take the risks of exploration, she was undeterred, if not untroubled, by the size and intransigence of the historical problems she set herself to clarify. She would fling herself at them, 'jump in and splash around', as she put it, relying on her own exertions and on the help and guidance of those she trusted where she knew herself to be out of her depth. Entering the past through an intense imaginative effort and in a sympathetic spirit, she recreated its intellectual life by insights and arguments that upset accepted ways of thinking and opened or reopened many doors that had been judged either not to exist or to have been sealed for good.

Frances Yates's qualities as historian had been nurtured and sustained within a rather secluded, liberal, enlightened, serious but not unsociable, closely-knit, observantly Anglican and intensely English small family; later, she would write appreciatively of its Arnoldian valuation of poetry, its unpriggish highmindedness, sense of duty and exaltation of individual 'effort'. Her consciousness of herself was not fundamentally altered by association with the Warburg Institute during almost the last fifty years of her life, though she was always ready to acknowledge what she owed to its members and their approach. Both family and Institute fostered her preoccupation with ideas and her choice of subjects that were either uninvestigated—in English at least—or had been investigated by routes calculated not to fall foul of those whom Aby Warburg had derisively described as the border guards of the academic disciplines.

Nevertheless, the way that Frances Yates made, she made largely for herself. Born in Southsea on 28 November 1899, she was by some years the youngest child of a naval architect. James Alfred Yates, her father, began life with no advantages but, entering Portsmouth Dockyard at the age of fourteen, rose eventually to the rank of Chief Constructor. He took an important part in the shipbuilding programme of Sir John Fisher, supervising the building of the Dreadnoughts and, from retirement, called back to the Admiralty in 1916 for special service. His moves from dockyard to dockyard meant that Frances Yates's early formal schooling was intermittent; her education owed much to her family's discernment of promise and, in particular, to her mother and two elder sisters, one a graduate teacher who was also a novelist and the other a trained artist who became a missionary in Africa. In later life, each sister in turn saw to Frances Yates's domestic arrangements. Particularly after the death in action of her only brother in 1915, the family had centred its expectations on her. Following the setback of failure to follow her brother to Oxford, she began to work, from Worthing, for a London external degree in French. Helped by a correspondence course and a few classes at University College, she graduated with a first in 1924 and went on, this time as an internal student of the same college, to take her MA in 1926 with a thesis on the French social drama of the sixteenth century.[2] Her choice of French for both degrees must have been influenced by family Francophilia, expressed in holidays in France, and her concentration on the drama perhaps by family devotion to Shakespeare reinforced by a conviction of acting ancestry. To improve her spoken French she spent time in the Loire Valley.

In 1925 James Yates bought The New House in Coverts Road, Claygate, then an old-world village in Surrey. In it Frances Yates was to live uninterruptedly until a few weeks before her death on 29 September 1981. The move to Claygate improved access to London, where she had begun to use both the British Museum Library and the Public Record Office from Worthing; and she joined the London Library, always a main-stay. In 1930 finances were eased by a modest bequest from an aunt; and later there was a minuscule grant or two. Intermittent periods of teaching French at North London Collegiate School during the late 1920s and 1930s, however, were her only salaried posts until 1941, when Fritz Saxl made her part-time, ill-paid Editor of Publications at the Warburg Institute. She had been informally associated with the Institute since 1937 and, when it was incorporated in the University of London in 1944, she retained her post, being appointed Lecturer in 1950, promoted to Reader in 1956 and redesignated Reader in the History of the Renaissance in 1962. In 1967 she formally retired, to be welcomed back the same year as Honorary Fellow and occasional teacher and to continue so until the end. Her sister Hannah had long ago pointed out to her the advantages of her

---

[2] Of her life up to this time and indeed up to the 1930s there is little documentary evidence except the thesis itself, a teenage diary and the charming record of childhood and some other reminiscences, written in her seventies and early eighties. The diary and a copy of her thesis are among her papers in the Warburg Institute Archives; for her reminiscences, see *Ideas and Ideals*, pp. 275–322.

lack of success in applying for jobs and the freedom this had left her to exercise a preference for solitary reading and writing and a mild resentment at disturbance of her routine. Mondays and Thursdays were her regular days to see friends and visitors, to discuss their work with the pupils over whose progress and problems she would agonise, to consult sympathetic colleagues at the Institute about shared interests and her own writing, and late in her career to hold seminars; and she would also appear, a little reluctantly, on Wednesdays during term to deliver a public lecture or to listen: 'old bore' was her judgement on an eminent historian of cosmology. For the rest, inclined always to think of herself as an outsider in conventional academic circles, she felt most comfortable reading in the British (Museum) Library or reading and writing at home (impractical in many ways she was, until her very last days, her own typist). She trusted above all the reactions to her work-in-progress of her sisters and of individual Warburgians—Fritz Saxl, Rudolf Wittkower, E. H. Gombrich, Charles Mitchell and, especially, Gertrud Bing and D. P. Walker.

Family satisfaction in the publication of Frances Yates's first learned article, 'English Actors in Paris during the Lifetime of Shakespeare', in the initial volume of the *Review of English Studies* (1925), was enhanced by the *Times Literary Supplement*'s commendation of the 'new and lively light' it had thrown on the external conditions of contemporary drama. This new light having come from a Public Record Office document, she borrowed more from the same source (and from her thesis) in 1927, using her finds and Antoine de Montchrétien's play on Mary Queen of Scots, which considers Mary's fate both from the English and the French viewpoint, to illuminate specific intellectual as well as political issues. More State Paper discoveries led her to John Florio, second-generation religious refugee and language teacher, dictionary maker and translator of Montaigne; she began to pay special attention to English, French, and Italian rivalries in and out of the Sidney–Leicester circle (John Eliot in particular, with his assault on pedantry; the mysterious H. S., whom she identified as Henry Sanford; Gabriel Harvey, and Thomas Nashe). A couple of articles, one of them establishing Florio's close connection with the French Embassy in London, were followed in 1934 by her first book, *John Florio. The Life of an Italian in Shakespeare's England*, in which her verve and enthusiasm are already evident. Preparations for this first biography of Florio included teaching herself Italian with the aid of a grammar and a long forgotten novel, Tommasina Guidi's *Il curato di Pradalburgo* (Florence 1915); they involved family journeys in pursuit of John Florio's father Michelangelo, Protestant refugee and Italian teacher to Lady Jane

Grey; and they showed that Florio *figlio* had never himself been in Italy. They also introduced Frances Yates to Giordano Bruno, another religious refugee though (he maintained) a Catholic one, and also associated with the French ambassador.

What put *Florio* above the ruck of literary biographies was the concern for the extra-literary, European dimension which was to be Frances Yates's distinguishing mark. Here she was already the intellectual historian, exploring not only contemporary notions concerning language and their practical issue but also religious thought and experience. C. J. Sisson had helped her as she worked; G. B. Harrison recommended the book to Cambridge, who published it (with a subsidy from London); reviewers everywhere, from Desmond McCarthy, Harold Nicolson, and Mario Praz in the weekly press to the heavies, united in praise; the British Academy awarded its Rose Crawshay Prize. The book is still standard.

Included in Frances Yates's account of Florio was a summary of the *Cena de le ceneri*, in which Bruno describes a real or pretended philosophical discussion of the Copernican and the Ptolemaic world systems which had taken place in London, either (as represented in the dialogue itself) in the house of Fulke Greville or (as Bruno told his inquisitors) in the French Embassy. Florio was present, as the carelessly dressed Bruno's exposition of Copernicanism carried the day against a pair of magnificently robed, pedantic, mistakenly Aristotelian Oxford doctors. That was Bruno's account, at any rate; only long after Frances Yates had written was Oxford discovered to have hit back with an account of his Ficinian plagiaries there. With hindsight, she was inclined to self-castigation for not having immediately recognised the true significance of Bruno, let alone the importance of Hermes Trismegistus, who is not even mentioned. Bruno was still present in her immediate attempt to follow up initial success, but still in a supporting part to the language teachers and even more to the leading man. 'It's all aimed at Willie, you know' she would sometimes say, facetiously, about her life's work, which was to culminate in the comprehensive book on Shakespeare that she never wrote. This was to have seen him by the light of the intellectual conditions in which the poems and plays had been written and performed and to which they had themselves contributed.

What Frances Yates had then to say about Shakespeare was incorporated in *A Study of Love's Labour's Lost*, published in 1936, again by Cambridge, in A. W. Pollard's and J. Dover Wilson's Shakespeare Problems series. Early notices were respectful, with reservations. William Empson called the book's argument 'wandering but fascinating', seeing 'its great interest in the view it gives of the Elizabethan intellectual climate' but finding its biographical suggestions about Shakespeare 'very doubtful'.[3] She had proposed to add to the already accepted shadowy presences in the play the Wizard Earl of Northumberland; John Eliot as opposer of the pedantry represented by Holofernes-Florio; Bruno as Florio's fellow-critic of English barbarism and ignorance and, more particularly, the upbraider of Sidney for writing sonnets to Stella (whence the insistence on the connection of stars and ladies' eyes). Subsequent Shakespearians have united in rejecting these, judging longer accepted connotations with the so-called 'School of Night', Harvey and Nashe and the Gray's Inn Revels to be sufficient. Frances Yates herself was equally dismissive later of this classic case of second book syndrome. Though she never quite abandoned the Holofernes-Florio identification, which had first been advanced by Warburton in the eighteenth century, or the conviction that the play reflected current attitudes to poetic and pedantic language, she lamented her lack of grasp in the broader context of Renaissance thought and, despite the space Bruno occupies in the book, her ignorance of his true importance.

She continued, all the same, to believe that 'this apparently rather ridiculous play' might 'touch on something deep', the choice between ways of life, for example; it might even have a bearing on the contemporary politico-religious situation in France and on contemporary ideas about how it might be improved. In it, the King of Navarre urges the formation of a sort of academy, whose learned investigations of the arts of peace, laying bare the intellectual and spiritual bases of cosmic harmony, would show the way to compose wars and factions. Following up this perception by asking herself whether such academies had existed Frances Yates went, as her custom was, directly to the original sources named in by then outdated accounts. *The French Academies of the Sixteenth Century* was something new, a first mature demonstration—she was already nearly fifty when it appeared—of her powers in her own genre, the analysis of movements of thought and sentiment as political forces, no less real for their invisibility or their frustration. The French author of one favourable review of *French Academies* found it a little humiliating to his countrymen that such a study should appear in English; she was herself disappointed that it was not translated into French in her lifetime (not until 1996). No other critic uncovered more than minor false

---

[3] *Life and Letters Today*, Sept. 1936, p. 204.

emphases in her account; it too has never been surpassed or superseded. It is the first comprehensive description of a particular milieu, in which Medici-Valois court ceremonies and festivals, conceived as the serious embodiments of aspirations to politico-religious peace, were nourished by encyclopedic learning, with the accent on music and poetry. Tracing the French Renaissance academic tradition, which retained the medieval objective of a synthesis of religion and philosophy but aimed to achieve it by the way of Neoplatonism rather than that of Aristotelian logic, she showed how it developed ultimately from the example of Marsilio Ficino's Platonic Academy in Medicean Florence. She mapped the routes by which this new academic approach had been transmitted to France and the Pléiade by Symphorien Champier and others. Baïf's Academy of Poetry and Music, founded in 1570, was followed, in the days of Henri III, by the Palace Academy and that was in turn succeeded at Vincennes in the penitential phase of Henri's attempt to bring about reconciliation between Huguenots and Catholics. Such academies could, she showed, have existed only at a time before the discarding of certain assumptions about the nature of the universe and the consequent partition of the encyclopaedia of knowledge into self-contained disciplines. As theorist-in-chief of the earlier French encyclopaedic ideal, she identified the humanist bishop and scholar Pontus de Tyard. Tyard was the intermediary between painters and poets; his efforts to draw together poetry, music, natural and moral philosophy were comprehended within the ambition to recover the 'effects' of ancient music, to use the almost magical power of music to temper the soul to a perfect condition of goodness and virtue and the state to political and religious harmony. Her demonstrations of how all the disciplines—the visual arts, rhetoric, poetry, music, philosophy, and religion—were expressed in commemorative or celebratory festivals, elaborate funerals or religious processions, culminated in her description of the most famous of court entertainments, the *Balet comique de la Royne* of 1581. To form a just estimate of the size and originality of Frances Yates's achievement in this study, it is necessary to remember not only that this was a new field but also that she was turning to triumphant advantage the virtually complete destruction of conventional documentation during the Wars of Religion: the immense detail of her narrative had its source in contemporary descriptions of ceremonial, in the music which was so important a component, and in the writings, poetic and theoretical, of the academicians themselves.

The book's journey to publication had been long. Beginning in the question she had asked herself about the existence of such academies, it had first taken form in lectures delivered at the Warburg Institute early in 1940, the first of them to an audience of less than half-a-dozen in a freezing, lightless, and transportless London. The invitation to lecture had come from Saxl and from Edgar Wind. Saxl's influence as she worked, she said, had meant most to her; she took greatly to heart his infinitely laborious attention to accuracy and detail and his humility, both as a person and in his attitude to the past; Wind's philosophical knowledge and flair made a large contribution. Writing was complete in 1941; publication was impeded by the endemic money and paper shortages that were also holding up Praz's two volumes of *Studies in Seventeenth-Century Imagery*, on revising which Frances Yates had spent much time and energy. When *The French Academies* finally came out early in 1948, she acknowledged in her preface both her relief and the difficulty of recapturing 'the atmosphere in which the French academies of the sixteenth century first presented themselves as a steadying subject in a disintegrating world'.[4] She had done what she could in a practical way to arrest disintegration, contributing to the financial support of an Italian Jewish scholar, for instance. She joined first-aid classes and the ARP scheme, exchanging experiences with her friend K. M. Lea, of Lady Margaret Hall, who described to her how she had put on her gas mask to read Ariosto, so as to discover whether she would be fit to drive an ambulance while wearing it.

As she continued her own reading and writing, Frances Yates found her sympathy growing with what she called the encyclopaedic ideal of the Warburg Institute, not least the article of its faith which held that the documents of history were visual as well as verbal. A feature of all her work came to be the skilful use of the evidence to be found in works of art. Her innate tendency towards *histoire à part entière* was enhanced, too, by Warburgian inclinations towards a European rather than a national view of the Renaissance, seen also in terms of applied humanism as well as pure. Perhaps finding a parallel with her own comparative academic isolation in her own country, she would later briefly perceive the Institute as in some sense a modern incarnation of the academies she had described. They had been introduced to each other later in 1936. That was almost exactly the moment when, the initial three-year period of its invitation to England—a blind to get it out of Nazi Germany—being about to expire, the Institute's adherents in this country were few and its

---

[4] *The French Academies of the Sixteenth Century* (London, 1947 [1948]), p. v.

foothold again precarious. She had got to know it as the indirect result of a meeting with one of its early English friends, Dorothea Waley Singer, wife of Charles Singer, the historian of science. Mrs Singer had responded to her appeal to fellow Brunonians, if any, in the *Times Literary Supplement* for help with the *Cena de le ceneri*, which she had been attempting to translate. Mrs Singer, whose own translation of Bruno's *De l'infinito* was much later published as part of her book on Bruno's life and thought in 1950, invited her to a house party at the Singers' home at Par, in Cornwall. There she met Wind, in his hand a copy of her *Study of Love's Labour's Lost*, 'which he appeared'—she later wrote mistrustfully—'to be studying'.[5] Wind invited her to the Institute, where she met its other members and began to use its library, finding there a comprehensive collection of works by and about Bruno which included both books and articles she had already used and many that were unknown to her. Most had been acquired by Warburg himself towards the end of his life; towards the end of her own life, she treasured a copy of *Degli eroici furori*, presented by Warburg to Gertrud Bing. Bing, from having been Warburg's assistant, had become successively the Institute's Assistant Director and then Director; she was to be Frances Yates's closest friend, ally, confidante, and critic outside her family. At that time the Warburgians were, Mrs Singer apart, virtually the only people in England with an interest in Bruno—or in ideas and their history, it has been suggested.[6] She found congenial and stimulating company, almost a second family, in a collegiate ambience where shop-talk about one's work and intellectual interests were the norm rather than the discouraged exception. Even when the Warburg Library had to be packed away and its staff and associates to take refuge in the Buckinghamshire countryside, there were still Saxl, Bing, Wind (for a time), and Wittkower to counsel and hearten her, and to draw her into the Institute's activities. She served, by her own account, a difficult but highly rewarding apprenticeship, mastering a huge programme of new reading; she also slaved at indexing and at Englishing essays more sophisticated in conception and vocabulary than any in her experience so far. Most had been written for the new *Journal of the Warburg Institute*; on her own account she published in its first volume an article on the Italian teachers of Elizabethan England and she remained one of its editors until death.

---

[5] 'Autobiographical Fragments', *Ideas and Ideals*, p. 313.
[6] By Arnaldo Momigliano, 'A Piedmontese View of the History of Ideas', *Sesto contributo alla storia degli studi classici e del mondo antico; Parte prime* (Rome, 1980), p. 329.

Though Frances Yates retained her interest in the refugee language teachers of Elizabethan and later England, especially those who were putting the Italian polish on uncouth natives, these were already, when she was introduced to the Institute, in a fair way to being replaced at the centre of her immediate concerns. She had become fascinated by Bruno's ideas and his significance in his time. Before the publication of *A Study of Love's Labour Lost*, to relieve the anxieties of her father's serious illness and convalescence, she had set about translating the *Cena de le ceneri* and expounding its signficance. The result, unreadable and unpublishable though she later judged it, revealed to her clearly a Bruno who differed radically from the received image of him; he was neither atheist and martyr to free thought, nor modern philosopher in conflict with reactionary medievalism. This was the beginning of the long process of revaluation which occupied so much of her time, energy, and imaginative strength for more than forty years. When Cambridge turned her translation down she found consolation in discussions with her new friends and mentors, who showed her that there was more to Renaissance ideas about the cosmos than she had gleaned from Pierre Duhem's admirable *Système du monde* and encouraged her reading in Renaissance Neoplatonism. She was able to salvage and expand parts of the introduction she had written to the *Cena* in three articles, all published in early numbers of the Warburg *Journal*: on Bruno's conflict with Oxford, on his religious policy and on the imagery of his *Degli eroici furori*.[7] These were her first attempts to see Bruno in his true international, intellectual-religio-historical context. The last, discussing *Degli eroici furori* in relation to Neoplatonism and the emblematic mode, gave to scholarship on Petrarchism, anti-Petrarchism and the Elizabethan sonnet sequences a thematic dimension, a concern with the nature of imagery and with the ideas and attitudes behind it which was lacking in the merely literary accounts of which she never ceased to be forthrightly critical. In the other two articles, she was still more original. She saw Bruno's disagreements with the Oxford doctors as critical of them for rejecting medieval philosophy as a whole rather than for retaining outmoded medieval beliefs; and she found, in his defence of the Copernican hypothesis against the Ptolemaic, a reference both to the Eucharist and to the eirenic religious policy proposed by one whom she would later call 'this rather threatening advocate of toleration'. She seems to have sent an offprint of the Oxford doctors article to C. S. Lewis. Lewis

---

[7] Republished in her *Lull and Bruno: Collected Essays*, 1 (London, 1982), pp. 134–209.

thanked its unknown author for diverting his mind from the current international situation and for confirming his view of humanist philistinism in
regard to philosophy in general; he concluded with the customary polite
enquiry as to the nature of the Warburg Institute. That Frances Yates's
and Lewis's estimates of Elizabethan Oxford have been shown to be
flawed in different ways does not diminish her impact. As ever, she had
opened up a subject.

To a little later belongs an essay, arising out of Frances Yates's interest in Bruno's unorthodox eirenism, on the role of England and Venice in
a political and religious configuration marked by the ascendancy of Spain
and by the post-Tridentine papacy's increasing assertion of its claim to
control secular affairs. 'Paolo Sarpi's *History of the Council of Trent*',
published in the *Journal of the Warburg and Courtauld Institutes* for 1944,
was a groundbreaking exposition of Sarpi's critical attitude towards Trent
and its failure to reunite Christendom; it made clear also how that critical attitude was echoed in James I's sponsorship of the book's publication. The Catholic Republic was maintaining under interdict its liberties
and its claim to an earlier Christian religious tradition; Protestant
England, likewise in defiance of the Pope, was likewise claiming descent
in the apostolic tradition. Here was an opportunity for eirenic leadership
from England, bringing the Anglican Church again into communion with
Rome. The chance was not taken.

Frances Yates's choice of Sarpi and his *History* reflects her own religious position at about this time, which she defined at the end of a
remarkable letter to Philip Hughes, apropos his *Rome and the Counter
Reformation in England*, as that of

> an Anglican, who takes the historical view that the Nazi revolution of 1559,
> and all the miserable complications which ensued, deprived me of part of my
> natural and native inheritance as an English Catholic.[8]

Later, though the religious sentiment, Anglicanism in particular, was
always of prime importance and the need for sectarian peace carried a
heavy emphasis in her historical investigations, she was only an occasional churchgoer. Her concept of the lost opportunity of the time and
circumstances in which the *History* was published in turn embodies what
was to become one of her great underlying themes. In her Sarpi essay, as
in the books she published during the 1970s, the reign of James I is seen
as embodying England's failure to act in the true larger interest, prevented

---

[8] Yates Archive, Warburg Institute.

from doing so by a sort of Counter Renaissance which acted in the wake of the Counter Reformation to stifle the reformed imperial idea, which had been embodied in Elizabeth I, James's Protestant predecessor.

Frances Yates's lifelong concern, almost yearning, for the ideal of a truly reformed and eirenic religion, visible in the Sarpi essay and in *The French Academies*, her understanding of the figurative and mythic dimension of the imperial idea, and her acquaintance with the serious intellectual content of court ceremonial were embodied about this time in another long and remarkable essay, also groundbreaking and still not surpassed for its vision and its grasp of implications. 'Queen Elizabeth as Astraea', published in the *Journal of the Warburg and Courtauld Institutes* for 1947, had begun as a lecture in 1945 to F. S. Boas's Elizabethan Literary Society which was, with *The French Academies*, her first real attempt to use visual evidence. Centred on Queen Elizabeth I, in whom the poets, dramatists, devisers of festivals, religious and political propagandists, and artists of the age had seen the virgin who would restore the Golden Age of justice and peace, it is perhaps the single essay of hers which has been most influential, on students of literature especially. The theme of spectacle and its significance broached here and in *The French Academies* evoked some of her finest and most cogent writing as she described the possibilities envisaged by those who were involved in such manifestations in England and in France. These matters continued to be addressed in studies of the allegorical portraits of Elizabeth and the tilts celebrating her accession day, of masquing costume and of the 'magnificences' at the wedding of the duc de Joyeuse, of the entries into Paris of Charles IX and his queen, and of the dramatic religious processions in the same city. In 1974 she published, with an introduction, a facsimile of Simon Bouquet's account of Charles IX's entry into Paris in 1572. The next year most of these festival essays, many of them based on lectures given during the war and in the immediate post-war years, were drawn together, much revised and expanded, in a single volume entitled *Astraea. The Imperial Theme in the Sixteenth Century*.

In 1975, also, there had been a second edition of her most sustained and exciting single exercise in the genre, her monograph *The Valois Tapestries*, first published in 1959 by the Warburg Institute, which shows at its best her ability to recreate the historical moment by understanding it. This great series of eight tapestries, woven in Flanders, is now in the Uffizi, having been taken to Florence by the granddaughter of Catherine de' Medici, Christina of Lorraine, on her marriage to the Grand Duke Ferdinand I in 1589, which was itself the occasion of splendid festivals.

The series is French in its reference to the richly dressed and often identifiable personages, the masquerade combats, the water festivals and *ballets de cour* that are figured. Reflected here, and in related drawings by Antoine Caron, are magnificences commissioned long before by Catherine, to glorify her progeny, on two separate occasions. The first was when she met her daughter Elizabeth, queen of Spain, at the Bayonne interview of 1565 and the second when she received, in Paris, the ambassadors who had come to offer the crown of Poland to her son, the future Henri III, in 1573. A prime difficulty is that, though the festivals recorded belong to the reign of Charles IX, there is no sign of him in the tapestries. Their record must be a memorial one and an additional political purpose must lie behind them. This purpose, it had already been conjectured, was revealed in the discrepancies between Caron's drawings and the tapestries, which indicated that the occasion for their weaving was the brief and disastrous intervention in the Netherlands of a less happy scion of the Valois, Elizabeth's suitor the duc d'Anjou, who appears in the tapestries but not in the drawings. Frances Yates boldly extended this hypothesis by identifying the artist responsible for other drawings, now lost, on which the tapestries had been based, as the Netherlander Lucas de Heere, working in the confidence of William of Orange. For her the weaving of these superb objects and their presentation to France represented a plea to Catherine and her son Henri III to continue a *politique* policy, steering Europe through the crisis of division into hostile factions after Trent and bringing together Catholic and Protestant; specifically, the tapestries embodied the hopes of moderate men and women and a request to support Anjou against Spain.

A large part of Frances Yates's legacy, hugely important among literary historians and critics in particular, is the result of this preoccupation with Italianate French and English festivals, the architecture, music, poetry, and prose that accompanied them and the records in word and image both of their physical aspect and their spiritual and political purposes. *The Valois Tapestries* and the revised essays in *Astraea* show her at her best in meeting the need for historical interpretation of sources which do not satisfy the precise and explicit criteria so beloved of high-and-dry historians. As she points out, no surviving document bears witness to the political purpose she defines for the tapestries, just as there had been none for the French academies. The tapestries are themselves the evidence, historical documents which, interpreted with knowledge, skill, and sympathy, will give access to historical, artistic, and spiritual movements at a deeper level than can be got from more conventional sources. Ultimately her legacy was Warburg's and her gift for this kind of research had been fostered by Saxl, Bing, and her other colleagues in the Institute, but she herself greatly enhanced it. She was its pre-eminent, for many years along with D. J. Gordon—also Warburg-influenced—virtually its sole practitioner in England, until those she had set on their way and encouraged—Sydney Anglo, Margaret McGowan, and Roy Strong in particular—achieved their own reputations.

In Frances Yates's understanding of the symbolic dimension in sixteenth- and seventeenth-century religion and politics, as manifested in these writings of the 1940s and 1950s, Giordano Bruno was a shadowy background presence; she had been worrying away at him intermittently since the 1930s. After the publication of *The French Academies*, she began to work on Bruno in earnest, fired by a new perception of his importance which she could not yet fully articulate. Reading prodigiously in his Latin works and, as was her way, taking copious notes and making explicit summaries, she found herself deflected by his frequent references to Ramon Lull. In *Florio*, referring in passing to Bruno's French lectures on the art of memory propounded by 'Lully', she had not concerned herself with the significance of the medieval Catalan mystic and philosopher. But she was always inclined to go back to beginnings and it was now clear to her that an investigation of Lull and Lullism was necessary in order to understand Bruno. Once again, she was on her own, in a phase of European history that was all but unknown outside Spain. As with Bruno, there was little that would guide her in scaling the 'huge, unclimbed mountain' of Lull's thought, let alone the nature of his European influence in the sixteenth century. In the England of the 1920s, there had been E. Allison Peers, but neither his biography of Lull nor his translations were a help with the nature of the Lullian Art; their concern, like that of Spanish writers, was literary, and more with Lull's works in Catalan. Nor was there much to be got even out of the monumental survey of Spanish philosophy from the thirteenth to the fifteenth century by the brothers Carreras y Artau of 1939–43. Neither the Majorcan Schola Lullistica nor the Raimundus-Lullus-Institut of the University of Freiburg-im-Breisgau had yet wrought their transformation of Lullian studies; and E.-W. Platzeck's two volumes in German would not be available until 1962–4. Her first article, however, soon brought her enthusiastic support and informed criticism from her solitary Lullian sympathiser in Britain, Robert Pring-Mill; he was followed by J. N. Hillgarth, whose study of Lull's influence in fourteenth-century France, published in 1971, filled an important gap in the story of transmission and by Anthony

Bonner, much later. For the moment, though, there was nothing for it but a solitary frontal attack. She embarked on the vast bulk of the Latin writings, using the eighteenth-century edition of Ivo Salzinger and eighty-odd manuscripts in Rome, Milan, and Paris—one at least of them superbly illustrated—and she taught herself to read Spanish and medieval Catalan as she went along. Uncovering for the first time the cosmological basis of Lull's philosophy, she showed how the Lullian universal Art or key, divinely revealed to him as the means to congruence with God, was built on the elemental patterns of nature which could be brought into accord with the divine patterns or attributes by means of a system of wheel diagrams. The Lullian Art, working on all steps in the ladder of being, had been intended by its inventor to give access to a truth so sure and irrefutable that Islam and Judaism both would be compelled to assent to Christianity and the world be made one again. Even when it had wholly or partially lost its missionary impulse, it could be shown to have retained importance for the history of the art of memory and, Francis Bacon's objections to it notwithstanding, for the history of method at large. Expounding the Lullian system unaided Frances Yates considered the hardest task she had ever undertaken; her account, published in the *Journal of the Warburg and Courtauld Institutes* for 1954, was long unrivalled as an introduction to the Art. It concludes with a ringing call for unsparing effort

> This article has concluded nothing, for it is not an end but a beginning. . . . My aim has been to re-open the problem of Ramon Lull and his Art through suggesting some fresh ways of approaching the problem. To prove these suggestions either right or wrong will involve stirring up, sifting, and bringing to light the Lullian material, and that is bound to be an instructive and illuminating process.
>
> Lullism is no unimportant side-issue in the history of Western civilization. Its influence over five centuries was incalculably great. . . . Surely it is time that we . . . should . . . try to learn more of the true nature of this great monument which towered for so long over the European scene . . .[9]

In a sequel of 1960, also in the Warburg *Journal*, she showed how this might be done by proposing that the connection made in Lull's art between elemental theory and divine attributes had its source in the broad tradition of Neoplatonism, and specifically in the work of the ninth-century Neoplatonist and translator of the ps-Dionysius, Johannes

---

[9] *Lull and Bruno*, pp. 66–7.

Scotus Erigena.[10] Erigena being also at that time far from adequately investigated, this was another characteristically bold and suggestive attempt to respond to questions not merely unanswered hitherto but not even proposed. Rather uncharacteristically, she circulated it widely, anxious for reactions to such a novel linking in a continuum of two philosophers who had been studied in isolation from each other, in so far as they had been studied at all.

Besides opening a new way, Frances Yates's Lullian studies gave her the hope of one day making clear, by a study of the occult accretions subsequently suffered by Lullism, how Lull might be said to have prefigured the Renaissance magus. This magus figure is omnipresent in her subsequent work. In the form of Bruno he dominates her next two books; in various guises, as John Dee in particular, he permeates the rest. There is a sense in which Bruno has an important role in everything she wrote, from *Florio* onwards, and one of her achievements is to have put study of him on a new footing, not only in Anglophone scholarship but also in both his native country and in France. In particular, Bruno links *Giordano Bruno and the Hermetic Tradition* and *The Art of Memory*, which are best thought of as two instalments of one book. The controversy aroused by these two sustained exercises in intellectual history was due to their re-evaluation of the larger Renaissance Neoplatonic tradition, which was essentially religious in character, in the light of magical belief and, in particular, of what she called Cabalism-Hermeticism, white magic.

When Frances Yates began seriously to study it, Hermeticism could not be said to be a new subject; she herself had even made passing reference to it in her book on *Love's Labour's Lost*, though what little modern publication there was concerning it was suspect as history. G. R. S. Mead could not be countenanced; Walter Scott's edition of the Hermetic corpus was much better, but not completely satisfactory. There had been progress in Paul Oskar Kirsteller's publication in 1938, which established a presence for Hermes Trismegistus in Italian Renaissance philosophy; and in the 1940s and 1950s his significance had been recognised in the work of Eugenio Garin and his circle. Between 1945 and 1954, as Frances Yates worked, A. D. Nock's and A.-J. Festugière's Budé provided a better text. Her contribution was to give Hermeticism a central relevance and to describe, in terms of intellectual connections, the powerful allure of the Hermetic fragments to the consciousness of Renaissance Platonists, who

---

[10] *Lull and Bruno*, pp. 78–125.

saw them in the double false perspective of a fictitious dating and of a fundamental religious truth. *Giordano Bruno and the Hermetic Tradition* was an attempt to define the character and trace the influence of Hermeticism's strange and aberrant gnostic mysticism. Chiefly, she showed it working towards a heterodox, illuminist, magical religion dominated by the stars, and offering initiates the possibility of transformation into powerful magi, interpreting and harnessing celestial influences. As she acknowledged, her perceptions were much indebted to the analytic work of Walker, especially to his *Spiritual and Demonic Magic from Ficino to Campanella* of 1958, but her interpretations went beyond his. She began by taking her story from the Hermetic corpus itself to Marsilio Ficino as, at the command of Cosimo de' Medici, he laid aside his translation of Plato into Latin in order to make accessible in the same language the Greek elements of the corpus. Ficino's role was decisive: he found in the Hermetic writings, especially the *Asclepius*, not only a reinforcement of Christianity but a guide to ways in which human powers might be strengthened by magical operations which would draw down to earth the life of the heavens. The Ficinian synthesis of Christian philosophy, optimist gnosis and animistic belief was decisive for the succeeding century and a half. His system, building on the relations believed to exist between macrocosm and microcosm, took on another dimension in the syncretic philosophy of Giovanni Pico della Mirandola, particularly in its conversion to Christian purposes of the Hebrew *Kabbalah*. This was further enhanced by Johann Reuchlin and Cornelius Agrippa, likewise applying Hebrew truth to illuminate Christian. Continuing into the later sixteenth century, despite theological and humanist objections, religious Cabalism-Hermeticism reaches a sort of apogee in Bruno, who in turn influences both Tommaso Campanella and, in England, Dee. All are united by their determination to harness magical powers for the amelioration of Christianity and humankind. Finally, after 1614, there is the legacy of a Hermes debased by Isaac Casaubon's demonstration that he had no place among the pre-Christian witnesses to a *prisca theologia*. This is the Hermes who survives, in varying forms and degrees, in such occult system-builders as Robert Fludd, the alchemists and, less centrally, in the Cambridge Platonists.

This remarkable, documented study of an important part of the Renaissance Platonic tradition which had displaced the Aristotelian-scholastic in so many contemporary minds places much emphasis on the unity rather than the diversity of the Hermetic tradition. Its value is seriously diminished neither by this nor by its special pleading; rather its

radically new view confirms doubts about the validity of attempts, such
as P.-H. Michel's, to put Bruno's thought into a sort of rational framework, as Kristeller had done for Ficino's. Bruno was to be approached
through the realisation, as one appreciative reviewer put it,

> that magic, astrology and myth form the core of his thinking and that it is only
> by working outwards from this more primitive world of powerful symbols that
> we can hope to understand his apparently more rational philosophical works.[11]

Like *Bruno, The Art of Memory* was both tour de force and the result of
long preparation. When she began she was, as ever, practically on her
own, apart from a couple of outdated German monographs; what is still
today the only other study in depth of the topic appeared after her own
was well advanced. Paolo Rossi's viewpoint in his *Clavis universalis: arti
mnemoniche e logica combinatoria da Lullo a Leibniz* of 1960 (English
translation, 2000) was, moreover, different from hers and his historical
vision less adventurously rich, so that *The Art of Memory* is still a pioneer
book. It is also one of her best in its demonstration of the relevance of a
seemingly unimportant and virtually unknown element in the intellectual
tradition deriving from Antiquity to larger issues in medieval and
Renaissance thought, in particular to those that concerned the making of
images and their deployment in verbal and visual structures. She traced
the continuum of the art of memory from its invention by the Greeks and
transmission to Roman rhetorical theory and practice, to its descendants
in the broad European tradition as far as Fludd and its application to the
development of scientific method. As she went, she considered the role of
Augustinian psychology and of Scholasticism, with accounts of the
Divina Commedia, Lullism, and Ramism as memory systems of a non-
Hermetic kind and, at length, the relation of memory images to talismans
in Giulio Camillo Delminio and in Bruno. To the Roman rhetoricians,
artificial memory had not been a mere technique of rote or verbal recall;
their concern was with how to form 'images' which, once indelibly
imprinted within the mind, would act by association forcefully to remind
a prosecutor of the points of an argument. An example she made famous
is the images recommended by the author of the ps-Ciceronian *Rhetorica
ad Herennium* in a prosecution for murder by poison: a man in bed (the
victim); a man standing beside him (the murderer); holding a cup (the

---

[11] D. P. Walker, in *Modern Language Review*, 61 (1966), 719–21. Among other favourable reviewers was the late H. R. Trevor-Roper (Lord Dacre of Glanton), to whose continued advocacy and
encouragement, practical as well as intellectual, Frances Yates was always conscious of a
particular debt.

poison); tablets (inheritance as a motive); and, dangling from the fourth finger of his left hand (*digitus medicinalis*), a ram's testicles (*testes*; witnesses). Recollection of these images, and so of the points to be made and of their sequence, was to be assisted by setting the images on 'places', the rooms in a building for example. The more graphic the images and the more familiar the building and its ground-plan the stronger the mnemonic power of both. Such a technique was clearly important in itself in the period before printing; then and later it was equally important in the invention of imagery and the broader field of intellectual conditioning. Consciousness of the artificial memory and its operations could thus be invaluable in modern study of medieval and Renaissance art, literature and philosophy. The lesson has been widely absorbed.

In demonstrating this, she had much at heart the hermeticisation of the art in Camillo and Bruno. By her own account it was in 1950, soon after she had begun in earnest on Bruno, that E. H. Gombrich put into her hands the book that made the difference, leading her to the assessment of the Hermetic tradition that would dominate her work for the rest of her life. This was the Hermetically influenced *Idea del theatro* of Camillo, first published in 1550.[12] She lectured at the Warburg Institute in 1952 on Bruno and artificial memory and on Camillo's memory theatre in 1955; in the latter year her seminal essay on 'The Ciceronian Art of Memory' appeared in a volume dedicated to Bruno Nardi, the Dantist and student of medieval thought, who was one of her heroes. In Cicero, memory had already been given a kind of ethical role as one of the components of moral virtue; this was accentuated when St Augustine made it one of the powers of the soul; and within Scholasticism's emphasis on order its ethical dimension was further enhanced. In Camillo's theatre, which is also Solomon's house of wisdom, the basically planetary images preserve eternally, in themselves and in their 'high and incomparable' placing, the eternal nature of things; in Bruno's memory system Frances Yates saw, along with a debt to Lull, a kinship to Camillo, a magical use of images and the adumbration of a new and eirenic universal religion.

In *The Art of Memory* Frances Yates ventured into the minefield of received opinion concerning Elizabethan theatre buildings with a chapter on Fludd's memory theatre and Shakespeare's Globe Theatre in Southwark. She continued her trespass the same year with a revised

[12] *Art of Memory*, p. xiv; cf. Hilary Gatti, 'Frances Yates's Hermetic Renaissance in the Documents held in the Warburg Institute Archive', *Aries*, NS, 2 (2002), 193–210.

version in *New York Review of Books*, following it in 1967 with another in *Shakespeare Studies*. At least one student of the Globe allowed that 'certain ideas' in Fludd's theatre engraving were 'too significant to be disregarded' and that Fludd's insistence on the use of real rather than imaginary buildings for artificial memory was a point in her favour.[13] She was innocently surprised, however, by the reactions of most traditional Shakespearians and theatre historians to her alternative to the native inn-yard tradition. Why, she wondered plaintively to a correspondent, had the mere attempt to say something new and different about the Globe aroused opposition of a sort that she had never before encountered in a long and blameless life of scholarship?[14]

This essay was followed in 1968 by a more general one on architecture and the art of memory and by her book *Theatre of the World* of 1969. Here she set out in detail her views on the applicability of ultimately Vitruvian architectural principles to English building. As ever, she was in quest of assumptions basic to Renaissance thought. Much influenced by what she had long ago learned from Wittkower, she introduced an intellectual element, demonstrating the importance and relevance of the theatre as metaphor for the universe, a microcosm consonant in its structure with the proportion and harmony of the macrocosm.

If historians of the theatre retain a certain wariness towards Frances Yates's ideas about theatre architecture, many are conscious that recent excavations and reconstitutions leave us still knowing less than had been thought to be known and other students have found enough in her expositions to trouble accepted notions and to extend consciousness. Her views on the Globe in Southwark are embodied in the Globe in Tokyo; they have influenced modern architects, such as Sir Denys Lasdun at the National Theatre on the South Bank; and, as usual, they have fruitfully penetrated literary studies.

Theatre of the World, third of a series carrying the themes in Frances Yates's study of the Renaissance further than *Bruno* and *Memory*, is not theatre history as such. It is theatre history embodied, according to her habit, within the conceptual terms of the European tradition, history rather of thought and outlook, its ultimate aim an approach to Shakespeare. It sees in Fludd and in Dee the influential representatives of Renaissance philosophy in England. Dee is the more powerful, as math-

---

[13] C. Walter Hodges, *The Globe Restored. A Study of the Elizabethan Theatre*, 2nd edn. (London, 1968), p. 119.
[14] Yates Archive, Warburg Institute.

ematician and, in his apprehension of the power of mathematics, magus as well. His importance is encapsulated in his mathematical preface to Billingsley's Euclid of 1570, its praises of architecture drawn from Vitruvius and from Leon Battista Alberti making it a seminal text for the transmission of 'Vitruvian subjects' to Fludd and so to Inigo Jones. It is also the means of transmission of these ideas to practical builders.

Dee remains a key figure in the next stage of Frances Yates's advance in the thought world of Shakespeare. This was initially by way of her special Ford Lecture in Oxford in 1970, which took for subject James I and the unhappy outcome of the marriage of the Princess Elizabeth, the Winter Queen, with the Elector Palatine, Frederick V of Bohemia. In the ensuing book of 1972, *The Rosicrucian Enlightenment*, she argued for the importance of a phase she detected in European civilisation at just that time. Its fundamental documents, mysterious in origin, were the so-called 'Rosicrucian Manifestoes' and the spiritual ancestor, in the Bohemia of Rudolf II, was Dee. She would have nothing to do either with modern Rosicrucianism, as presented both by its devotees and in the historically unreliable writings of such authors as A. E. Waite. Nor was her enlightenment the more tangible and fully documented Enlightenment of the eighteenth century. What she described, in a brilliantly sustained balancing act, was a movement intermediary between the Renaissance and the so-called scientific revolution of the seventeenth century, in which the enlightened liberal thought of the Hermetic-Cabalist tradition had received an influx from another Hermetic tradition, that of alchemy. Fludd again shares with Dee the leading role, as the brief reign of Frederick and Elizabeth becomes a Hermetic golden age, its philosophy nourished on Dee's *Monas hieroglyphica* and on the alchemical activity and writings of Michael Maier. Frances Yates's concern is with how this European 'Rosicrucian' movement, with its striving for illumination and for the advancement of knowledge, failed in its effect and slipped out of history when disowned by James I.

In the last decade of Frances Yates's life there were essays and reviews on her favoured people and themes—Bruno, Copernicus, Cornelius Agrippa, Dee, Erasmus, Lull, Nostradamus, Rabelais, artificial memory, festivals, Hermetist-Cabalist magic, iconoclasm, the idea of an imperial reform, religion and magic's decline. It also saw two more books, best thought of as the last two parts of her synoptic investigation into the influence—and its frustration—on Renaissance thought of hermetic-cabalistic and hermetic-alchemical preconceptions. *Shakespeare's Last Plays: A new Approach* appeared in 1975, the same year as her revised

Astraea, and four years before her final attempt at a synthesis at book length, *The occult Philosophy in the Elizabethan Age* of 1979. In the first, which is based on the Northcliffe Lectures in Literature at University College, she explained *Henry VIII, Cymbeline* and *The Tempest*, with Ben Jonson as a foil, in terms of Shakespeare's intellectual situation 'amid the currents and cross-currents of magic and religion, Reformation and Counter-Reformation, whipped up . . . towards the oncoming storm of the Thirty Years' War'. The plays are interpreted through the typically Yatesian concept of a Europe profoundly affected by the failure of an Elizabethan revival in contemporary Bohemia—Frederick and Elizabeth—and Jacobean England, with its vision of a wide imperial peace about to be realised—Prince Henry, Michael Drayton, Inigo Jones, court masque and courtly chivalry. This liberal revival reaches a peak of poetic expression in *The Tempest*, with its masque symbolic of chastity; it is nullified by Counter Reformation absolutism, reflected even in the Jonsonian masque. The hard heads win again as James takes the Spanish line in keeping England out of the fury of war and leaving Protestant Europe to lament the loss of a leader.

There is no doubting either the originality of the thesis that, in the background to Shakespeare's last plays, there is a late outburst of the esoteric and magical thinking typified in Dee, in a world where such non-conformist ideas were in danger, or the ardour with which it is argued—or the perilous leaps required in pursuing it. Frances Yates was always at her best and most exciting in describing what might have been. *The occult Philosophy in the Elizabethan Age* is the final rapid summation of her long ponderings on the thought behind the religious and political history of the sixteenth century. Comparison of this brief, radical and summary historical study with her book on *Love's Labour's Lost* of 1936 and a prentice piece on Shakespeare and the Platonic tradition of 1942 show how far her own thinking had come since then. Her title borrows the title of Agrippa's most famous book, *De occulta philosophia*, at once defining the mystical, white-magical *philosophia Christi* that had long been her central preoccupation and rescuing Agrippa from the vulgar, denigratory image of him as diabolist black magician. Fundamental to the occult philosophy itself are Hermetic Neoplatonism as revived by Ficino and christianised Jewish *Kabbalah* as added by Pico; this synthesis, tending towards liberalism and reform in religion, reaches a peak in Reuchlin, is continued in the magi Agrippa, Bruno, and the Franciscan Francesco Giorgi (the last, as influencing Edmund Spenser, the subject of her lecture to the Society for Renaissance Studies in 1977), Fludd and Dee as the prophets of a Protestant-cabalistic messianism, culminating in Milton. Her admiration for the great expert on Jewish mysticism Gershom Scholem, another of her heroes, and for Chaim Wirszubski, which had been making itself felt for some time, is particularly strong in her emphasis on the decisive influence of Jewish thought in Europe from Ferdinand and Isabella's expulsion of the Jews from Spain in 1492 to their return to England in the seventeenth century.

Some of the directions in which Frances Yates had been taken as she wrote she described as unexpected by herself, even alarming. Rejecting the dissuasions of friends, worried that her reputation might suffer from the sweep of her argument, the length of its historical perspective and the audacity of its connections and conclusions, she insisted on its essential rightness. As her best seller, it has carried her ideas, in this condensedly suggestive form, more widely than any other of her books.

The broadening of Frances Yates's reputation, beginning with the stir made in 1964 by *Bruno*, had borne out her hopes. Her position had been quickly consolidated by an invitation to contribute to the then newly established *New York Review of Books*, which became an important new forum for her. Continuing her long-established appearances as occasional reviewer in the learned journals, the monthlies and quarterlies and the *Supplements* to *The Times* she had now, for almost the last two decades of her life, a regular platform and a larger audience, for which she was deeply grateful. Joined in the *Review*'s pages first by Gombrich, whose obituary tribute to her was published there in 1983, and later by Walker, she made it seem like a sort of fief of the Warburg Institute.[15] Her first essay, appearing in the issue for 19 November 1964, was a critical account of the unacceptable narrowness of Kristeller's concept of humanism and the history of philosophy as represented in his *Eight Philosophers of the Italian Renaissance*. Her last, laudatory piece on Charles Nicholl's *The Chemical Theatre*, sub-editorially titled 'An alchemical Lear', was published posthumously seventeen years later to the day, in the *Review* of 19 November 1981. In between, that journal's liberality, coupled with her own willingness—not always confident, as her intermittent, skeleton diary entries show—to grapple with whatever was presented to her, her facility in expounding complicated issues, her readiness in forthright restatement of her ideas about intellectual historiography, not to mention her scrupulous meeting of deadlines, resulted in more than twenty

---

[15] Gombrich's obituary is reprinted as 'The Evaluation of esoteric Currents' in his *Tributes* (Oxford, 1984), pp. 211–20.

substantial essays, besides the piece on the Globe Theatre. These concerned over thirty books: Felix Gilbert on Machiavelli and Guicciardini, a translation of Guicciardini's *Ricordi*, Craig Thompson's translation of the *Colloquies* of Erasmus and P. E. Memmo's of Bruno's *Eroici furori*, C. G. Nauert on Agrippa, J. A. Mazzeo on Renaissance and revolution, Herschel Baker on the race of time, Rosalie L. Colie on paradox. A. Bartlett Giamatti on the earthly paradise and the Renaissance epic, Giuseppe Prezzolini on Machiavelli, Werner Gundersheimer on Louis Le Roy, Paolo Rossi on Francis Bacon, Brian Vickers and Joan Webber on seventeenth-century prose, Bacon's included, Mikhail Bakhtin on Rabelais, George Huppert on the idea of history, Peter French on Dee and Wayne Shumaker on the occult sciences in the Renaissance, Walker on the ancient theology, John Phillips on iconoclasm, Charles Webster on the Great Instauration, Marion Leathers Kuntz's translation of Jean Bodin, Brian Copenhaver on Symphorien Champier, Robert Klein's Renaissance essays, and Michael Dummett on the tarot. Many were republished in the final two volumes of her *Collected Essays* (1983–4); she is often at her liveliest and best in them, despite an increasing preoccupation with her own interests and unease with other approaches than her own.

These *New York Review* essays played their part in the almost cult status that Frances Yates had achieved internationally by the end of her life. In her own language she reached a wider readership than most scholars. Her books were translated into Dutch, French, German, Italian, Japanese, Norwegian, Polish, Russian, and Spanish (in Latin America); she even makes brief appearances in contemporary fiction. Posterity has enhanced her reputation. To it, her living presence was an appropriate match: unselfconsciously dignified and impressive, it reflected a seriousness that was without guile concerning important issues in scholarship and in life, offset by a certain public and private shyness. Once she was sure of her company this would be dissolved into laughter by an almost schoolgirl sense of the ridiculous. She was deeply attached not only to her family but also to their house, which became hers, and to its garden, with its weeping willow which she liked to believe had sprung from a slip of a tree beside Napoleon's grave on St Helena. She was deeply attached also to her friends, who were beneficiaries of numberless acts of kindness and consideration—tea or Sunday lunch in the garden at Claygate, little lunch- or dinner-parties at her or her sister's club in London, where she would regularly stay a few nights for shopping, a lecture, a play or an opera; gifts of books, or of wine from that family recourse, the Army and

Navy Stores (usually Pouilly-Fuissé, a favourite, along with the Chianti demanded in an Italian context). She enjoyed congenial company, but was happiest working alone. The greatest of her pleasures was reading, which she names in *Who's Who* as her recreation, along with travel (in France, Italy and Britain); for music she had old favourites on her gramophone.

On her 'days' at the Warburg Institute she would arrive about eleven and stay often quite late in her study in South Kensington or Bloomsbury, discussing their work with pupils or receiving visitors; more often than not with a cigarette—Craven 'A', for as long as the brand existed—jutting from its holder and with her hands in motion to assist the making of an especially important or abstruse point. Or she would progress through the Library, pupil or visitor in tow; ranging along the shelves there and elsewhere before seizing the book she needed 'like one of the more ample gun dogs'.[16] She would collect great armfuls, carloads almost, of books to carry home; it was not always easy to reclaim them. In public, she had always to control her diffidence but had been from quite early days an effective lecturer, clear-voiced and upstanding, her hair always threatening to escape from its securing pins or from the hat which she would sometimes wear for really formal occasions. Besides her Warburg lectures of the 1940s and 1950s, she made memorable contributions to symposia on Sidney and on Chapman at Reading; when she came into her own after the publication of *Bruno* and *Memory*, she had much success in London and in Oxford, as well as in the USA. During one triumphal American tour in the spring of 1966 she lectured at Johns Hopkins, the Folger Shakespeare Library, Bryn Mawr, Columbia, Harvard, MIT, the Newberry and Chicago and Northwestern Universities before winding down with a restful week at the Princeton Institute for Advanced Study. She was visiting professor at other universities, notably Cornell. At the Warburg in the 1960s and 1970s she gave postgraduate courses: festivals and empire again; or seminars on the hermetic tradition; in addition to weekly small reading parties on individual texts—the *Nicomachean Ethics*, Macrobius on the *Somnium Scipionis*, *The City of God*, Luther and Erasmus, and two presentations of academic study as useful rather than the reverse: Bartolomeo Delbene's *Civitas veri*, dedicated to Henri III, and Bacon's *Advancement of Learning*. Dante's *Convivio* and *Monarchia* were also considered, Dante being always an object of

---

[16] Elizabeth Mackenzie, *The Brown Book* [of Lady Margaret Hall], 1982, p. 37.

reverence. A little souvenir-shop image of him stood on her desk; one of
her finest earlier essays was one in the Warburg *Journal* of 1951 on the significance of the story of Ugolino and the Tower of Hunger from the
penultimate canto of *Inferno* for writers and artists in England during the
eighteenth and nineteenth centuries.[17] The *Divina Commedia* is important, also, in her account of the medieval phase in the theory and practice
of artificial memory. At her death she was planning a further study of the
Commedia in relation to the Thomist synthesis of knowledge and its
visual manifestation in the Spanish Chapel of Sa Maria Novella.

Despite being somewhat taken unawares by fame and despite a certain
lack of comfort—rather surprising in a student of ceremonial—in public
manifestations of it, Frances Yates enjoyed the translation to eminence
which the impact of her books had won for her. She was always firm,
however, in rejecting invitations to write little books on The Renaissance
and the like. Her honorary doctorates from Edinburgh, Oxford, East
Anglia, Exeter, and Warwick, her foreign membership of the American
Academy of the Arts and Sciences and the Royal Netherlands Academy,
her Senior Wolfson History Prize in 1973, and her Premio Galileo Galilei
in 1978, as well as her Honorary Fellowship of Lady Margaret Hall, gave
her much pleasure. Likewise her OBE in 1972 (announced at the end of
'columns of very small print about footballers, dentists and other worthy
and deserving citizens') and the DBE which followed in 1977. There was
deeper satisfaction in her London D.Lit., awarded by due process of
examination and assessment in 1965, on the basis of published work.

The source of Frances Yates's distinction and her influence was the
fecundity of her laborious explorations of other times than her own. She
was unique in her repeated demonstrations of the vitality and animating
power in their own time of ideas condemned by later ages as baseless and
futile. For her, possibilities were not less great and less significant for having been denied. If her sense that she was merely opening the way for suc-
cessors to follow was sometimes overtaken by overstatement, her insights
had huge influence in making occultism, historically considered, a legiti-
mate and illuminating object of study. There is, in any case, ample com-
pensation in the inspiriting example of a scholar undaunted by difficulty,
transparently honest and single-minded in her ambition to chart the history of the West European Renaissance. Her work was done in a mod-
estly circumstanced life of apparent calm but spirited and constant

---

[17] *Journal of the Warburg and Courtauld Institutes*, 14 (1951), 92–117; repr. in her *Renaissance
and Reform; The Italian Contribution: Collected Essays*, 2 (London, 1983), pp. 30–58.

intellectual activity, continued to the end, even after operations for cataract in 1978.

Frances Yates was a frank and severe critic of her own work and of that of others. Those who had got it right included, as well as selected Warburgians, Italian historians of thought such as Nardi, Garin, Cesare Vasoli and Paola Zambelli (she loved Italy and there are ways in which her approach was Italian or Italo-French rather than English). Unwilling to modify her views in any essential way, she was never afraid to indicate where others had got it wrong, however cross with her—a favourite expression—'they' might be made by this. She did it largely by restating her case, sincere in the often-expressed belief that her work was there to be developed by 'nackwacks' (= *Nachwuchs*, the new generation). Her initiatory talent is nowhere more apparent and influential than in her dealings with the secret heart of ancient philosophy as represented by the Hermetic strain of Renaissance Neoplatonism. If she was inclined to overinsistence on this one component of the tradition and to large claims for its centrality to politico-religious experience and action, she opened up an area virtually unknown to English-reading historians. She herself would deny the existence of the 'Yates thesis' in the crude and easily refuted form extrapolated from her writings by her critics, and much opposed by them; it was not an essential part of her endeavour to propose—as they accused her of doing—the origin of modern science in occult belief. Rather, she wanted to show how occult belief, permeating the thought of the Renaissance, had accompanied the slow growth of science, if only sometimes as a stimulus *per contrariam*. Sharing with her friend and coadjutor, Walker, a distaste for the excesses of lunatic-fringe esotericists, modern believers in astrology and magic, and misguided modern Freemasons, she shared with him also a firm conviction that belief in the possibility of magical manipulation of the correspondences had been a profound motivating force. As a component of the thought system of the Middle Ages and the Renaissance, in greater or lesser degree compatible with philosophy, science, and religion, as the means of mental and emotional orientation in the human condition, it was worth historical investigation. Its intangibility, increasing the difficulty of interpretation, made it more important. For Frances Yates, as the 'mere' or 'humble historian' she liked to call herself, what was thought to be, or hoped for, was as significant as what modern opinion selects to characterise progress. She attempted above all to describe the almost inseparable combination of the irrational with the rational in the thought world of the Renaissance, still discernible in the Newtonian symbiosis of alchemical myth, apocalypticism, astrology, Neoplatonism, and the principles of mathematics, as it had been in the mixture of eschatological detritus and navigational skills in the mind of Christopher Columbus. She concerned herself with how that combination had been arrived at in specific instances, and how it had manifested itself in specific contexts, rather than with the rise of modern science in general.

Frances Yates created her own discipline.[18] Wrong-headed or wrong she could sometimes be; but there is always a kernel, an aperçu, always 'something there'. Her investigations, supported always by courageous and agile argument, are profoundly suggestive and challenging to accepted notions, especially in their adumbrations of relationships and of consequences. The conditions she experienced for protracted, individual, pure research and reflection have vanished, along with the worlds in which she moved, physically as well as imaginatively. Of her it could be written, as she wrote of Gertrud Bing, 'She staked a claim for humanity and learning and unflaggingly defended it to the end. That was her true work, a work infinitely important and invisibly lasting.'[19]

As well as enlivening the past, Frances Yates heartened the present; she was an earnest, impulsive, modest, warm, humorous, and generous human being. Her care extended to the future, her final act of generosity and vision being her bequest to the Warburg Institute, which ensured that her personal library would be incorporated in the Institute's Library and her working papers in its Archives, while her residual estate would be used to found research fellowships there in her name.

J. B. TRAPP
Fellow of the Academy

Note. I am indebted to Sydney Anglo, Kay and Michael Baxandall, Jocelyn Hillgarth, Frank Kermode, Christopher Ligota, Margaret McGowan, and Elizabeth McGrath for advice and criticism.

---

[18] H. R. Trevor-Roper, quoted by J. N. Hillgarth in Frances A. Yates, *Ideas and Ideals*, p. 277.
[19] *Journal of the Warburg and Courtauld Institutes*, 27 (1964), p. [vi].